CHARLES 'DOUGIE' USHER

CHARLES 'DOUGIE' USHER

A Remarkable Man

by

KENNETH USHER

'Usher — a wonderful leader of men'

F.S.V. Donnison

For

Peter, Katerina, Jack, Alexandra and Sophie

FOREWORD

By Lieutenant-General Sir Peter Graham K.C.B., C.B.E.

IT is an honour and pleasure to write the Foreword to this fascinating biography of one of my Regimental heroes, Colonel Charles Usher, D.S.O., O.B.E., *Légion d'Honneur, Croix de Guerre.* Charles, or Dougie, as he was known in the Regiment when I first met him in 1959, was a wonderful character who was extremely kind to a young Gordon Highlander. I knew little about him then, but over the years have come to appreciate what an amazing, energetic and talented man he was.

Relatively few who excel at school do so later in life. Charles Usher did. At school he excelled academically, was fluent in French and German, with a ready ear for languages. An accomplished athlete, rugby player, cricketer, boxer and swimmer, he had interests besides sport—the Scientific and Field Club, photography, and responsibility as a School Prefect.

This was the solid grounding for an extraordinary life. Commissioned from the Royal Military College, Sandhurst into The Gordon Highlanders in 1911, he played rugby for Scotland and went on to captain the side, and captained the Scottish fencing team. He became an excellent piper and Highland dancer, tutored by the world famous Pipe Major G.S. McLennan, with whom he remained friends until 'GS' died in 1929.

Captured in August 1914 with the rest of the 1st Battalion, Charles Usher ran a 'spy ring' in his prisoner-of-war camps, getting the information back to the War Office. After the First World War he was decorated with an O.B.E. and then served in England, Scotland, Northern Ireland, Gibraltar and Singapore, mainly at Regimental Duty but with responsibility for Physical Training at Eastern and Scottish Commands.

The start of World War II saw him in command of the 1st Battalion The Gordon Highlanders. He took the Battalion to France and in early 1940 was promoted, and commanded an area around St. Malo. The German blitzkrieg resulted in the British evacuation from Dunkirk. Six miles south is the town of Bergues, the key to the southern approach to Dunkirk. Bergues was held by Usherforce, a scratch assembly of diverse units and detached individuals under Usher's command, for seven days against a German mechanised division, thereby ensuring that many thousands of soldiers could escape from Dunkirk. He too ultimately got away, only to be given a staff appointment in Scotland. Later in the war, after D-Day, he commanded the Civil Affairs units which supported the French authorities in Caen while the German army still held it—an extraordinary feat which resulted in two French decorations.

Before the war ended he was in charge of the military government of the Minden region of Germany.

The war over, Charles Usher became Director of Physical Education at Edinburgh University, and remained hugely involved in sporting matters, piping and the welfare of retired Gordon Highlanders. He was a gifted person who led a 'Boys Own' adventurous life, and how fortunate it is that it has been recorded by his son Kenneth for posterity.

The story of its compilation is almost as strange as some of Charles' own exploits. During his lifetime he collected many photographs, cuttings, letters and documents relating to his own life and family. When he died, his son inherited them and kept them carefully in a substantial summerhouse in the garden of his home in Buckinghamshire. On a July day in 2006 a garden contractor left a bonfire unattended which spread to the summerhouse and then to the cedar roof of his home. Together with a neighbour, Kenneth aged 78, went into the roof and directed the Fire Brigades where to concentrate their efforts. Some thousand books were lost and months were spent sifting through the charred and sodden heap of family papers. He began to write with the fragments as a starting point, supplementing these with visits to Bergues, Caen, the Gordon Highlanders Museum in Aberdeen, the National Archives and Sandhurst. This story is the result. The Gordon Highlanders owe father and son a great debt.

CONTENTS

LIST OF ILLUSTRATIONS

Maps

Illustrations

Photographs

Frontispiece - Colonel C.M. Usher, D.S.O., O.B.E.

(Between pages 168 and 169)

Photographs (continued)

Pre-War Map of Caen

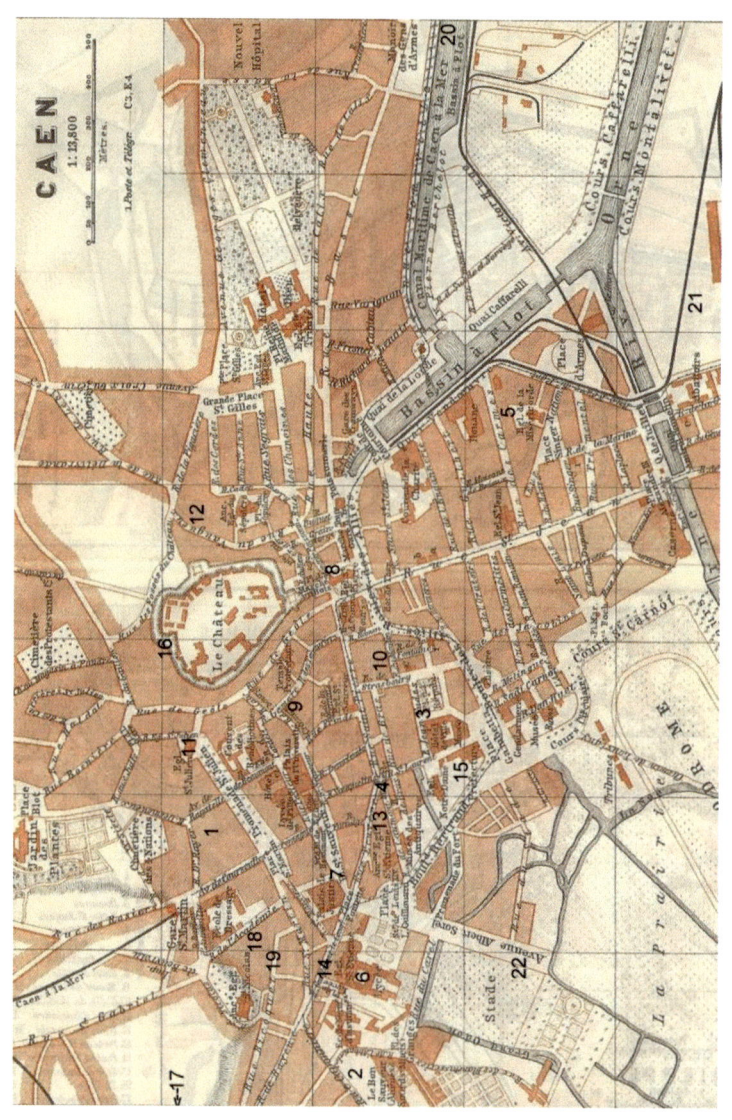

Key to Caen map

CHAPTER 1

EARLY DAYS

CHARLES Usher was the third son of Henry Usher, a member of the family that established the Scottish brewing and distilling companies that made the name 'Usher' famous[1]. As well as his brothers, James and John, he had two elder sisters, Ina and Elsa. Henry (Harry) Usher died in 1898, leaving his widow to bring up the family on her own.

Charles Usher started his education at a prep school, Stanley House, at Bridge of Allan, where he won the prize for excellence in English and Latin. This talent for languages would be of great benefit to him during his military service. Unfortunately, his time at Stanley House was blighted as he was subjected to bullying, a circumstance which, though undoubtedly traumatic for a small boy, would seem inconceivable to those who knew the powerful, athletic, intellectually robust sportsman he would become. As a result of the bullying he was taken away from the school. In 1905 he went to Merchiston Castle School[2] in Edinburgh, under the distinguished Headmaster, George Smith, a product of Ayr Academy, Edinburgh University and Trinity College Oxford, and former house master at Rugby. Smith greatly improved living conditions at Merchiston by installing electric light and proper baths (with hot and cold water) to give boys two baths a week.

Like the best Scottish schools, Merchiston was run on the basis that a good education struck a balance between academic achievement and physical fitness. Hard work in the classroom was followed by hard work on the sports field. Usher thrived in this regime, and proved to have a particular gift for languages, becoming fluent in French and German[3]. His academic career at

---

[1] See Appendix 1 for the Usher family genealogy.

[2] Merchiston relocated in the 1930s to fine new buildings and a large open campus in Colinton. When Usher attended it was still based in the tower house Merchiston Castle near the 'Holy Corner' junction of Colinton and Morningside Roads.

[3] In later years he mastered Spanish, learned basic Russian from Russian fellow prisoners of war in World War I, and even attempted to learn Gaelic.

Merchiston was of the highest standard and he excelled in many subjects.

On the sporting field Usher proved adept at rugby, cricket, hockey, boxing, swimming and track events, and was also a fine gymnast. Excelling at all, it was in rugby that he gained most renown, going on to become a distinguished Scotland rugby internationalist.[4]

The curriculum included boxing and swimming. Boys learned swimming and lifesaving, and played water polo at the Warrender Park Swimming Baths, where swimming before breakfast was very popular, although it entailed a brisk walk to Marchmont from Merchiston Castle. There was an annual swimming competition in the cold River Forth at Granton. Usher's Prefect's tail-coat did service at Ascot, weddings and funerals for the next half century.

Leisure activities flourished. Usher took a great interest in photography, taking and developing pictures in the dark room. He enjoyed carpentry, and his training in those skills was to prove unexpectedly valuable a few years later. He was the Secretary of the Scientific and Field Club, organising parties to such places as a linen factory in Dunfermline, Dryborough's brewery at Duddingston and the power station at Tollcross (where they went underground to see the cables).

With its balanced approach to education, Merchiston encouraged those with an academic bent to take part in physical activities, and those with a sporting talent to apply themselves to academic studies. Inevitably, however, some preferred to remain in the comfort zone of their particular talents while ignoring the other. Usher remembered one boy he recalled seeing only once a year, at prize giving, and even then it was difficult to make him out. All that could be seen was a large pile of books walking down the aisle with a pair of feet projecting from beneath.[5]

Usher left Merchiston academically and physically fit. His guiding lights were Kipling's poem '*If*' and the morality of the New Testament. Throughout his career, wherever he was stationed, a framed copy of the poem hung on the wall behind him. The final verse of the poem sums up the man who was Charles Usher.

---

[4] See Appendix 2 for details of Usher's remarkable sporting career.

[5] The book balancer became the Governor of Assam, a knight, and Chairman of the Scottish Gas Board.

If you can talk with crowds and keep your virtue,
Or walk with kings—nor lose the common touch,
If neither foes nor loving friends can hurt you,
If all men count with you but none too much;
If you can fill the unforgiving minute
With sixty seconds' worth of distance run,
Yours is the Earth and everything that is in it,
And—which is more—you will be a Man, my son!

Usher went to the Royal Military College, Sandhurst in 1910, where he captained the rugby XV in 1911 and won the Golf Cup. To his regret he could not emulate his cousins, experienced horsemen Stuart and Clive Usher, who had won the Saddle[6] at Sandhurst and Woolwich respectively. It was not for want of trying. After giving 'a polished display of horsemanship', he ruefully admitted that his instructor had informed him that 'a hegg couldn't fall off the 'orse you're sitting on'—and that was not the one he was tested on!

Usher was commissioned, on 4th March, 1911, as a second-lieutenant in the Gordon Highlanders, a regiment where, though the highest standards of performance and presentation were expected, a large private income was not a prerequisite. He was posted to the 1st Battalion at Gujarat Barracks, Colchester. Lieutenant-Colonel the Hon. F. Gordon handed over command in July 1911 to Lieutenant-Colonel F.H. Neish, an experienced officer who had seen action in Nubia, the Nile Expedition and the Boer War.

It was a good choice of regiment. The Gordon Highlanders had produced great sportsmen, winning trophy after trophy throughout the Empire. In the Peninsular War, so the story goes, the 92nd was quartered at Amunjuez on the River Tagus, where a grand fête was held. A renowned Spanish hammer thrower and shot putter challenged anyone to beat him. Major Colin Campbell and his servant Dugald Mor rose to the occasion. Dugald 'although an old man with silver hair' won the shot while Campbell threw the hammer over the rooftops to the astonishment of the Spaniards, who were convinced that he had been assisted by the 'Evil One'[7].

---

[6]   The prize for horsemanship.

[7]   When the 92nd landed in Lisbon in 1810 there was no Major Colin Campbell on its strength, but it is noted that Captain Dugald

In 1898 the 2nd Battalion football team had won the Army Cup, the blue riband of Army football. In the same year, in India, they won the Lucknow Murree Cup, while in 1902-3, after the 2nd Battalion returned to India after the Boer War, they won the Murree Cup again, the Punjab Cup, the Lucknow and the Delhi Cup, open to all India. The 1st Battalion won the Punjab and Murree Cups in 1896 and the 2nd Battalion won the Indian Football Association Shield in 1909.

The Officers Heavy-Weight Boxing Championship was won by Major C.J. Simpson[8] in 1896, and by Captain J.R.E. Stansfeld[9] D.S.O. in 1903 while Captain R.B. Campbell[10] was Middle-Weight Champion in 1908.

The 1st Battalion had some well known cricketers in Colchester, one of whom, Lieutenant H.M. Sprot, was at that time captain of Hampshire. As for golf, the death occurred that year of Major Meiklejohn, V.C., who had played brilliantly despite having only one arm.[11]

The Gordons had many fine athletes and cross-country runners, and they excelled at swimming and rowing, consistently winning Aquatic Championships at the garrisons where they were stationed. They had shown considerable prowess at polo in India and at home.

Beauvoir de Lisle, in *Tournament Polo*, maintained that 'even the most impecunious subaltern should have at least two polo ponies'. Usher, though in comparison with other subalterns

---

Campbell had not yet joined from the 2nd Battalion. Dugald Campbell served with the 92nd throughout the rest of the campaign in the Peninsula, and was at Quatre Bras, where he was wounded, and Waterloo. He retired on full pay as brevet-major. Before enlisting he was a blacksmith, so he would have been a man of considerable strength. It is possible that the story refers to him.

[8] Wounded at Mons in 1914.

[9] Killed at Loos in 1915 while commanding the 2nd Battalion.

[10] Later to be Inspector of Physical Training in the Army, and Director of Physical Education at Edinburgh University, in which latter post he was succeeded by Usher in 1946.

[11] Major Meiklejohn had lost his arm in the Boer War when he won the V.C. He was on parade in London when his horse panicked and bolted, charging directly towards a nursemaid wheeling a baby in its pram. To prevent the horse hitting them Meiklejohn selflessly pulled the horse round, into some cast-iron railings. He was thrown from the horse, and died shortly afterwards from his injuries.

clearly in the 'impecunious' bracket, duly acquired two ponies and a groom, Binnie. The second-hand polo boots, bespoke for their previous owner, must have been extremely uncomfortable, as the left one was considerably smaller than the right!

As expected in a Highland Regiment, piping held a special place in regimental life. Piping was taught by the incomparable Pipe-Major George Stewart McLennan, known throughout the piping world simply as 'GS'. The greatest Pipe-Major the Gordon Highlanders ever had, he made a lasting contribution to the world of piping. His genius was very real in addition to being the stuff of legend. Usher and GS struck up a deep friendship which lasted until McLennan died. When Usher was on leave in Edinburgh he would get lessons from GS's father, John.

A detachment occupied a camp in Regents Park on 6th June, 1911 under the command of Major F.H. Neish for the Coronation of King George V on 22nd June. In blazing hot weather, Usher found himself standing in full dress outside the East India Club, listening to the sound of ice tinkling in the glasses of members crowding the windows behind him.

Usher had been a very fine rugby player at Merchiston (as were his brothers James and John, the three known in Scottish circles as the 'rugger brothers'), and he had been considered for selection for Scotland while still at school. Wise counsel prevailed, however, and it was decided to wait until he was older before calling him into the national side. Shortly after joining the Battalion, Usher, along with Lieutenants L. Richmond and D.R. Turnbull, introduced rugby to The Gordon Highlanders. There were no facilities, no ground, no teams to play against, and only two men (apart from officers) who had played before, but these difficulties were surmounted. A ground was found, teams such as the London Scottish came all the way from London to give the Gordons a game, and men in the Battalion 'were falling over each other in their desire to learn the game.' The two men who had played before were Corporal Harry and Lance-Corporal Marchbank. Much credit was due to these two N.C.O.s, whose keenness and enthusiasm, together with their sportsmanship, sealed the success of the game in the Battalion. After lengthy deliberation jerseys were chosen, with the regimental colours in horizontal stripes, the yellow broader than the others. The reasoning was that it made the men look bigger, and the result was effective! Blue shorts and blue stockings with yellow tops were worn.

The chance to play for Scotland came in 1912, and in the last match of the season Usher played against England in the Calcutta Cup match, which Scotland won. In 1913 he played in all four international matches, against France, Wales, Ireland and England, but he was only able to appear in one match, against England, in 1914. The promising international career that lay ahead was to be cruelly interrupted by the First World War.

In September 1913 the Battalion entrained for Plymouth, where it joined 8 Infantry Brigade in 3 Division. They were housed in huts, poor accommodation after the modern quarters of Colchester, but if the quarters were indifferent, their neighbours were not; the Royal Scots at Crownhill, the Royal Irish and Middlesex Regiments at Devonport, and the Royal Navy were agreeable companions and sporting opponents.

On 22nd June, 1914, the Battalion went to Willsworthy for musketry training on the ranges sited on the edge of Dartmoor. Usher was pleased to score a 'possible'[12], having got up late with only just enough time to put on overalls over his pyjamas. The Battalion remained at Willsworthy until 29th July, when it received orders to return to barracks and to take up the 'precautionary period' in view of possible mobilisation. Detachments went to predetermined defences and stations, and awaited developments.

---

[12] In military terms a 'possible' means that every shot hit the target in the 'bull's eye', thereby achieving the highest possible score.

CHAPTER 2

OUTBREAK OF WAR AND CAPTURE IN FRANCE

CHARLES Usher kept a diary from the declaration of war on 4th August, 1914, when he was stationed at Plymouth, up until 25th August, just before the surrender of the 1st Battalion. Later events were added in prison camps. The diary covers the military situation, and touches on the unfortunate disagreement between the Commanding Officer, Lieutenant-Colonel F.H. Neish and the Second-in-Command, Brevet Colonel W.E. Gordon, V.C., with the former making the hard, but inevitable decision to surrender, and the latter arguing to continue fighting while attempting to withdraw. Entries from Usher's diary and corroboration from other Gordon Highlander accounts are used to describe this short but intense period.

Usher records the start of the war in a brief and unemotional manner.

4th August. Mobilisation ordered about 6 pm. England[1] declared war on Germany about 11 pm.

Usher was tasked with collecting the horses required to pull the Battalion transport. On 5th August, the first day of mobilisation, he set off at 6 am with a sizeable detachment of men under Corporal Lamont to take a train to Totnes, where the horses were held. This took three days, during which Usher stayed at the Seven Stars Hotel. Throughout the 6th and 7th of August he toured the countryside 'in a huge Sheffield Simplex car which was lent to us'[2], and collected 58 horses in all. The return to Plymouth on 8th August was frustrating, as it took four-and-a-half hours to get the horses loaded on the train.

Over the next three days the Battalion trained, with route marches and an inspection by the Brigade Commander on 11th August. On the 12th the Battalion left barracks to entrain for Southampton, where it would sail to France. Usher recorded an incident on the way to the station.

---

[1] Usher uses the convention, current at the time although incorrect, of referring to 'England' when the correct term was 'Britain'.

[2] The Simplex tourer was one of the great Edwardian marques. It had a straight six-cylinder, side-valve engine of 6982 cc, developing 45 hp, with a top speed of around 50 mph.

There was rather a bad accident on the way to the station, one of the A.S.C.[3] drivers lost control of his horses, which bolted. I rode on and warned the people in front and then waited. As the runaway wagon approached, my own horse got restive and swerved across the road, at the same moment the wagon dashed into a lamp-post just behind me. It was a very narrow escape. The wagon was broken to matchwood. None of the horses or men were killed. The horses were able to proceed. We managed to get the kit which the disabled wagon contained carted to the station in a motor van.

Usher lists the officers who entrained for Southampton.

CO	Lt. Col. F.H. Neish
2i/c	Bt. Col. W.E. Gordon.
A Company	Maj. W.M.K. Marshall
	Capt. W. Neish
	Lt. H.L. Pelham-Burn
	Lt. Hon. A.A. Fraser,
	(Master of Saltoun)
	Lt. D.W. Hunter-Blair
B Company	Maj. C.J. Simpson
	Capt. G.H.S. Fowke
	Lt. L. Richmond
	Lt. W.A.F. Sandeman
	2/Lt. D.R. Turnbull
	2/Lt. A.D.L. Stewart
C Company	Maj. P.S. Allan
	Maj. A.A. Duff
	Lt. A.P.F. Lyon
	2/Lt. J. Houldsworth
	2/Lt. I.B.M. Hamilton
D Company	Capt. C.R. Lumsden
	Capt I. Picton-Warlow
	Lt. C.M. Usher
	Lt. M.V. Hay
	2/Lt. A.W. Robertson
Machine Guns	Lt. J.K. Trotter
Transport	2/Lt. R.D. Robertson
Quartermaster	Lt. J. Macdonald.

---

[3] Army Service Corps. It became the Royal Army Service Corps after World War I.

Usher's diary entry for 13th August describes the departure from Britain.

> We arrived at Southampton after a miserable journey at 9 am. The morning was spent in embarkation. Our boat was the *Abuisi*[4] which was very comfortable. We left Southampton at 2 pm.
>
> Our departure was very different from what I had imagined it would be. There was nobody to see us off. General Smith-Dorrien and his staff sailed with us. I was rather touched when men started singing '*I'll take the high road*'. Looking around I saw all the men in good spirits and health and all the horses which I had collected—little did they know what was in store for them. I wonder how many of them would see an English stable again. We did not know our destination, everything was secret.
>
> We were held up off Ventnor while enquiries were made. We passed a torpedo boat which gave us three cheers and signalled good luck. We made Boulogne at 5 am after a beautiful crossing.

As the ship neared Boulogne a lamp on the quay threw a meagre light. From the darkness a voice roared, instructing the pilot with colourful oaths. There was not much room for the ship to turn in the narrow harbour, and by the time it was alongside the night was past.

The few citizens in the streets of Boulogne at that early hour watched what must have seemed a strange procession. As the pipes played at the head of the marching troops, all down the steep, narrow street heads appeared from every window, flags were waved and enthusiastic cries of '*Vive l'Angleterre*' (an error of identification perhaps excusable in French citizens) rang out.

The streets of Boulogne were soon very busy. At the quayside, transports arrived and unloaded soldiers. Cheering crowds lined the passage of the troops, but the people seemed to show anxiety rather than excitement.

The way through the town was long and steep, and by the time the Battalion reached the top of the hill the sun had risen and was making its heat felt. They passed long lines of market carts waiting to enter the town, and half a mile further on, beyond the last few straggling houses, they came to Camp St. Martin. In a large field stood four lines of tents. The ground was fresh and clean, for the Gordons were the

---

4   This was probably the Elder Dempster liner RMS *Abinsi*, which is recorded as having been stopped and checked by HMS *Sapphire* off St. Alban's Head on the approaches to Southampton on 12th August.

first to arrive there. The Gordons and the Argyll and Sutherland Highlanders were together in the camp.

The camp offered extensive views over the sea, and further up the coast the lighthouse at Étaples could be seen, while across the English Channel, looking through field glasses, the coast of England could be seen as little more than a shadow on the horizon.

The following days were busy. The Battalion was transported by train to Aulnoye, then marched to Taisniers, about four miles away. D Company was billeted with the mayor, and Usher records 'he put up a lot of red wine for our consumption. Our stay would have been pleasant but for a horrid old dirty woman who would come in at meal times.'

On the 20th August the Battalion marched off for St. Aubin, and on the 21st marched some fourteen miles to Gugnies-Chaussée on the French-Belgian frontier. Here, Usher records:

> The people where my platoon was billeted were very kind and allowed the men to eat as much as they could out of a very large orchard. I also managed to get a lot of new potatoes which were greatly appreciated.
>
> On the march we passed through Maubeuge. Thousands of men were hard at work on the trenches and putting the place in a state of defence. I thought it looked very strong but did not see any guns. Some of the battalion were billeted in France and some in Belgium.

On the following morning, 22nd August, the Battalion marched off at 6.30 am and after eight miles reached Hyon. That night D Company 'messed with H.Q. but we slept in the coach house. This was the last time we saw our valises.'

The Battle of Mons

The 1st Battalion, The Gordon Highlanders, was about to come face to face with the might of the vast German Army. Usher records:

> We stood to arms at 3 am and marched off at 7 am to take up a position about 2 km from Hyon to the east from Mons. 'D' Company's position was along the Mons-Binche road with 'A' Company on the right and 'B' on our left. We worked hard entrenching ourselves, and my platoon got well dug in. We had an easy for dinners at about 1 pm. The war dog was in great form as there were a lot of hares in the field.
>
> It was very hard to believe we were going to have a battle and [that] it was not company training. The trenches were soon

completed and quite good. They were also quite well concealed (fortunately).

About 2.30 pm the expected battle began. A shell burst in the wood behind us and we discovered that a battery of artillery had taken up a position just behind my trenches. They started firing and the report of the guns nearly blew us out of our trenches, the guns were so close. Private Taylor was the first man to get wounded; he was hit by a splinter of wood from the trees around the battery. It got him in the nape of the neck and the lower part of the back of his head and knocked him out for the rest of the day. He lost a lot of blood.

Next we saw large masses of Germans going across our front at about 1,700 yards away. As they were such a huge target I opened fire, and may have done some damage.

The artillery duel went on hard all day and I heard a tremendous amount of rifle and machine gun fire on our left. The fighting seemed to sweep round from left to right. We got quite a lot of shooting and Sgt. Craig and I did some very good practice. The most interesting event of the afternoon was when we managed to knock out a couple of German machine-guns coming into action. We spotted an officer standing in a gap in the hedge and pointing to his left. We waited, and taking the range accurately, got all the rifles laid on to the place. Sure enough, in a few minutes two pairs of men appeared, carrying machine-guns—they looked like stretcher bearers. We let them go about 15 yards and then gave them 'rapid until further orders'. They went down and never got up again.

We got quite a lot of shooting all the afternoon. There were lines of German infantry going across our front and we fired at them, with a range of about 650 yards. We were subjected to heavy artillery fire all the afternoon, but did not get much rifle fire against us. Our artillery relocated at about 4 pm As it got dark the Germans dropped some shells on to a small house about 400 yards to our left front and set it on fire. However it did not burn. Some Germans came and poured petrol over it and started hacking the roof to pieces. There were women and children there, and their screams were dreadful. I could see Germans clearly defined against the background in the dark but did not fire, as I was afraid it would give our position away and I knew I could not do much good.

While Usher and D Company engaged the Germans, the other rifle companies were also heavily involved. Between B Company and Mons, a distance of over 1,000 yards, there were no troops at all, but the field of fire was excellent. The platoons to the right rear of B Company (including Usher's) were firing before B Company saw any Germans, but soon a considerable deployment was observed about 1,500 yards to the north-east, followed by another from the wood directly north at about 1,000 yards; then greater numbers were seen pouring over the slopes to the north-west. A strong patrol of about a dozen Germans to the north-east at 350 yards received the first volley fired by Second-Lieutenant Alexander Stewart's platoon, which wiped them out in a moment, scarcely one escaping.

The Royal Irish and the Middlesex pulled back from the canal in extended order through B Company, suffering heavy losses from concentrated artillery, rifle, and machine-gun fire. They were cool and disciplined, and their behaviour was magnificent, but they had lost heavily on the canal. The Gordons covered their retirement with fair success as many Germans were seen to fall.

Usher's account continues:

> Lumsden came along and told me to prepare for an attack. He also told me that Leslie Richmond and Simpson had been killed[5] and that Allan had been wounded. We got out of our trenches and lay in front of them, bayonets fixed. I had great difficulty keeping the men awake as they started snoring dreadfully. I suppose it was the relief after the noise of battle during the day, and the strain of the first battle being over which accounted for this. Owing to the magnificent way in which the men worked at the trenches, in spite of the soil being none too easy, we suffered only two casualties. At twelve o'clock we retired, and I met Sandeman on the road. As we walked along we exchanged views of our first battle. We were both greatly affected by the sad news of Leslie Richmond, and it seemed hard to believe that we would never see him again.
>
> After some wandering to and fro we joined up with the Royal Scots and started to march south. After about 4 miles we went into a field and lay down to sleep. We were wakened about dawn by the enemy's guns, firing at some position on our left.

24th August.

> We discovered we were close to the village of Nouvelles, and some of our guns opened fire behind us. This, of course, brought fire on to them, and we then had the unenviable task of returning

---

[5] Major C.J. Simpson had been badly hit carrying ammunition to his company, but survived, and went on to command the 1st Battalion after the War.

through the village with shells bursting all around. If the Germans had known, they could have knocked all of us out. I have since found that we were surrounded on all sides, and the enemy were only yards away.

We got safely through the villages and I met Griffiths (Blackheath and Yorkshire) who was supporting us with his battery. We passed the time of day and he galloped away. We marched on, left Nouvelles, and at mid-day we got orders to entruck at a place called Quevy-le-Petit.

Then we saw a very interesting artillery duel between one of our heavy batteries and a German one. The shells went right over the top of us, and after we got accustomed to them we took them as a matter of course. We stayed there about 4 hours and then retired. After messing about we finally got on the move and marched to Bavay, where we arrived at about midnight and lay down. We were to have had some food, but lay down for the second night running in the open. It was cold and miserable but we were very tired and went to sleep. I wish we knew what was happening but we were kept absolutely in the dark. There was a tremendous amount of transport and it must have been an advanced park or refilling point.

25th August.

We started off about 5 o'clock and continued to march without breakfast. Hungry and tired, we set off on the longest march we were to do. We marched all day and late in the evening. After many wanderings, and having done about 30 miles, we arrived at Audencourt. After a lot of worrying we managed to get into dreadful billets. We were all soaking and I confess I was rather down on my luck.

During the day we passed through 11th Brigade and I saw Lionel Tennyson. Also, in the course of the day, I saw Hab Rankin (R.A.M.C.), afterwards killed, and Jack Fulton (Lancashire Fusiliers).

26th August.

Next morning we were going to continue the march, but these orders were countermanded, and we were ordered to take position in front of the village of Caudry. The position occupied by 'D' Company was between the village and the Cambrai-Le Cateau road facing it about 400 yards back. 'D' Company (less Robertson's platoon) was detailed to carry tools around to the other companies, as we were to take up a position on the unexposed flank. When we arrived Lumsden told me to join up the Company. Just as we got into close [formation], four shells burst over us—we could tell by the sound that the guns were not far off. We continued to entrench and clear the foreground, under shrapnel fire. It was a marvel that no one was hit seriously. I was struck on two occasions by spent shrapnel, which hardly hurt me at all. We finally got fairly well entrenched, and a tremendous fire opened away on our left. A little while afterwards Trotter came along and said that the 4th Division were doing very well on our left. This was the last time I spoke to the 'Old Colonel'. He was killed later in the day. The battle now started in earnest. Before this we had been able to get the men breakfast.

The German infantry first came into view crossing beetroot fields on top of the hill on D Company's right front, where telegraph poles gave the 1,200 yard mark. They advanced in close formation until disturbed by a machine-gun. German troops, debouching from a little wood, advanced across the stubble field on top of the hill, moving to their left across the Gordons' front. They were extended to not more than two paces, keeping a very bad line, evidently very weary and marching in the hot sun with manifest disgust.

The command, 'Five rounds rapid at the stubble field 900 yards,' jolted the Germans back to reality. They hopped into cover like rabbits. Some threw themselves flat behind the corn-stooks, and when the firing ceased got up and bolted back to the wood. Two or three remained motionless.

The Germans, having found that the Gordons were dangerous at 900 yards, then crossed the stubble-field in short rushes and reinforced their men who were advancing through the beetroot fields on the right.

Great numbers of German troops appeared on the ridge between Bethencourt and the little wood. They advanced in three or four lines of sections of ten to fifteen men extended to two paces. Their advance was direct on the village of Audencourt, so D Company could pour an enfilade fire upon them. They advanced in short rushes across pastureland which provided no cover, and offered clearly visible targets even when lying down. Throughout this action the German gunners kept up a steady stream of shrapnel, which burst just in front of the D Company trenches and broke over the top like a wave. Shooting at the advancing enemy had to be timed by the bursting shell.

The Gordons adopted a procedure of firing two rounds and then ducking down, at intervals determined by the arrival of the shell, but the shooting of the battalion was good enough to delay the enemy's advance. From the 900-yard mark they took more than an hour to reach the *Route Nationale*, 400 yards from the nearest Gordons' trench. Here they concentrated in great numbers, as the road ran along an embankment behind which nothing but artillery could reach them. This was the situation at four o'clock in the afternoon. The enemy were beginning to cross the road; D Company fixed bayonets. It seemed that they would have little chance against the large number of Germans behind the embankment.

For nearly an hour the British guns had been silent, but they had not all retired. With a white star-shaped flash two shells burst right over the road behind which the Germans were massed. Those shells must have knocked out forty or fifty men. The enemy fled back up the hill to the 900-yard mark, followed by rapid fire and loud cheering all along the line.

Usher describes this period:

We were subjected to tremendous artillery and machine-gun and rifle fire. This went on all day and Sgt. Craig, McAlister and I had some good shooting at 500 yards. There was no communication between companies. We got it very hot in the afternoon and the enemy seemed to be firing at point-blank range with field and machine-guns at a range of about 400 yards. The high explosive shells were the worst and stunned us for a minute or two if they burst. About 4 o'clock we all thought that our number was up. At that time I admired my platoon more than I had ever done before. We were subjected to tremendous shell fire—high explosive shrapnel, and also the enemy seemed to have got round the flank, for every now and then a bullet would come into the trench from behind. The men never turned a hair and though they realised the situation, they carried on as though they were on the range at home.

As at Mons, I was very lucky, not only in my position, but also with the nature of the soil. We had a very splendid field of fire, and the only fault was that being in a turnip field several men were hit by turnips which were dug up by the shells. At about 6 pm a message came through from Warlow asking me to go and see him. When I got to his trench I found poor Lumsden lying dead, Warlow hit in the arm and suffering from loss of blood and Hay hit in the head. Warlow handed the Company over to me as all officers senior to me were killed or wounded.

I tried to communicate with the rest of the Company without success and sent a man to find them, I sent Sgt Skelly to try to locate Battalion H.Q., and I got in touch with 'C' Company on my right. The next few hours I will remember for the rest of my life. It was cold and wet. Wherever I moved I kicked poor Lumsden. It was very hard to keep awake. We expected to be attacked at any moment. The men were very good. They had been continuously in action since 6 am and had withstood all hostile attempts, both frontal and flanking, to drive us from our trenches. They had to suffer a concentrated and continuous bombardment, with no British guns to reply They were under enfilade fire at intervals. They were suffering from the fatigue and exhaustion of the previous retreat, and they were hungry and thirsty. Sgt Stewart was splendid. He and I kept watch by turns. We had two men with us but in spite of all efforts they would go off to sleep and slip down to the bottom of the trench. At about 10 pm I received the order to hold myself in readiness to retire at about midnight. I warned the Royal Irish who were on my left. Finally at about 11.15 Houldsworth came along with the order to retire about midnight and the rendezvous was a small wood to our right rear. We were to leave everything except rifles and ammunition. I personally went all along the Company and also made sure that the order was communicated to the Royal Irish. It was about 11.15 when we got the men ready to move. In addition to being dead beat they were depressed and dismayed on hearing that the army, the rest of the Brigade and three platoons of 'B' Company had retired early in the afternoon and we had been left on our own[6]. But they rose manfully to the occasion and with unflinching discipline evacuated the trenches quietly and in perfect order, despite pitch darkness and incessant enemy fire.

Captain C.R. Lumsden and Lieutenant J.K. Trotter were killed and Captain I. Picton-Warlow, Major A.A. Duff and Lieutenant M.V. Hay were wounded during the day.

I went along to Robertson, and by the time I got back we had started off. Warlow managed to walk and Hay was helped by two men, but we had to leave him to his fate. I thought he would never live.[7] The Company arrived at the rendezvous and Colonel W.E. Gordon, V.C. got the column of Royal Scots, Royal Irish and Gordon Highlanders on the move at a fast pace. I was in the rear of

---

[6] The message from 8 Brigade to withdraw never reached the Gordons, apart from three platoons of B Company which were instructed to withdraw by the Brigade Major personally. This left the Gordons, and parties of other regiments, dangerously isolated and eventually surrounded.

[7] Lieutenant Malcolm Hay survived, was repatriated and later wrote an account of his war, *Wounded and a Prisoner of War*.

the column, and at one of the checks I went to the head of my Company and remained there. Villages were on fire all around, and men groaned in the trenches as we passed. It was evident that we had the enemy on both sides and behind.

When nearing the village of Bertry violent fire broke out on both flanks and in front and the men seemed to surge back. I went up to investigate, and getting mixed up in a melee I was hit in the back of the head and couldn't remember anything for three or four hours, but I was helped to my feet by one of the men who told me all officers were wanted at the front, and on the way forward two or three bullets came and hit me through the clothes. When I arrived all the men had their hands up and the Gordon Highlanders had surrendered. The name of the place was Bertry. When I came to I was a prisoner-of-war.

During the last fight we suffered the following casualties:

Killed:	Lt. A.P.F. Lyon
Wounded:	Lt. R.D. Robertson
	Lt. A.W.M. Robertson.
Escaped	Major W.M.K. Marshall

Captain W. Neish and self were also *hors de combat*, badly stunned. At midnight on 26-27 August I realised I had become a man.

Usher's memory of the last moments of the 1st Battalion is understandably limited, as he was clearly concussed from his wound. The death of Lieutenant Lyon occurred in the following manner.

During the final moments before the 1st Battalion, The Gordon Highlanders, left behind by the retreating British Army and surrounded by overwhelming numbers of Germans, was forced to surrender, their fighting spirit was as high as it ever had been. The remnants of the remaining companies, led by Colonel Gordon, were proceeding along a road leading to the village of Bertry when they ran into the Germans. At the first meeting, in the dark, a German officer, speaking French, tried to convince the Gordons that they had met up with French forces, but the Gordons quickly saw through their subterfuge. The German officer flew at Colonel Gordon, and they rolled in the road together, more Germans joining in and viciously kicking Colonel Gordon. Other Gordons, led by Second-Lieutenant Stewart, came to his aid and freed him, capturing the German officer in the process. Stewart shot a tall German officer and disabled another German by hitting him in the face with the butt of his revolver. The Germans to the front opened fire at about four yards range, but the

British replied with heavier fire and drove them off. Colonel Gordon shouted for all officers to follow him up the road towards Bertry, and they attacked a party of Germans, shooting several, and pushed them back as far as the first house in Bertry.

Lieutenant Lyon shouted 'There are Germans in here!', and he and Stewart entered the house, forcing open the first door on the right inside. Two Germans raised their rifles, but Stewart shot them dead with his pistol. Another German armed with a rifle jumped from behind the door and aimed the weapon at Lyon, who grappled with him. As the doorway was very narrow Stewart was unable to shoot the German for fear of hitting Lyon, who appeared to be getting the better of the struggle. However, Lyon's foot slipped in a pool of blood, when the German he was grappling with fired his rifle, hitting Lyon in the left lung. Lyon 'came back with a rush and fell into the arms of some other officers who had come into the house.' Stewart shot the German. The door of the room was then slammed from inside. As the Germans refused to come out, Stewart went outside and got three or four men to fire through the windows, which flushed out the Germans. Standing at the door Stewart shot both as they came out.

Despite this valiant attempt to break out, it was to no avail, as the Gordons were surrounded by large numbers of Germans, and the inevitable end was surrender and capture.

Into Captivity

Usher's account of the move to a German prisoner-of-war camp is reinforced by accounts of other Gordon Highlanders on that journey. They were taken by train to Germany, in conditions that were uncomfortable for the officers, but almost unbearable for the men. First, however, they had to endure an arduous march, under armed guard, from Bertry to the railhead.

In the first forenoon of the march the more fortunate got a small piece of bread and meat and a drop of gravy, but many got nothing. At noon they marched about two miles to Troisville, where they got bread—one loaf for every 10 men. On the next day they were marched to Le Quesnoy, where they were accommodated in the barracks at the Fort. They made themselves fairly comfortable as there was a good supply of straw for beds. During the evening of the following day they reached Quiverain near the Belgian frontier, where they were herded into a church and given coffee. The next day they paraded and marched off at 6am, and after about 18 miles reached Mons, where they were put in a shed at the railway station, and almost stifled by the heat and dirt.

They marched for 12 miles on the next day, and arrived at Soignies, where they were accommodated in a splendid old church, but there were no cooking arrangements. On the following day they marched to Halle, about five miles south-west of Brussels, and were put in a grain store. At 8 pm on September 2nd they received a hurried order to move and marched to the railway station. After much muddling they were crammed into a train. In one carriage were 15 French, 19 British, and two German sentries. The prisoners were packed like sardines, and the heat and stench were almost unbearable.

The train taking the prisoners into captivity left Halle railway station at 6 pm on Monday 31st October, with the officers accommodated in second-class corridor carriages and the wounded on straw in rows in luggage vans. The train passed through Brussels, Louvain, which was in ruins, then through Liège and into Germany. The prisoners soon encountered the hatred that propagandists had whipped up against the '*Englander*', and there was an ugly demonstration when one of their guards held up a pocket knife with the marline spike open, showed it to the German soldiers in an adjacent troop train, pointed to the British Medical Officers and claimed that this was used to gouge out the eyes of wounded German prisoners. Their colonel even shouted 'out with them!' but fortunately the incensed soldiery were restrained by a civilised junior officer. The civilian spectators, including a couple of priests, women and children showed their horror at being in the presence of such vile criminals.

No refreshment was provided by the Red Cross at Dusseldorf, Essen, or any of the other stations they stopped at on their way to Dortmund. All that occurred each time was that the doors were flung open to display the wounded. They came to Dortmund at 8 am the next morning. Some of the officers were fortunate to be given some hot soup and bread and butter by a couple of kindly but correct ladies who could understand English. Usher was not so fortunate. He got soup, but only after the German Red Cross woman spat in it. (He was never again very keen on soup of any sort.) The next three days were spent on the train, and those who could were permitted to buy a meal at the station refreshment rooms.

When the train reached Sennelager the officers were separated from the warrant officers, non-commissioned officers and men, and sent to a different camp.

Usher describes the final part of the journey:

On [7th] September the train finally reached Torgau, some 450 miles from its starting place at Mons and 60 miles south of Berlin, on a blazing hot day. The prisoners were marched through the town escorted by guards with fixed bayonets. There was no help to carry any of their meagre belongings and anything they couldn't manage had to be left behind. All the way they were accompanied by the townspeople [making repeated rushes at us, armed with every agricultural and household weapon of offence], calling them every possible kind of *schweinhund* until they finally crossed the bridge over the Elbe and reached the Brückenkopf fortress.

Usher was put in a 'sitting room' with four Russians, two Belgians and eight British colonels, until he was housed in a large shed along with some sixty subalterns, amongst whom were brother Gordons the Master of Saltoun (Second-Lieutenant Hon. Alexander Fraser), Lieutenants H.L. Pelham-Burn and D.W. Hunter-Blair.

As a prisoner-of-war Usher faced an unknown future of months, even years of incarceration with no apparent purpose, apart from surviving. The biggest enemy was despair, aided by boredom, inertia and lack of stimulus, physical or mental. It would be only too easy to fall into a meaningless unproductive routine based solely on passing time. Charles Usher was not prepared to accept this bleak vision of life in prison, and he devoted all his talents to stimulating physical and mental activity, for himself and his fellow prisoners. He also determined to do what he could to help the British war effort, and to endeavour to escape.

The subalterns' dormitory was used for Divine Service by the Anglican chaplain, Benjamin O'Rorke, who was imprisoned by unfortunate chance, for under the terms of the Geneva Convention he should have been returned to his own side. A suitable loft in an outbuilding was assigned for use as a chapel, and everyone with carpentry skills (with Usher, who had assimilated well his woodwork lessons at school, to the forefront) lent a hand in constructing an altar, lectern and pews. An old saw, a chisel, a pair of pincers together with a hammer and nails were, with some bribery, borrowed from German carpenters working in the fort. These 'skilled' volunteers included Pelham-Burn and Hunter-Blair, who also joined a twenty-seven strong choir. O'Rorke had a Bible that incorporated a hymnal and psalter. Lance-Corporal Higgins, Gordon Highlanders, was the church orderly. The work was completed on St. Luke's Day and the chapel was accordingly dedicated to the saint.

Mail and clandestine Intelligence

On 6th October, Colonel W.E. Gordon, the Senior British Officer, announced that officers could send postcards home. These were double-sided with, on one side, printed statements, such as 'I am in good health, a prisoner-of-war etc' (with no news of military operations), and six lines to write the bare minimum; the other side for a similarly laconic reply. Soon, however, censored letters were permitted. Prisoners wrote in a way that the recipient would understand but, it was hoped, the censor would not.

With the first letters from home Usher heard from his mother that she had returned safely with his sister Ina from America, where they had been on holiday to see relations (Usher had obtained special leave from Colchester to see them off). In reply he asked that warm clothing and food should be sent to his servant, Private A. McAlister, a prisoner at Sennelager. This last comment throws light on the close relationship between officers and men in The Gordon Highlanders, and the continuing concern of the officers for their men.

Usher found a way to write to his mother that avoided the official censored mail system. A 'secret mail' system was developed, where letters, set out in almost microscopic hand on very thin paper, were sewn into the clothing and headgear, or concealed in buttons and footwear of severely wounded French prisoners who were repatriated. The system also used little artefacts, split in two, hollowed out to accommodate the letter then glued together and painted to conceal the join. The French were good at this. On arrival in Paris these artefacts were posted home. The problem was how to let the recipient know, so that the artefact would be broken open and the message retrieved. This was solved with the help of the padre. References to scripture gave clues of where to look. This sudden interest in religion gratified Usher's mother, but that became concern that he was suffering a nervous breakdown or developing a religious obsession. When she consulted her minister, however, it all became clear.

Throughout his time in German prisoner-of-war camps, Usher passed back to Britain, through his mother, information that he gathered on German troop strengths, movements and morale. He read all the German papers, and later at Burg and at Mainz on the Rhine he was able to study rail and river traffic movements. A fluent German speaker, he chatted to German workmen brought into the camps and collected all the gossip and little snippets of news that they let slip. His letters, including an appreciation of the build up to the Battle of Loos in particular, were forwarded to the War Office. All his letters were numbered, as they could arrive home out of sequence.

An extract from a coded letter to his mother explains how he would send coded messages in his letters.

If you have anything important to say to me in a letter—writing a sentence containing either of the following words, 'start', 'beginning' or 'commencement' then every 6th word write a word of the required message. As a double safeguard, put the number of the letter in a square instead of the usual brackets or circle.

Part of one such letter survives. With the letter F in a square and sent from Friedberg on 13th January 1917 (with every sixth word shown here in italics) it reads:

This is the <u>start</u> of another year in captivity. *Robertson*[8] seems to be most grateful. *Prison* life seems to go on *for* ever on the same lines *year* after year. We have not *complained* but what is the use *because* we cannot alter our lot. *Parcels* seem to have arrived and *not* to have stopped. I duly *distributed* all your messages as requested—*now* the shock is over and *gets* easier to bear I see *no* danger for Aunt Bon. The *packets* of sticky sweets practically always <u>finish</u> up here in a bad state. I got the two photos of Wattie & Marchbank....

[The message it contains is: <u>Start</u> 'Robertson prison for year complained because parcels not distributed now gets no packets' <u>finish</u>.]

A letter to Usher's Aunt Caroline (Carrie) in January 1915 contained paragraphs thanking her for stuff which was presumably contraband, recounted by allusion the fighting on 26th August 1914, the successful accounting for a number of the enemy that day, the surrender, loss of contact with the battalion, bullets through clothing, wounds to the leg, the standard of comfort of the prison room, the monotonous pork diet and prison conditions that did not bear favourable comparison with Peterhead, the infamous Scottish prison. This letter probably did not go through the official post but was concealed on the person of a repatriated French prisoner, in which case the content should not be compromising if discovered.

Dear Aunt Carrie,

I never wrote and thanked you for the splendid parcel which you sent to me, it was <u>very</u> useful indeed. Did mother tell you about the great grouse drive they had on Aug: 27th? They had been having very good sport up till then with two really big days.

---

[8] Corporal James Robertson was a piper, later promoted to Pipe Major, and known in piping circles as 'James Robertson of Banff'. He had been court-martialled by the Germans for destroying a piece of machinery on which he had been working in the prison camp, and sentenced to a year's imprisonment.

Glenord's youngest child[9] seems to have come off well on both and to have got going really well seeing it was his first time out. As you probably know the 26th was a very big day and most of the men were very tired; however the drive on the 27th was a dismal failure. The parties were badly let down by the underkeeper and only started walking when it was miles too late. However they did a tremendous lot of good, really, by not getting a move on, though of course they did not appreciate or realise that fact at the time.[10] I believe young Glenord got in the way of one of Willie's pals, he was very lucky indeed that his clothes were the only thing to suffer. Give Jean Usher my love and tell her I hope she was not bothered by the <u>leg</u> again this Xmas as we both were last and I was this . . . . There are now 18 of us in our bed/wash/dining/sitting room. 5 Russians, 2 Belgians, 8 French and the three of us. The room is quite a large one the same size as your drawing room with six windows. You know what travelling on the Continent is like!

The next time you go to Tobermory you might congratulate 'Old <u>Isaiah</u>' on his 65th birthday.[11] I wonder where his <u>four</u> sons are now.

Tell Mother that all eatables are more than acceptable

It is getting harder to keep cheerful here now. We have now done 5 months. When we all left for the front we <u>did not</u> count those left behind lucky. Peterhead would be a welcome change.

With much love to all.

Ever your loving nephew

Charlie

Keeping up morale

Life in prison camp was dull, boring and monotonous, and ways had to be found to keep people active and sustain morale. Daily life revolved around sport, amateur concerts and plays, lectures, debates, and reading.

The padre, Benjamin O'Rorke, who was eventually repatriated, describes in his book, *In the Hands of the Enemy,* published in 1915, how leisure hours were spent at Torgau in both intellectual and physical pursuits and he singles out Usher in the following passage.

---

[9]   Usher himself—Glenord was his mother's address.

[10] This refers to the failure of 8 Brigade's order to withdraw to reach the Gordons.

[11] A reference to the monotonous diet of pork. Isaiah 65:4 'Which remain among the graves, and lodge in the monuments, which eat swine's flesh, and broth of abominable things is in their vessels.'

Athletic diversions were the earliest and most natural and probably in the circumstances the best. They took many forms, beginning with physical exercises under the direction of an expert, Lieut. C.M. Usher, Gordon Highlanders, who was an ideal instructor.[12] [Usher] led his pupils by graded exercises from the simple to the strenuous and concluded each day's programme with a game. Sometimes it would be 'leap-frog' sometimes 'French and English', sometimes 'twos and threes', and in later days Highland dances. He made a very detailed study and careful notes on these. In the afternoon football was played. The heat of the German autumn was no discouragement to ardent spirits. Association, with extemporised goal-posts, was the usual game, and occasionally an international contest with the French would be held. On certain days in the week the English orderlies competed with the French orderlies and nearly always beat them. Once the game, peculiar to Eton College was played, the number of Old Etonians being nearly enough to form the two sides[13].

For prisoners with neither the desire nor the talent for sporting activities there were less arduous pastimes, such as seeing who could grow the best Kaiser Wilhelm moustache!

Prisoners wounded before capture were attended by Allied Medical Officers among the prisoners. Those whose wounds were sufficiently healed were further helped to recover through Usher's skills as a sports masseur, and his invariably cheerful and positive manner.

A bumpy tennis court was laid out and the game was played into the depths of winter when it was very cold and snow lay thick on the ground. As there was no wire surrounding the court many ball boys were required, which kept them warm.

Prison journalism

In October 1914 a group of officers decided to produce a magazine, which they named *The Torgau Lyre*[14], to entertain their fellow prisoners. The Editorial Staff comprised The Hon. Rupert Keppel, Coldstream Guards, who had been wounded in the head at Landrecies,

---

[12] Gym apparatus was available and the P.T. Class had 35 members.

[13] Usher, a Merchistonian with no connection to Eton, was one of five Gordon Highlanders to take part in this game. See account in *The Torgau Lyre* in Appendix 3.

[14] A pun on the word 'Lyre'. As well as meaning a small harp-type musical instrument, its phonetic use cast doubt on the veracity of the printed content of the journal!

C.M. Usher, Gordon Highlanders, H.A. Cartwright, Middlesex Regiment, Conrad F. Ffrench, Royal Irish Regiment and L.F. Sloane-Stanley, Middlesex Regiment. The *Torgau Lyre* played a large part in sustaining morale and maintaining a sense of humour among the prisoners. Its cleverly drawn sketches and cartoons brought smiles to its readers, but also mocked their German captors through a series of caricatures that blunted German ire as they were invariably seen alongside caricatures of the British themselves.

There were three editions of the *Torgau Lyre*, which speaks highly of the journalistic outflow and editorial drive of the team, which fulfilled its commitment of producing a fortnightly magazine. The editions came out on 17th and 31st October, and 14th November. When the prisoners were moved to Burg *bei* Magdeburg the magazine was produced there, but it changed its name to *The Iceberg*.[15]

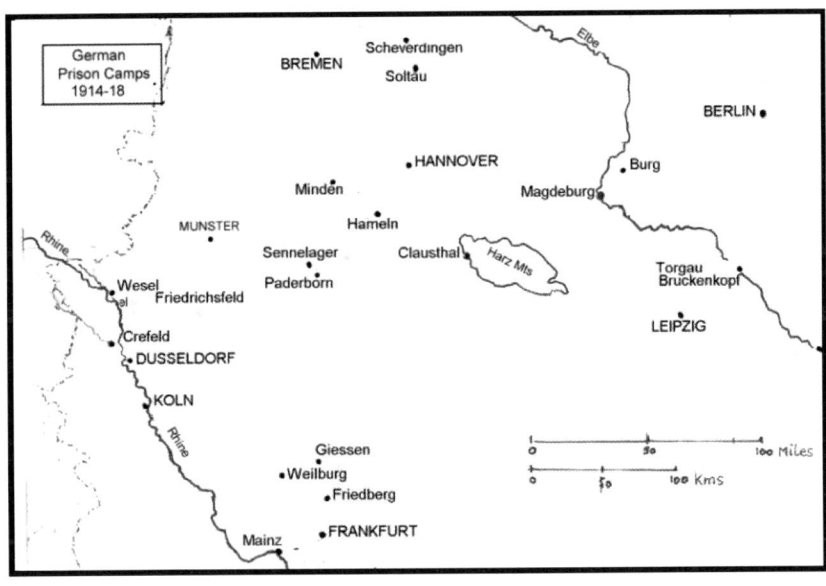

Prison camps that held Usher and other Gordon Highlanders shown in lower case

Moves to other Prisons

The prisoners' ranks at Brückenkopf were swelled by some 230 British and 800 French officers, including four generals. They brought

---

[15] Some editions of *The Torgau Lyre* and *The Iceberg* were brought home at the end of the War and are held in The Gordon Highlanders Museum. Extracts are reproduced in Appendix 3.

information about German troop movements, and this was transmitted back to the War Office by Usher, via his secret mail to his mother.

On 25th November, 1914 the Commandant announced that the British would be transferred the following day to Burg *bei* Magdeburg, 20 miles north east of Magdeburg. Despite the short notice the chapel was dismantled and all that was readily transportable, such as the altar hangings and furnishings, were distributed amongst those departing, with Usher entrusted with the Bible, which he packed with his kit. Anything not transported was left to the French.

There was regret, as many friendships had been forged. The quarters, though crowded, were adequate and the regime had been humane. There was inevitable uncertainty about what might lie ahead.

It was snowing when some 80 officers, of many regiments and corps, clad in a motley collection of British and German greatcoats and Burberrys, formed up in two ranks. Some were bare-headed, some had balaclavas, all were carrying precious possessions, including loaves of bread that they would need on the journey ahead, and which they had not risked entrusting to the cart conveying the heavy baggage. They stood in the snow for half an hour and, although cheering was forbidden, they were given a heartfelt send-off by the French. After being counted three times, and with guards armed with loaded rifles and fixed bayonets in front and rear, the party, headed by the Senior British Officer, Colonel S.C.F. Jackson D.S.O., Hampshire Regiment, tramped out shortly after mid-day through the heavy iron gates and over the planks of the bridge over which they had come in three months previously.

The column of prisoners provided entertainment for a rapidly expanding crowd waiting to jeer the *schweinhunde*, although they were much less insulting than they had been previously. At the station they were squashed, five to a carriage, in third-class, together with three German soldiers, each with a loaded rifle.

The train went through Wittenburg, where Martin Luther had once been imprisoned, and Magdeburg, to their new destination, which they reached at 9.30 that night. They were immediately surrounded by a howling mob that had awaited their arrival with relish. The crowd sang *Deutschland, Deutschland über alles* with gusto and shouted their approval when the guards, putting on a display befitting the occasion, yelled '*schnell, schnell*' at their charges and prodded the slower ones with their rifles. This caused some of the overburdened prisoners to drop bits of their kit, which they were not allowed to retrieve, and which were seized upon as souvenirs by the rabble.

As soon as Camp Burg was reached, Irish Roman Catholic officers were called forward, allocated the largest and most comfortable rooms, and interviewed individually to see if they would be prepared to serve against Britain in the German Army, but there were no volunteers. Soon after, three-quarters of the British and Russians were moved to other camps in the area and replaced by 200 French and 100 Belgian. The Irish were left alone; Germany hoped to profit by bitterness between Great Britain and Ireland. The Home Rule for Ireland Bill had received Royal Assent but the war had led to the suspension of the Act and the 'Irish Question' simmered. The Germans were puzzled when they found that they had Major A.E. Haig, K.O.S.B. amongst the prisoners. They thought that he had been shot in reprisal for his order to fire on rioters in Dublin before the war, and were bewildered to find that he was as popular with the Irish as the other prisoners!

Keeping fit and producing the magazine

The recreation area at Burg was only 160 yards by 30, and in January 1915 Usher felt himself getting out of condition, due to the diet and lack of exercise. Breakfast at 8 am was one slice of rye bread—*kriegsbrot* made out of rye meal and potato—some jam and a cup of coffee. At 1.00 o'clock there was soup, 1 oz pork and potatoes and at 7 pm supper of *kriegsbrot* and cheese, with raw fish on Fridays. This cost 1/6d a day, deducted from pay. Food parcels sent from Scotland helped, with tinned meat, chocolate, soup, tea, coffee and cocoa from Gibson's, in Edinburgh's Queensferry Street, and McVitie's. 'Eggo' powdered egg could be made up into scrambled eggs. Later in the war there was bread from Switzerland and Denmark, the latter preferred and obtained, through Usher's Aunt Lizzie, from the Red Cross and the Order of St. John in Copenhagen. So generous were the amounts received by some officers that they eschewed prison fare altogether.

Usher held a P.T. class each morning, with 14 attending, including two colonels and a major. There had been 35 at Torgau where there was more space.

Undeterred by the bitter cold, ice and snow of the hard winter, Keppel and his companions from *The Torgau Lyre* carried on their journalistic efforts where they left off, amending the title to *The Iceberg* and commencing with a Christmas number. Many of the illustrations were in colour.[16]

---

[16] The front covers of and some illustrations from *The Iceberg* are reproduced in Appendix 3.

Russians and fresh air

A very favourable impression was created by the 300 fine looking Russian officers in the camp. They had been warned that the British were peculiar about fresh air. The padre related:

> Although we were allies against a common foe, and as time went on became close friends, it must be acknowledged that on one point we were at first obliged to join issue with them. To have the window open by day or by night in the winter time was to them as one of the deadly sins, whereas to us it was the very breath of life. So much was this the case with us that one of the things we had done on the previous evening was to go straight to the windows on our side of the room and open one of them. This had the effect of bringing a Russian officer out of bed in protest. He closed the window in the politest manner possible, gesticulating with his hands because the language difficulty made it impossible to explain by word of mouth. Captain W.L. Dugmore, Cheshire Regiment, whose bed was next to the window made gesticulations likewise to the effect that the opposite side of the room was the Russian quarter, and this the British. Again our friend moved his hand rapidly to and fro in front of his body . . . the offending officer seized it in a friendly fashion, shook it firmly and bowed. The Russian also bowed, returned to his bed, and the Englishman re-opened the window. A peaceful settlement was thus happily arrived at.'

Usher was an enthusiastic participant in the game, which also involved the French! The battle between those who wanted fresh air and those who wanted a good fug was unceasing. Writing from Friedberg in 1916 Usher said:

> The temperature in the different rooms here, especially in winter, is very varied. The Russian rooms are like ovens in a crematorium, the French like a hothouse, while the English remind one of the North Pole. The Englander does not keep his windows open because he likes shivering, but from a sense of duty. Having gained his reputation after inhuman struggles in many a frosty continental railway carriage, he must keep it up. At Torgau, I remember, we made a complaint about a shortage of coal in the cold weather. The old barrack warden, who rejoiced in the name of Mossy (actually universally nicknamed 'Mossy-face', a kindly soul) appeared to solve the mystery. He was horrified to observe that although the stove was alight all the windows were open. This

was too much for him and despite an impromptu lecture on hygiene from a member of the R.A.M.C, he went away wringing his hands and muttering about mad English.

Tit-for-tat incarceration and another move

In the Spring edition of *The Iceberg* the Editor jokingly referred to the 'not unlikely case of the staff being arrested' and on 13th April he and nine other officers were arrested, but for an entirely different reason. Captured officers and men of two German submarines, who had sunk British ships without making any attempt to save the crews, were placed in solitary confinement in Portsmouth. The Germans decided to do the same and took those arrested to gaols in Burg and Magdeburg. Gordons in the party were A.D.L. Stewart[17], D.W. Hunter-Blair, A.W.M. (Alistair) Robertson and A.A. Fraser, the Master of Saltoun. Pelham-Burn was selected but excused as he was ill. Usher told his mother why he thought he was not included, but this was blue pencilled by the censor and is therefore not known. He said that he was 'green with envy'. It was considered a great joke and 400 officers gave the party a rousing send-off, to the disapproval of the Commandant, who stopped the sale of beer and wine. The reprisals officers appreciated the peace and quiet it gave them for the next seven weeks, but their company was missed as the time passed.

Correspondence and parcels were coming through freely, including a haggis from Usher's Aunt 'Phee' and, in due season, Easter eggs. He gave one to a huge Russian in his room, Nikolay Leonidevich Miloradovich, who asked that Usher should write specially to his mother as he was so touched. Mail from Russia was infrequent.

Russia was such a vast country that the apocryphal story was readily believed that when a fellow prisoner, a reserve lieutenant, received a telegram from the Czar ordering him to the front with such men as he could come up with, he duly marched his men many hundreds of *versts* across the steppes until he came across the smoke and fury of battle. When he encountered an important looking officer, he saluted, gave his name and rank in the Imperial Russian Army and reported for duty. The officer returned the salute, gave his name and

---

17   While in Magdeburg, Stewart helped in the escape of two other officers. For this he was transferred to prison camp at Weilburg, from which he escaped with another prisoner, hoping to steal a German aircraft and fly it back to Allied territory. They were recaptured and sentenced to imprisonment in Friedberg jail, but escaped from there in a daring daylight escapade. Unfortunately they were both quickly recaptured.

rank in the Imperial German Army and said 'You are my prisoner, sir!'

The condition of the other rank prisoners was a matter of continuing concern to Usher, in particular Private Andrew McAlister at Crefeld, Sergeants A. Stewart and Charles F. Troup at Sennelager, Sergeant W. Lamont at Schneverdingen, Corporal James Connolly at Sennelager, Private James O. Elliot at Hameln, Private Peter Binnie at Sennelager, Sergeant W. Harry[18] in Minden, Corporal James Robertson at Hannover, Private J. Beattie at Soltau and Corporal A. Corbett at Friedrichsfeld. There were Canadians too; Corporal Fred Bone, 48th Canadian Highlanders[19] at Giessen and Private Robert Johnston, 15th Canadian.

Usher was upset that he was cooped up and only able to write dull letters about being a prisoner-of-war and not one about hair-raising fighting adventures, derring-do, narrow escapes etc; war still held some glamour and he wanted to be part of it. 'Please congratulate Turnbull's wife on his D.S.O.' he wrote. In March the news came through that Lieutenant-Colonel H.P. Uniacke had been killed leading the regiment. Usher expressed his sorrow and said that Uniacke had been really kind to him when he joined, but it 'was glorious leading the Regiment to victory'. All the other Gordons, save Pelham-Burn, who was sick, had now gone, and he felt lonely.

Morale was helped by clothes sent on from Torgau and kit sent out by Meyer and Mortimer (the London firm of British Army tailors). Usher, a confirmed Presbyterian, assisted with the Padre's services and described the room used as a Church as unique, with three altars, Church of England, Roman Catholic and Greek Orthodox. Like everyone else, Usher was deeply impressed by the unaccompanied Russian singing. O'Rorke rejoiced that 'the three branches of the Catholic Church were worshipping one God in the same room'.

On 20th June 1915 Usher was moved to Mainz, twenty-five miles southwest of Frankfurt. After a 22-hour trip from Burg, Usher arrived at *Offizieregefangenenlager Zitadelle* Mainz at noon on 20th June. The Citadel was situated on the south side of the town and overlooked it with a view of the Rhine. Napoleon said goodbye to Josephine here in the courtyard before he set off for Russia. On the 18th June the local papers had all been full of Waterloo!

---

[18] Sergeant Harry was one of the two soldiers who were in the 1st Gordons' first rugby team at Colchester in 1911. See Chapter 1.

[19] The 48th Highlanders of Canada were affiliated to The Gordon Highlanders.

Casualties and education

The Battle of Loos was fought between 25th September and 8th October 1915, with 48,267 British and 191,767 French casualties. Usher's elder brother, John, was killed by a sniper while serving with the 9th (Pioneer) Battalion, Gordon Highlanders as the battle drew to a close. Never again could the Edinburgh sporting public enjoy the exploits of the famous 'rugger brothers' whom they had taken to their hearts. This was a crushing blow for Usher. 'Everything seems to be out of joint now since poor old Johnnie has gone, but if one is too sad I suppose one is selfish. He was splendid all his life and had a glorious death.' Writing to his mother he said that it was good to know that 'he died as he had always lived, uprightly, a credit to you, his family, to his school and to his country, but what a glorious memory. *Dulce et decorum est pro patria mori.*'

After John's death Usher opened his heart in a letter to his mother:

> I had made it a rule not to tell you anything about my physical condition until I was completely better. My head had been giving me pain, but the doctor could not find any bullet hole or splinter mark, so it was only concussion, and I had great luck in finding just 4 bullet holes through my clothing and some skin off my left leg.

In fact there was a shell splinter in the skull which remained lodged there for life.

The casualty lists were distressing, and many friends were lost. Among these were Captain Lewis Robertson, Cameronians, capped nine times for Scotland and killed at Ypres; Dr Watson, Lieutenants Huggan and Oakley who had all played in the last England v. Scotland International; Lieutenant Turner, great rugby flyer and place kicker, who represented Oxford against Cambridge for three years in succession, who took a bullet through the brain; Surgeon Greig, one time captain of Scotland against England; the dazzling 'Kenny' Macleod, remembered for his performance against South Africa at Glasgow; Sergeant Andrew Wemyss wounded by a bayonet thrust; Lieutenants R.F. Simson and James Ross hit at Calais; Lieutenant Bain of Edinburgh Academicals, capped eleven times for Scotland; Merchistonian Alan Wilson who had represented Cambridge against Oxford for three years in succession. Among others killed were Private Ian Mackay, Glasgow University; Private Kyle of Edinburgh's Royal High School, who played for London Scottish and Kelvinside Academicals and Private Jackson, the Langholm flyer.

Usher was studying French, 'a language so much more beautiful than German', with a *M.* Willaume, and he asked to be remembered to

Burgess at Merchiston for the sound grounding he had given him. Good progress was made in Urdu and Hindustani, taught by Jervis, who had been an instructor in India. German was 'swotted' with Davenport and amongst the newspapers studied were the *Berlin Tageblatt* and the *Frankfurt & Kölnisher Zeitung*. Learning Russian posed some difficulty with the declensions. Gaelic was taken up and Italian considered. Gaelic was soon discontinued as there was no one to help, and Italian remained a pipe dream.

Pipe and violin music for strathspeys and reels were a prime requirement. With his chanter he joined forces with a violinist, flautist, clarinetist, and a pianist. He thought there might be something wrong with the clarinet, particularly when the other fellows in the room threatened to buy a big drum in self defence.

In 1916, as the result of an agreement reached between the British and German governments, British officers were allowed to go for walks in groups outside the camp, provided they signed a document giving their word of honour not to attempt escape. Having given their parole, Usher and his fellow prisoners were not accompanied by armed guards, but were watched by police on bicycles who were under instruction to see but not be seen. They played a game, with points against if their policemen could not be seen for half an hour and points for if they were spotted.

The kilt was a great success with the local ladies' college. The guards referred to them as *bauermädchen*. Four months on the attraction was unabated, and even among the older ladies the most severe and spiteful looking were forced to smile. 'I think it must be the first joke they have seen in their lives.'

The Padre moved on and was replaced by a Free Kirk 'Meenister' who had enlisted in the Scots Guards and had served with the Royal Scots, not seemingly a man ever lost for words.

In January 1916 Usher started learning about cars with Captain R.F. Peskett. 'He is a bit of an expert. It is an awful grind but I am sticking it. I always felt such a fool driving a car and not knowing about the inside.' By March he was struggling, 'the motor lectures are dealing with "Ignition." As I know nothing at all about electricity I find it very difficult indeed.'

In February 1916 Usher gave a lecture on hockey to the French in their own language.

> They wished to play. It was '*bien passé*' except for the fact that unfortunately there was one 'Frog' there who talked English much better than I do French, and he was always trying to put his oar in. However, the result was the next day they '*essayed une partie*'.

They were quite comic. I was referee—not one of the safest positions. You see I did not like to take a stick to defend myself with. They only managed to hurt two players. The best incident was when one fellow (heavily bearded), knowing he was allowed to stop the ball with his hand, waited with the ball at his feet until an opponent came to attack him, whereat he picked up the ball and put it behind his back.'

Both the Russians and the French learned to play hockey. The ground was limited, with lots of stones, and it was a wonder that no one was killed. The Russians played in their ordinary clothes, with caps, boots, spurs and cigarettes. In March 1916 Usher wrote:

> The Russians had a great game of hockey the other day. From a spectacular point of view it was more like polo especially the play of the back who went leisurely towards his own goal swinging his stick above his head and preparing for a backhander! I believe they have challenged the Frogs—it is hard to say which of them is the most dangerous.

With his work on *The Torgau Lyre* and *The Iceberg*, and in the organisation of physical and sporting activities, Usher did much to keep up the spirits and the morale of fellow prisoners. Beneath his ever-active, outgoing and optimistic facade, however, Usher felt his loss of freedom deeply. His inner yearnings were revealed in a letter home, in which he wrote that he wished he could go to North Berwick in the wintertime; that he could go to his Aunt Carrie's place Kinechyle, Aviemore, for the lovely Highland air and where he could see the Spey and the hills in summer; and he wrote how much he missed his dog, Coolie. One telling remark brought home how he felt a responsibility for maintaining a cheerful demeanour that would help to keep up the spirits of his fellow prisoners. 'One's face got quite sore trying to keep smiling.'

Friedberg

In mid-1916 some of the British prisoners, including Usher, were moved again, this time to Friedberg. After a fatiguing journey accompanied by armed escorts, Friedberg, 15 miles north of Frankfurt, was reached on 19th June 1916. The room window looked out on to a *Düngerfabrik* (fertiliser factory). What was distressing, however, was that all the Russians had been left behind at Mainz. Some time later they did arrive, looking like living skeletons. They were allowed neither to receive nor write letters. The Russian Government objected to this and put all German officers in Russia into confinement,

Generals included. Usher wrote, 'We have got a real live Russian Major-General here. I read the paper to him every morning.' Usher's best friends among the prisoners, Lieutenants T.J. Dobson (Royal Naval Division), and Captain Ian M. Henderson (London Scottish) were repatriated through Switzerland, leaving Usher miserable, as he used to pass the hours every day with them with pipe lessons and massage[20]. A few days later another patient, Captain R.F. Peskett, Lincolnshire Regiment, who had been at Torgau, Burg (where he had tried to teach Usher the workings of the internal combustion engine), and now at Friedberg, went off to Switzerland. Many wounded and sick Russians were sent to Sweden. Usher, in the meantime, had mastered one thousand words of Russian.

In an effort to spice up the monotonous diet, snail soup was served up, but this turned out to be unpalatable. Prison diet continued to be supplemented from home and, asked what would be welcome, a shopping list for items which could be purchased from the Army and Navy Society export list groceries was drawn up:

> 3 tins Oaten Biscuits, 3 tins Water Biscuits, 2lbs Apricots evaporated, 2lbs peaches evaporated, 3 tins Choice Californian Apricots, 3 tins Lemon Cling Peaches, 1 doz tins Nestlés Milk, 2 boxes Verbena Soap.
> Tiptree Specialties:
> 3 tins little Scarlet, 3 Gooseberry, 3 Tongues Breakfast, 1 tin Truffled Terrines.
> Total £ 2 - 8/4d.

Allsop of the London Scottish, having been rejected for repatriation to Switzerland, brought a set of pipes with him. He was just learning to play, so Usher took them over and found them 'a great joy'. The class of young pipers now consisted of Pelham-Burn (whose talents also included being a good cook), Allsop, Graves (Royal Scots), Brown (A.&S.H.) and Moodie (Black Watch) of Fettes. They were all doing well.

Thirty-four marches, strathspeys and reels were mastered, and contact was maintained with G.S. McLennan for assistance with tunes (e.g. *Lochanside* and *Badge of Scotland*). Books on Highland dancing, particularly the *Seann Triubhas*, were requested. They had a great St. Andrew's Day, November 30th 1916, the subject of a letter from Friedberg dated 11th January 1917, included in *The Pipes of War* by

---

[20] In 1919 he was given a silver salver inscribed *'Dougie' from 'Dobber' & 'Hender' In grateful remembrance of Mainz & Massage 1915–1916.*

Brevet-Colonel Sir Bruce Seton, C.B., Bart., of Abercorn, and Pipe
Major John Grant:

> We organised an Exhibition of dancing which was a complete
> success. As the Scottish colony here is so small we asked the
> Russians to come and help us. This they did right well with dances
> and songs, the music being provided, in both cases, by the
> 'Balalaika' a Russian national instrument. For our part we danced
> two foursome Reels (dancing two different sets of steps), a Sword
> Dance and a Highland Schottische. In the latter dance we each took
> a Russian as a partner, they having been trained up for the event.
> We sang *'Bonnie Dundee'*, *'Lassies of Scotland'*, *'Macpherson'*,
> and finished up with *'Auld Lang Syne'*. For the Reels my Russian
> friend provided the music on the piano. Our costume was of course
> improvised. Kilt, shoes and hose we had, we wore white shirts with
> lace cuffs, a strip of tartan fastened at the shoulder with a brooch to
> do duty as a plaid and a black velvet band with a lace ruffle falling
> down in front, round our necks. Our sporrans, with the exception of
> one which was made out of local rabbit, all came from home.

Dancing shoes were sandshoes (gym shoes or 'trainers'), with
buckles made from biscuit tins. Nikolai Sokolow, a firm friend,
painted Usher performing the *Sword Dance.*[21] Sokolow was an
accomplished painter, despite having lost an eye at Tannenberg.

In a letter home of 16th December, the dancing Exhibition on St.
Andrew's Day was described as a complete success. The cast was
Younger, Sokolow, Gillespie, Shoste, Usher, Vinogradow, Pelham-
Burn, Brown, Graves, Pachensky and Private Bone, who was in
charge of the improvised plaids for the sword dance.

The programme was:

> Overture on the piano. Russo-Scottish Airs – Vinogradow.
> Foursome Reel. Pelham–Burn, Gillespie, Brown, Usher.
> Song. *Lassies of Scotland*. Graves.
> Russian Dance (balalaika accompaniment by Mikhail Shoste).
> Song. *Bonnie Dundee*. Younger.
> Sword Dance. Gillespie accompanied by Usher on the goose[22]
>   (bagpipes sadly arrived 5 days late).
> Russian Dance, accompanied on the balalaika, Vinogradow.
> A Comic Song, accompanied on the balalaika. Pachensky.
> Foursome Reel and Finale.

---

[21] See Illustration (e) between pages 169 and 170.
[22] Practice pipes, with no drones.

The Russians danced 'most awfully well but one of their dances seemed more like acrobatics'.[23] The Finale was the Highland Schottische, in which Usher was partnered by Sokolow. They had had three weeks practice and the Russians all joined in with 'wild cries'. 'Everyone, Russians, French and English joined hands for *Auld Lang Syne* sung with great gusto; the old Russian Generals were greatly astonished and must have thought it was our national anthem!'

The Pipes of War illustrates how absorbing piping and dancing became and how popular they were among fellow prisoners. In it Usher is quoted,

Though only a young player I play here every day and do not find people too hostile to me. The Russians, French and even the Germans greet me with great interest and seem to find pleasure in listening to me, though as I said I am no great player. The most unsympathetic are always to be found among the ranks of the '*Sassenach*'. I learnt to play in 1911, on joining my Regiment, under George McLennan, who was Pipe-Major at that time. While on leave in Edinburgh I used to have lessons with his father, Jno. McLennan. Up till now I have only attempted *The Glen is Mine* and *Struan Robertson* in *Piobaireachd*, but having been thoroughly taught by the McLennans I naturally follow their way of thinking. Yesterday I played to a Russian who is a very good player of the piano. He was delighted with the Pipes and I could not play too many tunes for him. Strathspeys and reels are greatly appreciated by all our Russian friends. I had several pretty compliments paid to me by the Russians and French, both on our costume and dancing. Five of us took part altogether. I wonder if it would be too much to ask you to send me instructions for dancing the *Lochaber Broadswords* and the *Seann Triubhas* in case we have the misfortune to spend another St. Andrew's Day here in Germany. If we do, we shall give another Exhibition and I would like to be able to vary it. I know only 12 Strathspey steps and 8 Reel steps. Since I have been a prisoner I have taught 30 people to dance the Reel, including two Frenchmen and one Russian, and at present I have five pupils on the chanter. We are 16 Scots here, so can you say we are losing our national distinctions? I have only told you this because I thought it would interest you.

---

[23] This may have included holding a sword at both ends and jumping back and forwards over it, which became incorporated into the routine for the Certificate of Physical Proficiency at Edinburgh University gym!

As if all this were not enough, there was a garden to tend, and bulbs (with instructions) were requested from home. In December after much rehearsing they staged a pantomime, *Cinderella*, with 23 people taking part.

Usher was deeply unhappy about the Russians, whom he held in high regard, and who received practically nothing from home, while he got so many good things; food, clothing, uniform, sports equipment and books—even Tolstoy's *War and Peace* in Russian. He was most impressed by their chapel in the attic filled with flowers, pictures, incense, its intriguing sectioned-off altar and the superb unaccompanied singing which he found 'very complicated for a simple Presbyterian'.

1917

In February, 1917 temperatures plummeted, and there were 25° of frost. The tennis court was flooded for skating. With 400 wishing to take part it did not give much room for figure skating! The Russians were expected to excel but surprisingly did not, the Canadians being much better. The Germans, seeing the prisoners skating on the flooded tennis court, were scandalised, and seeing them *enjoying* themselves, put a stop to this recreation for three weeks.

On 23rd February, 1917 an account was received of the crushing defeats of the Russian army, riots in St. Petersburg and the abdication of Czar Nicholas.

Now Usher could tell his mother things which would otherwise be censored. Any reference to the French or Russians was immediately struck out. He told her about his capture, the treatment of prisoners in the immediate aftermath, and in the ensuing years.

On coming to after being hit on the back of the head at Le Cateau it was as a prisoner. We were kept in a church for two days and then marched back through the country passed through before the battle. Mother, I do not wish to whine, but what I'm about to say is fact. We were kicked, spat upon and hounded like dogs. At Cologne station the Red Cross nurses were ordered to take water to the wounded, who were almost mad for want of food and drink. They took it to the men and then poured it out on the platform before their eyes. They were told to take soup to the men. This they had to do but they spat into each bowl. Wounds were not dressed. We arrived at Sennelager and were separated from the men, who were made to stay out in the open all day and all night in the rain— not a blanket—nothing to eat. There were no arrangements at all. We were taken to Torgau. More insults. We were nearly mobbed.

At Torgau the Germans had made no arrangements for feeding or anything and we were treated as private soldiers. Burg was overcrowded, filthy and beastly beyond description, sanitation positively revolting—food practically uneatable. The officers were rude and insulting. One instance—a British colonel had his cap and his Bible on his bed—there was no other place to put them. A German officer entered, commenced to yell and scream, as is their custom, then picked up the Bible and hurled it across the room at the same time calling the colonel a *SWINEHUND*. Another British officer, who, owing to bad treatment in hospital, developed blood poisoning and had to have his finger amputated, was made to walk carrying his kit two days after the operation, but these are nothing compared with what happened in France and Belgium. They are too terrible for me to recount. I myself passed through Louvain while it was still burning. The treatment in the camps is the worst thing of all—no food—no clothing—conditions filthy—bullied—shot on the least excuse. One story, a private in the Guards, wounded in the leg was marching with a fatigue party but, unable on account of his wound to keep up, he turned to the guard to say so. The guard (ignored him), a little after the man again turned to say he could not proceed further. This time the guard shot him dead. I have seen the men come from the camps, lousy, haggard, in rags. Above all the Red Cross officials have been the worst for cowardly unchristian and brutal behaviour. This is for you and you only, to know how the other side work. How many British soldiers would now be alive were they not tended by German hands. The British are made to do all the filthiest tasks. The *Continental Times* is distributed to the men. It is in English and all our defeats are magnified. I know it is all lies—am angry and depressed having to read it. What of the men? Sir (name deleted)—I hope to God they hang him—went to a camp where they had collected all the Irish soldiers exhorting them to join an 'Irish Brigade' to fight the British. The men were threatened with prison if they would not go. The N.C.O.s who went round persuading the men NOT to go were punished, left hungry, in rags and maltreated. No wonder a <u>few</u> poor devils betrayed their country.

British orderlies at Mainz were abused and everything a coward and a bully can do has been done. It is a nightmare. The Russians get maltreated, they cannot get parcels and they have no money. It is impossible to live on the filthy food supplied. They die like flies, are sent to munitions factories and to dig trenches near the front in defiance of the Geneva Convention. If they refuse they are sent to prison. I could write many more things worse by far. They mix the different nationalities and endeavour to make us fight, but the effect has been to make us the greatest of friends. When they have a victory, flags are put up in the camps. While we have clothes we have no means of washing them. We were locked up in indescribably dirty and overcrowded conditions for whole mornings at a time. Many outrages were committed at Magdeburg. Officers had their personal possessions and watches taken from them. We had to salute German officers five paces before we reached them and keep the hand up for two paces past them. Newly captured prisoners have their greatcoats taken from them. The operating tables are covered in lice. You cannot imagine what a hospital here is like. Peskett, who has gone to Switzerland was very ill, yet he could not get one small cup of milk, the thing he needed most. If he had not got away I think he would have died. In fact, the whole miserable story is too sordid to think of. Whatever you hear people say and whoever they may be—you believe your own son, who, having been all through it, knows the truth. Again I repeat don't worry on my account. I am big enough to look after myself. My knowledge of German has stood me in good stead on more than one occasion.

The condition of the men is very bad and they are made to work like dogs in factories. They survive on account of their spirit. They never complain and it makes the Germans furious. As regards ourselves, this is a filthy place but we are well organized. We know the country is very badly off for food. We live on our parcels and have done all along.

The Germans are trying to make things a little better now that they know they cannot break us, but I can never forget what they did to us at the beginning. It may be un-Christian but there are limits. It is easy for people at home to say love your enemies—but not after 1914-15 in prison in Germany! Any pictures you may see are taken from favourable angles and on a fine day with the dirt and squalor hidden away for the occasion.

The fellow I mentioned in my [letter] Z was called Newman. He was flying near Dunbar and just met Iris and Cousin Lizzie. He is now in my cell. We are 7 in this room. Younger, Sampson (Royal Fusiliers), Le Hunte (Hampshires), Burrows (5th Dragoon Guards), Walker (Royal Flying Corps), & Newman [Royal Naval Air Service]. We live together and take turns at cooking. Now we are getting more ambitious, that is why I sent home for extra stores. The order to the Army and Navy Stores was for the French

Commandant. He was very pleased to get the things. I was so afraid to write his name in case the censor might take that out. He is Curt Berthélon (Cdt Berthélon, 68 Regt Inf. Le Blanc (Indre) of 48 Rue de Gazomètre, Tours (Indre et Loire)). He has been awfully kind to me and gives me an hour and a half's lesson a day and asks for nothing in return.

2/Lt Frédéric Eberlé, 37e Régiment d'Infanterie, Troyes (Aube), is a nice chap and please write in French to his mother at 20 Avenue Carnot, Montbéliard and act as a channel of communication. If she wants to send letters through, the method is to get a tin of biscuits, carefully remove them, put the letters in the bottom and replace the biscuits.

I am not going to do anything foolish but if the chance occurs one would look such an idiot not to take it. Send me maps from here to Switzerland and wire cutters. The last should be put in a box soldered shut. Maps in Baedeker. Hide things in cakes and cologne. Don't worry about me. I have stuck it for three months and I can stick a bit more now as I am 100% better and fit and I have, thanks to you and my friends, plenty to eat. I have made three attempts to get away. All failed. Once I got into a laundry van and got outside the gate, I told you in one of my letters. I was seen but I managed to get back to my room without being discovered. Now it is impossible because of the weather.

I am still cheery. I am so used to being a prisoner that I manage to pass my time without noticing very much what is going on around me. I seem however to have lost the desire for society and I am content to be with Pelham-Burn, Gillespie and a few friends. I have three real friends here Younger, Gillespie and P-B. I always used to be fond of going round with different people but now they bore me and I only want to be quiet. The great event since I last wrote you is that I have become very great friends with Pelham-Burn. It seems to make things easier to bear. The next time you write to Mrs P-B tell her that I am taking very good care of him.

Yet another Prison

Usher, by now promoted to Captain, was sent to his sixth camp, said to be brand new and for British only. He did not welcome the move as he would be losing old friends from France and Torgau. The camp was at Clausthal *am* Harz, which he reached on 23rd March 1917. Among the inmates were two generals, who arrived from the prisoner-of-war camp at Crefeld.

As in previous camps, Usher organised a programme of physical activity to keep the prisoners fit. His efforts received a boost when a consignment of tennis balls arrived from home in July. A Grand Tennis Tournament was immediately organised, with Usher as the driving force. He, of course, took part himself, and with his partner, C.K. Hutchison, won the first prize, an engraved silver cigarette box.

The many golfers among the prisoners bemoaned their forced separation from the golf course. The concept of a golf course within a prison camp seemed unimaginable, but, nothing daunted, 130 enthusiasts set about constructing a course. It may have extended to an area only the size of two tennis courts, but it had six holes, bunkers, tees and grass, trimmed with nail scissors and hair clippers. The longest hole was 20 yards and the shortest and most difficult, 7 yards. The greens, christened *Künst*, were a mixture of mud and granite siftings, and putted very true, providing great satisfaction to those who could not take more strenuous forms of exercise. A Grand Tournament was held, which had its own particular problems as the majority of the 130 members wished to play at the same time. Eventually, some sort of order was established and the tournament was completed, having given much enjoyment to all. At the end of September an Inter-Regimental Tournament was held.

For active prisoners Clausthal had a squash court. Membership was fully subscribed, but Usher sent for a racquet and balls in anticipation of a vacancy, so that he could get regular exercise throughout the winter. Membership came in October, and fencing classes were started in that month. Usher was a first-class fencer.

Piping, one of Usher's many talents, and a growing source of satisfaction to him, played a part in camp activities. He describes some of these in a letter dated 23rd July 1917.

My pipe class increases. It now consists of 9 members. I gave, it was very ambitious, a concert on the pipes. Two of my pupils performed. First Stirling played a slow march called *The Land of the Trees* and Allsop played *The Glendaruel Highlanders*. I played two sets. The first, *The Piper of Duneveg*, *Because he was a Bonny Lad* (strathspey), *Sandy Duff* (reel) and *Hielan' Laddie*. The second, *My Home* (slow march), *My faithful Fair One*, *Miss Drummond of Perth* (strathspey), *The Piper of Drummond* (reel) and *The Earl of Mansfield*. As encores Stirling played *Allan Water* and I played *The Skye Boat Song* and *Blue Bonnets*.

It was not the idea to dance but people insisted, so my dancing class performed. They were a little short of practice but did v. well. The whole evening was a great success; of course the audience was only composed of pipe lovers. Kynoch Cumming did me credit by his dancing. He is getting on well with his piping and already shows signs of turning into a piper. He is keen and conscientious which is more than half the battle.

On 28th July, 1917 a Bagpipe Concert was held in the squash court, somewhat restricted in size, whose acoustics made for some interesting harmonics! The progamme was:

1. March. *Orange and Blue*. Captain T.K. Allsop (London Scottish).
2. Highland Fling. Usher.
3. Song. *Mo rùn geal, dìleas*. A. McCuish (Cameron Highlanders).
4. Sword Dance. J.J.K. McEwen (Cameron Highlanders).
5. Reel. Captain A. Stirling (A.&S.H.), W.A.S. Brown (A.&S.H.), Captain H.L. Pelham-Burn (G.H.), J.K. Cumming (Cameron Highlanders).
6. March. *The Wind has blown my plaid awa'*. Captain Stirling.
7. March: *92nd Welcome to Edinburgh*, Strathspey: *The Market Place of Inverness*, Reel: *Christmas Carousing* and March: *The Cock o' the North*.

An orderly, Robb, a Gordon Highlander, gave an impromptu rendering of two of Harry Lauder's songs, to enthusiastic applause.

Usher maintained his interest in the welfare of the other ranks, and he was pleased to get a photo of the sergeants, who all looked well turned out and healthy. He noted that Colour Sergeant Isaac Bell should be sent 'tobacco etc' for Christmas. Private R. McDonald of the Seaforth Highlanders needed a Glengarry, size 7 with badge, which Usher's mother was asked to send.

In October came the sad news that Lieutenant-Colonel Dudley Ralph Turnbull, D.S.O., only 25 years old, had been killed in action while commanding the 20th Battalion of the Manchester Regiment. Commissioned into the Gordon Highlanders in 1912, he had played rugby for London Scottish. Having asked his mother, in 1914, to write to Turnbull's mother to congratulate him on his award of the D.S.O., a much more difficult letter had to be written to express Usher's profound personal sorrow.

Towards the end of 1917 parcels were held up, very few getting through. The prisoners were short of everything and Usher, the ultimate physical exercise and sports advocate, recommended that if they kept physical exercise down to a minimum it would be possible to exist on minimal rations. To this end boxing and fencing were stopped.

November, 1917 saw the Russian Revolution. Known in Russia as the 'October Revolution' because, in the old Russian calendar it took place in the month of October, it led to an armistice between Russia and Germany. Apart from the effect this was to have on releasing large German forces for redeployment on the Western front, the terms of the armistice included an exchange of prisoners. Russians in German prisoner-of-war camps were returned to the uncertainties of life in the new Russia.

While rejoicing in their release from the prison camps, Usher was sad to lose so many Russian friends. In addition to those mentioned earlier were A. Jarsanoff, Vasily Bereslavsky, Igor Makovetskiy, Pavel Meier, a long-term friend who went to Paris and worked in a bank there, Boris Naskin, Ivan Rink, Alexandr Leonid Vasilijev (affectionately known as 'Vaseline', and the recipient of shortbread from Usher's mother), Captain Nicolas Purshinn, and Lieutenant Boris Tichanow.

Usher never lost his desire to escape, and his handiness at carpentry was put to good use. A tunnel, so sound that it was still intact in 1945, was dug, but betrayed by an Irish informer. Usher, the eponymous 'tail end Charlie' was extracted from the tunnel at bayonet point.

Davies, an Indian Army officer, wrote a clever play called *Dale Sahib of Dustypore*, a production taking many hours of hard work. Usher and his band of pipers imitated Indian music on the chanter, which gave a surprisingly realistic Indian tone to the production.

Freedom—of sorts

Throughout the war there had been exchanges of prisoners, usually the seriously wounded and those deemed unfit for active service. Towards the end of 1917 agreement was reached between Britain and Germany that long-term British and German prisoners would be sent to Holland, where they would be interned, and not treated as prisoners.

Usher was eligible for transfer to Holland as an exchange prisoner, and he prepared for the move. He acquired a pair of boots fitted with continental-style blades for figure skating on frozen canals, and obtained a new Gordon kilt, made by Sergeant E. Robertson of the 1st Battalion. It is clear that communication between officers in one prison camp and other ranks in other camps was not only possible, but permitted.

The transfer took place in March 1918. On arrival in Holland Usher lost no time in organising a pipe band in the Dutch internment camps, with two pipe majors and eleven pipers. This was rewarded with a magnificent silver-topped sporran with a Celtic design, inscribed with the Usher badge on the front and, on the back, the words *'Presented to Capt. C.M. Usher Gordon Highlanders by the Pipers of the Hague Caledonian Society as a token of their appreciation and esteem'*.

Good tailoring enabled the British to keep up standards in public, and after years on a restricted menu the offerings of the excellent fish restaurants were hard to resist.

In February 1918, internees had published the first copy of *The British Empire* fortnightly, a magazine for interned of all ranks, with a cover price of 25 cents per copy and a quarterly cost of 1 florin 50 cents, post free. It was initially published on trust, first of all as the possible demand was unknown, and secondly, if the demand justified it, how were sufficient copies to meet the demand to be produced? Thanks to the ready support of the British Community in The Hague, civil and military, who underwrote the project, it was an instant success, and the staff, presided over by Corporal Holland and manager Lieutenant R.G. Malby, met the demand 'under difficulties which have to be seen to be realised'. The Editor, Captain H.S. Jervis, when he eventually moved on, heartily thanked them and the Sub-Editor, Mr Price, for producing the journal in the face of enormous difficulties. It was well supported by some three dozen local advertisers; hotels, restaurants, chemists, hairdressers, tailors, hatters, shoemakers, cigarettes, patent medicines, taxi services and much more. One advertisement was for *The British News*, the only daily newspaper in Holland published entirely in English. The Dutch combined hospitality with an appreciation of business opportunities, and the advertising budgets duly benefited.

The British Empire was a cross between a regimental and a parish magazine, with a touch of humour. There were notifications of coming events such as a fête in aid of the Red Cross Society of the British Empire, due to be held at Clingendaal by courtesy of Baroness de Brienen, who had done so much for the internees. There were serious articles, commentaries in verse, and reports on the progress of the war. In the edition dated July 26th, 1918, there was an analysis of the war, the authors, responding to criticism that the publication had not touched much on this subject, pointing out that they lacked the intelligence available to the generals about the logistics of conducting hostilities spread over such vast territories. Their last predictions had been confirmed by events, and even accepted military critics got it wrong. They would, therefore, only summarise past events, even though the best time to do this would be at the end of a year rather than in the middle. There were one or two interesting matters, and they referred to their comments made earlier on March 18th, which were:

To those who expect a triple offensive in France, (Belgium, the Somme, and the Vosges) resulting in a dissemination of facts. [Attacks by the Central Powers against the weakest link in the Entente chain.] Should the Germans attack the British Army in France they will be attacking the strongest part of the enemy's line. We dare hardly hope that Hindenburg will play into our hands quite so obviously.

The British Empire edition of July 26th expanded on those comments in the light of the historic events which had happened so soon after they had appeared in the March 18th edition.

Three days after this article appeared the Germans attacked the British line from Arras to La Fère and broke through, with the result that the present Amiens salient was formed. The article was adversely and somewhat severely criticised, but now that we can view the incidents of March from some small distance, does it appear that the remarks quoted were unjustified?

Does any Briton disagree with the statement that our front is the strongest part of the Western Front? We doubt it. Does anyone hold that the enemy would not have achieved more had he attacked a weaker part of the Entente front? Again, we doubt it. Then surely we may congratulate ourselves that he attacked where he did, the heavy losses he sustained slowing up the advance far quicker than would have happened had he chosen a weaker front to break.

We do not wish to minimise for a moment the importance of the success he achieved. His rapid initial progress was a most unpleasant surprise to us, and we still hold that we were not unreasonably optimistic in hoping that an advance of ten miles would be the utmost achieved against our armies then, as it has been before and since.

This year we expected the enemy to attempt to repeat his successes against Italy. After the tremendous debacle of 1917 there is no doubt that this objective promised the Central Powers results of the greatest magnitude. With ten or fifteen German Army Corps to 'point the spear', a break-through on the Piave front would have been easily within the reach of the enemy, and this would have necessitated a withdrawal from the Asiago heights, the abandonment of a broad strip of fertile country, and a retirement behind the Brenta.

A success of this sort must have meant a tremendous bag of prisoners, as, even now, the North Eastern Italian front forms a sharp salient from which it would have been very difficult hurriedly to withdraw. A second blow promised even greater results than the first, and it is not pleasant to contemplate what would have been the final result of a concentration of the Central Powers against Italy, if carried out with the determination which has characterised their other movements against our weaker allies. It might have resulted in forcing Italy to surrender, thus not only endangering our Mediterranean communications, but releasing practically the whole Austrian Army for service on the West Front.

Surely this was tempting bait. Why then did Hindenburg not take it? We think that he had three main reasons for this, one wrong, the others right. In the first place he probably thought that by a blow of the first magnitude he could break through the Western Front and gain a complete victory within three months. The second reason was that 1918 was the last year in which Germany could hope to win the war, thereafter the balance must be tilted more and more against her, furthermore that an Italian campaign would not leave sufficient time for the final blow on the West Front, the same summer. Thirdly, that Austria-Hungary would probably decline to send her armies to France to participate in the final blow when the threat to her own frontiers had been definitely removed.

It is the old story. Victory on the West Front means victory everywhere and in the same way victory over the British Army would mean victory on the West Front. On the other hand a French defeat would still leave the British to be dealt with, and so Hindenburg decided to go for the *fons et origo mali*, and he accordingly staked his all on one mighty throw in France. The next four months will decide whether he was right or wrong. We onlookers can but await the result with that confidence in the valour of our soldiers, which has so often spurred them on to achieve the apparently impossible.

This assessment of the progress of the war, at the end of July 1918, was undoubtedly optimistic, but it was also remarkably accurate. The assessment of Germany's options for attack, with the added strength of the 40 divisions brought from the Russian front, allied to the necessity of achieving victory before the full force of America could be brought into the field, was not far from actual reality.

There was nothing the internees could do about the progress of the war, apart from observing it, and they made the most of their life in internment. There was plenty of entertainment, both in town and in camp, and the other ranks put on entertaining productions, as the following account shows.

We have much pleasure in publishing a page of sketches, drawn by Leading Seaman Bygrave, of some old favourites in the N.C.O.'s entertainment world. Everyone who has been to the group concerts will recognise a great number, if not all of them.

The most famous character is without a doubt Mr. Fred Gwyn, 'the man with the india-rubber face', who has spent hours of his fellow prisoners' existence. On his arrival in Holland he lost no time in popularising himself not only with the interned, but also with the Dutch public, among whom he has now quite a following.

Mr. Andy Cutting, of the Royal Naval Division will be remembered for his excellent performance as Pooh-Bah in the *Mikado*, produced in May last at the French Opera House. 'Miss Dana Norton', a very prepossessing young lady is much in demand at the group concerts, where she is highly appreciated. Mr. Fred Baynton has an easy style, and sings light comedy songs with a very pleasing voice. Anyone who has seen Uncle Heard in his amusing 'Fireman' and 'Coon' songs, has only one wish, to see him again.

Messrs Tim Randall, Hennell, and Bert Hill are all excellent types of the good old English comedian, such as we used to love and applaud at the *Empire* or the *Tivoli* in pre-war days. They bring back to you the hoots of the taxis, the cries of the newspaper boys, and all the sights and sounds of London, as we knew it. Incidentally they make you laugh properly and without restraint— which is always good for the soul.

We wish that space allowed us to print a few more sketches of the many artistes, who have worked so hard and so disinterestedly to add to our gaiety.

We should like to mention especially Messrs Marshall and Neighbour, a baritone and tenor, who possess excellent voices and know how to use them. If at any time the P.O.W.'s produce another opera, such as the *Mikado*, they should prove invaluable.

We conclude with a word of thanks to those organising the Group Concerts. Week in, week out, during the whole of our stay in Holland, never in the lime-light but with unceasing energy they have laboured for our amusement. The success of their efforts is the best testimony to their work. May the best of fortune attend them.

All this good living, after the shortages and deprivations of prison camp life, meant that people got out of condition. Usher and some fellow enthusiasts set about putting this right, and on Saturday, July 13th, a large gathering watched the opening of the New Gymnasium Church, built by the Y.M.C.A. on the *Tentoonstellingsterrein* in Scheveningen. Among those present were Sir Walter and Lady Susan Townley, Brigadier-General Graham-Thomson, C.B., C.M.G., and the Baron and Baroness van Heeckeren van Kell. After the Dutch and British National Anthems, General Graham-Thomson performed the opening ceremony. Addressing the audience, he remarked on the importance of physical training, and the great part it played in the training of a soldier. He called attention to the fine work performed by the Gymnastic Staff in France. He referred to the valuable work of Captain Henslow, Captain Wand-Tetley, and Captain Usher, and paid tribute to the Y.M.C.A., to which credit was due for the building. He declared the building open in the name of the British Prisoners of War. After the ceremony an exhibition of boxing and fencing, a demonstration by the Gymnastic Staff, and a display of physical training were given. The smartness and efficiency of the physical training class were noted, receiving considerable applause.

This was followed by the Imperial Services' Athletic Meeting, at the *Tentoonstellingsterrein*, on July 20th, which was most successful. The ground was decorated, with flags and gaily coloured bunting all round the enclosure. About six thousand people were present, and the arrangements for their reception were admirable. The organisation of the meeting reflected great credit on Captain Henslow, officer in charge of Sports, and on Lieutenant Oliphant and the N.C.O.s under his direction for the preparation of the ground. On both days the military band played, which was much appreciated and added a welcome contribution to the meeting.

Despite the heaviness of the ground, and the recent imprisonment of the competitors in Germany there were some good performances. In the officers events Mr. Oliphant won 1st prize for the 100 yards race, the 200 yards and the quarter mile. The 100 yards was won, by inches only, from Captain Graves in the excellent time of 10.35 seconds. Captain Graves, besides 2nd in the 100 yards, easily won the 120 yards hurdles. Captain Bowring won the mile and Mr. Haymen the high jump, clearing 5' 3¼", and also finishing 3rd in the 100 yards. The donkey race caused great amusement, the efforts of the competitors to urge their unwilling steeds into anything faster than a walk causing much hilarity. The race was won by Mr. Haymen. In the events for W.O.s, N.C.O.s and men the 100 yards and 220 yards went to Corporal Anderson in 10.25 and 23.15 seconds respectively. Both were splendid races with excellent finishes, and the time for the 100 yards, considering the conditions, was extraordinary. The 3 miles, won easily by Sergeant Eccles, earned the Ladies of the Y.M.C.A. prize for the best individual performance during the meeting. No. 4 Group carried off the inter-Group Relay Race and Tug-of-War, and the British Consul General prize for the best group aggregate. The Irish team, who also came from No. 4 group, won the Empire Relay Race. The Y.M.C.A. prize for the highest individual aggregate was won by Corporal Holman of the Australian Imperial Force. There were many good performances, notably that of Lance Corporal Dawes, who won the half-mile and mile races. The results were highly creditable from competitors who had been on poor rations, and in confinement for some years.

At the close of the meeting the prizes were presented by Sir Walter Townley, who congratulated the competitors on their fine performances, and paid tribute to the excellent work of the fatigue parties of N.C.O's. The serious side of the prize-giving was relieved by the arrival of Fred Gwyn, who kept the crowd in fits of laughter with his comic antics.

One of the organising officers proved a highly entertaining and persuasive recruiter for the gym, and sport in general. It is not recorded who it was, but if it was not Usher it may well have inspired him at Edinburgh University some 28 years later! (It can reasonably be assumed that 'The Jerxpert', appearing in *The British Empire*, with his vast sporting repertoire and addiction to photography, was none other than Captain C.M. Usher. *Ed.*)

The Jerxpert

It was very difficult to find the Jerxpert. He is a man of such intense energy and such varied accomplishments. We were told that we should see him at the cricket marquee, but there a hot and exhausted XI languidly removed its glass from its lips and informed us that he had just gone off to the new gym. At the gym he had certainly left traces; a group of breathless athletes, a boxer with a bleeding nose, a broken sabre, and a general atmosphere of departed vitality, all spoke of his recent presence there. We ran him to earth in the Hexham Abbey Hut, where he sat with a cup of tea in one hand and a strawberry cake in the other, beaming at the motley crowd that surrounded him.

We approached with the deference due to greatness 'Good afternoon', we faltered.

'*Good* afternoon', he replied genially. 'Do you want to enter for any of the sports. No? Not even the donkey race? Lot of distinguished officers going in for that. No? Well, may I put your name down for a subscription,' he continued with a smile, that would have wrung a guinea from Scrooge himself. 'Thanks very much. Now what can I do for you in return'.

'Could you give us a few of the impressions you have received during your sojourn in The Hague'.

'Certainly, certainly. Very pleasant place The Hague, what! Charming people the Dutch. But don't you think it's a little bit dull. Not much to do'.

We suggested that with his numerous activities his time ought to be fairly well occupied. 'O well, of course boxing, and fencing, and cricket, and tennis and gym and bathing before breakfast help to fill up the day. But what we want here is some form of exercise. Not enough room for long runs of course. And then bathing inside a three mile limit, Childish! What we want are two games every day of really strenuous American football, no rules and no referees. Then one might have a chance of getting fit. But people won't do it; so confoundedly slack, captivity, I suppose. Well I must be off now. Got a tug-of-war, and two tennis matches and a dance at the *Kurhaus* to attend to. But before I go, must allow me to take your photograph. Always photograph everybody I meet. Snap-click; Thank you very much. So long.'

He was off like a whirlwind, leaving us rather limp and with an uncomfortable feeling of our worthless indolence.

There was fun to be found in Holland. The British let off steam occasionally by pushing Germans leaning over the parapets of canal bridges into the water, and then running to catch a departing tram. Not, perhaps, a gentlemanly thing to do, but understandable after the experiences of the preceding four years! There were many concerts, and at one of these Usher struck up an abiding friendship with Emil Huitfeldt, a Norwegian who had been Danish Ambassador in Berlin at the outbreak of war, and his wife. Twenty-one years later they lent him their house, Hollow Dene, in Frensham while Talavera Barracks, Aldershot was vacated by the Regiment in preparation for going to France with the B.E.F. for the second time.

America entered the war on 6th April, and on 29th September Ludendorff recognised that defeat was inevitable if he did not pull out first. With the Armistice six weeks later was born the myth of the undefeated German Army, the first seed of renewed conflict twenty years on.

On 9th October the Kaiser abdicated and went into exile in Doorn, Holland, followed by railway-wagon loads of personal treasures and household goods from the *Alte Palais* at Potsdam. He had been Colonel-in-Chief of the 1st Royal Dragoons since 1898. There is a vast silver salver, dated 1914,[24] bearing the signatures of the officers.

On 10th November Usher's brother, James, lost a leg to one of the last shells fired by Germany during the war. The 'rugger brothers' had paid a heavy price for their patriotism and sense of duty—one dead, one maimed and one incarcerated for four years.

At 11.00 am on 11th November the guns fell silent. Usher was repatriated on the 18th, when his long years in captivity came to an end. During that time he had sent home valuable intelligence, devoted time and energy to the welfare of British, French and Russian prisoners-of-war and spent much of his meagre prison pay assisting the men in many ways. Many dear friends and relations had been lost, but the fluency he had gained in Russian, French and German would prove invaluable in the years to come. He had not allowed despair, boredom or dull routine to prevail, and had spent those years helping others in so many ways.

With the Armistice, men and women at the Front, together with prisoners-of-war, could now return optimistically to a 'land fit for heroes' and to their homes in the Dominions and Colonies overseas.

---

[24] The Kaiser was removed from this position in 1914, so the silver salver must have been presented shortly before!

CHAPTER 3

THE INTER-WAR YEARS

MOST prisoners returning home after long periods of imprisonment found difficulty in adjusting to freedom and resuming a way of life that had seemed just a distant memory for so many years. Usher, who always took a positive approach to life, was delighted to see his family again, although there was shared sorrow and grief over the loss of his brother John in 1915, and the severe wounding of James on the last day of the war. He was welcomed back to the Regiment, and while he mourned the loss of so many fellow-Gordons, of all ranks, whom he had known before the war, he was joyfully reacquainted with those who had survived, and made new friendships among those who had joined during his long absence.

Back in the bosom of The Gordon Highlanders he threw himself into regimental activities, both military and social. He won first prize for the Highland Fling (Officers), which was not surprising, remarked some of his fellow-officers, as he had had plenty of time to practise! He also showed concern for the welfare of the Russian friends he had made in the prison camps, who had no home to return to after the Revolution, and who had fled to Paris to get jobs in banks, as taxi drivers or in whatever tasks they could turn their hands to. He helped them in their predicament by sending parcels of clothes, a contribution he maintained for some years.

He was soon in action on the rugby field again, and on 5th April 1919, when the Mother Country (the predecessor of the British Lions) met New Zealand at Inverleith before 15,000 spectators in the Inter-Services and Dominion Tournament, Usher was to the forefront. New Zealand won the match, although Usher scored a try for the Home Country. This was to be the precursor to a successful continuation of the international career that had been interrupted by the war.

In 1919 he was posted as an Instructor to the Royal Military College (R.M.C.), Sandhurst, where for the next two years his services were greatly appreciated by the Gentlemen Cadets of F Company. During this time he taught H.R.H. Prince Henry, Duke of Gloucester, to box, and they remained in touch for the rest of their lives. (Usher was delighted when the Duke of Gloucester was appointed Colonel-in-Chief of The Gordon Highlanders in 1937.)

1919 was a significant year in Usher's life, for that was when he became engaged to be married, to Madge Bell, step-daughter of Brigadier-General A.W.F. Baird, C.B., C.M.G., D.S.O., who was himself a Gordon Highlander. Baird had been awarded his D.S.O. during the Boer War, and had served gallantly during the First World War, commanding the re-raised 1st Battalion in November 1914 and going on to command 100 Brigade in 1918.

Madge, born on New Year's Eve 1897, was, in contrast to her future husband, a petite 5'3", and her hands could not span an octave. However, she could competently accompany her fine mezzo-soprano voice on the piano. While not physically strong, her spirit undoubtedly was, and she was to prove a great helpmeet throughout Usher's career.

At the age of one Madge stayed with her aunt and uncle, who had an estate in Buckinghamshire with a home farm and model dairy. It was before the days of tuberculin tested herds, and she contracted tuberculosis. Her parents consulted the great child specialist, Sir John Barlow, who prescribed sardine oil, chocolate, Brands Essence and a warmer climate. They took Madge to Biarritz. While her nurse wheeled her through the park, they met a kind old lady who was much concerned about how ill Madge looked, and who invited her to be walked daily with her nursemaid in her private gardens. Furthermore, the lady said, she should be fed on ass's milk. This encounter attracted press interest, which was not surprising as, unbeknown to the nurse, the old lady was Queen Victoria.

Madge's early childhood, with French and German nursemaids in her grandmother's flat in the *Rue Galilee* in Paris, summer holidays at Dieppe and long stays in Germany, where her sisters were studying music at Wiesbaden and Dresden, made her fluent in both languages. Childhood stays at Aviemore and Fortrose gave her a love of Scotland (and a crush on the gamekeeper at the Fortrose house which was only rivalled by her crush on Lord Roberts![1])

Sadly her parents were divorced after her father, whom she adored, lost all his money in an unfortunate South African

---

[1] Field Marshal Lord Roberts of Kandahar.

investment, and, dodging creditors, started life again making Turonne[2] in the Pyrenees.

Madge went with her mother to Mauritius before returning to school in London. When War broke out in 1914 she worked as a censor, and worked in the canteen of the French Red Cross in Belgium. Afterwards there was a spell in Paris at the *École des Beaux Arts* and film work as an 'extra'. While working in the Red Cross canteen she met troops who told of roadsides lined with crucifixions perpetrated by the Germans, and was convinced that *schrecklichkeit* (frightfulness) and *schadenfreude* (glee at the misfortune of others) were German national characteristics. She was even less well disposed to the Germans when her best friend in Paris, Susanne Fleurschem, a Jewess, died of starvation during the Occupation in World War II.

Madge's mother was disappointed that Charles Usher was not one of the 'rich Ushers', and had only his pay to support them. However, following a monumental stag party, the wedding took place at St. Peter's, Eaton Square on 17th December, 1919. Playing at the wedding were Pipe-Majors G.S. McLennan and James Robertson[3] (who composed a tune, *Captain C.M. Usher's wedding*, also known as *Glenord*), both of them Gordon Highlanders, Pipe-Major Jack Lawrie, former Pipe-Corporal of 1st Gordons until promoted Pipe-Major of the Argyll and Sutherland Highlanders, and Pipe-Corporal (later Captain) Donald Ross MacLennan, Scots Guards, half-brother of G.S..

Madge thought that 'Charlie', the name by which Usher was known in rugby circles was, in view of the hilarious comedy *Charley's Aunt*, undignified, and from then on 'Charlie' became 'Dougie', as he wore the Douglas tartan in mufti[4].

The economy honeymoon was spent in two locations. The first was in North Berwick, where Usher's mother took a suite in

---

[2]   A confection, typically made of honey, sugar, and egg white, with toasted almonds, usually shaped into a rectangular tablet or a round cake. It is frequently consumed as a traditional Christmas dessert in Spain.

[3]   This is probably the Robertson in Usher's coded letter to his mother quoted in Chapter 2.

[4]   Usher was almost certainly known as 'Dougie' long before this, as evidenced by the engraved salver presented to him by his friends Lieutenants T.J. Dobson and Captain Ian M. Henderson for his help when they were all prisoners of war together.

the Marine Hotel overlooking the golf course. Usher, who played golf with a handicap of plus two, gave his bride golf lessons, while battling the bitter winter winds blowing in from the Firth of Forth. Madge ran to her new mother-in-law in tears saying 'I hate golf' only to be rebuked by a sanctimonious admonition that 'you should hate nothing other than sin and the devil'. The new mother-in-law was a contrast to her own mother. Although she had a sporting background, and had ridden to hounds as a young woman, Usher's mother's spiritual home was St. Cuthbert's Parish Church in Edinburgh, while Madge's mother's spiritual home was the bridge tables of Monte Carlo! She was a keen golfer, but had not passed on her love of the game to her daughter.

The second honeymoon destination was Paris, Madge's home-from-home, to which she would escape as often as possible, and when absent would extol the city's virtues in French verse of her own composition.

In 1920 Usher was made an Officer of the Order of the British Empire (O.B.E.) 'for valuable services rendered as P.O.W.', which was greeted with some bewilderment by Usher. The Order of the British Empire had been instituted in 1917 by King George V to recognise people in the British Empire who helped the war effort, as either combatants or civilians on the home front. It was an appropriate award for Usher's tireless and unending work in the prison camps and in Holland, but it was unfamiliar to those who had been imprisoned, and therefore ignorant of its introduction. That it was given for his morale-boosting work with prisoners of war in organising sports and physical education, and easing war wounds and muscular injuries through sports massage was appreciated, but Usher had done that because it was natural for him to help his fellow prisoners, and he had never considered it anything but his duty. The lack of recognition for his work in sending back operational intelligence to aid the British war effort, an activity that could, if he had been caught, have led to charges of espionage, was a source of frustration and some resentment. He could not understand why he should be given an award for doing something within his 'comfort zone', but not for a clandestine activity that he had patriotically carried out throughout the war, which could have had severe repercussions had he been caught. That the award was announced beside one to an entertainer devalued it in Usher's mind, and when the official letter informing him of the award asked if he would like to have it presented at Buckingham Palace, he politely declined. The insignia duly arrived by post!

Returning to the rugby field in 1919, Usher found himself in Scottish colours once again when International fixtures were resumed. The match against France was held in heavy drizzling rain on Thursday, 31st January 1920, at the *Parc des Princes* in Paris before 30,000 spectators and Paul Deschanel, President of the Chamber of Deputies. Madge's friends in Paris were surprised to learn that, in order to keep the team at the peak of physical fitness, husbands and wives were separated. *'Quoi? Déjà divorcée?'* they asked incredulously. For Madge, the forced segregation before the match might have seemed a respite, as the marital bed could be dangerous when her husband, dreaming that he was in the trenches grappling with Germans, lashed out right and left. Usher led the Scottish team on to the field wearing the kilt over his shorts and playing the pipes, to a rousing welcome, followed by ecstatic applause when he removed the kilt.

The brilliant, but eccentric, Deschanel mooted a *Légion d'honneur* for Usher but, although he became 11th President of the Republic in February 1920, the proposal fell by the wayside after a bizarre episode. One night in May, at Montargis, just beyond Fontainebleau, Deschanel disappeared from the Presidential train and was found by a country station-master, in his nightshirt. Usher recounted that Deschanel knocked on a farmer's door, said he was the President and could he please have a bed for the night. The next morning he asked the farmer why he had showed no surprise the previous evening, and met with the reply that the farmer knew he was someone important as he had clean feet! Deschanel left office in September. It was to be another twenty-five years before the French decoration was awarded, for entirely different reasons!

The struggle for Home Rule in Ireland prevented Usher's selection for the match at Lansdowne Road, Dublin on 25th February. A post office branch had been the object of an armed raid, and there was a strong police presence in and around the ground, with a company of soldiers and armoured cars stationed near the entrance gates. Service personnel were not selected for the team on security grounds, and Usher missed the game.

In January, 1921 Usher was appointed Superintendent of Physical Training, Scottish Command, a job he held until January 1924. In those days officers in The Gordon Highlanders were not encouraged to go to the Staff College. Enough had reached the rank of General without having attended Staff College to make the qualification seem superfluous in the eyes of the Regiment, and Usher was not put forward for Staff College attendance.[5]

The Inspector of Physical Training in the Army was Colonel Ronald Campbell, C.B.E, D.S.O., who was to have a great influence on Usher's career in later years. Born in 1878, Ronald Campbell was an all-round schoolboy athlete at Bedford, where he won the Public Schools Boxing Championship and played rugby for the East Midlands and London Scottish. In the South African War he gained a field commission in the Duke of Cornwall's Light Infantry. He won the Army Officers Middleweight Boxing Championship in 1905 and, after transferring to the Gordon Highlanders, won it again in 1908. He was Superintendent of Physical Training, Southern Command in 1910, and in 1914 represented the Army at sabre and épée in Paris. He went to France with the Regiment, was severely wounded, made Brevet Colonel, awarded the D.S.O., the *Légion d'honneur*, four other foreign decorations and Mentioned in Despatches five times.

[The aftermath of the war had its effect on politics in Europe. In Italy Mussolini marched on Rome, but Victor Emmanuel remained on the throne. Mussolini took credit for making the trains run on time, and built up his power base steadily, but no-one took *Il Duce* too seriously.

November 1923 saw sinister developments in Germany. Adolf Hitler's failed Munich Beer Cellar *putsch* saw him sentenced to imprisonment in the fortress of Landsberg am Lech, where he started to write *Mein Kampf*, publication of which left little doubt as to his political programme and his hatred of the Jews. Significantly removed from the English edition, Hitler said that Germany 'Should be steeled for a final, active settlement

---

[5]   This was an unfortunate and short-sighted attitude. While Regimental soldiering was the first priority for officers, dissuading capable officers from attending the Staff College meant that their chances of employment outside the Regiment, and further advancement in rank were needlessly restricted. This would have an effect on Usher's own career, when promotion to higher command was denied him despite practical operational evidence of his outstanding abilities and command fitness.

with France in a death grapple for the realisation of German aims!' When the German Army marched home, honourably defeated but feeling humiliated and shamed, few doubted that they would be back. To add to anxiety the 'Bolshies' and 'The Yellow Peril' were never far from peoples' minds. The result was the development in Weimar Germany of a brittle, cynical, café society in which people lived for the day and well-known intellectuals fuelled a hedonistic lifestyle with cocaine, all the while flaunting this unfortunate and illegal lifestyle.

In Britain, however, most people preferred to ignore what was going on elsewhere, and concentrate on work and family, and getting what enjoyment they could out of life in a country that was still trying to recover from the exertions and expenditure of the war.]

The British Army concentrated on its peace-time role. Rejoining the 2nd Battalion in 1924, where he assumed command of B Company, Usher was stationed at Fort George, exposed to the north winds blowing off the Moray Firth. Musketry and platoon training occupied mornings, sport and leisure activities the afternoons. Usher, Madge and their infant son, Iain, set up home at Ardersier Cottage, in sight of the Fort.

The 2nd Battalion took part in the Scottish Command Bronze Medal Tournament at Redford Barracks, Edinburgh in March, 1925. Usher entered the fencing competition, in which he won the sabre and took second place in the épée and foil. He was in the Battalion bayonet team which beat the Royal Scots Fusiliers and qualified for Olympia. In bayonet competitions service rifles were not used, the bayonet being a spring-loaded plunger fitted in the muzzle end of a heavy wooden mock-rifle that was more like a Brown Bess[6] than the Mk III Lee Enfield rifle that was the standard firearm of the British Army!

As with the 1st Battalion in 1911, Usher was instrumental in introducing rugby to the 2nd Battalion in 1924. There was a core of rugby players among the officers, and many willing learners among the men. It was not long before the rugby team made its mark. In October 1925 the Battalion team defeated the East Lancashire Regiment 54-0, the Army Physical Training School, Aldershot 10-0, The Royal Aircraft Establishment 30-3, 17 Field

---

[6]   The smoothbore, muzzle-loading, black powder musket superseded by the inventions of rifling and breech loading.

Brigade, Royal Artillery 23-0, and after a 6-6 draw in the First Round of the Army Cup, defeated the 1st Pack Brigade, Royal Artillery 18-0 in the replay. In the Second Round of the Army Cup the Battalion drew 3-3 with the 1st Anti-Aircraft Brigade, Royal Artillery, but won the replay 6-5, a very creditable result considering that three of the most accomplished forwards, Usher, Lieutenant Pirrie and Second-Lieutenant Robertson missed the game through injury. This splendid run came to an end on February 3rd, 1926 when the Gordons, without Usher and Pirrie, lost heavily, 0-32, to the Gloucestershire Regiment. It had, however, been a splendid end to a first competitive season and thoroughly justified Usher's efforts in introducing rugby to a primarily football-orientated Regiment.

Madge formed the 2nd Battalion Concert Party, the 'Dandy Bees'[7], to perform in the Garrison theatre, in which Usher looked striking as a Pierrot! Her own singing, in a sophisticated programme, was extremely well received, and Lieutenant V.A.H. Denne[8] provided hilarious comic turns. The regimental magazine, the *Tiger & Sphinx*, reported:

> The 2nd Battalion Concert Party, yclept 'The Dandy Bees', which has been very ably organised by Mrs Usher, gave its opening concert in the Garrison Cinema at Fort George on November 3rd, meeting with unqualified success, and since then in the sacred cause of charity has been asked to repeat the programme at various local centres, such as Ardersier, Geddes and Croy.
>
> The organisation of the troupe, the designing of the dresses and scenery, the latter alone by no means a small effort, speaks well for the enterprise and ingenuity of Mrs Usher, whose talented singing is the *pièce de résistance* of the performance.

---

[7] The name 'Dandy Bees' was a phonetic anagram of the regimental motto 'Bydand'. The concert group was a feature of the 2nd Battalion throughout the '20s and '30s, until the onset of the Second World War brought it to an end.

[8] Victor Denne's father, Major H. Denne Denne, was at Tel-el-Kebir, Tamai and the unsuccessful Nile expedition to relieve Gordon at Khartoum. He was killed at Elandslaagte in 1899. Victor Denne was captured with the 2nd Battalion in Singapore and worked on the Burma railway. He survived captivity.

Madge's activities were not confined to Battalion concerts. She played a full part in the social life of B Company, and presented the prizes at the annual Company games. Usher, in addition to his duties as B Company Commander, was also the Pipe President and in this role oversaw the pipe band, with responsibility for both pipers and drummers. This was an ideal role for an officer who took such an interest in piping, and who was himself a good piper. He competed in Piping Competitions at the Scottish Command Athletic meeting and Highland gatherings two years running, where he achieved 2nd place on both occasions for marches in the officers competition.

In April 1926 Usher handed over B Company to Captain G.E. Malcolm, M.C. The Company bade him farewell in the *Tiger & Sphinx*:

> It is with regret that we mentioned the departure of Capt. C.M. Usher, O.B.E., to the command of Headquarter Wing. In saying goodbye to the Company, Capt. Usher remarked that no matter what he called upon the men to do, whether in their own time or not they always responded manfully and nearly always succeeded in their efforts.

Usher took with him from B Company Lieutenant J.B. (Jack) Robertson, an accomplished athlete and rugby player. In 1927, Usher and Robertson took a 115-strong party, principally the Drums and Pipes, to the Royal Tournament at Olympia. Shortly before a battle was due to be staged between the Picts and Scots, it was noticed that the two sides were missing. With only minutes to spare they were rounded up from the nearby pubs, and the fiery realism of the subsequent performance drew the admiration of the Princess Royal, who called Usher up to offer him her congratulations!

In December, 1927 Usher handed over Headquarter Wing and took command of A Company, which welcomed him with open arms. This coincided with a welcome addition to the family, Kenneth, a brother for Iain. The birth was noted in the next *Tiger & Sphinx*:

> Our heartiest congratulations to Capt. and Mrs Usher on the birth of their son at Edinburgh on December 8th. May we hope that he will follow in his father's footsteps.

In the welcoming family that was The Gordon Highlanders, two brother officers were delighted to be asked to be godfathers. One was Jack Robertson[9] and the other was the wonderful raconteur Kenneth O'Morchoe[10]. 'A' Company was no less forthcoming in its delight at this new (honorary) addition to their ranks:

> Congratulations to our Company Commander on a new arrival. Will he also one day play for Scotland, or be a boxing champion, or both?

Boxing, another of the sports that Usher oversaw, thrived in the Battalion. In the Army Championships Private J. Garland retained his title as bantamweight Army Champion, and created a very favourable impression on the Amateur Boxing Association officials[11]. Boy Davidson was just beaten in the final of the Boys' Featherweight and Sergeant Jamieson lost by the narrowest of margins in the semi-final after having won four fights. After the meeting Usher received a letter of congratulation from Major Wand-Tetley[12], who said he had never seen a regiment put up a better show.

In April 1928 Usher left the 2nd Battalion on appointment as Officer Commanding the Regimental Depot at Castlehill Barracks in Aberdeen. This was a significant step in his career, where he would be responsible for training recruits for both the regular battalions, and with additional responsibility for overseeing the whole recruiting process.

The Depot was a hive of industry, with the crash of recruits' boots on the barrack square under the eyes the Regimental Sergeant Major (this post was held by WO1 J. Chalmers and then WO1 J. Dunbar), rehearsals of the Pipes and Drums and Military Band, and non-stop work from the cobbler's shop, the kilt makers and tailor.

---

9   Lieutenant J.B. Robertson, who, as a Lieutenant-Colonel in the London Scottish, worked on the planning for D-Day, for which he was awarded the MBE.

10   Captain K.G. O'Morchoe, known in the Gordons as 'The General', who briefly commanded the reformed 1st Battalion after Dunkirk.

11   Private Jack Garland was the Bantamweight Champion of the 2nd Battalion, 1927 and 1928, the British Army, 1927 and 1928, the Imperial Services Boxing Association, 1927 and 1928 and the Amateur Boxing Association, 1928. He also represented Great Britain at the IX Olympiad in Amsterdam, 1928.

12   Wand-Tetley was interned in Holland in 1918 alongside Usher, and was an old friend.

The Gordon Highlanders looked after those who had completed their engagement and returned to civil life. The Depot worked hard—and no-one harder than Usher—with the business community and the Gordon Highlanders Associations of Aberdeenshire, to secure employment for time-expired men. Many had qualifications that could be useful in civilian life, and this was very important in the face of world economic depression in 1930. Madge did her bit by holding musical concerts in aid of the Child Welfare Centre.

Advances in technology greatly impressed visiting senior officers. In 1929 General Sir William Peyton, G.O.C. Highland Area, arrived unexpectedly, having come to watch gun practice at Torry Fort, but owing to bad weather conditions the exercise could not take place, and he came on to Castlehill instead.

The telephone message received in the Orderly Room was that General Peyton would inspect the Depot *gardens* at 11 o'clock. As everyone was otherwise occupied, Mr. Connell, the Officers Mess Steward, found himself responsible for horticultural duties. With tender care he 'sponged the soot off the wallflowers in the window-boxes of the Officers Mess'. The result was magnificent, and all was ready for inspection, but the G.O.C. showed little interest in garden or window-box. It transpired that the sender of the telephone message came from County Cork, and his pronunciation of 'Guard' sounded to Aberdeenshire ears like 'gardens'! The General inspected the barracks, which were in good order, but his greatest interest was in the electric mincer in the cookhouse, ably demonstrated by the chief cook, Sergeant Morrison.

The annual inspection was carried out by Major-General Sir W. Thomson, who watched the recruits march past in column of route. Afterwards he too went round the barracks, and he in turn was impressed by the electric mincer, demonstrated once again by the stalwart Sergeant Morrison.

There was delight when the Colonel of the Regiment, General Sir Ian Hamilton, G.C.B., G.C.M.G., D.S.O., T.D., came to inspect the recruits. In an inspiring address he waxed lyrical. They were chips off the old granite block of Aberdeen, he said. He did not think it was well enough understood what a splendid stepping off place for a successful career the army was for a young fellow who would keep steady and make good use of his opportunities.

Everywhere he went, he found Gordon Highlanders. He had found one running the whole show in a great railway hotel. They all did extraordinarily well, because a man who took a military career sensibly and learned to take orders learned also how to give orders.

He had recently visited an American military school and found young fellows whose parents paid £500 a year for having their sons there. What were they educated in? Why just what the recruits in the Gordon Highlanders were learning. Those American millionaires were sending their sons to military schools to learn to take and give orders.

Finally, he told them to keep their tempers and put on as much weight as they could, a piece of advice that reflected the times. There was no obesity problem in the country, where a square meal could be a real treat.

To the great disappointment of everyone, as time was getting short and Sergeant Morrison was absent on duty, the electric mincer was not exhibited. However, Usher recorded that a hearty vote of thanks was accorded by all ranks to the new innovation!

In 1928, the Depot, represented by Pipe Major Stephen, Corporal Aitken, Pipers Mitchellson, Geddes, Simpson and Thompson, under Usher's eagle eye, won the Scottish Command Inter-unit Piping and Dancing Cup, beating the 2nd Battalion, The Black Watch into second place. Dancing was the deciding factor, being judged 'correct' from a Highland point of view. Usher himself was 2nd in the Open Marches (Officers only). At the Scottish Command Bronze Medal Tournament at Redford Barracks in Edinburgh, Usher won all his events—sabre, épée and bayonet. Every member of the Depot team featured in the prize list.

In a concession to modern technology a wireless set was installed in the Sergeants' Mess so that they could keep in touch with momentous events in the world.

In February 1929 Usher was promoted to major. On April 25th 1929, that greatest of pipers, Pipe Major George S. McLennan wrote a poignant letter addressed to Major C.M. Usher, O.B.E., Clinterty House, Bucksburn[13].

---

[13] An imposing house kindly lent to Usher and long since burnt to the ground.

Dear Sir, Please accept my heartiest congratulations on your promotion to rank of Major. Although somewhat late, I am sure you know that they are none the less sincere. Of course you know also that only my illness prevented my writing at the time. I am enclosing a march, which, subject to your approval, I would like to dedicate to you. You should have had it years ago but I found there were too many 'Captains' Usher, so I decided to wait—I knew it would not be long—until I could dedicate it to *Major C.M. Usher, O.B.E.* I hope you will like the tune—I think it will sound very well in the band.

Yours respectfully, George S. McLennan.

At the bottom of the score McLennan wrote 'Hand and Eye just about done. G.S.M.'. The march, written *in extremis*, reflects the genius of G.S. McLennan![14] It was the last tune he wrote, and he passed away, aged only 45, on 1st June, chanter in hand. He gave his sons tuition for an hour each day, up until the night he died. Usher was devastated by the death of his old friend and mentor, who had done so much to help him develop his piping skills. The funeral, on 4th June, 1929 saw over 20,000 mourners lining the route to the station in Aberdeen. The gun-carriage bearing his coffin was led by pipe bands from The Gordon Highlanders Depot, the British Legion and one formed by competitors. The hearse was followed by his two sons and brother, Usher, Pipe-Majors George Findlater, V.C., James Robertson and George Cruickshank and Piper Bob Nicol. At Edinburgh the coffin was met by his brothers, Duncan, John, William and Donald, and by Colonel William Robertson, V.C. leading the many Gordon Highlanders there. His favourite *piobaireachd*, *Lament for the Children* was played by his friend, Pipe-Major Robert Reid.

G.S. McLennan's pupil, Charles Usher, a considerable authority on piping and Highland dancing, was in great demand to judge these disciplines at Highland Gatherings in the North East of Scotland.

Sporting activities featured high at the Depot, and Depot teams entered many competitions and tournaments. At the Royal Tournament, Usher won the Officers épée. He won the Scottish

---

[14] The letter and tune are now in the Gordon Highlanders Museum in Aberdeen.

Command sabre, and the 18-hole golf medal handicap at Turnberry. The Depot won the Highland Brigade Inter-Depot Golf meeting against the Argyll & Sutherland Highlanders by 23-0. On February 23rd, 1929, the Depot played against the Richmond Hockey Club and won, 5-0. Usher played a full part, and featured in the hockey team in most of their games.

Twice a year the Depot was represented at the Feeing Markets, where recruiting teams offered an attractive alternative for farm servants seeking re-employment on farms in the regimental area, in particular in the Mearns and Buchan, by signing on for a term with the Colours. The Feeing Markets were held twice a year, in May and November, a week before the end of the six-month term for which farm workers signed on with employers. This allowed them to terminate their current farm employment and find a new one, if so desired. Sometimes there was a feeing market in July for the coming harvest, but that was usually only for women and children. The principal markets were in Aberdeen, Huntly and Turriff, with others occasionally in Aboyne, Inverurie and Stonehaven. The farm servant ('servant' was the term for a farm worker) was paid at the end of his six month term. When taken on, the farmer would usually give him 2/6d, which would most likely be spent on beer at 6d a bottle. This sometimes helped the recruiting teams as the farm worker might get 'pootered' (drunk) and then enlist. The Pipes and Drums from the Depot, or one of the Battalions if it was in Scotland, all added to the attraction and glamour to put the potential recruit in a receptive frame of mind towards the Gordon Highlanders. Faced with the sight of smart, healthy and confident soldiers in uniform, with experience of soldiering throughout Britain and the Empire, the recruit could not help but compare their life with his. There were good arguments in favour of signing on. His life was one of unremitting toil, working through all daylight hours. He was fed and accommodated, but his accommodation was usually a bothy that was little more than a primitive hut. He worked in all weathers, driven by the needs of sheep, cattle and horses, or by nurturing growing crops.

As a Gordon Highlander, he would get regular pay, three meals a day, decent clothing and a smart uniform, clean accommodation with hot and cold running water, adventure, travel and comradeship. He would have the opportunity to secure a 1st, 2nd or 3rd class Certificate of Education. The courses included map reading and musketry. (One answer to a musketry question suggested that a Gordon recruit was capable of what is now known as 'lateral thinking'. He asserted that it was better to aim in the rear of a moving man. When asked why, he replied 'Weel, it would mak' him jump, and when he settled doon you would hae time to tak' a steady aim and shoot him'.)

There were new skills to be learned as clerks, tailors, kilt-makers, armourers, cooks, farriers, grooms, waiters, storemen and, for a lucky few, drivers. Experience in the Regimental Police could lead to employment in the civil police force on conclusion of their engagement. The recruit served with men from his own area and background. There was always the chance that he might get killed or wounded on active service, but to young men this was an attraction, bolstered by the belief that it would happen to someone else and never to him. If disabled, life could be hard and there was not much of a pension to look forward to, but exactly the same future faced a farm servant injured on a farm.

Although agricultural wages were depressed and harvest was in, it was hard getting men to join up, because some of the Labour Government wanted to grant the dole to farm servants, offering subsistence payments without the need to work rather than committing to a military life, albeit with a better wage.

Usher assisted the recruiting staff by sending the Pipe Band and his gymnastic display team to the principal markets, and by allowing recruits in training to recruit in their home areas. At the November Feeing Market over 100 men were obtained for the Army, but 40 were rejected on medical grounds. Of the 60 recruits raised for the Gordon Highlanders, 31 were obtained personally by N.C.Os. and men of the Depot.

Recruits would often bring in their friends, as recounted in the *Tiger & Sphinx,* in November 1930, as 'Overheard in the Castlegate'. This is a notional encounter, with a sense of humour, but it reflects the comparison between life in the ranks and in a society where employment was becoming increasingly difficult to find.

Geordie: 'Hullo, Tam! Yer lookin' braw. Far did ye get the new shuit?'

Tam: 'Oh, I'm in the Gordon Heilenders noo; an' I get fourteen bob a week, an' as I've got naething tae dae wi' it, I bocht this shuit'.

Geordie:	'Gosh, man! I hae twa pown ten a week an' it taks ma aboot twa year tae buy a shuit like that'.
Tam:	'Oh, aye. I dare say, but ye hae lodgin's, claes and beets an' a' yer extras tae buy oot o' that, an' I get the hale lot for naething'.
Geordie:	'Fin yer a sodger I aye thocht ye hid tae weer yer sodger claes'.
Tam:	'Sae I hive; but gin ye behave yersel' they lat ye weer civvies fan yer oot, and fin I ging hame they ga'e ye a cheeper ticket on the train'.
Geordie:	'Fat dae ye dee wi a' yer siller fin ye hinna got onything tae buy?'
Tam:	'Och, I files send puckles hame tae ma mither an' I'm keepin' the rest o't for ma month's holiday fin I get it'.
Geordie:	'Man, yer a right lucky divil! I've hid an affa time wi' weet weather an' I'm fair scunnert. Fu auld hive ye tae be tae jine'?'
Tam:	'Oh, echteen tae five and twenty if yer teeth's gweed. Come awa' up tae the berrecks recht noo an' get yer denner wi' me and we'll see the recruitin' mannie. Mebbie I'll get ye inta ma room if ye pass'.
Geordie:	'Come awa', Tam'.

Photographs of recruits from the Feeing Markets show rows of happy young men, some still in cloth caps, but most proudly kitted out in smart uniforms. Inevitably, new recruits found Army ways somewhat confusing, especially how to address their Instructors.

Sergeant-Major (*to recruit in civilian clothes*): 'What's your name, boy?'
Recruit: 'John Macduff.'
Sergeant-Major: 'Say "Sir" when you talk to me.'
Recruit: 'Sir John Macduff.'

Recruits were vaccinated against the dangerous diseases of the day. Going for 'jabs' was an ordeal, and remained so right through the Second World War. One recruit squad reported that, although at full strength, they were not yet formed because most were still attending hospital with sore arms owing to vaccination!

The Annual Inspection in 1929 saw the Depot at the peak of efficiency, with the high standards set and demanded by Usher maintained. The Inspecting Officer, Major-General Sir W. Thomson, G.O.C. 51st Highland Division, 'complimented Major Usher and his fellow officers on the high state of efficiency which he found in all quarters.' This was nothing less than Usher expected.

Some items of Regimental interest were presented to the Depot Officers Mess, among them a set of pipes from the 1st Battalion, found on the battlefield of Dargai, presented by Lieutenant-General Sir Walter Campbell, who had been Adjutant of the 1st Battalion during the campaign, and an Afghan knife, picked up outside the cantonments at Kabul by Private A. Gammel, 92nd Highlanders, on December 23rd 1879, and presented by Major C.M. Usher, O.B.E.

In March 1930 a Depot team competed in the Scottish Command Bronze Medal Tournament at Redford Barracks, Edinburgh. All the Scottish Regiments were represented, and competition was very keen. All the Depot competitors appeared in the prize list, but Usher, the Commanding Officer, won all his events—sabre, épée and bayonet. In April, at the Highland Brigade Inter-Depot Golf Meeting, the Gordons Depot met the Seaforth Depot and won by five holes, four won by Usher. In the final, against the Argyll & Sutherland Highlanders Depot, a close match had been expected, but the Gordons Depot proved easy victors by 23 holes, seven won by Usher.

While Usher was at the centre of all military activity at the Depot, Madge had a regular input. In August 1930 she organised a costume concert to raise funds for the Child Welfare Centre. She designed the ladies' dresses, which were described as being 'correct in every detail'. The report went on to say 'it is hard to single out any individual, but Mrs Usher did not let the cares of management and organisation interfere with her own singing, which was delightful and full of technique, grace and charm.' Over £40 was raised for the Child Welfare Centre, a considerable sum in 1930.

There was a sad event early in 1931 when Madge's stepfather, Brigadier-General A.W.F. Baird, C.B., C.M.G., D.S.O., was killed in a road accident. General Baird, a former Gordon Highlander, was a brother of Lord Stonehaven, who had recently been Governor-General of Australia. The funeral service took place in Fetteresso Parish Church, Kincardineshire. The coffin, draped with a Union Jack on which were placed General Baird's hat, sword, Orders and medals, was born from the church by sergeants of the Gordon Highlanders and was taken to the burial ground at Urie.

In May, 1931, Usher handed over command of the Depot. He had enjoyed his three years there, training recruits and preparing them for service in the 1st and 2nd Battalions. He had also ensured that everyone took part in sporting activities and physical education, and saw the Depot achieve highly creditable results in competitions and tournaments. There was an added dividend in that, when he returned to either of the Regular Battalions, there would be a wide spread of trained soldiers in every company who knew him and understood his methods and philosophy.

Usher took a short break to undergo a successful minor operation, then rejoined the 2nd Battalion, at Ballykinler, in County Down, Ulster. He took command of C Company, which welcomed him warmly. Usher took the opportunity to see his cousin, Sir John Milne Barbour, Minister of Agriculture in the Northern Ireland Government, who lived in the magnificent Conway House at Dunmurry[15].

In March 1932 the 2nd Battalion left Ballykinler and moved to Aldershot, but not before Usher's C Company won the inter-company bayonet fencing competition and the inter-company hockey league, giving them a commanding lead in the prestigious Gardyne Shield Champion Company competition.

Usher was sent on a three-month course at the Senior Officers School, but before going he had time to play rugby (at the age of forty!) for C Company against C Company, 2nd Battalion, The Queen's Own Cameron Highlanders. On his return he continued leading sporting activities from the front, shining at golf in a drawn match against the London Scottish in which he won his games in the Four-Ball and the Foursomes. In the cricket match against the London Scottish he was the Gordons' top scorer with 39 not out. He played in the C Company hockey team that played their Cameron Highlander counterparts, and scored in their 4-1 victory. His training and coaching led to the C Company boxing team winning the Byng Cup.

---

[15] Conway House was subsequently blown up by the IRA, rebuilt, blown up a second time, resurrected as a hotel, blown up again and finally demolished.

In September 1932 the Military Band, and the Drums and Pipes had a successful appearance at the British Exhibition in Copenhagen. The party was under command of Major G.T. Burney, M.C., but during the visit Major Burney's father, Brigadier-General H.H. Burney, a former commanding officer of the 1st Battalion, died. Major Burney returned home and his place was taken by Usher.

In May 1933, after nine years in the Regimental fold, with tours in the 2nd Battalion and the Regimental Depot, Usher was appointed General Staff Officer for Physical Training at Eastern Command in Colchester. C Company said farewell to him in the *Tiger & Sphinx*:

> It is with very genuine regret that we bid *au revoir* to our Company Commander, Major C.M. Usher, O.B.E. Rumour has had it for quite a long time that he was due to take up a staff appointment sometime in the near future, but we had hoped that the rumour in this instance would prove false. However, he [left] us on May 1st to take up his new appointment, and one and all would like to take this opportunity of congratulating him on the appointment, and wishing him every success. Taking as he did, such an active and keen interest in every branch of sport, and setting such a splendid example himself, his place in the Regiment will be a very difficult one to fill.

[Events in the outside world took a sinister turn. In 1931 the Japanese invaded Manchuria, and dormant concerns about the 'Yellow Peril' now grew into a very real and worrying apprehension. On February 27th 1933, the *Reichstag* fire in Berlin, engineered by the Nazis, gave them control. By the time Usher took up his Staff appointment in Colchester, the Third Reich had been born, bringing in a regime of terrorism, brutality, and imprisonment of those who opposed Hitler in the newly constructed concentration camp in Buchenwald.

On June 30th 1934 Hitler's S.S., under Heinrich Himmler, ruthlessly executed the leaders of his personal Brown Shirt army, the S.A. (*SturmAbteilung*), including Hitler's friend Rohm, *Reichsminister* and S.A. Chief of Staff, *Gruppenführer* Karl Ernst. Prominent people were shot, including former Chancellor, General Kurt von Schleicher and his wife. Hitler made no secret of what he had done, as ruling by fear was his *modus operandi*.

Germany and the world knew about concentration camps, with nearly 50,000 inmates, although the real horror was not even dreamt of. Himmler had a free hand but Hitler ensured that he kept the details to himself. The German people knew about Jews trying to escape the terror by seeking asylum abroad, and about Himmler's eugenics programme to produce pure 'Aryan' Germans. They, especially women, were ecstatic about Hitler, who, they believed, had given Germany new hope and pride.

On August 2nd, 1934 Hindenburg died, and Hitler became Head of State. General von Blomberg, the Minister of Defence, and the General Staff did not object to taking the new oath, not to the German State, but to Hitler himself:

> 'I swear by God this sacred oath, that I will render unconditional obedience to the Leader of the German Reich and people, Adolf Hitler, the Commander-in-Chief of the *Wehrmacht*, and that I will, as a valiant soldier, at all times be ready to stake my life for this oath.'

But the world just wanted Germany, where almost everyone from the leadership down was in some uniform or other, contained and it hoped for the best.]

Usher threw himself into his job, his sporting ability and appreciation of how best to achieve physical fitness standing him in great stead. He oversaw physical education in Eastern Command, guiding and helping officers and physical education staff in all the units in the district. In this, as in every endeavour, he was successful.

In autumn 1934 the 2nd Battalion handed over its barracks in Aldershot, earning great praise for the handover. There were only two articles deficient in the entire barracks, the total value being 10s. 2d., very possibly a record for any battalion, and the state of the quarters and barrack rooms was 'highly satisfactory'. The Battalion boarded the troopship *Somersetshire* and sailed to Gibraltar. The *Somersetshire* was to be the vehicle for a unique occurrence in the history of the Gordon Highlanders, when, bringing the 1st Battalion back from Palestine, it berthed at Gibraltar on 5th January, 1935. The troopship remained in Gibraltar overnight, and a mass parade of the two Battalions was held on the Alameda parade ground on Sunday, 6th January. The importance of the occasion, only the second time the two Battalions had met in peacetime, was enhanced by the presence of General Sir Ian Hamilton, the Colonel of the Regiment, who journeyed from Britain in order to be present.

A thick 'peasoup' fog enveloped Liverpool in November 1935 when Usher, Madge and their younger son, Kenneth, embarked on the Anchor Line SS *Britannia* bound for Gibraltar, where Usher was to be Second-in-Command of the 2nd Battalion, The Gordon Highlanders.

Four days later, after a safe passage through the Bay of Biscay, they arrived, and stayed at the Rock Hotel, before being allocated a quarter at 45 Engineer Lane, at the foot of the steps to the Moorish Castle. It was a secluded house with a little garden and an orange tree, entered through a gate that opened on to the street. On one side were the frosted windows of the synagogue and a large water tank. At night they heard the raucous shouts of '*caliente*' from street vendors, and the smell of hot olive oil wafted on the evening breeze. The Rock was well-ordered and tidy, as a garrison outpost should be. In the springtime it was redolent of a blend of narcissi and cigar smoke, and later in the year, when riding down to the frontier through an avenue of eucalyptus trees, the strong scent of the ripe fruit was everywhere. In Gibraltar it seemed always cheerfully sunny— except when the Levanter[16] struck, which brought with it 'flu-like symptoms. Officers had square canvas beach tents on the otherwise deserted and idyllic Sandy Bay where, in addition to sand and clear sea, there was the diversion of swimming round the headland into the caves. Child beggars in La Linea lined the passage that families took to the wild shoreline of the road to Malaga for picnics. To get to the sea they had to negotiate marsh and scrub, dotted with pools populated with terrapins, which turned the outing to an adventure for young children.

In Gibraltar, while military training was carried out on the limited training areas available, opportunities for sport and recreation abounded. The Gordons competed for, and usually won, a collection of cups for tug-of-war, boxing, polo, bayonet fencing, point-to-point, rowing, hockey, water polo and cricket. Usher played polo with Captain B.J.D. 'Joe' Gerrard and Lieutenants Pirrie, More-Gordon, Ross, Buchanan, Adam, Findlay-Shirras and Gordon-Duff at Royal Calpe, which was also the venue for the point-to-points.

---

[16] The cool, moist easterly wind that blew in from the Mediterranean.

Usher's insistence on physical fitness and participation in sport as essential elements of a competent soldier soon made itself clear. The *Tiger & Sphinx* commented:

> We welcome Major Usher, who is by no means a stranger to the Wing. In his capacity of Senior Major, we see very little of him, but there is no question as to his presence. Physical-training kit figures more in our range of dresses, and quite a few of us wish we had been born sooner. The benefits of physical training will be felt in a very short time, *i.e.*, when we descend on North Front Ranges.

[In 1935 the German army marched into the Saar, and Mussolini invaded Abyssinia from Eritrea in defiance of the League of Nations. The world was shocked when Mussolini, dissatisfied with progress, authorised Marshals Badoglio and Graziani to use mustard gas. The League was seen to be ineffective, and German and Japanese expansionist plans proceeded unchecked.]

In the light of these events it was decided to show the British flag in Egypt, and in June 1936 the Battalion was taken there by the battle cruisers HMS *Repulse*, *Exeter* and *Shropshire*. The Headquarters Wing and one platoon of D Company were on *Exeter*. The Royal Navy, as always, was extremely hospitable, and made everyone feel at home. The Gordons, anxious to be more than just passengers, helped out with some of the everyday duties, and on one day the Gordons took over the 'upper deck' and the sailors the 'lower deck'. While the seamen cleaned and polished down below, the Gordons holystoned the quarterdeck and 'chipped' paint to their hearts' content. The holystoning party was led by Sergeant Lloyd, the Gordons' Master Tailor, who, when giving a spirited exhibition of the hornpipe, trod on the soap, abruptly terminating the dance!

Usher and Madge often spoke of 'Hooky' Bell, of HMS *Exeter*, who would later acquire great renown as its Captain at the Battle of the River Plate. The voyage was enlivened when a man fell overboard from the *Shropshire*, an event described in the *Tiger & Sphinx*:

> Immediately the man was in the water, rumour started in; the biggest estimate being two sailors and two Gordon Highlanders overboard! No sooner had the alarm been given than the ship changed from 24 knots to full speed astern, and the illuminated lifebuoys were in the sea and searchlights

turned on; the *Exeter* stood by. The boats were lowered without any fuss or bother, and very shortly the lights picked up a man swimming strongly in the water. It proved to be A.B. Milne, who, by a coincidence, came from Aberdeen. Luckily the sea was calm, but even so the Navy say it is only a 50:50 chance of saving a man.

The Gordon Highlanders were the unwitting cause of this accident, as a signal from HMS *Shropshire* explains:

> During exhibition of sword dance given in waist by Gordon Highlanders, several men clambered into cutter to see better. One man slipped and fell overboard, and it was thought that he might have taken someone else with him. Man was Ordinary Seaman Milne, who was picked up swimming strongly and is none the worse.

Despite this incident, which added excitement to the cruise, it was a congenial voyage for all ranks, who were happy to work on deck for their keep. On arrival they encamped at Sidi Bishr. The political situation demanded nothing more than the Gordons' presence, and activities were organised to keep the men gainfully occupied. Sport figured largely, and Usher featured in cricket games against the Royal Navy ships and other army units in Egypt. After a month 'sitting in the sand at Sidi Bishr' it was decided that the situation in the Middle East was stable enough to allow the Battalion to return to Gibraltar, and it sailed on HMS *Repulse*, arriving back on 24th July, 1936.

By the time the Battalion got back to Gibraltar the Spanish Civil War had broken out, which was to cost half a million lives. The Germany and Italian air forces fought for Franco's Nationalist rebels, and the Soviet Air Force fought for the Republican Government. The three powers used the war as a training ground. The Spanish people suffered appalling privation. Prisoners taken near La Linea by the Nationalists were given the choice of drinking a pint of castor oil and being chucked out into no-man's-land, or a bayonet in the stomach. They were rescued and placed in compounds just inside the Gibraltar Frontier. From their barracks, the Gordons could see the Spanish Government battleship *Jaime Primero*, supported by cruisers, bombarding the Carnero Point battery and Algeciras. The *Primero* was bombed by the Nationalists and the Republicans replied with anti-aircraft fire.

Foreign fleets paid courtesy visits to Gibraltar. The German pocket battleship *Admiral Scheer* and the heavy cruiser *Admiral Hipper* stood off shore, and there were mixed feelings when their smartly turned out sailors went shopping in the High Street. The Italian cruiser *Cortiglione Gorizia* came alongside in the dockyard, and the officers proved charming hosts. The arrival of the Home Fleet, with HMS *Hood, Nelson, Barham, Orion, Rodney, Renown*, the aircraft carrier *Furious* and the submarine *Oberon* was a tonic. The might of the British Empire on the doorstep was reassuring. There were parties on board, and the flag lieutenant made a great hit with the ladies. A party of Gordons acquired a new skill—coaling ship!

Inevitably conversation turned to what Hitler might do next, where the German quest for *lebensraum*, and the reunification of ethnic Germans lost as a result of the Versailles Treaty would take them. The undermanager of the Rock Hotel was German, and a Nazi. He admired the nursemaid, pretty, busty, blonde and very Aryan in appearance, whom Madge had employed to look after her younger son, and whisked her off to the Third Reich!

The Battalion welcomed the news that it would be posted to Malaya. While it had enjoyed Gibraltar, the small and crowded area in which it was confined was a source of frustration, limiting opportunities for realistic military training and, since the outbreak of the Spanish Civil War, off-duty visits across the frontier. In 1937 the Battalion sailed to Singapore, that fascinating and exciting island at the southern tip of Malaya. The Gordons were stationed at Selerang Barracks, Changi, at the east end of the island. Although based in Singapore there was plenty of opportunity to see Malaya. Field firing was carried out at Kuala Lumpur, and the men were kept fit by frequent route-marches, many of them across the causeway into Johore State. There was opportunity for sport in Singapore, and for off-duty travel to much of south-east Asia. Usher, on leave, took Madge on expeditions by ship and train to Bali, and to Cambodia where they visited the ruins of the ancient city of Angkor Wat.

[In July 1937 Japan invaded China and demonstrated her supremacy in the air and on land. Everyone in Singapore was on the lookout for spies, with the ubiquitous Japanese hairdressers particularly suspect. In Europe the Rome-Berlin Axis was formed.]

Usher was informed that he was to take command of the 1st Battalion in 1938. He had served in the 1st Battalion when he was commissioned in 1911 and had nominally remained with it until 1919, but as he had been a prisoner throughout the war, his actual regimental service with the Battalion had ended in August 1914. He was overjoyed at the prospect of commanding the Battalion. Towards the end of 1937 he returned to Britain and enjoyed a period of leave before being promoted to Lieutenant-Colonel and taking over command from Lieutenant-Colonel J.M. Hamilton at Redford barracks, Edinburgh on 16th January, 1938.

[The expansion of Hitler's Reich was now extremely unsettling, with the real prospect of war. In March 1938 the *Wehrmacht* marched into Austria, which ceased to be an independent state. In September the notorious Munich Agreement was signed by Neville Chamberlain, and at the end of the month wireless stations throughout Europe were regularly reporting on the progress of the impending calamity; Hitler's speech in the sports stadium, Mussolini's at Verona, Roosevelt's appeal to the *Führer*, the mobilisation of the Fleet and the call up of Belgian reserves all seemed to make conflict appear inevitable.

In October 1938 the *Sudetenland* area of Czechoslovakia was ceded to Germany, and in November *Kristallnacht* took place. Jews were sent to concentration camps.]

In March 1938 the 1st Battalion left Edinburgh and moved to the austere Talavera Barracks in Aldershot, where Usher proved that his fencing skills were still well-honed when, at the Aldershot Command Annual Bronze Medal Tournament, he won the épée event.

War seemed possible. There was hope that negotiation and compromise could avert conflict, but the Armed Services, woefully underfunded for so long, strove manfully to prepare, although the training showed little concept of the fast-moving mechanised warfare that was to stun the world two years later. In The Gordon Highlanders training stepped up almost to fever pitch, and was only halted, momentarily, by a visit in April by King George VI and Queen Elizabeth.

Incessant clanging came from the Motor Transport (M.T.) Section, as it learned how to handle and maintain new vehicles and equipment. Weapon training was intensified, especially for the Bren gun, the Army's new light machine-gun that would prove such a potent weapon in the war that was soon to come, and in learning about the 'Boys' anti-tank rifle, that was to prove much less successful[17]. To the clamour was added the hoarse commands of drill sergeants and the crash of ammunition boots.

The Bren gun, on its bipod, with a cleverly designed spring mechanism that reduced recoil to an insignificant level, was a stable weapon system that was remarkably accurate, yet some found it difficult to master. The *Tiger & Sphinx* records:

> Many and long are the wails regarding our new targets and weapons. The Bren gun seems to get everyone down—down to the lowest possible score, if nothing else. One bright individual was heard to say, 'Well, the bullet left this end all right. The fault lies in the butts.'

Usher, fists clenched and shoulders shaking, hissed like a snake through his bristling regimental moustache when the high standards he demanded were not met. He knew what lay ahead, and insisted that only the best would do in every facet of military training. Athletic and sporting achievements that fostered team-work, however, always mellowed him and brought out the benevolent streak. *Mens sana in corpore sana* and Kipling's *'If'*, the latter always displayed prominently behind his desk, were the principles that drove him. To be thought of as a 'wash-out' was the kiss of death. Major R.G. (Dick) Findlay-Shirras[18], one of his subalterns, put it succinctly 'You were all right if you played rugger. I was fortunate, I played rugger'.

As well as a pipe band, Highland Regiments had a brass band, known as the 'Military Band', which, in unconscious anticipation of the radio programme *Music While You Work* (which cheered workers in factories and kept morale high during the war), made its presence felt every morning, with practice on the barrack square below the windows of Usher's quarter. (After

---

[17] The Boys anti-tank rifle, named after its designer, Captain H.C. Boys, was a 55 mm weapon, weighing 36 lb, that was to prove ineffective against German armour, but more successful in attacking machine-gun nests and pillboxes, and in long-range anti-personnel operations.

[18] Findlay-Shirras was a subaltern in Gibraltar when Usher was second-in-command. He had a great sense of fun and like his friend, David Niven in the HLI, was never one to miss a good party. He was taken prisoner at Tobruk by the Italians and then fell into German hands when Italy surrendered. He fell foul of the Gestapo, who were at a loss to appreciate his sense of humour.

the war both bands would, on occasions play together, a practice which piping purist Usher could never abide.)

In September 1938 Germany claimed the Sudetenland from Czechoslovakia, and the 1st Battalion was warned for deployment there. The men welcomed this opportunity for foreign service, and the Battalion was at six hours notice. As diplomatic negotiations went on, notice was reduced to 12 hours, then 48 and finally, to the Gordons' disappointment, they were stood down. The people with the most trying time were the draft, who had embarked at Southampton, only to be recalled next day.

The clouds of war did not interfere with the 1938 and 1939 Royal Tournaments, in which the Battalion took part, and which Usher helped to organise and make a memorable success. The officers team won the Aldershot Command épée competition.

On 1st September, 1939, Germany invaded Poland, and only a miracle could save Britain from becoming involved. Usher's elder son Iain, at home from the Royal Military Academy (R.M.A.) Woolwich (known as 'The Shop'), before he joined The Royal Engineers, had a home-made wireless set rigged up on the ground floor, with an aerial wire trailing up the three flights of stairs to the top of the house. He had been more interested in the engineering than the military aspects of his instruction, and even confessed to being somewhat pacifistically inclined, until he heard of the brutality of Nazi attacks on women and children. On the morning of 3rd September, with his younger brother Kenneth beside him, the electricity was switched on and there was an anxious pause while the valves slowly glowed red. After a few whistles and crackles it was tuned in and ready for the all-important broadcast. At 11.00 am Prime Minister Neville Chamberlain came on the air.

I am speaking to you from the Cabinet Room at 10 Downing Street.

This morning the British Ambassador in Berlin handed the German Government a final note stating that, unless we heard from them by 11 o'clock that they were prepared at once to withdraw their troops from Poland, a state of war would exist between us. I have to tell you that no such undertaking has been received and that consequently this country is at war with Germany.

Iain was now as resolved as his father for the grim years that would lie ahead.

CHAPTER 4

1939-40—THE 'PHONEY WAR'

IN September 1939 the future looked bleak. The prospect of jack-boots marching on British streets seemed all too real, as did the spectre of the Gestapo rounding up and liquidating people on the Nazi blacklist. Britain braced for bombing and gas attacks.

For Charles Usher, memories of 1914, with the deaths of brother officers and men, and long years of imprisonment, were still clear, as were the loss of his brother John and so many good friends, and those destroyed in body and mind like his brother James.

The Gordons vacated Talavera barracks, the Quartermaster reclaimed the Army furniture from the house, and Usher arranged for the family's possessions to be sent to his mother's flat at 32 Drumsheugh Gardens, Edinburgh, where they were stored in the basement. The family moved into Hollow Dene, the house in Frensham lent to them by Emil Huitfeldt, Usher's good friend from internment in Holland.

Hollow Dene, a welcoming and comfortable house, with an intriguing priest's-hole in the attic reached through a secret panel, was an ideal retreat for the short embarkation leave. The Huitfeldts were in Oslo, and the generous loan of the house, which came with housekeeper and gardener, was in exchange for looking after the huge, boisterous Irish wolfhound, Viking, who got excited to fever pitch when confronted by anyone wearing a civilian gas mask, which made a rude noise when the wearer exhaled.

It had been a glorious summer, with endless sun and blue skies, and fruit trees heavy with fruit. The hens, and the sow in her sty with her offspring, were happy and contented. There were tennis parties with Reginald Dorman-Smith, the Agriculture Minister, and his family. The white flannels would not see the light of day for a long time, and as they were packed away the inevitable thought was, 'Who would survive?'

There was one last walk across the fields with Madge, who wondered if she would ever see Usher again. She also worried about Iain, who would be involved in the war that loomed. Their younger son, Kenneth, was preparing for any German assault by hurling carbide-filled apples across the garden!

On 20th September 1939, Usher said goodbye to Madge. He took the 1st Battalion from Aldershot to Southampton, from where they sailed on 28th September, landing next morning in Cherbourg. The journey to Templeuve, south-east of Lille, was long and tedious. Some went by road, but the main body faced a long uncomfortable journey in goods wagons. Some straw was obtained to ease the journey. During this journey the news that Warsaw had fallen came through. Everyone knew that Hitler would turn his attention to the French and the B.E.F. in the west.

They reached Arras on the 30th, marched to Neuville, then went to Sainghin-en-Melantois for a welcome five-day halt, with the chance for recreation and baths. The battalion reached Templeuve-en-Pevele on 10th October, and work started on fortifying the town and setting up a mortar practice range. Three companies were detached to Cysoing on the 29th, a day after a visit, filmed by Movietone News, from Lord Gort, Commander-in-Chief, an old friend of Usher's, and the commander of 1 Division, Major-General (later Field Marshal) Alexander.

Lord Gort was met by Usher, lean and fit, immaculate in service dress, tartan riding breeches, riding boots and glengarry, and armed with his ashplant[1]. Together they set off at a brisk pace on their tour of inspection. Following on behind, the general's entourage was accompanied by regimental officers, also in service dress, but with kilt and dress hair sporrans whose gleaming brass mounts had so fascinated Boer snipers at the turn of the century.

First stop was trenches dug by a sergeant and his Jocks, in kilts, distinctive looped red flashes in their hose tops, smart khaki jackets with polished buttons and brass 'GORDONS' shoulder insignia. They wore their T.O.S.'s (Tam o' Shanter bonnets), with the 'Bydand' cap badge, but discarded their belts. For security reasons the commentator would only disclose that Lord Gort was visiting a 'famous Scottish regiment'. He took the salute from the kilted guard, and chatted to them.

Then followed a change of scene, a reminder of what was to come. The Jocks, steel helmeted, with blackened faces, gas masks on chests, rolled gas capes secured above the small packs

---

[1] The walking-stick made from ash wood that was part of the uniform of officers in The Gordon Highlanders.

on their backs, were busy wiring, encouraged by a piper, a man who in battle heartened the men, frightened the enemy and who, being most conspicuous, was the bravest of the brave.

In November Major-General the Duke of Gloucester, Colonel-in-Chief of the Gordons, whom Usher had taught to box at Sandhurst, inspected the battalion, followed the next month by HM King George VI, who was given a rousing reception. The weather was terrible, with alternate heavy rain and frost, which then thawed—not ideal for digging trenches and anti-tank ditches to improve their sector of the defences along the Belgian border, from the Western end of the Maginot Line to the sea.

A blow to morale and Highland pride came with the order that the kilt would not be worn until the end of hostilities, which incensed Usher and all Highland officers. Battledress might be more practical, but it was an insensitive and unfeeling directive.[2]

The Gordons made friends with the local population, and the Pipes and Drums played Retreat weekly in the village square. There were Christmas and New Year festivities, and home leave until January when the big German offensive was expected.

On 9th February, 1940, the battalion marched 18 miles to line the route taken by *M. le Brun*, the French President, as he made a tour of inspection. There was enemy air activity, and Regimental legend has it that Usher rushed down the line and demoted the Corporal Piper on the spot for his well-meaning but ill-advised attempt to raise morale during the air-raid by playing '*Run, Rabbit Run*' on the pipes, thus denigrating the *ceol mhor* that he should have been playing![3]

On 22nd February Usher handed over command of the 1st Battalion to Lieutenant-Colonel Harry Wright[4]. He had achieved one of his ambitions, to command a battalion of his Regiment. He felt lucky to have been given the command, as the Colonel of the Regiment[5] (General Sir Ian Hamilton) told him at the time

---

[2] The kilt had a habit of turning up wherever the Gordons served throughout the war, from North Africa through Sicily and Italy, and through France, the Low Countries and Germany.

[3] *Ceol mhor,* 'great music', *i.e.* classical pipe music.

[4] Son of Colonel Harry Wright, veteran of Afghanistan, 1st and 2nd Boer Wars and World War I.

[5] The Colonel of the Regiment was a senior Gordon Highlander, usually (but not always) retired, who represented the Regiment at the highest levels, ready with help and advice for serving Gordon

that it had been a close contest. Usher wished Wright, his brother officers and the men of the 1st Battalion all the very best for whatever might lie ahead. He 'was given a great send off. With pipers leading the way, his car was pulled along the cobbled streets by a team of sergeants; it was a fitting tribute to an officer who had given 29 years' devoted service to the Regiment'.

Usher was employed in the Lines of Communication (L. of C.), a vast organisation employing 78,000 men under the Quartermaster General, which included amongst its duties bringing in ammunition to Fécamp, St. Malo, Brest and St. Nazaire. Promoted to acting Colonel, he was appointed Area Commandant St. Malo in Brittany, far from the fighting troops of the B.E.F. Here Usher was in charge of the docks where the stores, shipped in from Fowey in Cornwall, were unloaded and sent to the Front.

This posting was short-lived, however, and on 1 April 1940, Usher returned east to command a sub-area of the Lines of Communication, with the simple title of 'X' L. of C. His headquarters (H.Q) was at Avesnes, with Major Thomas 'Harry' Jefferies as D.A.Q.M.G.[6] The H.Q. at Avesnes would administer the units left in the rear areas vacated by the B.E.F. when it moved forward into Belgium. This involved the administration of units, detachments, guards and individuals who had previously formed part of the three British Corps[7] and G.H.Q troops. The railheads at Avion (stores and supplies), Aubigny (ammunition), Saulty (stores and supplies), Beaumont (personnel), and Écoust (ammunition) would supply the area. Unit dumps were left in practically every village in the area, and in addition large dumps of petrol were established at the ammunition and petrol railheads. With the exception of one

---

Highlanders. He had an input on decisions on officers selected to command the regular battalions, and also assessed and advised on the recruitment of young officers to the Regiment.

[6] D.A.Q.M.G. - Deputy Assistant Quartermaster General.

[7] In the Second World War British military formations had a standard form, although this could be changed when circumstances so demanded. An infantry brigade consisted of three infantry battalions, and the necessary supporting Arms. A Division consisted of three brigades and the appropriate supporting Arms, while a Corps had three divisions and the appropriate supporting Arms. An Army was formed of a number of Corps, with three being the standard number.

section of a troop-carrying company, 16 lorries left behind by II Corps and one vehicle per detachment left behind by I Corps, there was no transport available.

The area was administered through area commandants of each Corps rear area—in the Douai area for I Corps, around Lens for II Corps and around Béthune for III Corps. I and III Corps left adequate staffs, but II Corps left only one officer, who was detailed for this duty on the day prior to the Corps marching out. Colonel Usher's task was to keep the troops at G.H.Q and in the three Corps supplied with men and material, and to handle personnel going the other way—sick, wounded or due leave.

Usher quickly got to grips with this disparate and wide-spread collection of men and material. An efficient system was quickly introduced, ensuring that equipment, supplies and men got to their destination, whether forward to their units or returning for replacement, repair or leave. As with everything he did, Usher set up and maintained an effective system. He was everywhere, ensuring that officers in charge of the various activities understood their duties and responsibilities, and were working efficiently. He also met the soldiers carrying out these tasks, encouraged them and made sure they were kept up-to-date with the situation at the Front. He got by on a few hours sleep every night, and had boundless energy.

The task, though demanding, was straightforward. It was supporting an army in the field by making sure that supplies, men and materiel were sent forward when required, and where required. Although facing the German Army, the French and British were not yet in contact with it, and there was no disruption to formations and dispositions. Usher's task was the administration of established procedures.

The expected B.E.F. response when the Germans eventually attacked was Plan D, a march of 60 miles through Belgian territory to the River Dyle east of Brussels. The name 'Plan D' was derived from the first letter of the river, 'Dyle'. This was based on the French belief that the German attack would come through the Low Countries, replicating the Schlieffen Plan of 1914. Lord Gort, V.C., Commander-in-Chief of the B.E.F., whatever his own interpretation of the situation, was under command of the French General, Georges, so had to deploy the B.E.F. in accordance with the French Commander's plans. The Germans, for their part, were well aware of French expectations, and had no intention of obliging them.

CHAPTER 5

1940—DUNKIRK

O N 10th May Adolf Hitler issued an Order of the Day to the German armies waiting to launch a devastating surprise attack on the French and British.[1]

At 5.35 am, German Army Group B, under General von Bock, invaded Holland and Belgium, and the *Luftwaffe* bombed allied airfields and G.H.Q. at Arras. This was in keeping with French expectations of the German attack, and they reacted accordingly, activating Plan D at 1.00 pm. Gort established his command post at Wahagnies and exhorted the War Office to remedy his acute shortage of ammunition[2]. At home, Prime Minister Neville Chamberlain resigned and Winston Churchill formed a National Government.

But the main German effort was not through the Belgian plain, where the strongest Allied forces in the north had been stationed to meet it, but through the Ardennes, where the weaker French 9th Army faced it. Von Bock's Army Group B, facing Holland and the Belgian plain north of Liège had been given only twenty-eight divisions, three of them armoured. South of Liège, von Rundstedt's Army Group A, facing Luxembourg and the Ardennes, had forty-five divisions, including seven armoured (*Panzer*) divisions under General von Kleist.

Army Group A, with General Heinz Guderian's XIX Corps, comprising 1st, 2nd and 3rd *Panzer* Divisions, which were lined up on the Luxembourg frontier, moved forward. XIX Corps, covering 45 miles, reached Martelange and Libramont that night and entered the Ardennes, which the French thought was impassable to tanks. Sedan fell to the 1st and 2nd *Panzer* Divisions, which had covered 60 miles in two days, and it was not until two days later, 12th May, that Gort received the 'disquieting news' from the Ardennes.

---

[1] The Order of the Day is at Appendix 4.

[2] Ten days later Guderian noted that 2nd *Panzer* Division at Albert had captured an R.A. battery drawn up neatly as on parade with only training ammunition at its disposal.

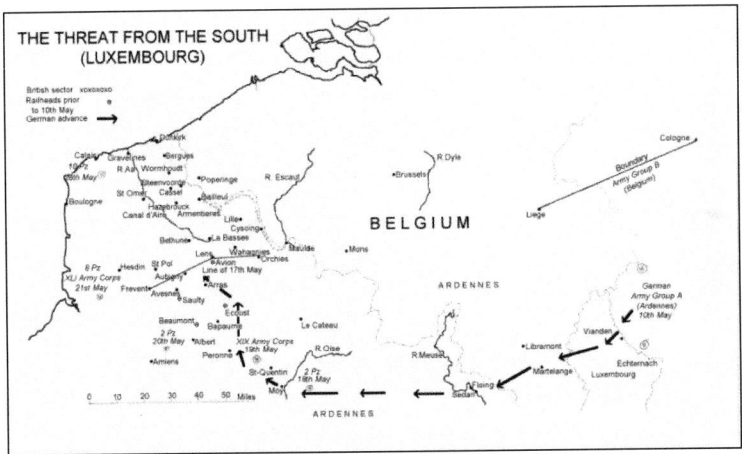

The situation from 10th to 26th May

On 13th/14th May Guderian, having defeated the French 2nd and 9th Armies, crossed the Meuse at Floing and advanced 45 miles, threatening to outflank the Allied position on the Dyle. While the British forward divisions concentrated on their immediate front, Lord Gort had to look over his shoulder at events in the south. The B.E.F., which had been successful in contact with the Germans, now found itself in a similar situation to that of its 1914 counterpart. Having held its own against the enemy, and performed well, it found its right flank vulnerable after the German breakthrough in the Ardennes. The B.E.F., to conform with the French withdrawal, found history repeating itself as it conducted a fighting withdrawal.

On 15th May Usher learned of the developing threat against the right flank and rear. He had tried without success to get authority to clear the area, but the proximity of the Germans made it essential to concentrate all non-fighting troops further back, to prevent them falling into enemy hands. Usher wanted to swing the tail of 'X' L. of C. north, so that communication with the B.E.F. could be based at Calais and Boulogne. This was agreed at H.Q. L. of C. on 17th May, when the grave situation in the south was at last appreciated, and enemy armoured forces had crossed the Oise. Usher visited General Staff (Operations) to argue for the move to be put into immediate effect. Accordingly, all troops south of Orchies-Lens-Frévent were ordered to move north of this line. The Germans were at Moy on the Oise, 45 miles away. Orders for the move were issued by despatch rider

(D.R.) at 02.30 on 18th May. By 07.00 hours units and detachments had started the move, most of them on foot.

In spite of a strongly worded plea to Brigadier Greenslade at G.H.Q, no extra transport could be provided, and many stores had to be abandoned. To Usher's great regret, stocks of whisky were set on fire to prevent them falling into German hands!

On 18th May Gort conceived his special forces to cover the evacuation of the B.E.F. These were to be formed from all arms of detached fighting and non-fighting units. They were to defend the canal line from St. Omer to La Bassée and the Dunkirk bridgehead until divisions from the east could take over.

The formation of these improvised 'forces'[3] is a feature of Lord Gort's conduct of the campaign which has sometimes been criticised. Such 'forces', hastily organised from miscellaneous and often ill-equipped units, had little chance to make sound administrative arrangements, or to ensure an effective system of communications. There were obvious disadvantages, but no alternative. Until the main B.E.F. retired from the Escaut to the frontier no infantry divisions could be freed to protect the flank and rear. Behind the front were considerable numbers of men who could make up the deficiency in fighting divisions. There were Royal Engineers working behind the front—construction companies, tunneling companies, chemical warfare companies. There were the staffs of training and supply depots, and men of the R.A.S.C. and R.A.O.C. Lord Gort directed that these scattered groups should be gathered into 'forces', to each of which he added as much artillery as could be spared, and such infantry as could be found without weakening the divisions fighting at the front. The 'forces' were in addition to the divisions, whose composition was not affected. Their formation, under commanders who could act on their own initiative once they had been given a general directive, gave a measure of organisation and fighting value when otherwise these units in the rear areas would have been uncoordinated and incapable of establishing effective defences. The resistance they put up was

---

[3] Initially Frankforce, commanded by Major-General H.E Franklyn, Petreforce, commanded by Major-General R.K. Petre, Macforce, commanded by Major-General F.N. Mason McFarlane and Polforce, commanded by Major-General H.O. Curtis. These forces had formations of brigade and even divisional strength under command.

sufficient to persuade von Rundstedt that the Canal Line was held, and made him hesitate to use his armour against it. In the time gained Gort was able to bring stronger forces up for its defence.

On 19th May[4], the greatest urgency was still in the south, where Lieutenant-Colonel Viscount Bridgeman, G.S.O 1 [Chief of Staff] at Lord Gort's Headquarters, and Brigadier Sir Colin Jardine Bt., D.S.O., M.C. were visiting H.Q.s to plan the moves to counter the German threat. German Army XIX Corps took Péronne and was advancing on Amiens. All units were ordered north to the line of the La Bassée Canal. It was chaotic. There was great difficulty getting orders to units on the move, and to other widely scattered units.

There was no transport to move personnel, and Usher and Major Jefferies were particularly concerned about the large numbers of men at Corps reinforcement camps, who were in a dangerous position. Messages were sent to Corps placing these troops under the command of the Corps, and Usher and Major Jefferies attempted to visit each Corps H.Q. to ensure that this arrangement was satisfactory. Only the H.Q. of II Corps could be found (at 01.30 hours) but reception camps and advanced H.Q. were visited.

Usher's H.Q. moved from Avesnes to Béthune. The roads were congested with refugees, and enemy air activity was intense. An air-raid at Avion when Usher and Jefferies were there destroyed two railway bridges and set houses on fire. They decided to continue to use Avion as a supply railhead and as much petrol as possible was taken by R.A.S.C. from Beaumont, only 6 miles from where 2nd *Panzer* Division had taken Albert, to dumps north of the La Bassée Canal. The R.A.S.C. personnel worked without rest, night and day, and large quantities were moved. The successful operation of the Avion railhead was largely due to the energy and efficiency of Captain Shobrook, R.A.S.C.

On 20th May, Brigadier Jardine visited Usher's H.Q. and ordered leave and reinforcement personnel to revert to their Corps. In the absence of motor transport, Usher tried to get trains for foot soldiers who had covered 50 miles in three days. Trains

---

[4]   On 19th May the possibility of evacuating the B.E.F. was discussed in London.

were arranged to arrive at Pérenchies, Armentières and Berguette.

All motor transport was ordered to rendezvous in the St. Omer area, animal transport to Bissezeele and H.Q. 'X' L. of C. Sub-Area to Steenvoorde, midway between Poperinge and Cassel. Béthune was blocked with refugees. Usher sent officers to the three railway stations to organise loading, but no trains arrived.

Unknown to those on the ground, 20th May was the date when Gort realised he would have to withdraw to the coast, and the War Office started discussing with the Admiralty how to evacuate at Dunkirk.

At 01.00 on 21st May Usher went to Armentières station with Major Jefferies, and found that troops were still waiting there. Determined to get these troops out of the area, Usher took control, commandeered a local train, embarked the troops and sent them to Boulogne.

That same day Frankforce, comprised of elements of 50 and 150 Divisions, under Major-General H.E. Franklyn, staged a brilliant counter-attack at Arras, which had been hemmed in on three sides. Determined thrusts were made against the enemy by 15, 17, 150 and 151 Brigades. Great acts of heroism and considerable sacrifice influenced the final outcome by significantly delaying the German advance. Rommel, taken aback by the ferocity of the assault, was convinced that he was up against a much superior force.

It was imperative to make arrangements to get all personnel out, but Usher's visits to Q (Maint.), then at Hazebrouck, were of little value. All that could be obtained was the general direction in which troops were to move. Little information on enemy movements was available, and the situation was obscure.

On 22nd May, 2nd *Panzer* Division fought its way into Boulogne and reached the sea. It could now turn north-east along the coast to Calais, then on to the river Aa, Bergues and Dunkirk. The encirclement of the Allies was complete.

At 1800 hours H.Q. 'X' L. of C. Sub-Area moved to Socx, just 1½ miles south-west of Bergues, which in turn was 6 miles south of Dunkirk. Usher organised Socx as a defended locality, taking under command all troops in the area. In addition to those originally under command of 'X' L. of C., many other units had moved into the area, some without orders, and others with no instructions what to do on arrival.

At Socx information was received, and passed to G.H.Q, that the enemy was west of the river Aa between Gravelines and St. Omer. Holding the east bank under command of 'X' L. of C. were 6th Green Howards at Gravelines, 1st Super Heavy Battery at St. Pierre Brouck, 3rd Super Heavy Battery at Watten and 52nd Heavy Regiment, R.A. at St. Momelin.

The situation from 23 May 1940

The 6th Green Howards, commanded by Lieutenant-Colonel M.R. Steel, D.S.O., M.C., at Gravelines who, by their own account, had been part of a 'pick and shovel brigade' a week earlier, repelled a determined attack on the afternoon of the 22nd. Their dogged resistance was bolstered by the arrival of a cruiser tank that had escaped from Calais and promptly joined in the fight. The gunner had been killed, but the H.Q. Company cook, Sergeant Gibson, took over and knocked out an enemy tank. At 6 pm Usher ordered them to Bergues where Major Dixon reported to the French Garrison commander that they were coming to defend him. He found 'the old gentleman' enjoying a brandy and confident that he could hold on without British assistance. The Green Howards moved at 9 pm, but the Germans had crossed the canal on their exposed left flank. They closed with the Germans and engaged them in hand-to-hand combat, killing and wounding many, and took many prisoners, including a company commander and the signals officer, both wounded. Second-Lieutenants Hughes and Carr were awarded the Military Cross, and Private Laidler the Military Medal for their parts in the heavy fighting at Gravelines which successfully delayed the enemy for three days while the defences of Bergues were completed.

A Supply Officer, Captain Shobrook (the same officer who had successfully run the Avion railhead), volunteered to go to St. Omer to find out what was happening there. Nothing more was heard of him, but it emerged later that he had been taken prisoner. Signalman Hutchings successfully took orders for the 6th Green Howards through heavy bombing, was wounded but returned, stopping on the way to buy cigarettes for his friends in Bergues.

The night of 22nd/23rd May was a busy one on the 15-mile front. Major Jefferies was visiting sentries until 01.30 on 23rd, but rest was interrupted at 03.00 with a message from 52nd Heavy Regiment announcing the imminent arrival of the Germans. The message read:

> 'I am at St. Momelin H1458 swing bridge which is swung open. I have a telephone with 1 Super Hy Bty at Watton H1263, 2 A.A. Bde [Brigadier E.W. Chadwick] is Renescures H2250, 2 Searchlight Bn are about H2354[5]. Am arranging W/T with them. 23 Div is at Bellezeele H2065. C.R.E. 23 Div is preparing all bridges for demolition from Gravelines H0731 to St. Omer H1453. He says 46 Div [Major-General Curtis] take on from there South Eastward. Col. of French Territorials in St. Omer reports enemy strength 1 Bn with some motorcyclists and five or six tanks advancing on St. Omer from South East this afternoon and two larger columns moving Westwards having come from St. Pol H1612.'

This message was sent to G.H.Q. at Hazebrouck and repeated to G.H.Q. Troops. Troops at Socx consisting of H.Q. 'X' L. of C. Sub-Area, Det. 23 Div. Sup. Col. [Supply Column], Det. C. Park[6] V.R.D. [Vehicle Reserve Depot] were 'stood to' and defences strengthened and re-organised from 04.00 hours.

At 05.20 hours many units, not under command of 'X' L. of C, but whose locations had been obtained through a report centre

---

[5] This was the village of Haut Schoubrouck, five miles east of St. Omer.

[6] A logistic park manned by officers of any Arm together with men from the Supplementary Reserve.

at St. Omer, were in a dangerous area north-west of St. Omer. Usher sent a special officer messenger, with despatch riders, to warn them to move. At 06.15 hours Major Hudson was sent to liaise with 23 Division (under Major-General W.M. Herbert and comprising 69 and 70 Brigades) at Bellezeele to obtain information.

At 09.00 hours 23rd May Captain Campbell, from Q Maint., visited H.Q. and confirmed the message from 52nd Heavy Regiment. He then said that G.H.Q. wished Colonel Usher to take command of all troops in the area, including 23 Division, and hold the line of the River Aa from Gravelines in the north to St. Omer and the Forest of Clairmarais, with the French 1st Army, Macforce and Polforce on the left, until Divisions withdrawing from the east could take over. Usher coordinated his forces with the French General Fagalde, who had regional troops, equivalent to a weak division. This was the western section of the outer line of the French defences of Dunkirk, based on the peace-time organisation of the *Secteur Fortifié de Flandres*. Ahead was the French 68 Division, and opposing them were 8th *Panzer* and S.S. *Verfugungs* Divisions. Behind them were 1st and 6th *Panzer* Divisions, von Kleist's Motorised Division and 41st Armoured Division. H.Q. 'X' L. of C. would be confronted by the enemy on 15 miles of the river Aa to St. Omer[7].

Usher was instructed to move his H.Q. to Bergues, where the garrison consisted of a collection of various units and detachments, and several senior officers. The garrison was disorganised and out of control. Colonel Usher was to re-organise it, and in addition to his command in the field, put Bergues in a state of defence.

Bergues, six miles south-east of Dunkirk, was an old fortified town. The Bergues Canal, running north to Dunkirk alongside the main road, formed a western boundary of the British sector of the Dunkirk perimeter, for the French were to hold the sector west of this line. It was a strong defensive position. The land around the town was easily flooded, low-lying and criss-crossed with ditches. It was impassable by tanks or guns except on conspicuous built-up roads, with ditches either side, which well-sited guns could make unusable.

---

[7] Ironically regarded in 1914-16 as a fine trout river in its upper reaches by A.D. Greenhill Gardyne and other Gordon officers.

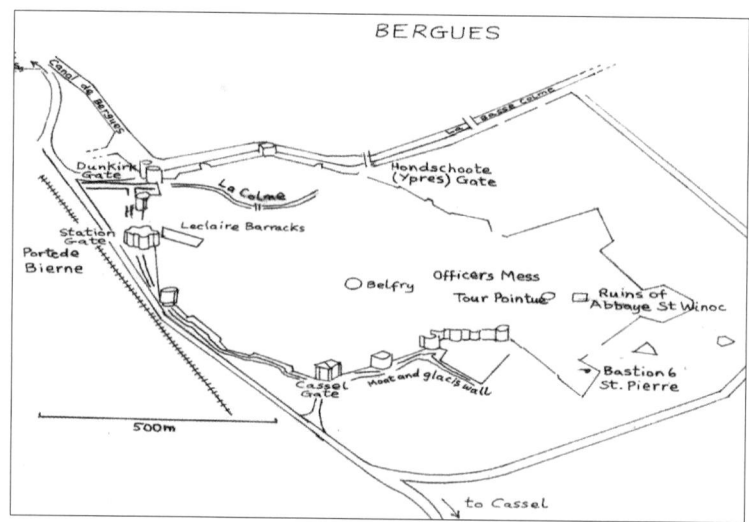

Plan of Bergues

With the large number of troops under command, and with Colonel Usher's H.Q. the only one capable of functioning as such (not to mention the somewhat confusing title of 'X' L. of C. Sub-Area), it was decided to re-name the force as 'Usherforce'[8]. Usher's first order, issued at 10.40 hours on 23rd May, was an instruction to 23 Division to blow up all bridges from St. Omer to Gravelines and take up positions with all available forces to hold the approaches from St. Omer from inclusive Broxeele to the road and river crossing at Les Rois, a little over six miles to the south-east. This fifteen-mile front was to defend the road and rail links from G.H.Q. Hazebrouck through to Wormhoudt, Bergues and Dunkirk against being cut at Cassel by the German forces advancing from St. Omer through the Forest of Clairmarais, which would leave G.H.Q. with no escape route.

At 10.50 hours Usher instructed the Reception Camp at Broxeele to evacuate all unarmed personnel to Dunkirk, and take the remainder to assist 23 Division. At 11.10 hours 23 Division Supply Column and C. Park V.R.D. were instructed to move all vehicles to Proven, south-east of Bergues, except for vehicles blocking the roads at Socx. Men capable of using weapons were to be left at Bergues. At 11.50 hours Usher sent orders to the

---

[8] Unlike Frankforce, Petreforce, Macforce and Polforce, Usherforce had no units larger than battalion size, and only one formed infantry battalion under command.

Officer Commanding the Construction Battalion at Killem, with about 10-15 construction companies, to organise them into companies of 100 fighting men.

At 14.00 hours the order to blow the bridges over the River Aa was countermanded by Lieutenant-Colonel Lord Bridgeman, and a message from G.H.Q. ordered that 23 Division was not to come under command Usherforce. As Usher's order to 23 Division had not reached them there was no alteration except that the gap had to be filled by troops under Lieutenant-Colonel Cobbett, commanding the Reception Camp.

H.Q. Usherforce moved to Bergues to strengthen the French Garrison and General Barthélémy's H.Q. Bergues was a great fortress, standing four metres above flat countryside that was drained by canals. Six hundred years earlier it had been on the point of an isthmus into the sea, and it had a formidable glacis and a moat. There were three bridges, the *Porte de Dunkerque* to the north, the *Porte de Bierne* to the west and the *Porte de Cassel* to the south. To the east was a further wall beyond the moat, to the north was the *Canal de la Basse Colme*, which ran into the *Canal de Bergues* which in turn went north to Dunkirk. The XVth Century Belfry in the middle of the town provided superb all-round views of the countryside, including Dunkirk; a good Observation Post (OP) but vulnerable under fire.

The garrison was in the Leclaire barracks immediately inside the *Porte de Bierne* and handy for the railway station, while the *état-major* and the officers mess were at the other end of town near the *Tour Pointue* next to the *Abbaye Saint-Winoc*. The town was 600 metres north to south and 1,000 metres east to west.

Major-General A.F.A.N. Thorne, commanding 48 Division, comprising 143 Brigade, (Brigadier J. Muirhead), 144 Brigade, (Brigadier J.M. Hamilton[9]) and 145 Brigade, (Brigadier Hon N.F. Somerset), sent 144 Brigade (2nd Battalion, The Royal Warwickshire Regiment, 5th Battalion, The Gloucestershire Regiment and 8th Battalion, The Worcestershire Regiment) to bolster the defences at Bergues, and assist at Wormhoudt, 6 miles south.

The road to Bergues near the gate of the fortress was blocked with motor transport, three abreast. There was a heavy air raid and drivers abandoned their vehicles to take cover in ditches.

---

9   Brigadier Hamilton was a Gordon Highlander. He had commanded the 1st Battalion before handing over to Usher in January 1938.

Usher, Major Jefferies and Usher's driver, Lance Corporal Carle[10], got out of their car, got the drivers back into their vehicles and got the traffic moving. Carle, showing complete indifference to personal danger and fatigue, drove several of the vehicles out of the way himself, and through his example the men returned to the task and cleared a passage, in spite of bombs falling close by.

An Animal Transport Company and a number of refugee vehicles were blocking the road, and movement was hindered by terrified refugees struggling along in every direction while enemy bombers screamed down on them. By hard work, cajoling, threatening and sheer physical labour, and not least by personal example, Usher cleared the road, shoving unusable wagons and vehicles to the side and directing refugees off the road and into the adjoining fields.

At 16.15 hours Usher ordered Reception Camp personnel under Lieutenant-Colonel Cobbett to take up position astride the road at Bellezeele, five miles up the road from Watten, which was under attack by the S.S. *Leibstandarte* Division[11]. One hundred men were sent in lorries from Bergues to hold bridges in the St. Momelin sector of Usherforce's stretch of the Dunkirk defensive perimeter.

The 24th of May brought intense excitement and strain. Units, detachments and stragglers arrived in Bergues unannounced, some without arms, having been without food for two days, and having marched considerable distances. Usher deployed those who were armed and able to fight into the defences, and sent the rest back to Dunkirk. He was everywhere, inspecting defensive positions, encouraging the defenders, driving them when necessary, and instilling in them the belief that they could face the Germans and destroy them when they attacked. He seemed never to rest.

The enemy reached the left bank of the River Aa and their 1st *Panzer* Division made several attempts to cross, but were repulsed time and time again by Usher's forces, the 6th Green Howards, detachments of the 3rd Searchlight Regiment and the 52nd Heavy Regiment under Major Strudwick. With his mixed

---

[10] William Carle, a typical stolid, reliable Gordon Highlander from Aberdeenshire, was described as a 'red-haired, freckle-faced loon fae Mintlaw'.

[11] The 1st S.S. Panzer Division.

force fighting as infantry at St. Momelin, Strudwick vigorously defended the bridge against determined enemy attempts to cross, until he handed it over to the French.

This was the day the German Supreme Command intervened, with results which, Guderian later wrote, were to have a disastrous—for Germany— influence on the course of the war. Von Rundstedt stopped the mobile armoured forces west of the River Aa. Dunkirk was to be left to the *Luftwaffe*[12]. Sepp Dietrich, however, disobeyed orders and ordered the *Leibstandarte* Division and the *Gross Deutschland* Regiment[13] to press on towards Wormhoudt and Bergues.

German Army practice was to advance along main roads. The only way for German forces to get to Dunkirk was along the road from Wormhoudt through Bergues, which stood in the way just six miles from their objectives, the mole at Dunkirk harbour, the beaches and La Panne, where Lord Gort had his final H.Q. Von Kleist's orders were to make a pincer movement on Dunkirk and to take out the troops on the beaches. If, together with the 29th Motorised Division and the *Gross Deutschland* Regiment, with the S.S. *Adolf Hitler* Regiment[14] in close support, Dietrich could defeat Usherforce and take Bergues, then the troops in Dunkirk and on the beaches would be swiftly overwhelmed before the B.E.F. could be evacuated. Bergues, therefore, was the critical link in the chain of defences around Dunkirk. It was the point at which the British and French sectors met, and there would have to be good liaison to ensure that the respective defensive lines linked up effectively, with mutual support.

Usher had under command:-

> 6th Green Howards, holding the River Aa from the sea to the railway line south of Gravelines.
>
> 1st Super Heavy Battery, holding the east bank of the river at St. Pierre Brouck.
>
> 3rd Super Heavy Battery, holding Watten.

---

[12] Hitler 'agreed entirely with the view that east of Arras an attack had to be made with *infantry*, while the *mobile forces* could be halted on the line reached'. After Hitler had visited his Headquarters, von Rundstedt issued a directive which read: 'By the Führer's orders . . . general line Lens–Béthune–Aire–St. Omer–Gravelines will *not* be passed.'

[13] Four battalions of motorised infantry.

[14] Three battalions of motorised infantry.

52nd Heavy Regiment, holding St. Momelin.

Cobbett's Force, holding a position astride the road St.Omer/Bergues, about Bellezeele, two miles south-west of Socx.

Troops at Socx, under Major Lewis R.W.F.

The Bergues Garrison of about 3,000.

4,500 men of Polforce—12 Construction Companies and 4 Field Companies R.E.

Usher set up the defence of Bergues, and the gate defences were manned and organised. Each gate had a commander, with 50-100 men, one or two anti-tank rifles and Bren guns, but there were no anti-tank guns at all. The streets were barricaded with wardrobes, bedsteads, tables and other furniture from abandoned houses and shops.

There were visits from and to the French H.Q., amid several air-raids on Bergues, called down by von Kleist. The 'X' L. of C. Supply Column was bombed just outside the town, with four killed and eight wounded.

It was a day of alarms, the situation vague with conflicting reports, no definite information and many visitors, most gloomy and all in trouble. Rumours circulated but Usher paid little attention to them. Calais, heroically defended by Brigadier C.N. Nicholson, was surrounded by the 10th *Panzer* Division and, against overwhelming odds, refused to surrender. Since 10th May the German armies had covered over 400 miles. The B.E.F. was squeezed between German forces on the east and west into a narrow 60-mile corridor, 13–25 miles wide, stretching from the French 1st Army in the south to the sea. British forces in the south and the west were outnumbered five to one. Half of these were Territorials, non-combatant or under training.

Three Army Field Workshops came, having been shot up by German tanks and having had to abandon everything, swim the River Aa and walk twelve miles.

On 25th May, Major Reeves, Royal Tank Regiment, arrived with one cruiser tank and two light tanks, having shot his way through the German lines, accounting for eight German tanks with the loss of only one of his own. The exhausted men had been without food for 24 hours, were out of ammunition and had very little petrol.

At 03.00 hours, 25th May, Frankforce, Petreforce, Polforce and Macforce were disbanded, leaving Usherforce as the only remaining 'ad hoc' force still involved in the fighting. At 05.00 hours, a captured German operation order disclosed that the *Leibstandarte* Division and the *Gross Deutschland* Regiment were advancing on Wormhoudt and Bergues.

Usher quickly drew up a plan to hold the Bergues perimeter. The timely addition of four 25-pdr guns and four 2-pdrs from 48 Division gave support to the companies on each bridge. These guns made the defence of Bergues feasible. Enemy armour could only approach along the roads, and would be an easy target for properly sited guns. If the guns could prevent the armour getting close enough to influence the fighting, the Germans would have to rely on infantry assault against well dug-in defenders. Usher was confident that he could contain and repel the German infantry. There was no news, however, of the remaining two battalions of 69 Infantry Brigade ordered to report there.

Brigadier Jardine brought news that the commander of 48 (South Midland) Division, Major-General Thorne, was now in command of all the British troops in the area, and that all non-effectives (with which the defence of the Aa had been maintained for the past two days) were to be evacuated through Dunkirk. Arrangements were made with the French General Barthélémy that French troops would take over from Usherforce on the line of the River Aa. Great stress was laid on a proper handover taking place.

On 26th May[15], 52nd Heavy Regiment finally withdrew from St. Momelin, with some 30 casualties. It was now Usherforce's responsibility to form a shorter perimeter from the sea at Fort Mardyk to Spyker, to Socx and on to the canal immediately north of Warhem, east of Bergues. This line was to be held by 6th Green Howards, the remaining two battalions of 69 Brigade and the RE Construction Companies under Colonel Pool.

Information on 69 Brigade was discouraging. The 6th Green Howards were already under command, but the remaining battalions, 5th East Yorks and 7th Green Howards, had lost their commanding officers and had still not arrived. On 25th May, the 6th Green Howards had withdrawn to hold Fort Mardyk.

Usher visited Major-General Thorne, commanding 48 Division, who later that day established his H.Q. at Bergues. There was a severe air-raid on Bergues, causing much damage,

---

[15] On 26th May the decision was made to evacuate as many of the B.E.F. as possible from Dunkirk.

although two German bombers were brought down by anti-aircraft fire. In the afternoon, Hitler, who had stopped the advance of the left wing on 24th May, now allowed it to advance and the fighting increased in intensity, but the Germans had lost two vital days.

Confusion arose over division of responsibility between French and British for the defence of the area. French forces were under General Fagalde, commander of the French XVI Corps, whose H.Q. was at Dunkirk. Under him were two sectors, A and B. Sector A was under General Beaufrère, commanding the 68th French Division, with H.Q. at Rosendael. He was responsible for holding the line of the Mardyk Canal and the *Canal de la Colme*, which included Bergues. Sector B was under General Barthélémy whose H.Q. was at Bergues. He was responsible for holding the line from the sea to St. Omer.

There was little definite division of responsibility between the two Allied forces; British and French detachments could be found holding the same line, but not under one command. One evening Usher agreed plans for the following day with the neighbouring French general, only to find him gone the next morning, leaving Usher's flank exposed.

When Major-General Thorne arrived at Bergues he noted that Usher, commanding such a large and motley collection of troops, had organised them into such an effective and aggressive defence that all German attacks had been successfully repulsed. He gave Usher the acting rank of Brigadier, with responsibility for the defence of Bergues. The defences were further strengthened and troops withdrawing through Bergues were allocated to groups manning the defences.

On 27th May, it became apparent that the whole of the B.E.F. was to be evacuated, and Usher was instructed to send all non-effectives to Dunkirk. He had prepared for this, and a plan had been worked out by Major Jefferies during the night of 26th/27th May, but on the morning of the 27th the general plan for the evacuation was issued from Gort's Headquarters by Lieutenant-Colonel Lord Bridgeman. Usher updated his plans and issued orders in compliance with G.H.Q. 6th Green Howards spent the day controlling the traffic on the Bergues-Wormhoudt road. 7th Green Howards had tried to get through, but on 27th May they were north of Poperinge, to the south-east of Bergues.

Captain Martinson, Deputy Assistant Provost Marshal, was sent out with his motorcyclist Military Police to put this plan into effect until such time as 6th Green Howards and Polforce could carry out their orders. He set a great example by keeping the motor cyclists operational throughout continual air-raids.

A heavy air-raid on Bergues at 15.30 hours resulted in fires in the town. The effect of the bombing was noticeable on the men manning the defences, who were largely non-effectives from the Pioneer Corps and R.A.S.C. Understandably shaken by the raid, they nevertheless stuck to their tasks, encouraged and supported by Usher's calm and reassuring presence.

It was now possible to arrange for the relief of non-effectives manning the defences of Socx under Major Lewis, by 120 officer-led trained men, formed from those withdrawing past the gates of the town. Major Lewis was told that French troops in front would withdraw through his position, and that he was to pull back to Bergues, preferably under cover of darkness, only if continuing to defend Socx become untenable.

Usher sited commandants, with basic staffs, at three points south of the *Canal de Bergues* with orders to collect full ammunition and supply vehicles sent back by the three Corps. He established similar organisations north of this canal at Bulscamp, Les Moeres and Teteghem to collect withdrawing fighting troops to man the defences, and to despatch the remainder to the beaches between Dunkirk and La Panne. Polforce was instructed to evacuate 1,000 men per day from the Construction Companies under command.

On 28th May, when the B.E.F. had retreated from east of Brussels, and it was known that they would be evacuated by sea and could provide no further assistance, King Leopold accepted that Belgium could not resist the invader alone. At 09.50 hours General Derousseaux, for Belgium, and Colonel-General von Reichenau, Chief of the General Staff of the German Army, signed the unconditional surrender of the 500,000 strong Belgian army. The German army could now sweep down from the north-east to the Yser unopposed, through a 20 mile gap from the sea to the left flank of II Corps at Boesinge.

At Hazebrouck, where the rump of G.H.Q. went after leaving Arras on 23rd/24th May, documents were burned and communication was cut.

Von Kleist pressed on through Cassel and Wormhoudt towards Bergues. Enemy pressure at Socx forced the withdrawal of the garrison there at 06.30, and the Cassel Gate Bridge at Bergues was blown.

Usher determined to hold Bergues to the last man and the last round. 9th Sherwood Foresters, under Colonel Lancaster, took up position behind the *Canal de Bergues*. The town was shelled continuously by 5.9″ enemy artillery, and the enemy reached the Cassel Gate. Captain C.H. Nicholson, commanding C Company, 2nd Warwicks, although exhausted, commanded the Cassel Gate defences. With great coolness and leadership he so motivated his tired but determined men that their dogged resistance in the face of heavy fire and fanatical assaults repulsed the advance guard of an enemy column, taking prisoners who provided valuable intelligence. One enemy officer complained bitterly to Usher that he should be the German's prisoner, not the other way round. Another showed his frustration by discharging his small .22 personal protection automatic pistol. Neatly stamped with the swastika, it was kept as a souvenir by Usher.

The Germans were incensed by their inability to get through the Cassel Gate, which came in for special attention from Stukas, heavy bombing, mortars and flame throwers. The Gate was close by the casemates of Bastion 6, where townsfolk who had not escaped took refuge. The conditions were appalling, with no proper light, food, fresh air or sanitation. The casemates were built one on top of another, and a bomb, striking the top one, plunged through, killing seventeen people, mostly women and children. The Germans sent a heavy calibre shell though the Belfry tower, setting it alight.

Major-General Thorne did not know how long 48 Division was expected to maintain its extended position. Even if the garrisons of Socx, Wormhoudt, Cassel and Hazebrouck could hold out, enemy penetration between them would seriously interfere with withdrawals farther east. He appealed to General Headquarters for reinforcements. Brigadier Norman's 1st Light Armoured Reconnaissance Brigade and the 1st Welsh Guards were put under his command, as were also 6th Green Howards from Usherforce. Usher now had to defend Bergues with even fewer troops.

The enemy attacked all of 48 Division's strongholds during the day, and by six in the evening the road between Bergues and Cassel could no longer be used, Socx had been lost, Wormhoudt had become untenable, and communications with Cassel and Hazebrouck lost.

In Bergues, many houses were on fire, and the gate garrisons were fatigued and strained, but casualties were relatively small in the face of ferocious enemy action. By the following day, May 29th, the enemy was at Nieuport and Furnes in the east and at the gates of Bergues.

German Army Group A proposed that Dunkirk be attacked through Bergues by mobile forces, as von Kleist's left wing could make little headway due to stubborn British resistance, but the proposal was not accepted. Instead 4th Army directed von Kleist to close in and shell Dunkirk with 10cm guns. Von Rundstedt's decision was influenced by the nature of the terrain, unsuitable for tanks, and by the ferocity of Usher's defence, which had already inflicted heavy casualties on the attackers. The *Panzer* divisions had only 50% armoured strength left, and their equipment was in urgent need of repair. In only a few days time he had to be ready to attack south over the Somme–Aisne line to achieve the comprehensive defeat of France, which was his prime objective. He felt that his current mission, the defeat of the B.E.F., had been successfully completed and, having suffered considerable losses in attacking Usher's forces in Bergues, felt there was no need to suffer further casualties in a major assault that would inevitably cost him more of his precious tanks.

Usher's stubborn defence of Bergues continued, and further digging-in was completed, while the stream of British troops withdrawing past the Ypres Gate went on unabated. Major Jefferies diverted 600 effective fighting men from this procession to the defence of the town, and Majors J.E. Gunter and Beadle each recruited volunteers from the unattached personnel and brought them into the town to swell the numbers of the defenders. Non-effective personnel, who would hinder rather than help the defence, were sent back to the beaches for evacuation. A heavy enemy air-raid on the Ypres Gate of Bergues at about 17.00 hours saw two bombs land on the bridge behind the gate, but they failed to destroy it. The enemy's object was to prevent the garrison getting away.

At 05.00 hours on 30th May Brigadier Usher was ordered by Major-General Thorne to withdraw from Bergues. Warning orders were issued, but at 08.00 Major-General Curtis, commanding 46 Division, asked Usher to hold Bergues at all costs. Usher accepted this revised task, and later in the day went to III Corps, and then to I Corps where he spoke to the Corps Commander, Lieutenant-General M.G.H. Barker, to ascertain whether the order from 48 Division was to withdraw at once or to withdraw on being relieved. Usher's command now consisted of one company of 2nd Warwicks, one platoon of Welsh Guards, 80 men of the Royal West Kents, about 250 men from various units, and one French company of 250 men under Captain d'Halluin of the *Dépôt de Cavalerie*.

General Barker told Usher that the intention was to regularise the defence of the line, and that Bergues would be a significant strongpoint in the defences. Usher was to hold Bergues until it could be relieved, when it would come under Brigadier Constable, who was responsible for the defence of the Bergues Canal line to the rear of the town. Once Constable had taken over responsibility for Bergues, Usherforce's mission would have been completed, and it would cease to exist. The various components were to revert, fighting units to their original formations and miscellaneous troops, including Usher and his Headquarters, to Dunkirk for evacuation.

Until relieved by Brigadier Constable's troops, Usher was still responsible for the defence of Bergues. Many automatic weapons and anti-tank weapons had been collected from units withdrawing past the town, and at one sector practically every man was armed with a Bren gun. Reserves in the town were established as 140,000 rounds of small arms ammunition, 14,000 rations and 5,000 gallons of petrol. The Station Gate, the Dunkirk Gate and a secondary gate over the canal near the Ypres Gate, were blown, to deny all road access to the town from the German-held area.

Brigadier Usher and Major Jefferies visited the Sherwood Foresters H.Q. behind the *Canal de Bergues* during the day, and were fired upon at point-blank range from across the canal, but emerged unscathed.

At about 20.00 hours on 30th May the relieving battalion, 1st Loyals, arrived at Bergues, and command of the company of the Warwicks and the Welsh platoon was transferred to it. Captain d'Halluin, commanding the company of French troops, volunteered to remain behind at Bergues. D'Halluin had gladly promised to remain with Usherforce '*au dernier homme*'.

Lieutenant-Colonel Sandie, commanding 1st Loyals, reported to Brigadier Usher at 1800 hours with his battalion, to reinforce the garrison. Corporal Morgan, of a depleted D Company, recalled that they got through the Ypres Gate under heavy shelling that continued while they took up their positions.

Earlier that day The Loyals, after an arduous fighting retreat across country, had successfully reached Bray Dunes and had even got 50 men embarked when, because of a false report that the enemy had broken through at Bergues, the Commanding Officer had the disagreeable job of telling them they had to turn round and mount a counter-attack. The Loyals' Medical Officer, Richard Doll, discovered that one of the reasons for the successful defence of the town was the 100 feet deep maze of cellars where the Regimental Aid Post and makeshift hospitals were established. There was also an abundance of food and wine, enough to feed a battalion for several weeks, in stark contrast to the conditions in Bastion 6.

On 30th May orders were issued for the garrison to withdraw, those on foot at 23.59 hours, and the Motor Transport column at 00.30 hours, 31st May. Early in the morning the columns arrived on the beach east of Dunkirk, which had been shelled throughout the night.

The group that marched from Bergues to Dunkirk, apart from several who volunteered as stretcher-bearers, embarked from the mole in Dunkirk harbour on the SS *Hythe* at about 10.00 hours. The ship, surviving artillery and air attacks, made it back to Britain, and on arrival the Bergues group was dispersed in different trains to unknown destinations. Their successful evacuation was due in large measure to Captain R. Smalley of the Kings Own Royal Regiment, who was G.S.O.3, 'X' L. of C. and Usherforce.

Usher stayed in the heavily shelled area at Dunkirk until all the men under his command were clear, finally getting away in the evening. At Bergues he had rated his chances of getting away as slim. With memories of imprisonment in World War I, he determined that the enemy would not take him alive. After the last round had been fired he would don a French suit of clothes and beret, together with a revolver that he had buried against that eventuality.

On arrival at Dunkirk he helped to organise the beaches. Getting off them was far from easy. Usher and Carle, his driver/batman, would have to swim, but Carle could not swim. With full packs on their backs, Usher took Carle on his back, and swam with him to seven boats, two of which were bombed when they were on board, before finding one to get them home, where they landed on 1st June. The highlight of the trip for Usher, was that he kept a pack of his lavatory paper, Bromo, from falling into enemy hands!

On 2nd June the Germans entered Bergues, torching everything in their path in frustration at finding that they were unopposed. Contemporary photographs vividly illustrate the severity of the bombardment and fighting in the defence of the town.[16]

Of the 400,000 troops in the B.E.F., 338,000 battle-hardened men returned from Dunkirk[17]. Churchill had believed that 20,000, or at most 30,000, might get away. However, British material losses were grave, including over 1,000 field guns and others of higher calibre, 600 tanks, 500 anti-aircraft and 850 anti-tank guns, thousands of anti-tank rifles, many lorries, cars, motorcycles, and tons of ammunition and stores.

Lord Gort, who fought a gallant and successful withdrawal in the face of a collapsing military situation, deserves credit for getting a sizeable part of the B.E.F. back to Britain, but he never commanded an army again. His appointment as Governor of Malta, however, was significant. The air-raids on Malta that began in May 1940 culminated in a relentless attack from June 1942 to February 1943. The combination of bombing and near starvation almost brought Malta to its knees. But just as he had saved the B.E.F. on the beaches of Dunkirk by the formation of the ad hoc forces that stemmed the Nazi advance for a week, so Gort denied Rommel the supplies he needed to win the desert war and take Cairo. The collapse of Malta would have severed the only allied link between Gibraltar and Alexandria.

Usher and Carle made it back to Britain, and Usher eventually arrived, still dripping wet, at The Caledonian Club in St. James's Square. Usher recorded that his first task was to dry off the precious packet of Bromo lavatory paper which he had saved in his pack, before settling down to write a *'Brief Report of the Operations of 'X' L. of C. Sub Area, Usherforce and The Bergues Garrison'*. In the report Usher wrote:

> I should like to place on record the excellent behaviour under heavy and almost continuous fire of the various units and detachments under my command, many of whom were not fighting units, but at all times put up a stubborn resistance

---

[16] For a German account of the capture of Bergues see Appendix 5.

[17] Including those evacuated before 27 May, 366,000 troops returned to Britain from Dunkirk. Not all were from the B.E.F.—226,000 were British and 140,000 French.

and repulsed all enemy attacks. I would especially mention the defence of St. Momelin by 52nd Heavy Regiment under their Commanding Officer and Major Strudwick.

It is impossible to estimate casualties, but as far as I am aware, they were not excessive compared with the constant enemy action encountered.

The official account says that Usher:

. . . found himself near Bergues, in command of a communications area, at a time when enemy attack was imminent. Realising the seriousness of the situation he organised the defence of the river from Gravelines to St. Momelin with such troops as were available. He then organised the defence of Bergues, which was held against heavy enemy attack, shelling, bombing and mortar fire. Its retention was vital to the evacuation of the B.E.F., and that it was not captured was due to the determination of Brigadier Usher, the soundness of his dispositions and his success in organising the defence with a number of small parties of troops, many of them only partially trained. The mixed garrison was defended doggedly, and held firm against continual bombing and shellfire, and more and more volunteers came along to join in the fight; all German attempts to cross the canal at Bergues were frustrated.

Usher conscientiously drew up recommendations for awards to the members of the units and detachments who had behaved so well at Bergues.

Usher and Carle had remained in France until the last of the men Usher had commanded had embarked for Britain. No one in Usherforce knew that Usher and Carle had got away until they reached England. Lt. Col W.F. Simpson wrote from the Durham Light Infantry at Brancepeth Castle on 10th June to say that on 31st May all of 'X' L. of C. and the rest of the garrison of Bergues were safely removed to Dunkirk without a single casualty on the march. They were only on the beaches for five hours. The mole and ships were shelled heavily and fragments hit his boat, but again none of the troops was hit. Many officers wrote to Usher to thank him for getting them away safely, and said they were concerned that he had got away too.

Press news of the success of Usherforce in holding Bergues, vital to the successful evacuation, brought in a flood of telegrams and correspondence. Recognition came from all quarters, and Usher got news about those who had fought with 'X' L. of C., Usherforce and the command at St. Malo. There were also fragmentary accounts of the fate of officers and men of the 1st Battalion, The Gordon Highlanders and the other battalions of the 51st Highland Division trapped at St. Valery, and the efforts to re-form the Battalion at home. In addition there were the heart-rending *cris de coeurs* of the widows of those killed and the wives of the wounded or missing in action. Worst of all was the agony of those wives and mothers left in suspense by the absence of any news of their loved ones.

The importance of the five-day action at Bergues did not escape the attention of fellow Scot, Air Marshal Sir Hugh Dowding, G.C.B., G.C.V.O., C.M.G., later Lord Dowding, who had, together with Air Vice-Marshal Park, organised the air cover for the evacuation of the B.E.F. Fragments of a telegram sent by Dowding to Usher read 'my very best on your splendid [work in defence] — Dowding'.[18] Before the war Dowding had worked tirelessly to prepare the R.A.F. for the coming conflict. Victory in the Battle of Britain, thanks to superior technology and a well-organised response strategy is his legacy.

Many were convinced that full use would be made of such an imaginative, innovative and inspirational soldier, and that an appropriate command for Usher would result. A letter from Banchory read 'You have done, and are doing, more for the army than almost anyone I know'. Many clamoured to serve in whatever command he was given.

Recognition came from all manner of men and women, typical of which was that of Tom Berry, the boxer who had helped Usher train the successful 2nd Gordons boxing team so many years before. He wrote to Madge

'I was like an overgrown schoolboy when I read of your Dear Husband and my old Pal. I knew all along it was coming to him. I've always felt that way. By my wishes to God, I am pleased to say all have been answered. May God bless you and all, and good luck. I remain, yours faithfully, Tom Berry'.

---

[18] This fragment of a telegram was rescued from a fire that destroyed many of Usher's records after his death.

Madge was relieved to learn of the safe return from Dunkirk of her nephew, Michael Shewell, who had been in action against the enemy some 18 miles south of Bergues during the retreat, typical of many gallant actions that delayed the enemy on the shrinking perimeter. Second-Lieutenant M.G. Shewell, with a T.A. commission based on his Certificate A from the Officers Training Corps at Wellington, together with Private W. Ray of A Company, was sent to retrieve the transport of 1st Battalion, The Oxfordshire and Buckinghamshire Light Infantry ('Ox & Bucks') stranded in Hazebrouck, and he had to extract his platoon from a perilous position in the town. He showed great bravery and leadership, and personally disposed of several snipers. Recounting the episode, he remarked that he felt at a bit of a disadvantage, and somewhat envious of his opposite number who was armed with a submachine gun. He did not even have a revolver as there were not enough to go round! At one point the platoon became split into two parties, and by using his head Private Ray led the detached party past several German posts to be reunited. On 28th May Captain Pallett and his detachment, at La Motte-au-Bois on the *Canal de la Nieppe*, took up a defensive position alongside two battalions of the Royal West Kent Regiment. The Germans, outnumbering the 1st Ox & Bucks three to one, crossed the canal and nearly surrounded them, but were driven out of the village and back across the canal at bayonet-point. After dark Captain Pallett led the party safely to Dunkirk. He and Shewell were awarded the M.C., Pte Ray the M.M.

When Usher handed over command at St. Malo prior to organising the defence in the Bergues area, the supply point there had found itself in the path of the inexorable German advance. J.F. Hopkinson wrote that he got a hole in his face and an eye knocked out although there was hope that it might be saved. Burgess and Harker were O.K. but Crossley and Deighton were missing. Corporal Little, the cook, was in hospital with shrapnel in his leg. Thirteen officers and 420 men got back, which left two out of three officers unaccounted for. How many were wounded was not known. Another officer bore some good news. 'Carslake and all your old friends at No. 2 docks asked him to convey their congratulations. We sent in advance our docks gear, baggage and the men's kit and the garrison baggage.'

Major Ellice from H.Q. 1 Division in Lincoln wrote, 'I wonder if it would be possible for me to see the Bergues

Garrison War Diary? I kept a very rough idea in my head but found I could not remember the dates when I got back to England. It was an interesting time! I hear George Ledingham is now in charge of an Infantry Brigade'.

On return to Britain, Captain R. Smalley was appointed Staff Captain to No. 2 Infantry Group. He told Usher that Lieutenant-Colonel W.J. Simpson and Captains Passingham and Lloyd (R.A.S.C.) had arrived at Tenby in the general mix up. Majors Jefferies and Gunter and Lieutenant-Colonel Cobbett had made it to safety. Major J.E. Gunter wrote from 45 Division H.Q. in Kent that he was now working with a T.A. Division who 'did not take their job seriously, and required kicking and verbal abuse'. All wanted to join up with Usher should the opportunity arise. One of his officers, Barton, wrote from York saying that it was already known that Shobrook was a P.O.W. and one would be sorry for him 'Good old 'X' L. of C. Don't forget my Gordon Highlander badge, I've already promised it to my very small daughter.'

Lieutenant-Colonel Cobbett, back at 4th Cavalry Barracks, said he had been re-posted there and was back to major 'but judging by the War Office letter that has just come in, I'm quite lucky not to have been retired!' He had a bad leg, which barred him from cavalry work, but was learning to ride a motorbike. Fortunately, the Commanding Officer was an old friend and the adjutant was in his regiment. He wondered if Usher had been given a job yet, and signed himself off as 'Yours ever, Oliver Cobbett'.

There was news from 1st Gordons via the wives. Lillian Alexander noted that Harry Wright, Philip Taylor and Jimmy Dunlop were prisoners. All hope had been given up for Freddy Colville. She herself had heard that her son Donald had been wounded but beyond that nothing. It was a terrible wait.

Freddy Colville had been shot at point-blank range by a German officer and was not expected to live. His wife Dorothy was distraught. He died later, as indeed did Donald Alexander, who, after receiving a bayonet wound, carried on, was wounded again by mortar fire, and stayed with his men until he collapsed. Corporal Groves and Private Knight were trying to carry him away when a German officer told them he would look after him. He was as good as his word, binding his wounds with his own field dressing, but sadly Alexander died. His subaltern, Barker, and Thom of The London Scottish, were wounded and taken prisoner[19]. Brigadier Burney was also captured[20].

In Aberdeen, Kenneth O'Morchoe had the task of re-forming the 1st Battalion. He was having 'a hell of a time trying to get things going'. Warrant Officers, Company Quartermaster Sergeants and N.C.O.s were his greatest difficulty, and he was having to make Second-Lieutenants with less than a year's service company commanders. He had Mike Du Boulay as adjutant. He pined for Eddie (Colville)[21]. O'Morchoe, the 'old leprechaun', looked forward to seeing Usher 'when he was commanding an Army Corps'.

O'Morchoe's letter was dated 6th [July?] as was another one signed 'Alex' (who took over O'Morchoe's company when O'Morchoe took on the task of command), which said there was an excellent crop of officers, O'Morchoe and Saunders as Company Commanders and they had Murphy, Hay, Du Boulay, McKechnie, Napier and all the young regulars except Gardyne[22]. When 'The General' [O'Morchoe] was asked what languages he spoke his reply was 'Swahili', which led to him taking charge of a German P.O.W. camp at Dingwall!

Norah Christie and Margaret Wright needed help getting money as their husbands, now prisoners, had always provided for them and Holts[23] did not answer their letters.

General Sir Ian Hamilton wrote to congratulate Usher, as did Colonel William Robertson, V.C., and Merchistonians, rugby players, piping enthusiasts and friends, some of whom expressed their views on suitable medals! Amongst the old internationals Chalmers Fahmy wrote 'Just what one expected from one who

---

[19] Second-Lieutenant C.N. Barker was wounded, but was evacuated to Britain, returned to duty after recovering from his wounds, and fought through the remainder of the war. He retired as a Brigadier.

[20] Brigadier G.T. Burney died in captivity.

[21] Not to be confused with Freddy Colville. E.C. (Eddie) Colville commanded the 2nd Battalion, The Gordon Highlanders in Normandy, was given command of a brigade and ended his career as a Major-General.

[22] Lieutenant (later Captain) D. Greenhill Gardyne, grandson of C. Greenhill Gardyne and son of A.D. Greenhill Gardyne, authors of Volumes I, II and III of *The Life of a Regiment*. He was killed in 1942 at El Alamein when serving with 5th/7th Gordons.

[23] Holts was one of the Army pay agents.

led us on to the field in Paris in 1920 with his kilt over his rugger kit!! What a day that was—and what a night'.

Many said they had joined the L.D.V.[24] Percy Brown[25] said he was busying himself with it and it was a case of making bricks without straw! A.G. Baird-Smith, at 74, wrote to say that he was too old to take an active part in home defence, that all Usher's old Clausthal comrades who had endured so long in captivity would be proud of him, and he liked to feel that many Scottish lads were seeing to it that no enemy secured a foothold in Britain.

A full list of recommendations for awards was sent to Brigadier Jardine, Military Secretary of the B.E.F. There seemed to be confusion about a suitable medal for Usher himself. Saunders had heard that he had been recommended for the V.C.

In June 1940, after the return of the final evacuees from Dunkirk, Major-General Thorne, now promoted to Lieutenant-General, recommended Usher for the award of the C.B.E.:

> As commander of a heterogeneous force collected from L. of C. troops, Base details and other formations in the rearward area of the B.E.F. he showed great resource, imagination and devotion to duty in organising these into fighting bodies and encouraging them to offer armed resistance for which in many cases they were untrained.
>
> He was the mainspring of the defence of BERGUES, the important pivot of the western flank defence which he successfully maintained until the majority of the B.E.F. had crossed the Canal into the DUNQUERKE Area.

This recommendation for the C.B.E. was passed up the chain of command, where it was downgraded to a recommendation for the D.S.O. In this form it was approved by the Deputy Chief of the General Staff. The rewritten commendation reads:

> Brig. Usher, while Commander "X" L. of C. Area, found himself located near BERGUES at a time when enemy attack was imminent. Realising the seriousness of the situation, he

---

[24] Local Defence Volunteers. See Chapter 6.

[25] P.W. Brown served with 2nd Gordons in the Boer War, was a Brigadier during World War I and commanded 2nd Gordons in Fort George, but was invalided out before Usher rejoined the Battalion there. His son, D.H.W. Brown commanded the 1st Battalion, 1968-1971.

organised the defence of the River Aa from GRAVELINES to ST. MOMELIN with such troops as were available.

He then organised the defence of BERGUES which was held against heavy enemy attack, shelling, bombing and mortar fire; its retention was vital to the evacuation of the B.E.F., and that it was not captured was due to the determination of Brig. Usher, to the soundness of his dispositions, and his success in organising the defence with a number of small parties of troops, many of them only partially trained.

Awards for gallantry and distinguished service during the fighting withdrawal to, and the evacuation from, Dunkirk were announced. Among them was an award for gallantry for Lance Corporal William Carle. Usher had felt that the Distinguished Conduct Medal (D.C.M.) was appropriate, but, aware that if this was turned down he might get nothing at all, put him up for the Military Medal (M.M.) instead. His recommendation read:

> Private Carle was driving the car carrying Brigadier Usher and Major Jefferies on 23rd May, when on the road to Bergues, near the gate of the fortress, the road became blocked with vehicles, three abreast, and all traffic was halted. The enemy began heavily bombing the road and all vehicles were abandoned where they stood by their drivers, who sought cover in the ditches and fields adjoining the road. Whilst Brigadier Usher and Major Jefferies were getting drivers back into their vehicles, Pte Carle drove several lorries in turn, moving them to clear a passage for the car. His example assisted in inducing men to return to their vehicles in spite of bombs falling in the closest proximity, and therefore contributed to the clearing of the block at this most dangerous time. This was not an isolated instance, for at all times Pte Carle showed a complete indifference to personal danger and fatigue when employed as a driver and servant.

Usher's boundless energy and determination to hit back at the Germans was to count for little when the War Office considered senior appointments in the post-Dunkirk Army. Charles 'Dougie' Usher, who had demonstrated outstanding organisational skills, an ability to improvise with limited forces at his disposal, superb tactical acumen and the leadership qualities to inspire battle-weary, disorganised and disillusioned men to turn and face an efficient and ruthless mechanised army, thereby holding up its advance for five days, was clearly capable of command at brigade and higher level, especially at a time when high quality leadership was required to prepare a disorganised army to face the expected invasion. Those who had served under him at Bergues had learned much about man-management, leadership and command, and many were now passing on these lessons to soldiers eager to learn. They confidently expected to learn of his appointment to a significant command post, and many were just waiting to apply to join him again.

Such a post was not forthcoming, however, and instead he was informed that, despite having held temporary ranks of Colonel and Brigadier, as a substantive Lieutenant-Colonel his services were no longer required in the Army. The fact that he had never attended the Staff College, and his staff experience was in the field of Physical Education undoubtedly figured in the decision of the Promotion Board, but that inexplicable, unimaginative and unfeeling decision was a devastating blow to a man with such energy, imagination, ability and leadership qualities.

CHAPTER 6

THE HOME GUARD

AFTER Dunkirk, Britain had ground forces amounting to 852,000 men, but this included the twelve divisions brought back from France, which had left most of their arms and equipment at Dunkirk. The rest were equipped for training but, for the most part, not armed for action, and some had not yet even learned to shoot. Churchill told the House of Commons in secret session that 'an invading force of 150,000 picked men might have created mortal havoc in our midst'. In fact, the German plan, Operation 'Sealion', was to land their 9th and 16th Armies on a front from Folkestone to Brighton, and their 6th Division in Lyme Bay. The proposed invading force amounted to 630,000 men, supported by some 650 tanks, 40,000 vehicles, 500 field howitzers and 52 anti-aircraft batteries. In planning the defence against invasion Britain also had to consider the threat of landings by airborne and parachute troops, and diversionary threats in the Thames Estuary, the Humber, the Firth of Forth and other points North to John O'Groats. Von Rundstedt was confident that, once a bridgehead was established, British generalship, inexperienced in handling mobile reserves, would not be able to counter the *blitzkrieg* that would follow, despite the expected dogged resistance from soldiers desperate to defend their homeland. Army commanders and politicians would be rounded up by the secret police, who would be responsible for the swift establishment of law and order. All able-bodied males between the ages of 17 and 45 would be transported to the Continent.

From the outset of war, ships bringing vital food and supplies around the Cape of Good Hope, and across the Atlantic to Britain had been attacked, and many sunk, by a fleet of 39 U-boats, mines, the pocket-battleships *Gneisnau*, *Scharnhorst* and *Graf Spee*, and the *Luftwaffe*. There was now a massive build-up of transports, barges, tugs and motor boats at every suitable port from Ostend to Cherbourg. A heavy bombing offensive was planned, to paralyse factories and demoralise the British people to the point of submission.

On 4th June 1940, just hours after the last ship sailed from Dunkirk, Churchill addressed the Nation.

I have, myself, full confidence that if all do their duty, if nothing is neglected, and if the best arrangements are made—as they are being made—we shall prove ourselves once again able to defend our island home, to ride out the storm of war, and to outlive the menace of tyranny, if necessary for years, if necessary alone.

At any rate that is what we are going to try to do. That is the resolve of His Majesty's Government—every man of them. That is the will of Parliament and the nation.

The British Empire and the French Republic, linked together in their cause and in their need, will defend to the death their native soil, aiding each other like good comrades to the utmost of their strength.

Even though large tracts of Europe and many old and famous States have fallen, or may fall, into the grip of the Gestapo and all the odious apparatus of Nazi rule, we shall not flag or fail.

We shall go on to the end, we shall fight in France, we shall fight on the seas and oceans, we shall fight with growing confidence and growing strength in the air, we shall defend our Island, whatever the cost may be. We will fight on the beaches, we shall fight on the landing grounds, we shall fight in the fields and streets, we shall fight in the hills; we shall never surrender, and even if, which I do not for a moment believe, this Island or a large part of it were subjugated and starving, then our Empire beyond the seas, armed and guarded by the British Fleet, would carry on the struggle, until, in God's good time, the New World, with all its power and might, steps forth to the rescue and the liberation of the old.

On 21st June France formally surrendered to Hitler, Goering, Keitel and Raeder, in the historic railway carriage at Compiègne, where Germany had surrendered in November 1918.

Britain now stood alone.

The nation was defiant. Everyone knew of the dire fate that had befallen the people of Holland at the hands of the invader. They were determined to defend their homesteads to the death.

On 10th and 11th May, the Home Defence Executive was set up to supervise a major overhaul of counter-invasion defences.

The Executive comprised the Commander-in-Chief Home Forces and representatives of the R.A.F. and Royal Navy. They had to determine how to defend likely landing areas, counteract 'fifth columnists', arm policemen against parachutists, intern enemy aliens and suspected sympathisers, arrange the removal of signposts, and form local defence forces. Any man between sixteen and sixty-five who had fired a rifle or a shotgun, and was capable of free movement, would be eligible for these forces, and those accepted would be embodied in an unpaid organisation called the Local Defence Volunteers (L.D.V.). Equipment would be an L.D.V. armband and a tin hat, together with one of the 100,000 rifles of various patterns and calibres available, failing which whatever weapon might come to hand—sporting rifles, old firearms, shotguns, or agricultural tools that could serve as a bludgeon. Newspapers showed how to make a Molotov cocktail. By the end of the month 300,000 volunteers had mustered. By the end of July, numbers had swelled to 500,000. The organisation was renamed the Home Guard, a force which reached 2,000,000 by the summer of 1943.

Although discarded for further service in the Regular Army, Usher's worth was recognised by those responsible for the L.D.V., and he was employed on the staff to help organise the new force, soon renamed the Home Guard. Very quickly Usher was appointed, in the rank of Colonel, as Area Commander, North Highland District, which covered everywhere north of the Caledonian Canal, and the Western Isles. On 29th June 1940, he also assumed the duties of G.S.O.1 (General Staff Officer, grade 1). Should the Germans attempt a landing they would face a formidable guerrilla leader. Usher had an office in the Iona Hotel, Inverness, on the banks of the River Ness, facing the castle. His Chief Clerk, Corporal A.N. Kerr, formerly Lieutenant-Colonel Alexander (Alec) Kerr, M.C., of the 17th Dogra Regiment, Indian Army, had distinguished himself in June 1916 with the 2nd Battalion, Kashmir Rifles at the Battle of Lukigura in East Africa. His son, John became a great friend of Usher's younger son, Kenneth, in the Far East a decade later.

Usher's responsibilities as the senior staff officer in the Home Guard north of the Great Glen included recruitment, training, provision of weapons and equipment, supervision of all Home Guard activities and liaison with local communities, from whom the men had been recruited. Usher was ideally suited for this, his military expertise and experience, allied to his easy charm, finding willing listeners, officers and men alike, when he visited units and detachments and spoke to them.

Home was Milton of Culloden, a two-storey farmhouse with additional attic bedrooms, forming a traditional T-shaped ground plan, on the shore of the Moray Firth, three miles east of Inverness. There was no gas or electricity, and cooking was on a range which also supplied hot water, and on a paraffin stove in the large kitchen. Coal and paraffin were rationed, but fuel was found by scavenging coal from the coastal railway, driftwood from the beach and sometimes some scrounged peat. Usher and Madge enjoyed family life for a while, reunited with their elder son, Iain, a Royal Engineer, when he could get leave, and their younger son, Kenneth, in school holidays. It was a beautiful setting with views across to Ben Wyvis. Permission was secured for rough shooting over to Bothyhill at Alturlie Point, where the bag might include duck, partridge and the occasional plover, and towards Culloden House. Rations were supplemented with a plentiful supply of rabbits, stalked in the sand dunes or bolted by a couple of ferrets named Romeo and Juliet, and the eggs from a dozen Rhode Island Reds fed on grain and household scraps (if egg production faltered, Usher encouraged them to start laying again by dosing them with castor oil). Usher's batman, Carle, lived in and the kitchen garden was very productive as a result of his labours. He had use of Usher's father's venerable brown, damascus-barrelled, Stephen Grant 12-bore. Before enlisting, Carle had poached salmon with torch and gaff, often pursued by the police, and he was gratified to be able to do it legally.

It was idyllic compared to much of Britain, subjected to continuous bombing by the *Luftwaffe*. There were constant reminders of the threat by the poles on the Moray Firth shore stretching out to the low tide mark, to thwart German airborne landings. Blackout screens were fitted to windows after dark, and everyone crowded round the wireless set, powered by a 12-volt car battery, to hear the news and Churchill's speeches. To lighten the gloom there was I.T.M.A.—*It's That Man Again*— with Tommy Handley making fun of wartime absurdities that affected everybody. At night, paper was put behind the glass of hand-held torches, and black slatted masks on car headlights meant slow progress over narrow country roads.

Madge worked as a censor, which gave her a sense of purpose in helping the war effort. Usher visited far-flung Home Guard units to supervise training, reconnoitre suitable checkpoints and defensive positions, and liaise with Regular units of the Royal Navy, Army and R.A.F. to provide assistance wherever and whenever required. Just as Britain did at Dieppe, the Germans were capable of raiding anywhere on the coastline to cause havoc, damage morale, and divert men and material from the Second Front. As the fortunes of war went against Germany, such raids would boost morale back at home. Besides supporting the Regular Army, the Home Guard had to be ready to impede enemy forces by such ploys as flooding roads with burning petrol, sabotaging behind their lines and conducting guerrilla warfare. In this respect the terrain favoured the defence, and the defenders could live off the land.

Usher found recruits and leaders by networking with the lairds, including Colonel Sir Donald Cameron of Lochiel, (the model for 'Ben Nevis' in Compton Mackenzie's *Monarch of the Glen*), The Duke of Sutherland at Dunrobin Castle, Flora Macleod at Dunvegan Castle, Alec Mackenzie of Farr, Findlay Mackenzie, the proprietor of the Lochboisdale Hotel, MacSween, the Principal of the Stornoway Technical College, Colonel J. Douglas Walker[1], founder of the Harris Tweed Association at Borve in Harris, and on Barra was Compton Mackenzie himself, writer and one-time agent in Greece. This list of prominent and respected figures shows the geographical extent of Usher's domain, and the distances he travelled to keep in touch with every Home Guard unit and detachment.

As a prisoner-of-war in the First World War Usher had tried to learn Gaelic, but without a tutor had not make much progress. Now, with so many Gaelic speakers in the ranks, he started again, with great enthusiasm, taught by MacSween, the Home Guard Commander in the Western Isles.

The Highlands north of Inverness was a Protected Area, the largest in Britain, out of bounds without an official pass, complete with photograph. There were particularly sensitive places, such as Commando training sites and the naval installations at Kyle of Lochalsh. As a Protected Area, any information concerning it was classified, and in contrast to other districts, very little has been published since. Usher, with Carle at the wheel of a small P/U ('pick-up' with a canvas canopy on the back), covered the territory comprehensively. On occasion,

---

[1]   Colonel Douglas Walker lost both his fighter-pilot sons in the Battle of Britain.

in school holidays, his younger son, Kenneth, accompanied him, concealed in the back under a rug with instructions not to move when passing through a check-point, or dropped off before reaching the check-point and told to climb up the hill behind it, go round the other side and get back in the vehicle. MacBrayne's provided the link to the Outer Isles across the often stormy Minch, on the old SS *Clydesdale* or the newer SS *Lochmore*, skippered by the redoubtable Captain Robertson. When Findlay Mackenzie opened a bottle of whisky for his guests in the Lochboisdale Hotel, they could not leave until it was empty. After visiting Mackenzie, Robertson, who knew every hazard in the treacherous waters, would be dunked in the Minch by the crew before being placed, dripping, on the bridge to take control. Years later, when Captain Robertson and his ship were replaced by a more modern vessel equipped with radar, many islanders felt it was safer to travel by air!

The SS *Politician*, inspiration for Compton Mackenzie's *Whisky Galore*, was wrecked on Eriskay, between South Uist and Barra. Some of the cargo was stoppered with cork and some with screw tops, and in the course of duty Usher was offered samples of both, saved from the attentions of the excisemen. The screw top was preferred as it was impermeable to sea water!

There was stalking and fishing at Amhuinnsuide Castle, and when Lord Bridgeman, who had worked closely with Usher at Dunkirk, reappeared in his new role of Director General of the Home Guard, they met up at Grimersta in Lewis, where John Gillies was Head Keeper. On 26th August, 1943 a 25lb cock salmon fell to a Kate fly presented by Usher, fishing his father's old monster greenheart. Interestingly, in a latter day context, the total bag for the day was over 30 salmon and a dozen sea trout. There was prolific fishing throughout Harris, North Uist and South Uist, at that time with few people about.

On the mainland, in the Highland glens, Usher could play the pipes in ideal conditions. Sometimes a reward was forthcoming in the shape of a cup of tea at an isolated croft.

The Duke of Sutherland was generous with fishing, stalking and walked-up grouse round Ben Klibreck at Loch Choire Lodge, which came with his great head keeper and stalker, Duncan. There was no shortage of salmon and trout in Loch Choire and the River Mallert, nor of magnificent trout in Loch Truderscaig. On occasion the family came too, as did Carle, who could now take a salmon legally. Sadly, one day the local exciseman investigated the telltale wisp of smoke coming from Duncan's still and he paid the inevitable price (incarceration 'at His Majesty's pleasure').

Other estates were just as kind, especially Alec Mackenzie of Farr, the Duke of Gloucester's factor at Farr. The Duke of Gloucester, Colonel-in-Chief of The Gordon Highlanders, was an old acquaintance of Usher's. There was generously given stalking in Glenmoriston, at Caennacroc and Corrie Lair amongst other venues.

At the end of 1943 the Second Front, for which Stalin had been calling ceaselessly to relieve the pressure on the Soviet Union's western front, where the Red Army was losing countless lives, was looming.

Although a long way from the 'hot war', the progress of battles elsewhere was on every mind. People crowded round the wireless to hear Churchill's eagerly awaited speeches on the B.B.C. The wait for the Second Front seemed interminable, and was made more so by concern for Usher's elder son, Iain, who had been defusing mines in the Western Desert with the 4th Indian Division. Usher felt great frustration while others were fighting the enemy, including his cousin Clive, who distinguished himself with a D.S.O. as a gunner Brigadier in Italy.

The 3½ years Usher spent with the Home Guard were challenging, through forming, training and operating a basic military organisation from non-military resources, satisfying, through the successful completion of the challenge, but ultimately frustrating, as the experienced professional soldier was excluded from active service, for which he was so well fitted and for which he longed.

In the Spring of 1944, however, Usher, officially too old for active service, was recalled from the Home Guard and re-engaged as an experienced officer and linguist, to become a Senior Civil Affairs Officer with the invasion forces for the forthcoming liberation of Europe, Operation '*Overlord*'. The *Military Manual of Civil Affairs in the Field* (February 1944) specified that Civil Affairs Officers required 'very high personal qualities'. The task would be demanding, and the *Manual* pointed out the requirements expected of a Civil Affairs Officer at all times:

He is always on duty, whether in his office, touring the district, taking meals at a hotel, relaxing at a theatre or in his quarters, or even when on leave outside of his own district. He must remember that it is by his conduct, even more than by that of other officers of the Army, that his country will be judged.

Civil Affairs officers were to abstain from politics, ensure that military interests came first, make changes slowly by adopting measures that had proved to work, have good relations, sympathy and patience with the local population and avoid favour or intrigue. They had to be self-reliant, with initiative.

Usher attended the commando course at Achnacarry, near Fort William, and it is a matter of conjecture who taught whom to climb ropes, run up walls, and carry out other physically daunting tasks! He brushed up his Russian when he took Madge and their younger son Kenneth to live with his sister, Ina, at 32, Drumsheugh Gardens in Edinburgh. Regular visits were made to an *émigré* Russian couple in a small flat, simply and tastefully decorated, off a malodorous common stair in a Tollcross tenement. Here Usher received intensive tuition in the language before going south to attend the Civil Affairs and Training Centre at Easthampstead and The Grand Hotel, Eastbourne.

The agenda covered the policies, principles and procedures to be adopted by the commanders and their subordinates who would exercise control over Civil Affairs in French territory liberated by the Allied Expeditionary Force. The staffing of Civil Affairs Detachments would be in proportion to the nationality of the different Allied units engaged in the theatre of operations, and Usher would be responsible for a detachment that would include a large number of American officers.

Every contingency was covered in detail. Usher would be responsible in his area for Politics, Finance, Public Safety, Police, Fire and Civil Defence, Health, Welfare, Civilian Supplies, Price Control, Rationing, Agriculture, Trade and Industry, Labour, Public Works and Utilities, Transport, Posts and Telegraphs, Fine Arts and Monuments, Archives, Education, Internees, Political Prisoners and Legal matters.[2] Financial

---

[2]   These responsibilities are in the *Field Handbook for Civil Affairs (France)*, of 16 June 1944. It was for use by British and American forces in the A.E.F. The first Handbook ran to some 353 pages.

precautions, which seemed sensible at the time, would give rise to a serious rift with de Gaulle[3].

In France, the fundamental Civil Affairs unit would be the 'Basic Detachment', a team of officers and soldiers that mixed general skills with specialist capabilities and self-administration. Each Detachment was to deal with problems on the ground as they occurred, and keep Civil Affairs Group staff aware of civilian matters so that they could anticipate problems. The Basic Detachment consisted of two generalist officers, two public safety officers, two clerks (one ideally an interpreter), one cook, one batman and two drivers. Detachments were commanded by a major. Most Detachments were given an increment of specialists, the number of which depended on the needs of the Detachment and who was available. The more significant Detachments (those working at regional and *Département* levels) were often commanded by a generalist Colonel or Lieutenant-Colonel, whose higher rank helped when working with senior French officials. French Liaison Officers were attached to as many Detachments as possible. Each Basic Detachment had one 3-ton lorry, one 15-cwt truck and two motor cycles.

Usher would have American officers as well as British under his command, and he had to work out how to deal pragmatically with different concepts of duties between the Allies. There were cultural differences, not least linguistic. It was realised, perhaps for the first time in an important context, that American English and British English differed significantly. The Americans had drawn up detailed instructions on how Civil Affairs within the Allied Military Government of Occupied Territories, (A.M.G.O.T.), should be conducted. The British Army's Lieutenant-General F.E. Morgan, Chief of Staff to Supreme Allied Commander, General Eisenhower, received one voluminous document which he read and re-read but could not understand; the words were undoubtedly English 'but in conjunction conveyed not one single thing'. He had to have the document translated into British military language.

To the Americans, Europe was a single entity, to be liberated regardless of national differences; each country should be put

---

[3]   In order to prevent shortage of currency, supplemental franc notes would be used to enhance the existing currency. That these would be legal tender was unacceptable to de Gaulle, because they would, in his view, constitute an infringement of French sovereignty.

under military government until it could hold fair and free elections to choose its own government. Distinctions between friend and foe did not occur to them. Countries like Norway and Holland had Governments-in-Exile which could legitimately represent their people. France, however, the first country in which Usher would have to operate, presented a serious problem for the Americans. They were not in the war when France fell in 1940, and when they entered it, in December 1941, they maintained diplomatic relations with the Vichy government until the Allied invasion of North Africa in November 1942.

On 16th June, 1940, with the assistance of the British Government, General de Gaulle had been flown to England and recognised as military leader of the Free French, who would fight with the Allies. In October 1940 de Gaulle set up a *Conseil de Défense de l'Empire* after a number of French colonies had declared for him. This became the French National Committee, but the British Government, backed by Roosevelt and Stalin, refused to recognise it as a future government of France. By D-Day negotiations about how civil affairs should be conducted in France remained unresolved. French liaison officers had trained for the re-establishment of civil administration in France before the Chief of Staff to the Supreme Allied Commander (C.O.S.S.A.C.) was appointed or Supreme Headquarters, Allied Expeditionary Force (S.H.A.E.F.) was established. The Allies' refusal to recognise his provisional government, the issue of Allied franc notes as legal tender and the wording of the Allied proclamation to the French people, led a furious de Gaulle to forbid members of the *Mission Militaire de Liaison Administrative* (M.M.L.A.) to be deployed with the invasion force. The French officers got on very well with their British and American counterparts while they all trained together at Wimbledon and Eastbourne. Usher and some of his British officers, instinctively Francophile, helped de Gaulle in his fight for recognition as the head of the government of a liberated France, and set him on the path to become President of the Republic.

CHAPTER 7

CAEN

USHER returned to France on D+4, shortly after the invasion. In the first week of June 1944 there had been a raging storm in the Channel, with low, threatening cloud and six-foot waves. Most of the invasion force was embarked and waiting in their craft. General Dwight D. Eisenhower, Supreme Allied Commander, met regularly with his Commanders-in-Chief, Admiral Ramsay, Air Chief Marshal Leigh-Mallory and General Montgomery at Southwick House, Portsmouth, to consider whether to give the go ahead for Operation '*Overlord*' or to postpone it. Their guiding light was Group Captain, J.M. Stagg, the R.A.F.'s Chief Meteorologist. At around 0415 on the 5th, based on information from his Atlantic weather stations (a service not available to the enemy), he predicted that there would be a brief break in the weather. A couple of hours later Eisenhower made the decision to go.

In Caen, all was quiet at the H.Q. of the German 716 Infantry Division, commanded by General Richter. The H.Q. was in two short streets, *Rues Leverrier* and *Bagatelle*, which the Germans had blocked at either end, and where they had requisitioned five or six houses in each. The only entrance and exit was at the bottom of the *Avenue de Bagatelle*, guarded by a sentry. At 7 pm Richter closed his weekly conference with his regimental commanders. He had received a warning that the invasion would come between the 3rd and 10th, but said dismissively that they had received the same sort of warning every full moon and every moonless night since April!

24 year old André Heintz, who had been a pupil at Bristol Grammar School for two terms in 1935, and who was soon to act as interpreter to Civil Affairs Detachments 201 and 209, was coming and going as usual from 7 *Rue Leverrier*, where he lived with his parents. He was a messenger for the pro-de Gaulle *Force Française de l'Intérieur* (F.F.I.), which fought just before and after the landing. His 'cover' was that he taught English at St. Joseph's private school. After dark he had to show his identity card and he recalled 'quite a thrill' every time he passed the sentry carrying documents, including identity cards for

people in trouble hidden in his socks, and messages written on thin paper hidden in the handlebars of his bicycle.

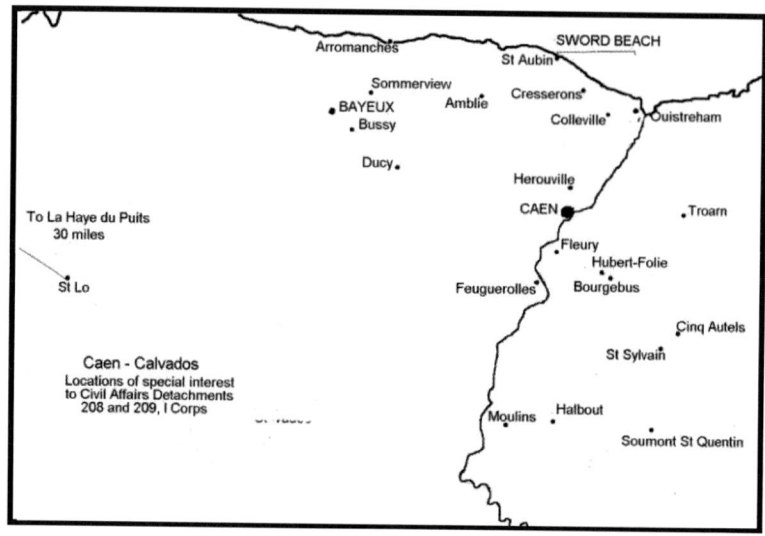

Area around Caen, June-July 1944

Waiting anxiously in the wings, and wanted by the Gestapo, was Pierre Daure. *M.* Daure had been *Recteur* of the University of Caen until 1941, when he had been sacked by the Vichy authorities for his opposition to the Germans. Around 5th May he received a note bearing the Cross of Lorraine appointing him *Préfet* of Calvados after the liberation. It was signed by de Gaulle and was with the approval of the Algiers government that had supplanted the Vichy government after North Africa had been liberated by the Allies. Disguised as a farmer, Daure was working for the Resistance and was hiding at Hubert Folie only a mile-and-a-half south of the outskirts of Caen on the Falaise Road, while his family were living on a farm a little north of Argentan, 25 miles further south. For his wife Marianne, going by her maiden name of Coulet, it was a harrowing experience. Short of cash and under police surveillance, she had her children, David and Catou, to care for. An Austrian officer billeted on the farm enquired after her husband from time to time, as the latter only made the briefest of appearances. It was a dangerous place to be.

[In Germany Adolf Hitler was entertaining senior Nazis with a Wagner concert at Berchestgaden. In Normandy, many senior

German officers and their staffs, reassured by the bad weather, were at a war game in Rennes. These included Generals Hellmich, 243rd Division, von Schlieben, 709th Division and Falley, 91st Division, all based in the Cotentin area. Ironically, the subject for study was an Allied landing in Normandy preceded by parachute drops. Because of the war game a practice alert scheduled for the night of 5th/6th June had been cancelled. H.Q. 7th Army tried to get the Generals to call off the war game, but to no avail. Admiral Kranke, commanding Naval Forces (West), left for Bordeaux. No German vessels could put to sea for night patrols. General Marcks at 84 Army Corps in Bordeaux was enjoying a midnight birthday drinks party, and General Speidel, Rommel's Chief of Staff, was entertaining guests to dinner at La Roche-Guyon.

Erwin Rommel was relaxing at home in Herrlingen, near Ulm, where he had gone for his wife's birthday on 6th June. He had left his H.Q. at 7am on the 5th, on the strength of the daily bulletin by Colonel Professor Walther Ströbe, chief of the Meteorological Section of the *Luftwaffe* in Paris, which predicted rain, violent wind and low cloud. Furthermore, because the Allies had not taken advantage of the three spells of good weather that had occurred, he could say with absolute certainty that there would not be any landings in the coming weeks. Friedrich Hayn, Intelligence Officer of 84th Army Corps, maintained that since the Allies had not taken advantage of the conditions in May, they would not move before August. The tactically astute Rommel intended to go on to Berchestgaden to try to persuade Hitler to move the two tank Divisions and the anti-aircraft batteries held in reserve close to the shore of the Cotentin Peninsula, which he considered inadequately defended. If, he maintained, they waited until the invasion had begun, it would make them liable to destruction by the R.A.F., which, in the event, was what happened. Had he got his wish the Allied task would have been much harder.]

Operation *Fortitude*, the Allied campaign of deception and disinformation to make the Germans believe that the main thrust of the invasion would be between Dunkirk and Dieppe, with diversionary landings in Normandy, was a brilliant success. The subsequent loss of life on both sides was appalling but had '*Fortitude*' not succeeded, D-Day could have ended in failure, and, although the Reich would probably have been defeated eventually, the added suffering and casualties would have been extensive.

At 9.15 pm on 5th June the French Service of the B.B.C. broadcast a 20 minute programme, twice as long as usual, of coded messages for the Resistance. The announcer said,

'Today the Supreme Allied Commander directs me to say this: In due course instructions of great importance will be given to you through this channel, but it will not be possible always to give these instructions at a previously announced time, therefore you must get into the habit of listening at all hours.'

This alerted the Germans, but in spite of all the evidence, including heavy shipping movements in the Channel and jamming of radar stations, General Blumentritt, Chief of Staff to Commander-in-Chief West, Field Marshal von Rundstedt, took no action. Rommel's H.Q. told his forces between the Orne and the Scheldt to stand to, but gave no orders to Richter.

At 0015 on 6th June a surprise preliminary airborne attack was launched by Major-General Richard Gale to secure the vital bridge over the Orne, and the Halifax bombers that had towed the gliders with the attacking troops went on to bomb Caen—a rude awakening indeed for the citizens of the town on what should have been their day of liberation!

By the afternoon of 6th June the Allies had successfully carried out landings on the beaches of Normandy. At 4 pm on D-Day, General Jodl, Chief of Operations Staff of the *Oberkommando der Wehrmacht* (O.K.W.)—German Supreme Command—telephoned and ordered that the bridgehead must be cleaned up not later than that night, and *Standartenführer* (Colonel) Kurt Meyer of the 12th S.S. *Panzer* Division, arriving at Major-General Edgar Feuchtinger's 21st *Panzer* Division H.Q. in Caen just after midnight, was sure that the enemy would soon be thrown back into the water. The British were little fish, he maintained, and no match for his men, who were the pick of the Hitler Youth and who would fight until the last man. A major offensive would be required to dislodge his men, and there were no Allied divisions available for a direct assault.

After the D-Day landings, the Germans shot 80 members of the Resistance in Caen prison and elsewhere in the city, rather than see them freed by Allied forces. Further executions were carried out, not discovered until after the liberation.

Caen and its 50,000 citizens suffered much from the earliest moments of the invasion. Caen was a vital road and rail junction, and its seizure would greatly hamper German ability to transport men and materiel across the battlefield. It was a vital Allied target, and its capture by D+1 was one of the early objectives. Part of the Allied strategy was to bomb German forces and positions in and around Caen, and the first bombing raids were carried out by the bombers that had towed the gliders that landed at Pegasus Bridge. There were further air-raids on the 6th, and a major air-raid was planned for 7th June. In the struggle for Caen these were to be the first of a series of Allied bombing raids[1]. Caen's ordeal over the following two months was truly horrendous, a nightmare of death, destruction and deprivation. The failure of the ambitious timetable to capture Caen by D +1 condemned the citizens to suffer through a long battle to take and hold the town.

The Deputy Mayor, Joseph Poirier, who was responsible for Civil Defence, kept a diary entitled 'La Bataille de Caen' from 6th June until 15th August. A digest of his personal recollections, [all French passages translated and paraphrased by the author] describing the start of the horrors which Usher would encounter in due course, is given below.

It was a terrifying battle, a nightmare, uninterrupted for sixty-five days, which turned the city into an enormous necropolis, destroying three-quarters of its infrastructure. Such was the torment that each day deserved an account of its own. 'How much sorrow, atrocities, deaths but also how much devotion, heroism and self sacrifice!' Poirier wrote. He felt inadequate to describe those dreadful days, when he saw the destruction of so much of the town, the death of so many friends, the suffering of so many unfortunates and the tears of mothers.

At two o'clock in the morning of June 6th he was awoken by a deafening cannonade in the distance. What was it? This was something quite unprecedented. Were the coastal batteries firing? Were bombs being dropped? Could it be the

---

[1] Caen suffered terribly in the two months following D-Day. As the Germans were determined to hold it, it was a legitimate target, but this condemned the citizens to a series of terrifying bombing raids that destroyed much of the town and killed many innocent civilians.

landing? There were planes in the sky and sirens sounding the alert and Poirier went to his Command post under the central police station. The populace besieged the bakeries . . . 'it is the long awaited landing! The Boches are going. One can smile at last and everything will proceed painlessly'. At 7am bombs fell near the station, with one person killed and two wounded. The rest of the morning was quiet except for the bombardment in the distance by Allied naval guns.

The R.A.F. flew overhead, and at 1 pm a large force of bombers dropped their bombs on the centre of the town. Many bombs fell in the quarters of the *Banque de France,* the *Rue Saint-Louis, Rue Saint-Jean, Rue de Gêole, Boulevard des Alliés,* and *Place Saint-Gilles, Place Courtonne, Rue des Chanoines, Rue Basse, Rue de Vaugueux, Place Blot* were cut off. When Red Cross teams got through they found many dead and wounded.

Everyone was shaken by the suddenness of the attack. A frightened crowd took shelter in the Civil Defence Command Post and the cellars of the Town Hall. The wounded were taken to the *Bon Sauveur* hospital and the horribly mutilated dead to a room at the central police station.

The raid only lasted ten minutes but there was much damage. The Monoprix Stores were in flames, and more than a dozen locations ablaze in the city centre. The Fire Service lacked the means to deal with them all. There was another short but violent raid at 4.25 pm. Bombs fell on the *Rue de Caumont,* completely destroying the annex to the *Préfecture,* the *Palais de l'inspection Académique* and *l'Ouvroir Notre Dame. Saint Etienne* suffered some damage. In the *Rue du Carel,* the depots of the *Couriers Normands,* together with all the vehicles garaged there, and the undertakers, holding around 500 emergency coffins, were reduced to ashes, leaving no coffins for burying the dead. About fifteen bombs fell on the *Bon-Sauveur* near to the *Rue de L'Abbatiale* and the *Place des Granges,* burying eight nuns and thirty patients in the ruins. The *Hospice de Saint-Jean* was destroyed. A bomb hit an ambulance crossing the Vaucelles bridge and the young Red Cross girl driver was killed and blown into the Orne. First Aid post No.1 was destroyed. Dead and wounded were everywhere. The Red Cross and Civil Defence were overwhelmed. There were not enough ambulances and stretchers, and the First Aid posts were unusable. Despite prodigious efforts, the medical services were unable to operate quickly enough on the wounded coming in a steady stream. More fires were breaking out, and a quarter of the town was in flames. Dynamite was needed to cut the fires. The Chief Engineer (Roads and Bridges) went to the mines at Soumont-Saint-Quentin to find some. His car was machine gunned, bombed and burnt out and he returned, fortunately unhurt, on foot unable to reach the mine. A mine engineer went to Fuegerolles and brought back 50kgs of dynamite and two technicians to undertake an enormous job, only to be killed two hours later.

There was a third raid at 10 pm, and the *Rue de Bras* was bombed, killing one of the *chefs d'îlot* and his wife. Flames were everywhere, getting closer to the houses next to Poirier's, and Poirier rushed to save some clothes and personal papers. Two hours later the conflagration was stopped, just ten metres away. He returned to his Command Post, climbed the Town Hall clock tower, to witness a terrifying scene. The church of St. Jean and the neighbouring quarters were on fire, and despite using the limited supply of dynamite, it was impossible to stop the fire spreading. The rumbling of aircraft went on all evening. Rescue teams struggled to get to victims calling out from under the ruins. There was not enough equipment or men to save them all.

At 2.40 pm on 7th June, the day Bayeux, only 12 miles distant, was liberated, Caen suffered its worst bombardment to date. More than a thousand Lancasters and Halifaxes carpeted the town from one end to the other with a thousand tons of bombs. The first string fell on the Fire Brigade barracks, killing the Commander, his deputy, 17 firemen, and destroying all their equipment. More than 20 bombs fell on the Town Hall, the *Place de la République* and the Museum courtyard. Everyone at the Command Post felt certain that their last hour had come. The façade, and then the whole of the Town Hall collapsed with a noise like an earthquake. Those in the cellar who survived emerged safe and sound in the *Place de la République*.

The Commandant of Police, his wife and baby and 14 of his officers were buried in their trench, which closed up after them. One of Poirier's friends was lying on the ground, decapitated. There were more than 50 dead in the trenches and 1,700 wounded were taken as fast as possible to the *Bon-*

Sauveur Hospital. The quarters of *Saint-Jean* and *Saint-Louis* were completely flattened.

The Command Post was lit by acetylene lamp. Telephone lines were cut and there was no electricity or water. The population, panic stricken, fled into the neighbouring countryside. People went round in bare feet and just a shirt. For several hours the town was hidden by yellowish smoke and the dust from collapsing buildings. It was infernal with the wounded groaning and screaming, carried on door panels and in bicycle trailers to the *Bon-Sauveur*, and the First Aid post in the *Lycée Malherbe* in the afternoon. Rescuers took mutilated, unidentifiable corpses and piled them in the central police station, with no idea of where, when or how they could be buried.

Poirier noted with consternation that many Civil Defence personnel had fled after the terrible bombardment they had suffered. His Command Post was threatening to collapse and he transferred to the *Lycée Malherbe*.

There were rumours that the British were at the gates of Caen. Poirier was concerned about what might happen to the remaining population of Caen and he wrote a message to the British generals, signed by the *Maire*, stating that the population had fled the bombed area and taken refuge in the *Lycée Malherbe*, the *Bon-Sauveur*, the *Quartier Saint-Etienne*, *Caponière* and the *Rue de Bayeux*. He begged them to spare this quarter, with 20,000 of Caen's 65,000 population. He asked *Lieutenant* Poinlane, a Resistance chief, to pass through the lines and deliver the message, which was duly received, and the *Quartier St. Etienne* was not attacked. Poinlane, the messenger, was to die heroically at the head of the F.F.I. six weeks later, leading his men at Lisieux.

Hour on hour the destruction caused by the bombing got worse. The *Miséricorde* clinic was heavily struck, and many nuns and all the nurses were killed. More than eighty corpses remained buried under the ruins for two months. All the fire-fighting equipment save for one small water pump was destroyed.

At 5am on 8th June there was a new bombardment, with many dead and wounded, at the *Place Louis-Guillouard*, the *Rue de Vaugueux* and the *Rue des Teinturiers*, which were then evacuated. A lone victim cried out in the deserted and silent street. The *Bon-Sauveur* hospital and the *Saint Martin* clinic overflowed with wounded. The health service was beyond praise for their care, with six surgical teams and two operating theatres, surgeons and physicians performing amazingly.

In the *Malherbe Lycée* Reception Centre, 4,000 refugees filled an area for 600, and 3,000 people were crammed into cellars designated for 600. A few days later the *Lycée* was sheltering 7,000. 2,000 refugees in addition to more than 1,700 wounded were at the *Bon-Sauveur*. All had to be fed, and, armed with requisition orders signed by Poirier, young men and women of the Red Cross and *Equipes Nationales* sought out sugar, wine, jam, lavatory paper and other necessities from the few remaining shops. Most shops had been destroyed, together with their stocks. Volunteers went out into the countryside to round up stray cattle, slaughter them and distribute the meat.

Fifteen hundred men, women and children were stretched out on straw in *Saint-Etienne*, the *Abbaye aux Hommes*, and at 6 pm the old *curé* gave them absolution, because the end appeared so imminent that there was no time for the last rites. All in the church felt close to death, and crowded round the altar. At that moment guns of every calibre, including those of the great battleships *Ramillies* and *Warspite*, opened fire on every road into Caen. André Heintz kept a souvenir, a huge chunk of shrapnel that hit his home in the *Rue Leverrier*. Poirier was reduced to tears when two great buildings in the *Place Saint-Sauveur* were destroyed. At 8 am bombing and shelling caused more casualties. At nightfall the bombing ceased, but the shelling continued. The Vichy Deputy *Préfet, M.* Triboulet, who had been secretly working for the Resistance and was a local landowner, offered his services to the Allies. He was treated with suspicion, and frustrated in his attempt to establish his credentials.

The shelters in the *Lycée Malherbe* were full to overflowing and it was decided to reserve them for women, children and old men. The Assembly Hall became a baby crèche; most of the babies had lost their parents. The fighting in the suburbs brought an unending stream of refugees.

There were more air-raids on 9th and 10th June. Many in the *Rue de la Deliverande* and the *Rue de Vaugueux* who had remained in their homes were killed. Refugees, who had had nothing to eat or drink for 48 hours, came to escape the ferocious battle in Hérouville, including a farmer in his cart drawn by a white horse with red crosses painted on its head, back and rump. Huge red crosses were painted with patients' blood on the *Lycée Malherbe*, the *Bon-Sauveur* and the *Lycée* for Girls, while others were painted on sheets of corrugated iron or pieces of cloth and scattered on the ground round about them. No bombs fell on them throughout the battle, but they were no protection against shelling. Two hundred shells fell on the *Bon-Sauveur*, 57 on the *Lycée Malherbe* and 19 on *l'Église Saint-Etienne*, killing 50 and wounding over 100. The Fire Service dragged living and dead from the ruins. Nine out of ten dead were unidentified, and buried where they lay under a thin covering of soil.

Meanwhile, the S.S. were engaged in an orgy of looting. They did not have it all their own way, however, as young Red Cross workers acted quickly to prevent them getting all the sugar stored in the *Societé-Normande d'Alimentation*, and rescued 45 tons against the 40 looted by the S.S.!

This was the situation in Caen when Colonel Charles Usher, Officer Commanding 208 and 209 Civil Affairs Basic Detachments, landed in France. Prior to sailing, he had received a Top Secret Second Army Civil Affairs briefing. His sailing date was D+4 (10th June), and he would land on Sword Beach, where his party would be under the command of the Senior Civil Affairs Officer (S.C.A.O.), I Corps. The increment for the voyage was composed of Captain van Brocklin (U.S.) (Labour), Captain Wilson (U.S.) (Relief), Major Kaplan (U.S.) (Supplies) and Captain Elliott (U.S.) (Medical). These were accompanied by seven other ranks, two x 3 ton lorries and two motor cycles. He was to hand over his party to the Officer Commanding 201 Basic Detachment.

Usher would remain under command S.C.A.O. I Corps from disembarkation until he came under the command of S.C.A.O. 2nd Army, and he was ordered to contact S.C.A.O. 2nd Army as soon as possible on arrival at 2nd Army Main H.Q. His own Detachments, 208 and 209, would land on D+6 (12th June) and further increments on D+8 (14th June). These Detachments had an increment consisting of officers to cover General Administration, Legal, Finance, Civil Defence and Fire, Labour (plus 34 O.R.s, seven 3 ton lorries, two 15 cwt and five motor cycles), Medical, Engineers, Communications, Trade and Industry, Supply, Food Production, Relief, and Road Transport.

The overall plan for the Civil Affairs organisation depended on the invasion timetable being maintained, and Caen being captured within the first few days. Usher was expected to start setting up his Detachments in Caen on 10th June. The timetable, however, fell behind from the first day, and Caen was still held by the Germans when Usher landed in France. He clearly could not enter Caen on the day originally planned.

The advance party of Detachment 201 landed at 2.30 pm on 9th June at La Brèche d'Hermanville on 'Sword' beach, west of Ouistreham, after suffering three days at sea in appalling conditions, with four-foot waves while anchored off the coast, nauseated by sickness, cold and wet. It was welcomed by enemy artillery fire, Captains Jenkins and Dale (U.S.) being wounded in the left leg and face respectively. The bad weather and congestion on the beaches prevented the other detachments from landing. The rest of 201 got ashore the following morning at 2.30 am and looked forward to getting to their intended billet at the *Hotel d'Angleterre* in Caen that night. Usher's intention was still to enter Caen on 10th June, the day of his landing on the beaches. He had with him a small advance party from Civil Affairs Detachment 208, together with Major E.J.W. Hellmuth, O.C. 201 Detachment, 2 Civil Affairs Group and 219 Civil Affairs Detachment (Refugee Control). In addition, several meetings had been arranged with the French authorities in Bayeux, which had already fallen to the Allies. However, the military situation meant that Allied entry to Caen was not possible until 9th July. Lieutenant-General Dempsey, Commanding Second British Army, had been ordered to capture the main road between Bayeux and Caen at the bridgehead east of the Orne, by the previous evening, 8th June.

They slept where they could in a ditch, and were then sent to reconnoitre Ouistreham, establishing their H.Q. at Colleville, just 6 miles north of Caen. They were in an enclave five miles by five, only a mile from troops of the German 716 Infantry Division and counter-attacks by Feuchtinger's 21st *Panzer* Division. By mid-day on 7th June the beautiful town of Bayeux, the destination of Detachment 202, had been liberated intact, but Caen was stoutly defended by Meyer's 12th S.S. *Panzer* Division, together with the 21st *Panzer* Division, with 228 tanks and assault guns, field and anti-tank guns and heavy mortars. Four anti-aircraft batteries were sited in the city itself.

Usher's Detachments had 35 officers, 46 other ranks, 9 x 3 ton lorries, 4 x 15 cwt lorries and 2 x motor cycles. There was no recorded increment of 2-seater cars, but jeeps appeared later. The task was to establish immediate contact with the Civil Administration for Calvados, in accordance with Civil Affairs General Instruction No 3, 'You are not in command of, but will work closely with 201 Basic Detachment. You have been phased in, in advance of your detachment in order that you can make the earliest possible contacts and appreciate your problems'.

The scope and complexity of the tasks were extensive. These included Resistance Groups, Special Security Instructions, Black and White lists, Finance, Post and Communications, Legal, and Ancient Monuments. A French Mission Liaison Officer would be phased in as soon as possible and be instructed to report directly after landing in France.

Usher's officers' responsibilities were for security while the fighting was going on, aid to refugees, food control, commerce, transport and traffic, civil engineering, clearance of roads, public works, industry, agriculture, manpower, health (water supplies and hospitals), justice, finance and the fine arts. Each officer worked alongside his French opposite number.

All that the 40-strong party of 201 Detachment could do, in the meantime, was to start work, re-establishing normality in Colleville and surrounding villages, bringing in food and medical supplies, clearing rubble and assisting the fire services, police and public utilities. Usher himself made it his business to establish contact with as many French officials and dignitaries as possible and to establish lines of communication for each of the areas of responsibility. His thorough grasp of French, his long-standing empathy with the French people and his natural charm and consideration all contributed to the establishment of harmonious and fruitful working relationships.

The situation in Caen, however, was desperate for the French civilians trapped in the beleaguered city, as Poirier's account describes.

The morning of 11th June was quiet. Amongst the refugees in St. Etienne, while Mass was celebrated a baby was on its pot by the pulpit, bridge fanatics were playing on the fonts, and an enterprising fellow was shaving in the church warden's pew; there had been no water for four days yet he'd found some! The afternoon saw tank battles in the suburbs and more shells falling than ever before, and gun fire continued all night, supplemented by the German *nebelwerfer* sited near the *Lycée Malherbe*.

On the next morning shell fire intensified, falling on the *Rue Ecuyère*, the *Palais de Justice* and the *Place Saint-Sauveur*. A naval shell struck the spire of the *Saint-Pierre* bringing it down bodily on the roof of the nave. In the evening air-raids struck the *Rue Elie-de-Beaumont*, the *Rue Saint-Pierre* and the *Rue de Geôle*, where a firestorm was started by incendiaries. Huge naval shells fell on the trenches dug in the *Fosses-Saint-Julien*, and although many were saved by the rescue services, many others were buried under vast quantities of earth. In the evening the wind got up spreading the firestorm.

When the ruins were finally cleared workers found the body of a man buried in his cellar, who had written a note before his candle burnt out and he died of suffocation. This read 'I know I am dying; it is terrible to think that I shall never see that liberation I have been waiting for so long, but since I know that because of my death others will be free, long live France and the Allies'.

[On 12th June the first V1 flying bombs landed on London. These, together with V2 rockets launched in August, had a serious effect on morale, which had been boosted by the landings in Normandy, when the civilian population thought it signalled the end of the *Luftwaffe* bombings. It increased the worries of troops in the field, concerned for their families at home. Eisenhower considered that if the flying bombs and rockets had made their appearance six months earlier, and if Portsmouth and Southampton had been targets, '*Overlord*' might never have taken place.]

Poirier's account continues the tale of Caen's ordeal.

In Caen incendiaries fell on 13th and 14th, by night and day. The *Galeries Lafayette*, the *Hôtel de la Place Royale* and the *Café de l'Hôtel-de-Ville* were one vast furnace, and at night all that could be heard was crackling flames and crashing roofs and walls.

Despite all this, the youth of the town helped the Fire Brigade, with their little pump, to halt the flames halfway in the *Rue du Moulin*, saving some buildings there.

Feeding the remaining 20,000 people in the town was becoming impossible, and what water that could be extracted from the wells was polluted. The *Préfet* appealed for people to escape across country to Trun, 25 miles south, by way of Bourgébus and St. Sylvain, and take refuge in the neighbouring districts. The German authorities undertook to keep the route clear but only a few departed. Some 1,700 remained, fearing that they might be machine-gunned on route or molested by the S.S., and they opted to remain in the ruins and face the inevitable carnage which would occur when the Allied assault met the furious German resistance. They had to be fed. Milk, cheese and meat from slaughtered animals were brought in daily by courageous souls dodging German transport and tanks, bursts of shell fire, and machine-gunning from the air.

In Bayeux, things could not have been more different. On 14th June a cheering crowd welcomed General de Gaulle with the *Marseillaise*. Accompanying him were two representatives of the Provisional Government, François Coulet, wanted for treason by the Vichy Government, who had been appointed Provisional Commissioner for the Rouen region and Colonel de Chevigné, Military Commander. De Gaulle spoke of the magnificent work of the Resistance Groups, and of France now being liberated by the French, which led Usher to nudge the French leader and ask whether he might not include the Allies as playing some part in the rescue![2] However, this was a great moment, with the *de facto* recognition of the Provisional Government as having authority for Civil and Military administration in the region, and ultimately for all France.

Twelve miles from the western outskirts of Caen, which was being battered to bits, it was an oasis of calm, with the Germans only three miles to the south and Isigny and the surrounding

---

[2] In 1957, F.S.V. Donnison wrote: 'At one stage de Gaulle paid a visit to Caen. He wanted to make a floodlit speech. Usher was much afraid the Germans would see. But he managed somehow, and de Gaulle was floodlit. [Usher] thought de Gaulle's speech ungracious in its omission of reference to what the Allies had done with emphasis on the exhortations that France must win the war.'

coastal area 15 miles west. De Gaulle had passed through Isigny on the 14th where he found every roof tile off, no glass in the windows and the streets strewn with blackened corpses.

Miraculously the people of Bayeux had not suffered at all from the war, and the change of regime was not to bother them either. There were few Resistance fighters or collaborators amongst them. The worst that anyone could be accused of was supporting their families by selling butter and farm produce to the occupiers. The shops were stuffed with all kinds of merchandise. François Coulet, the brother of Marianne Daure, acting as *Préfet* of Calvados, even ordered himself a black jacket and striped trousers so that he should look the part for the substitution of *M.* Triboulet[3], who had cycled in from near Caen, for Rochat, the Vichy *sous-Préfet*, in the presence of Cacaud, *Préfet* of Calvados.

The transfer of power was very dignified. Rochat, for the nine days since the landing, had carried out his duties punctiliously. He had visited all the local villages which had suffered in the fighting and together with the *Maires* had taken what measures he could to bring in food and care for the injured, while keeping his superior informed of his actions so long as it had been possible. Furthermore, he had put all his services at the disposal of the first British to arrive to their great surprise and delight.

Repairing to a small office with de Gaulle, General Koenig and Coulet, Rochat answered all the questions put to him calmly, concisely and quietly.

At this stage not everyone was overjoyed at being liberated. When Coulet received a visit from the Vicar General of the Diocese, he respectfully requested an audience with the Bishop of Bayeux and Lisieux, Mgr. Picaud. Picaud was old and had bad breath, but according to the Resistance chief, Mercader, and the newly appointed Gaullist administrators, Picaud had never collaborated and was stiffly formal in his dealings with the Germans. Introducing himself courteously Coulet said he had been detailed to ask for a *Te Deum* to be sung in the Cathedral on the following Sunday, 18th June. This was to be the first of the celebrations on French soil to mark the fourth anniversary of de Gaulle's call to arms, which might otherwise pass unnoticed in this part of Normandy.

---

[3] Throughout the Vichy years Triboulet, though a Vichy official, had been a secret member of the resistance.

The first person approached had been the President of the local Liberation Committee, who had a photo of *Maréchal* Pétain on display. He did not like the idea at all. He did not know what the 18th June was all about, and no one in Bayeux knew better than he the consequences of a party for the local authorities in the *sous-prefecture* gardens. Careless talk after a glass or two of bubbly *cidre mousseux* would attract inevitable German reprisals. The senior gendarme in the liberated area, an old Lieutenant whose brother had been a member of the *Conseil Supérieur de Guerre* in 1940, also feared that such a demonstration would invite military intervention by the Germans. The gendarme spelled out the risks if the Germans returned in force to throw the allies back into the sea!

Coulet patiently explained the significance of this historic appeal, adding that it was doubtful if Rommel, with everything he had to worry about, would find the time to thwart a modest garden party. Eventually the President of the Liberation Committee climbed down.

At 4 pm on 16th June, Coulet was admitted to the dingy little bishop's palace facing the south transept of the cathedral, the home of Queen Mathilde's famous tapestry. The bishop proffered his hand but showed no surprise that there was no kiss for his ring, because he had made enquiries about Coulet, and knew he was a Protestant. He frowned. It did not bode well for the success of the mission.

Coulet opened the conversation by expressing how glad he was that both the bishop himself and Bayeux had not suffered too much from the war, and followed by explaining the intentions of the Provisional Government that had succeeded the Vichy regime's usurpation of the French state. He presented the bishop with a portrait of General de Gaulle, and assured his host that the new administration had no agenda other than the re-establishment of the rule of law and bringing peace to all Frenchmen. Lastly he came to the principal reason for the visit which was to request a *Te Deum* in two days time.

Monsignor Picaud listened with darkening brow, and no sign of approval. At last he spoke. At his urgent request, Maurice Schumann, whom he had been pleased to receive a few days earlier, had told him everything, and now the Commissioner of the Republic, who was clearly not up to date with what was going on, barges into the Episcopal privacy, in wet battledress covered in sand, to tell him that he was spokesman for France.

Together with his vehement profession of his Gaullist faith he found it astounding.

After acid and recondite comments on the futility of revolutions Mgr. Picaud continued in a discomfiting tone, '. . . in addition to which I know and understand who you are. You are a Protestant like your brother-in-law, Monsieur Daure, the one-time *recteur de l'Academie*, and I swear to you that I am, with full justification, astounded that General de Gaulle has chosen someone belonging to the Confession of Augsburg to administer a region so profoundly Catholic as Normandy'. Coulet mused 'It was lucky he did not know that a Protestant Gaullist *sous-Préfet* had just replaced a Protestant Vichy *sous-Préfet!*'

The bishop went on 'You are also, if I'm not mistaken, the son of *recteur* Coulet, the first French *recteur* of Strasbourg in 1918, who had re-established the lay school in Alsace-Lorraine?' Coulet pointed out that all his father had done was to restore the laws of the French Republic in the lately German occupied regions, which was what he was endeavouring to do here and now.

Returning to the matter of the *Te Deum* the bishop was clear in his own mind, gesturing towards the magnificent stained glass windows, that there was a risk that when the Germans heard about it they would bombard the Cathedral.

The bishop was now in a quandary, because it was difficult to refuse to conduct a service thanking God for ensuring that Bayeux was spared. After a long and reluctant expression of his views he eventually revealed that there would be a great solemn Mass on Sunday over which he would be presiding—but it would not be a *Te Deum* Mass.

'But won't they sing the *Te Deum*?'

'Yes', grumbled the bishop, and after thanking him fulsomely Coulet departed to make the arrangements that would ensure the *Te Deum* would be a success. In the event the cathedral was packed, and to the bishop's surprise, the *Wehrmacht* did not exact revenge.

There were, however, some pleasant surprises. The people who had remained at home for four years, and who had suffered and fought their own private war against the occupation forces, were content to accept the right of de Gaulle's administration to take over. This even included those who had supported *Maréchal* Pétain. There was no need to chase the worst collaborators and traitors, or to intervene in the settlement of old scores between collaborators and members of the resistance. The legitimacy of the Free French was not questioned by the Allies or the Algiers government or the Pétainists. Some young women who had fraternised with the enemy had their hair cut off but suffered no other consequences.

Many liberated French avoided politics. Whether under German or Allied control was of little importance. This indifference had to be replaced with pride in citizenship. Others were deliriously happy to be reunited with fellow countrymen whom they had only heard on clandestine wirelesses over the last four years.

Vichy officials like Rochat in Bayeux, and Cacaud, *Préfet* of Calvados, the latter steadfastly sticking to his post under fire, had to be investigated before they could be considered for possible reemployment.

In Caen all the hospitals were full to bursting point, rooms and corridors filled with patients, yet none of the wounded complained. One patient was particularly memorable. Old Professor Barbeau of the *Faculté des Lettres*, who had an arm amputated in the *Bon Sauveur*, greeted the coming victory by waving his stump, laughingly proclaiming that it would not stop him teaching English to his students. His house had been destroyed and with it the manuscript of a new English grammar he had been writing. He had been long retired, but had volunteered to teach again in 1939 to take the place of the Professor of the English Department, who had been called up. Tragically, after Caen was liberated, he was moved to Bayeux hospital with the more seriously wounded and died there.

On 15th June the theatre, the *Gendarmerie* and the Department of Agriculture in Caen were all on fire, the fires probably started by the Germans. Artillery fire was unremitting. The S.S. looted blatantly—alarm clocks, vacuum cleaners, carpets, household goods, motor tyres, wheels and batteries and of course alcohol, ignoring the notices put up by the *Wehrmacht* police, the *Feldgendarmerie*, warning that 'Looters will be Shot'; the S.S. of the *Adolf Hitler* and *Hermann Goering* Divisions were untouchable! The German Governor ordered those who had stubbornly holed up in *La Maladrerie* to await the arrival of the British, to move out and, threatened with revolvers and sub-machine guns, they sought refuge in the *Bon Sauveur* and the *Lycée Malherbe*. The situation there deteriorated daily.

Not only were there 9,000 people to feed from kitchens designed for 600, but the business of the Town Hall—births, marriages (the ceremonies drowned by shellfire), and deaths all carried on.

As the days went by artillery fire intensified, hitting the *Rue Paul Doumer*, the *Rue Equyere*, the *Place Malherbe*, the *Rue Vauquelin*, the *Boulevard Bertrand* and the *Place Fontette*. Fire raged in the *Place du Marché-au-Bois* and the *Hôtel de la Victoire* burned from end to end. Civil defence and the fire service did what they could, despite progressively fewer men and increasingly unserviceable equipment. There were corpses and wounded everywhere, who could not be retrieved while shells were bursting all around. The *Préfet* once more appealed to the population to evacuate towards the Orne, but his plea fell on deaf ears. Everyone felt that after 15 days awaiting relief, the worst had to be over and why risk finding themselves in the shifting lines of battle?

The political situation among the Allies was resolved. De Gaulle's administration was accepted by the people as the Provisional Government of France, but not initially by the Allies. De Gaulle had taken a chance establishing his administration on French soil, because London and Washington refused to grant recognition. Other than war correspondents, the international press, following the White House line, were hostile. De Gaulle could only count on the support of some 16 out of the 60 reporters present in Normandy.

A press conference, complete with champagne and biscuits, was called on 16th June in the *sub-préfecture* at Cherbourg. Without any preamble an American journalist asked the inevitable question,

> 'They say that you and those who accompany you have set yourselves up here without the authority of the Allied governments, is that true?'

The Commissioner replied that that was indeed true but General de Gaulle had informed Montgomery, the Commander of the 21st Army Group, that his job was to look after the interests of the civil population. Anyway, why did the reporter think that the Provisional Government of the French Republic should find it necessary to ask friendly but foreign governments and allies for authority to exercise their legal authority on French soil?

'But how about Marshal Pétain's government?' they asked. 'Are you going to hold elections?'

This was an absurd line of enquiry. How could they compare a puppet government in enemy hands, which had exported workers to make bombs, corn to feed the *Wehrmacht*, encouraged people to don German uniform to fight the Allies and sent Jews to the incinerators, with a Provisional Government committed to ridding France of its occupying invaders? Were they not all fighting for the same cause? Yes, there should certainly be elections, but first they needed to find the ballot boxes buried in the ruins of the *Mairies*!

On 19th June the position of the Provisional Government was settled, pragmatically. A group of Generals, including Brigadier Lewis, called at the Commissariat to say that the presence of the Commissioner would be acceptable pending the instructions of their governments. They agreed not to interfere with each others' affairs, and Coulet made his position clear:

> 'I have been given the task, of administering the liberated territories in Normandy in the name of the French people, by the Provisional Government of the Republic and I will only renounce that by their order'

The delegation was taken aback by his declaration, but Coulet gave credit to the British for their recognition that at least one question had been settled, and in the days and weeks that followed, the relationship between the British, with Usher at the centre of Civil Affairs activity, and the French was harmonious[4]. They dined together over *filets mignons* cut from slaughtered cattle, and tucked into thick cream and *camembert* such as they had not enjoyed since 1940. Thanks to the American Colonel Gunn, Liaison Officer with the 1st Army Group, and Scanlon, the correspondent of *Time*, American resentment gradually disappeared. Brigadier Thomas Robbins'[5] intelligence and efficiency, the diplomacy and tact of the Scottish Colonels Douglas, Pirrie and Usher, and the goodwill of all the others

---

[4]   It took about a week before Coulet was convinced of the Civil Affairs organisation's good intentions. Coulet was convinced that this process was aided by the personal qualities of Brigadier Robbins, Lieutenant-Colonel Pirrie and Colonel Charles Usher.

[5]   Previously head of the Civil Affairs Staff Centre at Wimbledon.

contributed to full understanding, leading to an active and fruitful collaboration.

This *entente* contributed to keeping de Gaulle, whom Churchill only a month previously had wished to be put in chains and sent back to Algeria, on track to become President of the IVth Republic.

Coulet's next task was to sort out the American insistence on imposing what amounted to an occupation currency on France, a perceived affront to French sovereignty. On 9th July General Koenig, Commander of the French military mission to S.H.A.E.F., arranged a meeting with Montgomery in his caravan in an orchard outside Bayeux. Montgomery's H.Q. was concealed in peaceful quiet countryside. The general had plenty to think about. The Mulberry harbours had suffered badly in the storms of the third week in June, and reinforcements were held up. The enemy were fighting stubbornly, despite being continually machine-gunned from the air, and, with their communications sabotaged by the Resistance, they had difficulty bringing men, machines and supplies to the battle front. But the Germans still prevented him from taking Caen, which remained the first objective.

The caravan door was open, revealing a cage of canaries, and, in his famous beret, his habitual rollneck pullover and corduroy trousers, Montgomery bounded down the steps, followed by two fox terriers, to greet General Koenig, a comrade in arms from the desert. Koenig introduced Coulet, attired in his black jacket and striped trousers, as *'Commissaire de la République'* but before he could say more Montgomery, since his last meeting with de Gaulle wary of politicians, barked:

'He is a politician, what? You and I are soldiers are we not?'

'Yes,' replied Koenig, 'we are both soldiers, you and me, and he is a politician!'[6]

'What's the story behind all these bank notes which we have brought you? They say the people don't want them?

---

[6] Twelve years later Coulet volunteered for Algeria, commanded a parachute unit and was Mentioned in Despatches three times. He was awarded the *Valeur Militaire* with star and the *Légion d'Honneur*.

They must accept them. They must be made to. It's good money, understand? Our money, good money!'

In his best English Coulet rebutted this attack and said that the Provisional Government rejected these 'fantasy' notes as totally illegal. The Norman peasants had instinctively refused to accept them in payment, and those who initially had done so found that they were rejected by the *caisses publiques*, who were ordered to refuse them. As far as he was concerned, he would not press those under his jurisdiction to submit to a regime from which they had been spared under the German occupation. The points of view were irreconcilable and Koenig, who was upset at the unexpected turn of events when he had thought they were just making a courtesy visit, joined in and laughingly imitating Montgomery in English, said:

'Ah! You don't know Coulet. He is a very hard man! Ah! He is a Protestant!'

At a stroke, Montgomery, the son of an Anglican bishop, whose orders of the day were like sermons and whose victory announcements like Thanksgivings, turned to Coulet with his most gracious smile and said,

'Oh! really. So you are a Protestant, eh? A Protestant indeed! Very interesting! How many Protestants are there in France? What part of France do you come from?'

There was no further discussion about bank notes, and it was sweetness and light all round. Montgomery assured Coulet, whom he now addressed as 'Mr High Commissioner', that he would help him in any way possible should he have any problems.

On their way back to base, as Koenig laughed uproariously, Coulet recalled his reception at the Cathedral, and thought that perhaps in time of war it might be an advantage to belong to the Reformed Religion!

Thanks to François Coulet and *Sous-Préfet* Triboulet the Allies now entrusted administrative problems to the French authorities. Usher and the team in Bayeux resolved the matter of the *'francs supplémentaires'*, took over food control and got in contact with local administrations, including some still occupied by the enemy. The M.M.L.A. asserted itself and Major Hettier de Boislambert made everyone aware that it was fully operational.

Brigadier Lewis at the head of Civil Affairs, who had objected to the presence of the Provisional Government of the French Republic (*Gouvernement Provisoire de la République Française*, or G.P.R.F.), declared at the end of June that he would tolerate them and then in July actually praised Coulet for their good work. H.Q. S.H.A.E.F. acknowledged that the *de facto* recognition of the G.P.R.F. had gone extremely well, and on the 25th of August the U.K. and the G.P.R.F. signed an agreement recognising the latter's right to govern the French administration.

The battle, which had seemed to be getting further away from Caen now got closer, and there were tank battles in the western suburbs. The refugees who packed the nave of *St. Etienne* had no means of knowing what had become of their relations who had fled the city. The hospital operating theatre and the *Lycée* were hit in the intense artillery bombardments of 24th and 25th June. The *Maire* at last got Red Cross ambulances to take the old and infirm to the racecourse at Fleury, but this was later carpeted by German artillery fire. Those who remained sheltered, still in the clothes they were wearing at the beginning of the battle, under the ruins, in cellars and in holes in the ground. Flour supplies were all but exhausted and rich and poor survived mainly on beans, with the inevitable consequences.

By the end of June, Caen was a charnel house, but the Germans were determined that it should not fall to the Allies. An elegant S.S. propaganda officer appeared with assurances that the Allies would be thrown back into the sea, and the suffering of the people of Caen would be at an end. The might of the German Army was being built up daily by reinforcements, and the counter-offensive would lead to a glorious victory, liberating Fortress Europe. This was upsetting rather than calming; there was no trustworthy news about the military situation. Every morning came German news bulletins and proscribed B.B.C. reports. According to Radio Paris the Allies had been defeated and the bridgehead in Normandy was shrinking daily. News filtering in from the battlefront suggested a different scenario. Cherbourg had been taken, together with the whole of the north end of the Cotentin peninsula, and there was fighting at La Haye-du-Puits and in the outskirts of Saint-Lô. The Allied landings continued, but, bottled up in Caen, all were in a state of constant fear and uncertainty.

The Allies, who had not managed to break through the German defences, now sought to force the issue at Caen in an assault preceded by further bombing. After a quiet day on 7th July more than 1,000 Lancaster and Halifax bombers flew over in close formation, obscuring the sky, and submitted the town to the worst raid since 7th June. The raid lasted 45 minutes. The combination of bombs and anti-aircraft fire was deafening. Suddenly it stopped, followed by deathly silence. The whole town was shrouded in yellow dust, and fumes made it difficult to breathe. Corpses littered the ground and hundreds of dead and alive were buried under the ruins. Patients on the 4th floor of *Bon Sauveur* hospital panicked and begged to be taken down to the cellar, though this was impossible because it was already packed with wounded. The corridors and rooms up to the top floor were crammed full. One badly wounded patient was so desperate that he got out of bed, but could only take three steps before he dropped dead. The *Faculté* and the library were in flames. The noise of walls collapsing, the roar of the fires and the explosions of bottles bursting in the chemical institute could be heard for miles. The walls of 7 *Rue Leverrier*, a hundred yards away, were glowing red in the heat, but mercifully the house was not on fire. The *Eglise Saint-Julien* was razed to the ground. The Rector of the University was gravely wounded. Canon Ruel, *curé* of Saint-Pierre, and his vicar Abbé Poirier, *M.* Jager, sector Civil Defence Chief, together with his wife and assistant, *M.* Jaouen, with his wife and children, were among the 54 dead at 50 *Rue du Vaugueux*.

Early on that same day, unknown to Poirier, Usher, the Senior Civil Affairs Officer of 208 and 209 Detachments, together with *Capitaine* Ollivier (French Liaison Officer), Lieutenants F.P. Thomas and O.M. Street (U.S.) prepared to enter Caen, and Major Hellmuth, O.C. 201 Detachment, received warning orders to move with specialist officers for Civil Defence and Fire, Supplies, Relief, Public Health, Labour and Engineering.

There was nothing with which to put out the fires. The list of buildings destroyed and casualties was ever-lengthening, and Caen was a living hell. Early on the 8th July, however, after a short raid, it became clear that the Germans were leaving. Armour and hundreds of exhausted men, with clothing in tatters, crossed the town to ford the Orne at low tide, as only one of the three bridges had survived. The railway bridge high across the river was the only bridge remaining, and the Germans filled the space between the rails with faggots so that the tanks could use it to escape. The *Grand Cour* Footbridge, which had remained intact up to that moment, had been destroyed. The *Kampf-Kommandant* fled and early on 9th July the rearguard of lorries, cars, tanks and ambulances left under a hail of fire.

That morning a British Bren gun carrier was spotted in the *Place Saint Martin*, and around mid-day some motor cyclists arrived on reconnaissance. However, three German tanks were still in position at *Place de l'Ancienne-Boucherie*, machine-gunning the neighbouring streets. The people wondered if this was the liberation, or would there be a counter-attack? The Germans had abandoned their fortifications at the crossroads, so everyone hoped that there would not be any street fighting.

At 1.30 pm on 9th July, Major Hellmuth arrived in Caen in an armoured car, together with a security officer from 2nd Army. The road was blocked and the journey was completed on foot. Major Hellmuth, looking for the *Mairie*, was directed to the *Lycée Malherbe* by a Civil Defence worker, as the *Mairie* had been gutted and the *Préfecture* was under fire. He proceeded to the *Maire*'s parlour where he made himself known to Poirier and met the *Préfet*, *M*. Cacaud, and asked where he could find a good hotel and a hot bath. He was enlightened. Not a single hotel was left standing, three-quarters of the town was destroyed, the town's *Mairie*, university and churches were in ruins. Helmuth then explained his task to the *Maire* and told the *Préfet* that Colonel Usher would arrive later and call on him. Poirier had arranged a meeting with his *Chefs des Services*, but Hellmuth asked that a meeting be deferred until 8 pm that evening at which time plans would be laid for the next day.

What follows is drawn from André Heintz's recollection of events. The first French Canadians were advancing cautiously from the north-west, behind a tank which fired at anything that moved. Unfortunately it killed two men who had appeared at their doors to welcome them, close by the *Place de l'Ancienne Boucherie*. It also fired at two men from the Resistance carrying Sten guns but wearing Cross of Lorraine armbands who were coming to guide them. Fortunately they got out of the way in time.

Some while before a consignment of Sten guns had been parachuted in, but were now buried under the rubble. Only twelve were salvaged and accordingly six groups of 2 F.F.I., each armed with a Sten, were despatched to different parts of the city to act as snipers and mop up as best they could. Unarmed volunteers were sent to parts of the city where they could expect the Allies to appear. André was sent to the north. Suddenly a British patrol appeared; the leading man raised his rifle and took aim. Heintz was not displaying his identity so he put his arms up and shouted in English. They waved him towards the Intelligence Officer, who was on foot as the road was impassable to vehicles. He thanked André for coming, produced his map and asked where he was on it. It was hard to make him believe they were in the small lane he indicated on the map, as the whole area was so pitted with bomb craters and devoid of grass that it looked like a lunar landscape. The officer asked if there were still Germans around. André had seen some on his way there, which was why he had concealed his identity by stuffing his arm band and Cross of Lorraine in his pocket. 'Yes there were', he said, so the officer said 'You walk ahead and let us know if you see one!'

They did see one but he was dead. After half an hour they reached the castle, which, André told them, still held some Germans. The patrol said that this was where their mission, to open the way for some Civil Affairs Officers, stopped. It would help if he returned in half an hour to meet them, and show them the way to the *Hotel de Ville* (which had been destroyed) and introduce them to the local authorities (there was only *M.* Poirier left). They added 'You will recognise them easily, the Colonel wears a kilt'. When he returned as instructed there was no sign of a kilt but he found two 'strong, tall officers, Majors Hellmuth and Massey'.

> 'Where is the Colonel?' asked André.
> 'Oh, he speaks French so he went ahead'.
> 'But which way?'
> 'Down that road.'
> 'Which road?'

It was not a road, but the castle moat, and extremely unsafe on account of the German presence. There was no way out. It ended in a maze of brambles (which must have been rather prickly for the kilted Usher) behind the ruins of the houses in the next street. They rushed forward and shouted to Usher to get out. Then they went to the Old Abbey, which was called the '*Lycée*' because the *Abbaye aux Hommes*, founded by William the

Conqueror, had been taken away from the monks after the Revolution.

Usher asked the way to the *Hôtel d'Angleterre* to be told that it did not exist anymore, except for an archway bearing the Royal Arms with the motto '*Honi soit qui mal y pense*'. It was in a part of the city not yet liberated. Usher needed to set up his H.Q., and the party went off towards some buildings which had been used by the enemy and had not been targeted by them. As they went into the grounds of the first one they saw a pair of jackboots disappearing over the garden wall. At the next block, 1 *Rue de Hastings*, they found some young and frightened S.S. men in the basement garage, who seemed happy to be made prisoners-of-war. Birmingham policeman Major L.J. Massey went up to the fourth floor to check suitability. It had a grand view of the German positions at Fleury, but Massey told André that he thought it was too conspicuous. André was unsure what 'conspicuous' meant. While inspecting a bathroom a shell passed through the adjoining room; turning to André he said 'Now you know the meaning of conspicuous!'

No. 5 *Rue de Hastings*, the former *Luftwaffe* Headquarters, became the Detachment's offices[7] and 3 *Rue de l'Academie*, 100 yards away, was selected for the officers' billets. The back door opened on to the *Rue Bicoquet* and provided a short-cut to the offices.

The meeting Major Hellmuth had asked to be delayed until that evening took place. To it came Pierre Daure, accompanied by *Capitaine* Gille, *President du Comité du Liberation* and Resistance head, together with some of his F.F.I. men, *La Compagnie Scamaroni*. In muddy boots and dressed as a farmer, Daure announced that he was *Préfet* of Calvados. That was odd, thought Usher, as he had just met *M.* Cacaud, who had been introduced as *Préfet*, while he himself was *Préfet* until administration could be handed over to the French, hence there were now three *Préfets* in the room! He told Daure that he would send him to *M.* Coulet at Bayeux, and if the latter confirmed he was the right man then he would be appointed *Préfet*.

---

[7] Civil Affairs policy was not to use buildings previously used as German Headquarters as Civil Affairs Headquarters. 5 *Rue de Hastings*, a former *Luftwaffe* H.Q., was only accepted by 208 Detachment because the damage in the city meant there were no alternative options.

'Easy' said Daure. 'Madame Coulet is my mother-in-law'! He was sent by armoured car to meet his brother-in-law, François Coulet, in Bayeux. The next day Coulet brought Daure to Caen to install him. A small ceremonial parade was arranged for the event. Just before they arrived a shell dropped on the party knocking a number of them out but after the place was tidied up the parade took place without a hitch.

At Usher's meeting with his own staff it was decided that work would start sharp at 9.00 am the following morning, 10th July. Those attending included Wing Commander Wolser, Lieutenant-Colonel Hiles, Major Helmuth and Lieutenant Street. The officer in charge of security, seconded from the Metropolitan Police, would round up everyone on his list of residents suspected of collaborating with the enemy and bring them in for interrogation.

There would be daily meetings at 5 *Rue de Hastings*, with the object of taking charge of the town's Municipal Executive—the *Chefs des Services*—and getting them working immediately to deal with the chaos and carnage in the areas of the town free of German occupation. Plans would be drawn up for the German-held areas, to be put in action when they became accessible. As soon as possible, positions would be reversed; the French would take charge and Civil Affairs would revert to a supporting role.

On 10th July *Commandant* René Bertrand arrived and found that his job had well and truly begun. It was the longest day of his life! The town had been partially relieved, and the head of the M.M.L.A., the usually disgracefully disheveled (it was probably a pose) Hettier de Boislambert, briefed him on his new mission as *attaché* and counselor to the new *Préfet* of Calvados, who had just emerged from hiding. The noise everywhere was deafening. All was thick smoke and in every direction the horizon was a curtain of fire. There were very few people about and dead bodies lay every few yards, scattered like so many discarded puppets.

At the central prison the job was to find the bodies of patriots who had been killed the night before by the S.S., but all that could be seen was blood and brains *à hauteur d'enfants*, (as high as a child). Fortunately, the need to get out of the fallen concrete took the searchers' minds off the gruesome scene.

Despite continuous bombardment by German artillery and unremitting rifle fire, the civil population streamed out of their cellars. They were filthy and haggard but very happy, as the first people they saw were French Canadians and Usher. Everyone threw their arms around each other, while lots of little flags appeared from the burned out and ruined buildings, where it was estimated there were 6,000-8,000 dead. The Allies were amazed at their warm welcome having feared quite otherwise in the circumstances.

Now it was across the town to the *Bon Sauveur* in the north; the rest of the place, ruined and empty save for the dead, remained under enemy control. De Boislambert handed out cigarettes, and Crosses of Lorraine for Resistance fighters. A Canadian soldier fired off magazine after magazine at an invisible enemy and Bertrand asked him if he would 'make his music' further away! There were two more scheduled appointments, a medical conference at the *Bon Sauveur* and the installation of Pierre Daure.

The installation took place at the *Préfecture* during a furious bombardment. Boislambert, François Coulet, some officials, a party of Canadian soldiers and a group of partisans entered the seriously damaged *Préfecture* building on the border of No Man's Land. This was no mean achievement, as all the neighbouring buildings were on fire and collapsing. They found the *concièrges*, disabled *poilus* of the 1914/18 war, valiantly sticking to their posts, together with the Vichy *Préfet* Cacaud working in his office. Cacaud stood up when the party burst in. He was brave, very wan, stood very erect, and carried himself well, with much courage. Coulet deposed him in the name of the Republic and appointed Daure in his stead as the first *Préfet* of the liberation. Daure had arrived in cycling trousers and leggings moments before, and changed these behind the sofa in order to appear more formal! Cacaud said simply '*Je céderai donc à la force*'. In other words he had no option but to surrender in the circumstances. Whatever one might think, he was a true *Préfet*, and courageous. Doubtless happy not be shot on the spot, he was taken away and imprisoned.

Bertrand was appointed as *attaché* to the new *Préfet* in respect of his relations with the Allies. Major Chodron de Courcel, a Colonial academic, very aristocratic and very '*Quai d'Orsay*', gave him instructions from de Gaulle himself. These were to remember without fail that he was representing France, not a beaten country!

Foodstuffs, and quicklime for the corpses started arriving from Bayeux. Preparations were readied to receive all other essentials the next day. The Tricolour was hoisted over the *Lycée Malherbe*, *Capitaine* Gille spoke out for de Gaulle, tired British troops and F.F.I. presented arms, and all broke into the *Marseillaise* and cried '*Vive la France*'.

Work resumed at the *Préfecture*. It was just ten metres behind the last Canadian outpost in a previously German-occupied dugout, with the enemy close by, still in control of half the town. Bombing, shelling and mortar fire continued day and night. Bertrand organised an 8-man protection squad of soldiers, and guerrillas in civilian clothes sporting bandoliers, pockets stuffed with grenades, like Mexican desperadoes. The oldest one, ageless, tough and leathery, had served with the International Brigade in Madrid. Their job was to guard the *Préfet* against a nocturnal raid, because German patrols came and went each night through the Allied lines. The capture of the first *Préfet* in the bridgehead of liberated France would be a great coup. Daure worked on, oblivious to the battle and the mayhem going on all around. There was plenty to be going along with; 30,000 to 60,000 civilians to be evacuated from the *Bon Sauveur*, *Malherbe* and *St. Etienne*.

Usher, referred to fondly by Bertrand as '*le vieil*' (he was only 53!), burst in to take the '*diable du petit préfet*', as Bertrand called him, under his personal wing, make a quick getaway and shelter him half-a-mile to the rear at 5 *Rue de Hastings*.

At that precise moment a round of 155 G.P.F.[8] crashed into the middle of the *Préfecture* and exploded in the *Grand Salon*, filling the place with sulphurous fumes and killing a few people. Daure refused to go—he was plagued by the communist element in the Resistance and there were Pétainists to be rooted out—so Usher forcibly made himself clear; a surprise attack to take prisoners could be carried out that night. Finally the two friends agreed and went off together. From then on Usher took him back every evening.

On a reconnaissance that evening a shell exploded in front of Usher, leaving a large crater, but Usher, though blown to the ground and shaken, was unhurt. As the dust and smoke cleared a Canadian nearby was shot by a sniper. The shell-hole quickly filled with seawater, showing that the city's water supply had been contaminated when the locks on the *Canal de l'Orne*[9] were

---

[8] French field gun appropriated by the Germans.

[9] Actually the *Canal Maritime de Caen à la Mer*.

breached. Until repairs could be effected these craters would provide a useful public health aid as a temporary home for sewage.

The first meeting was held at the *Lycée Malherbe* at 9.00 pm that day (10th July). Present were *M.* Poirier, his *Maire Adjoint,* members of the French Committees, *Commandant* Zimmern, Usher, Major Hellmuth, *Capitaine* Ollivier, and members of Detachment 201. Extracts from the Minutes are below.

The most pressing needs were refugees, supplies, the fire service, hygiene, public works and security, both national and local. A central working committee was set up, composed of Civil Affairs members for Caen and Bayeux and their French opposite numbers. Refugees would be the responsibility of Captains Wilson and Gwin, the *Abbé* Noe and *Mme.* de Rothschild in Bayeux and *Messieurs* Hubert, Boysset and Tardif in Caen. Food supplies and rationing would be handled by Major Kaplan and Lieutenant Thomas with *M.* Raffy and the Liaison Officer, *Capitaine* Ollivier, in Bayeux and *Messieurs* Callet, Beriau and Dupuis in Caen. Major Massey together with *M.* Caudelier would be in charge of the Fire Service. Hygiene would be attended to by Captains Elliott and Patchett, by Major Zimmern in Bayeux and *M.* Sprit and Drs Digeon and Chauvenet in Caen. Captain van Brocklin assisted by *M.* Bournodon in Bayeux and *Messieurs* Jouverneaux and Lapouza were confirmed in charge of Public Works. National Security was in the hands of *M.* Leconte while Major Massey was responsible for police together with Lieutenant Genolarnomo, Chief of Police.

These Committees met at 6.00 pm daily at 5 *Rue de Hastings,* to report progress and plan for the following day. Functional Committees worked from then on under their own steam.

The major problem was refugees. Starting the next morning, 11th July, *Mme.* de Rothschild, with Captains Wilson and Gwin, would conduct a census, and evacuation of refugees had to start immediately, within the limitations of the military situation and the availability of transport, which was found by Civil Affairs. Field Security was to draw up a list of people to be evacuated, and together with the military, work out how they would be controlled, and the route they would take. All these arrangements were agreed with Civil Affairs. *M.* Aulong had already set up a Central Refugee Bureau in the *Lycée Malherbe* and a loudspeaker was at this moment touring the town.

'Hello! Hello! People of Caen! This is the Voice of the Allies! Here are some official notices for your information! Some foodstuffs for provisioning the town have now arrived and steps have been taken to ensure continuity of supplies. It is strictly forbidden to enter or leave the town while it remains an operational zone. When it becomes possible, plans will be put in hand to allow controlled movement out of the town. Experts are working on the water supply. For the time being please economise as much as possible. You are advised to boil or disinfect it when you can. The authorities subject to the *Commissaire Regional* and the *Préfet* of Calvados are working in complete accord with the military authorities to ensure the safety of the town.'

Dr. Cayla was confident on the medical front. There were 600 civilian wounded in the *Bon Sauveur* together with twelve British and six German soldiers. The Germans were to be transferred by the Provost Unit to a Military Hospital. There were 250 empty beds, partly due to the evacuation of some 150 people collected by transport from Bayeux. The evacuation of the wounded was completed by 11th July.

1,000 litres of petrol was needed immediately to run the electricity generating plant and 2,000 litres per month after that.

A list of medical requirements was prepared.

Brigadier Lewis, the Senior Civil Affairs Officer for 2nd Army, sent a present of cigarettes and confectionery for the French civilians, which was much appreciated.

Hygiene was the next topic, and just as they were getting going a lorry arrived with 1,600 lbs of soap, 150 lbs of louse powder, 60 gallons of creosote and 6 cwts of chloride of lime. Water was the big problem; water points had been found for military purposes but none was available for flushing lavatories. The civilian authorities were negotiating for an electrical pumping installation thought to be available at

Cherbourg, while a motor-driven Stella pump was requested from I Corps.

There were some 600 corpses buried under the ruins of the town. There was difficulty in obtaining labour to clear the debris because of the danger from unexploded bombs, unstable buildings, enemy shelling and questions of payment. A list of unexploded bombs had already been given to the police and The Royal Engineers would assist if need be. The modern sewage system functioned under air pressure, and Captain Patchett was trying to obtain a compressor.

28,000 rations were handed over to the civil authorities to feed the population of around 25,000. Fresh milk was restricted, but a delivery of further emergency supplies of tinned milk had been received. Civilian supplies of butter and cheese arrived from Bayeux and more, together with fresh vegetables, were expected the next day.

Usher turned to policing. Additional auxiliary police were provided by the Civil Authorities to check population movements. The *Mairies* of surrounding communes were to prevent movement towards Caen for the time being. There were no political prisoners, and consideration of the prison situation was deferred to the next day.

The lack of water, continued bombing and lack of personnel was an unsatisfactory state of affairs, but complete detachments of the Auxiliary Fire Service reported that day, sited near vulnerable parts of the town. Civil Defence was being overhauled.

The second Civil Affairs meeting took place at 6 pm the following evening, 11th July. Present were Usher, Brigadiers Robbins and Lewis, Colonel Lang, Lieutenant-Colonel Hiles, Major Helmuth, Major Kaplan (Supply), Major Massey (Police), Major Biddle (Finance), Major Fawcett (Post and Telegraph), Major Robertson (D.A.A.Q.M.G., L. of C. Sub-Area), Major Marwin, (Liaison Officer 21 Army Group), members of the Refugee Committee: Captain Wilson, (C.A.O. of the Refugee Committee), Captain Elliott, (C.A.O. Public Health), Captain Hickman, (C.A.O. Police), Captain Patchett, (C.A.O. Public Works), Captain van Brocklin, (C.A.O. Labour), Captain de Pury, (Liaison Officer C.A. 21 Army Group), *Commandant* Zimmern, (French Liaison Officer, Refugee Committee), *Commandant* Bertrand, (French C.A. Liaison Officer attached to

M. le Préfét), *Capitaine* Ollivier, (French C.A. Liaison Officer attached to C.A. Detachment 208), *M.* Poirier, (*Maire de Caen*), *M.* Tardif, (*Adjoint au Maire*), Mmes de Rothschild and Leon, (Refugee Committee), *M.* Hubert, (President of Refugee Committee), *M.* Bouisset, (Refugee Committee), Dr. Digeon and Dr. D'Anjou, (Public Health Committee), *M.* Callet, (Food Supply Committee), *M.* Bouton, (*Commissaire de Police*), *M.* Lapouza, (Public Works and Labour Committee), *M.* Jouverneaux, (*Ingenieur en Chef des ponts et chaussées*), *M.* Sprit, (Fire Committee), Second-Lieutenant Laurens, (*Gendarmerie*) and Second-Lieutenant Lucien, (French C.A. Officer attached 201 C.A. Detachment). Extracts from the Minutes are below.

The local paper, *Liberté de Normandie* should appear daily, be approved by the *Préfecture* and censored by the Intelligence Officer. The Editor would devote space to refugee information.

For the ceremony on 14th July, it was not possible under existing circumstances to accept the kind offer of a military band. A simple ceremony which would not entail a large gathering of people should be arranged, in conjunction with *M. le Préfet.*

250 refugees were to be sent to Bayeux, under the auspices of the Regional Refugee Committee, using civilian transport. 4-500 would be taken to St. Croix the next day, 12th July, for dispersal in the vicinity of Bayeux. Unfortunately, the census had not been possible due to a lack of stationery, which Brigadier Robbins promised to expedite. Security would be tightened up in the large refugee centres in the town.

Sixty more hospital patients were evacuated to Bayeux, while the British and German soldiers were transferred to Military Hospitals. Captain Patchett confirmed that there was an unlimited supply of water, if it could be reached, and water pumps would arrive the next day, but the main electricity plant was still controlled by the Germans and there was no immediate solution in prospect. As of the next day enough military labour would become available to clear a considerable portion of the town, and the unexploded bomb squad would start work.

Considerable quantities of fresh vegetables were coming in from local sources, and 13 trucks were allocated for distribution on a milk round basis.

There was still some small-scale movement of refugees, but there were now more Military Police, who were establishing 22 Control Points, with a local policeman attached to each. There would be a curfew for all civilians and military from 11 pm to 5 am, which could be further reduced as circumstances allowed.

Civil Defence and the Fire Services still could not cope, but some help would come from Army Fire Service canvas tanks, sourced from Corps.

Labour policy and wages remained unresolved, to be settled the next day.

The Telephone Exchange was almost intact, but when it was functioning again it would be limited to official traffic only. There must be an improvement in arrangements for sending letters and parcels to French P.O.W.s in Germany.

On 12th July *Mme.* Gagliardi, *M.* Daure's secretary, was hit in the arm, but bravely carried on regardless. At 6 pm the third and last meeting was held at Civil Affairs H.Q..

Present this time were Usher, Lieutenant-Colonel Hiles, Lieutenant-Colonel Ryder, (C.A. SO1), Major Shelley, (O.C. 219 Civil Affairs Detachment), Majors Fawcett, Evill, (C.A.O. Legal), Massey and Kaplan, Captains Wilson, Patchett, van Brocklin and Elliott, *Commandants* Zimmern and Bertrand, *Capitaine* Ollivier, *Capitaine* (*Mme.*) Leon, *Messieurs* Poirier, Tardif, Hubert, Jouverneaux and Prody, (Mines), Butillent, (Managing Engineer Bridges and Roads), Lapouza, Delacour, (Water, Gas and Electricity), Guenay, (Water and Sanitation), Marritt, (Fire Services), Caudelier and Sprit, Dr. Digeon, *M.* Callet, (Director of Food Control), *M.* Raffy, Second-Lieutenant Laurens and Second-Lieutenant Lucien. Extracts from the Minutes are below.

There were second thoughts about the ceremony on 14th July. A British Officer and the *Préfet* would lay a wreath together at the *Lycée*.

402 refugees were evacuated during the day and more medical equipment was delivered to fulfill immediate needs

The prospects for hygiene and sanitation were looking up, although the main water point was still under shell fire. With Royal Engineers assistance, two 3,000 gallons-per-hour filter pumps would be installed the next day, so the North East part of the town should have running water and proper sewage facilities. The hospital and transport authorities now had 11,000 litres of petrol and 8,000 litres of diesel in stock. Three tons of biscuits were delivered in lieu of flour, together with locally sourced potatoes. Getting hold of the large stocks of wheat in enemy hands on the other side of the river was anticipated. In general there was now some two weeks supply of food.

Arrangements were in hand, while the power station was still held by the enemy, to provide the town's administrative offices with paraffin lamps.

The 22 police Control Points were now in place and essential Civil Defence and Fire Equipment had arrived. The labour census was at last in progress, so the Labour Exchange could be opened shortly.

A temporary Post Office was in operation and Field Security would not stand in the way of delivering letters. Arrangements were in hand to clear the Telephone Exchange of possible mines and booby traps.

Biscuits, powdered milk, dried vegetables, canned food, butter, margarine, lard, flour, clothing, and vitaminised chocolate for pregnant mothers had to be distributed urgently.

The minutes of these meetings show just how much was achieved in only three days, a remarkable tribute to the drive, organisation, improvisation and diplomacy displayed by Usher. To get so many resources and agencies, British, American and French, working together with common purpose and achieving so much in so short a time was due largely to Usher. So successful had been the rebuilding of a civil administration and re-establishment of community services that Usher decided that the time had come for the French Authorities to take over complete control. He announced that in future the conference would be held in the *Préfecture* chaired by the *Préfet, M.* Daure.

To celebrate Bastille Day on 14th July, Daure, the Civil Affairs Officers, *Commandant* Bertrand and Poirier raised the Tricolour and lunched off corned beef, potatoes and preserves, in the superb, but windowless, dining room of the *Préfecture*, serenaded by the whistling of an immense barrage of 105 mm guns. Ignoring the maelstrom outside, Daure, imperturbable as ever, gave a speech that was completely inaudible. Just to please Bertrand and Poirier, Daure followed them down to the kitchen in the cellars, where they felt more secure, to continue their meal with added guests, the *concièrges*.

Two wreaths were placed by the Minister of the Interior and Colonel Montgomery on the flagpole at the *Lycée Malherbe*, in the presence of the Resistance Movement and a party of British troops. It had been an interesting day, with heavy shelling and mortaring the previous evening, increasing during the day, along with further bombing. A fire gutted a block of the *Bon Sauveur* hospital occupied by nurses and children. Shelling and mortaring intensified during a visit by Lieutenant-General Grasset and Brigadiers Robbins and Lewis.

While visiting the *Bon Sauveur* hospital, where the wounded were being devotedly nursed by the Mother Superior, Usher noticed some black sheets, and he was about to say something when there was a puff of wind and they turned grey. They had been covered in flies!

Before D-Day Caen was better off for food than places further inland, but now it was a different picture. There were three reasons for the shortage of provisions.

1. German troops moved into the town in force and the S.S. took control. In addition to an orgy of rape and shooting they looted householders' supplies.

2. The bombing raids destroyed many fine buildings including the *Hôtel Moderne* and the *Hôtel de Ville* and the stocks held in them.

3. The S.S. set fire to many properties which had survived the bombing, resulting in the loss of foodstuffs held in them. No meat was available, even on the now flourishing black market, and the food supply became still more critical. The bread ration was reduced from 275 gms to 100 gms. There was no soap at all.

Thousands of refugees, and D.P.s (Displaced Persons, like the forced labour used to construct Rommel's coastal defences), had to be removed before basic municipal services could be restored. Camps were set up at Amblie, Cresserons, Ducy and Bussy. As there were around 20,000 D.P.s some had to be sent to the

American Zone. Others had to fend for themselves. All streets and roads were filled with rubble, intermixed with corpses and body parts. Bulldozers drove a road through to permit the passage of military traffic. Labour had to be found to locate the bodies and give them a decent burial, for which gloves, boots and waterproof clothing were required. Prisoners-of-war were used, but German boots were not up to the job. Getting supplies in was difficult because of the terrain, and petrol shortage. Matters were made worse when it rained; blocked or smashed sewer pipes led to flooding and deep stinking mud. Replacement pipes had to be brought in and laid. Uncollected excrement left on the streets was a threat to public health, so empty biscuit tins were joined together with wire rope, filled and hauled out in an improvised wire basket. The assistance of the head of Caen's Civil Engineering department, *M.* Jouverneaux, was invaluable and a fine example of harmonious relations between Civil Affairs and the French authorities.

All water mains had been destroyed, and with no means of repairing them, Army bowsers were brought in. Standpipes were set up to give access to drinking water. Without gas or electricity everyone had to get by with candles, acetylene and paraffin lamps. This had the benefit of helping with the enforcement of black-out regulations. Electricity generators were found for refrigerating the milk and cheese depots. All jobs took longer to organise and carry out without a telephone service. Although a quarter of the houses in the city were still standing, most were roofless and there was no glass in the windows. Cardboard was needed for the windows, together with corrugated iron, tarpaulin and tar paper to make the premises temporarily watertight. The houses were devoid of any furniture or bedding.

No. 1 Civil Affairs Base Port Depot, next to the airfield at Sommervieu, held the foodstuffs, medicines, soap, clothes and blankets destined for the relief of Caen and brought in while the battle was in full swing. Unfortunately, there was maladministration, misappropriation and theft. Unable to recruit trustworthy manpower, the only satisfactory solution was to employ German P.O.W.s once again. Having his Civil Affairs efforts wrecked through ineptitude was intolerable, and Usher voiced his frustration and anger.

There had been widespread looting by the S.S., but there were also instances of Allied soldiers looting. Some contracted venereal disease. The security sections tracked down the source, the '*Trou Normand*', reserved for officers during the German Occupation. As a solution, the French police wanted to open a *maison de tolerance*, a brothel under their supervision, but Civil Affairs would not consider it.

Morale was a problem. The Fire Brigade needed resurrecting, and Usher decided that plant, consisting of two 15 cwt trucks and pumps from the Arromanches pontoons, be brought in and for the Army Fire Service to train local volunteers, but it was extremely difficult to find these, most people being too traumatised by events to show much enthusiasm.

A Second Army report credits Usher for the prevention of panic among the inhabitants:

> 'Much credit must be given to Colonel Usher who was in C.A. charge in the town, and was here, there and everywhere in his kilt'.

Pierre Daure, Usher's new-found friend, drove everywhere in a large car with an enormous tricolour, and it was difficult to dissuade him from doing this in parts of the town where he could be seen by the Germans who, from time to time, opened fire.

Poirier met Usher regularly describing him as 'a Highlander wearing the traditional kilt, with unequalled charm, courtesy, sensibility and affability, who did everything possible to make him (Poirier) comfortable.' At their first meeting in his office, seated to his right, he found an enormous cigar which Usher said was just like Churchill's! Usher ferried him back and forth by jeep, which Poirier thought practical but uncomfortable.

Usher was cheerful, smiling and indefatigable, sleeping scarcely three or four hours each night. Up at dawn, he would take a long walk, kilt flying, pipe in mouth. He practised what he preached and exhibited complete contempt for danger. He was most complimentary about the cheerful Texan colonel who was his deputy, and all the officers, British and American, who looked after food control, refugees, clearance, public works, hygiene, civil defence, fire service, policy, and did everything in their power to overcome problems.

Poirier observed that the Germans wished to delay the coming offensive, and the bombardment and casualties increased daily. By preventing a breakout at Caen, Rommel felt that he could compel Eisenhower to postpone a second landing. The men and weaponry in Rommel's five lines of defence from Bourgebus to Troarn, only six miles distant, were formidable; 98

'88s' and 12 heavy flak guns in dual anti-aircraft/anti-tank role, 194 field guns and 207 *Nebelwerfer*, 36 Tiger tanks, a medium tank battery of the 1st S.S. *Panzer* Division, and well-positioned *Wehrmacht* infantry with anti-tank guns, backed up by the six infantry battalions of the 1st S.S. *Panzer* Division, with 125 tanks.

The ruins of the railway and power stations in the *Faubourg Vaucelles* were controlled by the S.S. Everyone lived in fear of a German counter-attack; both banks of the Orne were machine-gunned, and grenades thrown at convoys in the *Place St. Martin* setting lorries ablaze. Canadians were killed and wounded, and buildings were destroyed.

Poirier thought the worst might be over, but to his horror, he found that the British offensive had been held up at the Orne; only half of Caen had been liberated. They were in the line of fire from the banks of the river, and S.S. fanatics were holed up in the ruins of the Hamelin barracks. The enemy were almost up to the gates of the *Préfecture*, which was under continuous machine-gun fire. Then German shells arrived, causing great alarm. Instead of withdrawing, it seemed that the Germans might counter-attack to retake the town. Poirier consulted Usher, who, with his charming and disarming smile, calmly said he did not think they would, but 'one must be ready for anything in war'. Poirier was not reassured!

The continuous crackle of machine-guns within a few hundred yards made the citizens fear a withdrawal by the Allies. What remained of Caen was decked out with tricolours bearing the Cross of Lorraine and pictures of General de Gaulle. Proclamations by the Commissioner of the Republic, the *Préfet* and the Liberation Committee were posted everywhere. What terrible reprisals would Caen suffer if the Nazis returned? This fear was heightened by increased enemy artillery fire and bombing of highways to destroy the material being brought in by the British. German batteries at Fleury rained shells around the *Avenue Albert-Sorel*, *Place Louis-Guillouard*, the *Tribunaux* and the *Lycée* kitchens. Between the 12th and 18th British lorries took 10,000 refugees towards Bayeux.

The Civil Affairs Officers were well placed to observe the performance of the Allies. By and large they, particularly front-line soldiers, behaved well, but there were inevitable exceptions. Major Massey was disgusted by the behaviour of some British soldiers in respect of German dead. On 17th July *Commandant*

René Bertrand (French Liaison Officer) had to stop a Canadian officer trying to climb up to the bell loft of the *Cathédral St. Etienne* to observe the enemy lines. He did not appreciate that this would attract German fire on to the church, where 3,000 refugees had been camped for weeks and which the Germans had respectfully avoided due to the huge red cross on the roof. The officer went red with rage, said 'I'm fighting and you can *** off.' Bertrand jumped on to the nearest Bren gun carrier and radioed the Sector Headquarters, who called the *'sauvage'* to order.

Bertrand thought the French Canadians were disagreeable, bumptious, growlers, thieves and not very courageous, and way below the British and the Americans. On the other hand, Usher just said that they 'scared the daylights out of him'. They asked him to take them on recces of the front line, which he did, but they seemed oblivious to the danger of gratuitously putting themselves (and him!) in the line of fire.

For two days, despite huge red crosses on the *Lycée*, the *Abbaye aux Hommes* and the *Bon Sauveur*, and aware that these were hospitals and refugee centres, the Germans rained down some 280 shells, causing extensive damage and many casualties. With shells falling on the *Abbaye*, it was finally evacuated. When food was being cooked in the grounds for the refugees in the *Abbaye* and the *Lycée*, a shell landed killing some cooks. Usher was everywhere, helping the wounded, encouraging the survivors and urging the remaining cooks back to work so soon after the shelling that the meal was only 15 minutes late.

On the 19th Vaucelles was secured, although the S.S. continued to fight fanatically block by block when common sense should have had them desist. The Royal Engineers threw up 12 bridges over the Orne in one afternoon and military traffic was re-established.

The Tricolour was ceremoniously hoisted in Vaucelles, but the *Luftwaffe* launched a heavy raid during the night of 23rd/24th July, damaging the *Place Saint-Sauveur* and the *Palais de Justice* and setting the Domin printing works alight. For five weeks Civil Affairs had to carry on their relief work under constant enemy fire, causing further damage, disruption to work, and the casualties described by Poirier. The period from 27th to 30th July was busy with the evacuation of the Fleury caves, when the old and infirm were moved to Amblie by ambulance. This operation was attended, amongst others, by the *Préfet*, the

Maire, the Senior Civil Affairs Officer from 2 Canadian Corps and *M*. Hubert. Daure addressed the inhabitants who were taken to the *Lycee Malherbe* for documentation, medical attention (including delousing), feeding, entertainment and sleeping. The French police took control of their movement when inside the building. On 31st July the refugees were evacuated from the *Lycée* for security reasons, but were not allowed back to their homes in Caen. In the evening Usher, together with Lieutenant-Colonel Hiles and Major Evill, visited his old regiment, the 1st Battalion, The Gordon Highlanders, who had already suffered casualties at Cazelle, near the start of what was to prove a long and costly fight all the way to the Baltic.

Sometimes oil had to be poured on troubled waters. On 6th August Usher called a meeting to deal with complaints about some British actions. The actual complaints and some of his reply are missing but how the problem was tackled is clear. This fragment of the speech, delivered in French, shows a man who tackled problems head-on, recognised and admitted failures and treated his audience honestly and sympathetically. He had no doubt that some of the complaints were justified, but they had to be viewed in the context of the time.

> Since our arrival Caen has remained in the front line for a long time. All Frenchmen engaged in the fighting will understand that it is difficult to control the behaviour of troops at the Front. The Allied soldier is no exception to the rule. Meanwhile, some of them are dying for the liberation—for France.
>
> Seen as of now your losses are enormous, but in the pattern of the operations as a whole they represent only a tiny part.
>
> You have lost materially—it is true—but equally you have lost the Germans.
>
> I can however assure you that the British will be generous, and without making any promises, I am sure that machinery and materials will be put in place to compensate you for your actual losses.
>
> In conclusion allow me to express my personal regret for all the inconveniences that you have suffered.

This wise, compassionate but honestly realistic explanation went down well with his listeners. All was forgiven and everyone went away happy.

One German the citizens of Caen were pleased to see the back of was Austrian-born pre-war Parisian waiter Gestapo *Hauptscharführer* Herbert von Bertoldi, nicknamed 'Albert', who worked out of 44 *Rue des Jacobins*. Concealed behind a charming appearance and manner, extremely attractive to the opposite sex, lay an unscrupulous monster who took part personally in the massacre of 80 members of the Resistance in the jail on June 6th. Anyone in the Resistance falling into his hands was tortured without scruple, and when the Germans were pushed out of Caen he continued to massacre and torture all the way to Rouen. He later escaped from American custody and fled to Argentina.

On 7th August the break-through to Falaise began; Rommel had not got his reinforcements in time. At midnight on 14th/15th of August, as a Parthian shot, the *Luftwaffe* dropped anti-personnel and heavy bombs on Caen, but the fighting was over. However, there could be a counter-attack, and Usher armed the Detachment as a precaution. Allied armour finally got through on 21st August. Usher found an abandoned German hospital, and brought all the equipment back to Caen.

On 9th August, 1944, the British Foreign Secretary, Anthony Eden, visited Caen. Usher took Daure to his house in Hubert Folie to retrieve the *Préfet*'s Anthony Eden-style hat. Carle cleaned and brushed it so that Daure could wear it when he met the always impeccably dressed British Minister. Unfortunately, when Eden arrived he was not wearing a hat. Everyone agreed that it was certainly 'one up' to the *Préfet*.

Bertrand found himself working closely with 'old Usher' whom he found to be a 'good chap, understanding, Francophile and effective'. This was high praise given the libelous comments Bertrand made about many of his colleagues. They went together to many locations, including the wrecked and looted steelworks, where Usher helped to cheer up the management, some of whom were in tears. On one occasion they found themselves in the line of battle amongst Guards tanks waiting to advance. Bertrand put his head through the roof to see better and realised he had left his blue *képi* behind but the 'old fox' said 'never mind—take mine', offering his glengarry! Carle, now quite an expert in the art, deftly extracted them from a worse fate by safely negotiating a minefield. Bertrand felt honoured to receive a letter from 'old Usher' making him an honorary member of his Mess.

On 22nd August, Usher sent Captain Jenkins and Sergeant-Major Mills to retrieve the Daure and Coulet families, Marianne, Pierre Daure's wife, their two children David and Catou and their parents *M.* and *Mme.* Coulet from behind enemy lines. They found the ruins of the house and collected some clothing

René Bertrand records that 'old Usher' found the entire Daure-Coulet family behind the lines and led them to safety. Usher, reluctant to take credit that belonged to others, gave his version, in a note written in French.

The Return to Caen of the families of the Préfet and the
Regional Commissioner of Liberated France.

On arrival in Caen we learned that the *Préfet*, *M.* Daure, had come through German lines dressed as a farmer. He left behind his wife, their two children and *M.* and *Mme.* Coulet, parents of *Mme.* Daure and *M.* Coulet, Regional Commissioner of the Republic. Because of the excellent relations established between *M.* Daure and Civil Affairs, we considered that the administration would be made even happier if the family was reunited. Three weeks passed before the Germans were chased from the South Bank of the Orne. Since the beginning of the retreat and the territory was recovered it was possible to undertake some reconnaissance. From time to time *M. le Préfet* had made enquiries. Cinq Autels, Moulines and Halbout were explored without success.

On 22nd August 1944 I decided to send Lieutenant Street (U.S.) on reconnaissance. The *Préfet* [said] that he had had news from a reliable source that the family were in (farms) (between) Trun and 4 Kms from Bailleul.

It was decided to search farms situated 2 Km north west of Villedieu les Bailleul. Lieutenant C.J. Hepburn, a fluent French speaker, would accompany Lieutenant Street, both instructed not to divulge the names of the persons they were looking for.

These two officers met Major Samuelson of C.A. detachment No. 220 at Falaise and with his permission questioned the Mayor. They were unable to find a large-scale map or any information regarding recent military events. The two officers then drove down towards Croucy.

On their arrival at Croucy they saw a local who directed them to the country doctor Dr. J.A. Madrus, who, he said, would help them. They found some refugees with the doctor, amongst whom was a lady who said that she had lived in the area they were then going to explore, and showed them where it was on the map. Bearing in mind that they were ordered not to divulge names they asked if there were any refugees in the area in question. She replied that she had left it to get through the lines since the Germans were still there.

The doctor, who was an active member of the Resistance, said that there were still pockets of German resistance in the surrounding woods. On this information they decided that it was inopportune to go there bearing in mind the state of the battle and the sort of vehicle they were using. I discovered later that serious fighting took place the same night in the locality.

The two officers returned to Caen and reported to me.

I sent Lieutenant Street to the *Préfecture* and he advised him of the current situation. It was decided to send *M. le Préfet* and his secretary *Mme.* Gagliardi, off the next day in the hope that the enemy would have been pushed back.

Detailed information reaching me in the night made me change the plan. I decided to make a reconnaissance further afield. The group would consist of Major Hellmuth, Lieutenant Street and me. L/Cpl Carle would drive an additional vehicle to bring back the family if we found them. The reconnaissance would be made by jeep.

I informed the *Préfet* that the military situation made it impossible for him to accompany the trip.

After finalizing the plan I was notified by the H.Q. L of C that an important American civilian would arrive the following morning at 11.00 am and that I would have to welcome him. Seeing that I could not now undertake the proposed trip, I asked Lieutenant-Colonel Hiles to go in my stead. The important civilian was none other than Ambassador Phillips. The rest of this story is thus best told by Major Hellmuth himself.

Arriving at Falaise, I left Colonel Hiles to examine abandoned German equipment and we agreed that Colonel Hiles would drive towards Trun and wait at a crossroads until we could possibly make contact with *M.* Daure's family. It was decided that we should endeavour to appreciate the very uncertain military situation due to the fact that there remained nests of German resistance still around.

I retraced my route to Trun then turned in the direction of Argentan. The road resembled a battlefield. No vehicle other than a jeep could get through. The debris of burnt out tanks and trucks, and human and animal corpses still cluttered the road and surrounding fields.

Finally we arrived at a cluster of farms 2 Km north of Bailleul. I asked if any refugees coming from Hubert Folie had anything to do with the University of Caen and I put it that the people I was looking for could have changed their names and it was difficult to get any firm news.

I visited numerous farms, and encountered many refugees without success. I thought of looking for the *Mairie* but I found it destroyed. However a guide showed up who would take me to the *Maire*. While we were going there some prisoners-of-war came up to us and warned us that there were numerous Boches still hiding in the woods around the *Maire*'s house. We decided to billet ourselves in the township and carry on our task of getting around the area.

The *Maire* told me that he didn't know the refugees because all the archives had been destroyed. However he found a list of allocations and there was the name Coulet. We were pointed in the direction of the secretary to the *Maire* who eventually showed us the farm where the family was. The *Maire* took us there and I had the honour and privilege to meet *Mme.* Daure and *M.* and Mm. Coulet and the children. I told them I had come to find them.

I gave them the news and had them get ready as quickly as possible so that they could all be brought out the same afternoon, after an exciting journey we returned to Trun where Colonel Hiles met us. We brought two vehicles to the farm and everyone returned to Caen where Colonel Usher accompanied us to the *Préfecture* where there was a happy party.

This report was signed by Usher.

This was a hazardous operation in territory where the military situation was fluid. On 22nd August Major A.R. Stewart-Grant commanding Det 208 (No2 Group Civil

1st Gordons Officers 1913

2/Lt. C.M. Usher, back row, right, Lt.Col. F.H. Neish, sitting, centre, Maj. W.E. Gordon, V.C., sitting 3rd from left, 2/Lt. A.D.L. Stewart, back row, 2nd right, Capt. C. Lumsden, back row, centre, 2/Lt D.R. Turnbull, back row, 3rd right, Lt. J.K.Trotter, back row, 4th right.

(Tiger and Sphinx)

a

1st Battalion, The Gordon Highlanders marching into Plymouth,
September 1913. Lt. Col. F.H. Neish on horse.

Gordon Highlanders Museum

1st Battalion holding Germans at Audencourt,
26 August 1914.

Gordon Highlanders Museum

Scotland v England, March 1912
Usher's first International cap.
C.M. Usher back row, second from left.

Usher family

J M Bannerman   J R Lawrie   W G Dobson   D S Davies   J C R Buchanan   G P S Macpherson
D M Bertram   H H Forsayth   A Wemyss   C M Usher (Captain)   A L Gracie   A Browning   W E Bryce
R C Warren   E H Liddell

Scotland v Ireland, February 1922.
Usher's last International season.
C.M. Usher front row, centre, Eric Liddell bottom right.

Usher family

c

Golf course made by C.K. Hutchinson and C.M. Usher
at Clausthal im Harz P.O.W. Camp, 1916.

Usher family

Hague Caledonian Society Pipe Band, 1918.
C.M. Usher sitting, in civilian kilt outfit.

Usher family

C.M. Usher performing the Highland Fling.
Painted by Russian P.O.W. Nikolai Sokolow.

Usher family

Major C.M. Usher with Maj-Gen Sir W. Thompson, G.O.C. Highland
Area during Inspection at Gordon Highlanders Depot, Castlehill, 1930.
Tiger and Sphinx

Major C.M. Usher with Lt-Gen Sir P. Radcliffe, G.O.C. Scotland,
at the Annual Inspection, Gordon Highlanders Depot, Castlehill, 1930.
Tiger and Sphinx

f

The Usher family, 1934.
From left - C.M. Usher, Madge, Iain, Kenneth.

Usher family

Lieutenant-Colonel C.M. Usher with General Lord Gort, V.C. at
Templeuve-en-Pevele, October 1939.

Movietone News

The Belfry, an ideal observation post, was struck by a German shell
during the siege of Bergues in May 1940, and callously destroyed when
the Germans withdrew in 1944. It was lovingly rebuilt and restored by
the citizens of Bergues after the War.

Colonel C.M. Usher and Civil Affairs Staff, September 1944.
Usher is flanked by Pierre and Marianne Daure, *Commandant* René
Bertrand front row, second left.

Usher family

Caen 1944 showing the devastation after the bombing raids and bombardments.

www.thefullwiki.org

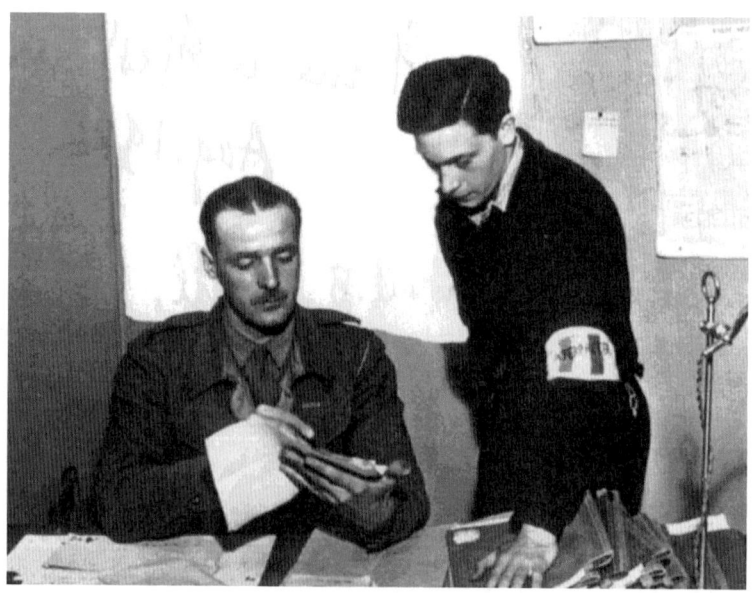

Major L.J. Massey and André Heintz, Caen 1944.

Usher family

Minden 1945-46. Compare with photos of Caen in 1944!

k

Colonel C.M. Usher, Senior Civil Affairs Officer
Regierungsbezirk Minden, 1945-46.

Usher family

Affairs), attended the funeral of six French civilians massacred by the Germans, and on the following day got the names of those suspected of the killings. One of the suspects got his desserts when he entered the house of *M.* Chretien, whose wife was one of the murdered civilians, told him he was a spy and six others like him had already been shot. The situation was tense, but *M.* Chretien engaged the German in conversation and offered him a glass of wine, which he accepted. Then, suggesting a refill, he went behind him and strangled him.

Stewart-Grant had to move on to St. Georges du Vievre to get help from the Resistance to keep the roads open and deal with their collaborator problems, which he managed to do despite being held up by a Tiger tank *en route.*

Heintz mentioned that Usher, in a report dated 15th September, stated that if Calvados had suddenly become a rear area as a result of the rapid Allied advance in August when the allies broke through at Falaise, it was still suffering bloodshed.

One Civil Affairs member expressed it in verse, ten verses of which survive:

> A captured town is a hell of a spot,
> Where Germans are dead or passed through,
> But when they still occupy the half of a place,
> No words of description will do.
>
> An administrative commandant had to be found,
> The job it was said was a peach.
> So they searched the sea shore and eventually found
> 101 Sub Area (Beach).
>
> What splendid perception, what vision, what ho!
> A Sub Area that's been by the sea,
> Is ideal to control the North bank of the Orne,
> And the South bank as well, maybe.
>
> So the Sub Area sent an H.Q. to the town,
> To the house of *M.* Pelpel;
> And mortar bombs flew and HE bombs too,
> And many a whistling shell.
>
> But 'tis not the endurance this H.Q. showed,
> That history books strive to relate,
> Nor how the town was redeemed from despair,
> From horror and hovering hate.

'Tis not the fact that the *Préfet* was brought
To share with a Colonel his bed;
Nor yet that the standard of France was hauled up
With speeches and wine and rye bread.

All this is a glorious pageant of life,
In Caen, now no longer in thrall;
But more strange and more wonderful even is this,
Which now I'm impelled to recall.

A Beach Sub Area fresh from the shore,
Was planted in Caen, and so
Troops from the base stood ready to fight,
Not five hundred yards from the foe.

For three nights and days about sixty Canucks,
Held two miles and a half of a stream;
And a Beach Sub Area in closest support,
Stood by (by mistake it would seem).

Now the Battle's moved on, the armour has fled,
The town has become a Base Port,
101 has moved out to find further renown
Among tanks of a different sort.

E.E.R. 1 Aug 44.

On 5th October 1944, *Mme.* Daure was told that 'old Usher' was off to Brussels for leave, and there was a touching scene. Before his departure *M.* Daure, addressing Usher, made clear, on behalf of the people of Caen, his appreciation of Usher's efforts, which had done so much to restore security and re-establish vital services, in a manner that restored and maintained the honour and dignity of its citizens. In his address *M.* Daure said:

> Since the beginning there has been no urgent task of support or charity with which you have not collaborated, whether it concerned the evacuation of refugees or the wounded, guaranteeing food supplies, organising civil defence, sanitation, clearing the ruins, setting the council services to rights again or to strengthen the morale of the population, tested appallingly, and while you have done a good job for the Allied Command you have done the same for Caen. You have always succeeded in your task while strictly respecting French prerogatives.

Everyone, including Daure, was moved to tears on the Grand Staircase. After Brussels 'old Usher' was transferred to Amiens, and in October wrote 'a nice letter' to Daure, which went into his personal archives.

Usher was heartbroken that it was beyond the resources of his Detachment to do more to relieve the disaster which had overtaken Caen and its citizens, so he got in touch with his friend, John Orr, Dean of the Faculty of Arts and Professor of French Language and Romance Linguistics at Edinburgh University, who in turn contacted Lady Roseberry. Between them they set up the Edinburgh–Caen Fellowship to collect basic necessities, such as clothing, bedding and pharmaceuticals for the dispossessed and exercise books, pencils and educational material for the school children and students.

Heintz records the enormous quantities collected and dispatched, (for example 80 tons in the following January) and the problems in getting them transported. Military traffic took precedence and it was a struggle to get the railways and port authorities to accept the quantities involved. At the French end, a one-time Head of English at the *Lycée Malherbe*, *M.* Prioux, organised storage and distribution from Saint Nicolas church, which was dry and vermin proof. Meetings between the British military authorities, *Commandant* Bertrand, the Mayor's representatives and the teaching profession took place at H.Q. 101 Beach sub-area.

The success of Anglo-French cooperation in Caen was rewarded by Usher being made a *Citoyen d'honneur* of the town and awarded a gold medal. A street leading to the University is named *Rue Colonel Usher*. When asked whether he would like a street named after him he quipped in his acceptance that there should be no brothel in it—so it was a very short street![1] Recognising his military input were the awards of *Chevalier de la Légion d'honneur* and *Croix de Guerre avec palme*.

Professor Orr was made *Docteur Honoris Causa de l'Université de Caen* and an *Officier de la Légion d'honneur* while Pierre Daure became a C.B.E., and a visiting lectureship at Edinburgh was provided for André Heintz.

Usher maintained that all he had done in Caen was his duty, but the truth is that he did far more than that. By establishing an

---

[1] Professor Orr also had a street in Caen named after him, and Caen boasts a *rue d'Edimbourg.*

empathetic and sympathetic relationship with French officials and citizens, and by listening to them and understanding the problems they faced and the traumatic experiences they had suffered, he was able to re-establish systems, procedures and protocols that enabled the French very quickly to assume responsibility for the administration of and rehabilitation of the devastated city. Not everyone could have achieved this, and it is a mark of Usher's ability, drive, energy, charm and diplomacy that he could do so much so well.

The failure to hold Caen, and the heavy losses in men and material sustained by the Germans in the battle for the city, allowed the American break-out from the West and the British push past Caen that decimated the retreating Germans in the Falaise Gap. That, in turn, led to the Allied advance to Paris, the drive through Belgium and Holland, the crossing of the Rhine and the final defeat of Nazi Germany.

After Caen and a well-earned leave, during which he took the opportunity to return to Edinburgh and discuss his proposals for the Edinburgh–Caen Fellowship, Usher was sent to Lille where he ran a Civil Affairs school, and then by way of Armentières and Tournai he made his way to Minden in Westphalia, Germany.

CHAPTER 8

GERMANY

USHER'S final task in the Second World War was to re-establish a viable civil administration in a region of Germany. The task could not have been more different from that in Caen. Rather than trying to rebuild the administration of a devastated city in a country that welcomed him as friend and liberator, he had to do the same in a defeated country whose people saw him as invader and occupier. He would need all his powers of diplomacy, charm and persuasion, backed up by firmness, strength and authority to rebuild the self-confidence of a scared and apprehensive population that feared retribution for the deeds of their misguided leader over more than a decade. The task was more delicate and fraught with political danger than that he had faced the year before.

After having successfully passed on the lessons of Caen at the Civil Affairs school at Lille, Usher found himself with the British 21st Army Group as it crossed into Germany for the last act of the War.

Around 20th March 1945, prior to crossing the Rhine, the British Second Army took responsibility for the area between the Rhine and the Maas, and Usher took charge of Detachment 507, under the Army Military Government staff. A formidable task lay ahead. When 21st Army Group reached the west bank of the Rhine it cleared the civil population (up to 30,000 people plus livestock) to a depth of 6,000 yards, to ensure secrecy for the impending operation. They were removed to tented accommodation around Bedburg, where the General Military Court was convened and Second Army Prison located. At the same time, military forces and supplies for crossing the Rhine poured into the area. The refugees at Bedburg were moved further back, and Bedburg was finally cleared of refugees on 23rd April.

In April, *Reichskommisar* Dr. Seyss-Inquart (sentenced to death at Nuremberg and hanged), wanted to surrender in view of the pitiful condition of the Dutch, but was ordered to continue resistance and inundate the country, and the German army there did not surrender until 4th May. The unconditional surrender of all German forces followed on the 7th and hostilities ceased on the 8th.

Usher's brief was to assume responsibility for all Civil Affairs matters in the *Regierungsbezirk*[1] Minden once the region had been cleared of German troops.

The Region around Minden that was Usher's responsibility

The Minden region was predominately Roman Catholic. When the German Army retreated the civil administration went with it, leaving no one in charge. The Catholic Church helped to fill the gap in Westphalia, of which the *Regierungsbezirk* Minden formed part. Graf von Galen, Catholic Bishop of Münster, was considered as the first *Oberpräsident*. He had courageously opposed the Nazis in face of Hitler's disavowal of religion. Hitler wanted no competition with the Reich in people's minds, and viewed the Vatican as a non-German international force. He hated religion, stating that if people wanted a God it should be Germany. He tried, but failed, to Nazify the Protestant Church, appointing a ferocious Nazi as *Reichsbishop* to 'coordinate' the Lutheran Church, which 'must be German and nationalist', but many Protestant pastors stood up for their religion and gave their lives for it.

---

[1] Region.

Germany had been comprehensively defeated, but there was no German Government to sign the surrender. A *Declaration of Defeat and Assumption of Supreme Authority* was signed and published by the Allied Commanders-in-Chief to establish a Control Council to deal with German matters. The Russians procrastinated, while removing to Russia as much industrial machinery as they could before negotiations began.

There was no constitutional government in Germany to assume responsibility for running the country. Until 1933 Germany had been in political and economic disruption, on the verge of civil war. The ineffective Weimar Republic was held in contempt. When Hitler formed a coalition between his National Socialist Workers' Party—the Nazi Party—and the Centre National Party, he achieved an absolute majority in the *Reichstag*. President Hindenburg, ruling under emergency powers, appointed Hitler Chancellor in 1933. The Nazi Party had private armies, the S.A. *(SturmAbteilung)*, the 'Brown Shirts', composed of inadequates, misfits, and unemployed ex-servicemen, who revelled in authority and power outwith the law, and the S.S. *(SchutzStaffel)*, the 'Black Shirts', Hitler's smart Praetorian Guard. The Nazi Party duplicated all offices of state, and Nazis filled key posts in the civil administration. The S.A. and S.S. took precedence over the civil police.

After the *Reichstag* fire of February 1933, the '*Law for Removing the Distress of People and Reich*' was passed, the deputies too afraid to vote against it. By passing this Act the *Reichstag* effectively voted itself out of existence. Hitler could make laws, amend the constitution and conclude treaties without reference to President or *Reichstag*. He controlled Central and Local Government and the Armed Forces. Local government consisted of *Länder* (States), the *Regierungsbezirk* (regions), *Kreise* and *Gemeinde* (districts and communities). Local officials obeyed the Central Government and the Nazi Party.

As the Allies advanced into Germany they came across the horrors at Belsen. It was imperative that control and rehabilitation, down to the grassroots of society, was established to reverse the *Führer Prinzip*—authority from the top down and obedience from the bottom up. It was a principle that suited German acceptance of authority and love of uniform.

The Allied Chiefs of Staff ordered that Military Government should be established as the country was occupied, with supreme legislative, executive and judicial power. The task facing Civil Affairs staff was significantly different from that in France

What was to happen to Germany? All agreed on the need to cleanse the country of Nazism, but views on how to achieve this differed. President Roosevelt favoured the Morgenthau Plan of splitting the country in two, stripping the Ruhr of all industry and closing the mines, so that Germany could not, for the foreseeable future, become an industrial power again. There would be no assistance to get the economy moving, except when in support of the Allied war effort. The Combined Chiefs of Staff more or less agreed this latter point, but were concerned that minimal relief supplies should be imported to forestall disease and disorder. At this point they were forced to decree that:

> Under no circumstances shall active Nazis or ardent sympathisers be retained in office for purposes of administrative convenience or expediency. The Nazi Party and all subsidiary organisations shall be dissolved.

However, the British insisted that:

> The administrative machinery of certain dissolved Nazi organisations may be used when necessary to provide certain essential functions, such as relief, health and sanitation, with de-Nazified personnel and facilities.

The Army's task was to save their enemies and revive public services. On 10th April, nearly a month before hostilities ceased, Detachment 507 took charge of *Regierungsbezirk* Minden, comprising Lübbeke, Herford, Halle, Bielefeld, Wiedenbrück, Paderborn, Höxter, Büren and Warburg, an area measuring 72 miles by 40 miles.

Potential administrators had to be screened to unearth membership of the Nazi party. Much interviewing was done, and on 22nd April Usher appointed Dr. Paul Zenz as *Regierungspräsident*. Dr. Zenz, married to a Jewess, had been barred from the Nazi Party. He was excellent in the job, and he and Usher enjoyed a warm and fruitful relationship for the next fourteen months. At his first meeting Usher addressed Zenz and his staff in German.

> I am Colonel Usher, I am the oldest officer of this Military Government and the senior commander of the Army garrison. Keep sight of the fact that we've come as victors. As

commander, I have appointed Herr Dr. Zenz as Head of Government and you gentlemen as his colleagues.

I have given up this evening to come to you to share my personal wishes with you. I have always thought that I understood German people well. I lived for six months with a German family as a young man in order to learn German. At the beginning of the last war I was wounded at Catson (Le Cateau) in France and taken prisoner. Despite my wishes to escape I lived in captivity in various camps for four years, which was a trying time for an active officer. In 1939 I went to France once again to fight Germany. After the Dunkirk battle I went back to England. We now come to 1945.

I have had nearly 40 years opportunity to see the German people and German troops in peace and war, in advance and retreat, in victory and defeat. Now I'm here, my task is that of an active officer. For myself, I have had enough of war. My task is to do everything possible to shun war and move on.

You have read this book. Everything in it is absolutely clear. Everything about it is without doubt.

I will always be just and fair, but positive with them [the local German population].

From today their government must function normally so that it will be possible to progress. A special task for your Administration is to help me provide for the many refugees and foreigners who have found themselves in the area. I know that Germany has enough provisions for these foreign visitors, not us.

I have Specialist Officers for each Department of Government. I have called you here today to introduce you to these officers. My officers' duty is to oversee the work of each Department. My officers are directly answerable to me, thus I will always know every ruling. The Government is directly responsible to me through Dr. Zenz. The appointments are provisional and they will be confirmed later by the *Oberbefehlshaber* [Usher himself]. You must discharge your duties in the best interests of the Army garrison, which I can assure you will also be in the interest of all your people.

I have four important aims:

First
Every form of National Socialism must be rooted out.

<u>Secondly</u>
Justice and Order must rule.
<u>Thirdly</u>
Provision for the refugees and Displaced Persons who are here.
<u>Fourthly</u>
No one here in Germany need go hungry.

I close by saying: The time must come when Germany, given freedom of speech and thought and cleansed of National Socialism and militarism, will take its true place in the world.

Major Clarke will now be willing to discuss any details with you.

The Archbishop of Paderborn was concerned about how the Military Government would operate, and Usher wrote to him on 5th May. He introduced himself as the oldest officer in the Military Government in the region of Minden. He said Paderborn had recently come under his control, which is why he would come to pay a visit. He said he personally belonged to the Church of Scotland. He hoped His Excellency would support him. His goals were in the best interests of the population, and he was sure that the Catholic Church could never have fully recognized National Socialism.

The goals were

To stamp out National Socialism and Militarism.

To look after all the many foreigners in the region of Minden (The screening and repatriation of D.P.s were an enormous problem).

To establish a basis for the re-education of the German people in order to avoid any future wars.

He hoped the Archbishop would not refuse him any help in this. Did he have any problems? Could he give him the limits of his areas of competence? Did he have access to a vehicle? If not he would see if he could be of assistance.

It is to be hoped that the Archbishop was charitably disposed to the Presbyterian Military Governor when he received this letter. The magnanimity of a member of a Church subscribing to the Confession of Westminster may have come as a welcome surprise!

The Russians were now in Berlin, and the first rumours came in about Hitler and Bormann—Hitler was dead—he had escaped to the Argentine—he was in disguise—he had a new identity! The Press was full of cartoons portraying how he might look. Zenz was concerned, and became agitated. Usher sent him a note on 21st May, the tone of which was firm and reassuring.

> Unfortunately I was not here yesterday evening but Major Gray has told me that you wish to see me. What is it concerning us?
>
> I do not know if Hitler is dead or not, but it is possible that he is still living. Hitler himself said that he would find a hero's death with his soldiers in Berlin. If he should be dead this is good; if he is still alive he has betrayed his people, so he can never become a hero! That Hitler would become a hero now or in the future would be dangerous—in my mind it is no more possible.
>
> Compose yourself (Relax!) *Herr Doktor*. It is not a matter to get worked up about!

Hitler had shot himself on 30th April. It was difficult to appreciate that the greatest threat to mankind that the world had known was now no more.

The Military Government went into action with Operation *Barleycorn*, the programme for getting in the harvest. Five hundred thousand agricultural workers were needed. These could only come from the German Armed Forces, and those selected were given priority discharge. A Control Centre at Herford dealt with *Wehrmacht*, supplies, transport and signals. German commanders were ordered to send a daily quota of between 500 and 1,000 men to Discharge Collecting Centres, from which they were transported to Dispersal Point camps by Military Government officers, with the provision of food, cooking facilities, water, medical and sanitary arrangements the responsibility of the German civil authorities.

It was essential to forestall the horrifying prospect of starvation, disease and ensuing unrest. Rations well above the minimum were desperately required by the miners of the Ruhr. This was an almost impossible task in view of the policy of no imports into Germany while the rest of the world was struggling to feed itself. Military Government officers were recognised by Sir William Gavin of the Ministry of Agriculture and Fisheries as having shouldered the biggest task of Civil Administration which any Military organisation had ever undertaken, in the face of almost incredible destruction and disorder.

There were eleven million refugees or D.P.s left behind throughout Europe. Used by the Nazis as slave labour or impressed into the Armed Forces, some two-and-a-half million were in the British zone. Among them were French, Belgians, Dutch, Russians, Poles, Czechs, Italians and Yugoslavs. The ultimate responsibility for them fell to the United Nations Relief and Rehabilitation Administration (U.N.R.R.A.), but initially they had to be provided for by the Civil Affairs officers in the Military Government. The German authorities were made to provide living accommodation at the expense of their own nationals. This measure, harsh though it might appear, was only fair, as Germany had been responsible for the problem in the first place. D.P.s without movement authorisation were collected at Assembly Centres, detained and subjected to security scrutiny, and their nationalities and identities registered—there were wanted men, who sought anonymity by hiding among the D.P.s, to be apprehended and tried by Allied Military Government Courts. D.P.s were medically inspected, deloused, immunised, clothed and issued with meal cards. Soviet D.P.s were repatriated, whether they liked it or not. By the middle of July there were over one-and-a-half million D.P.s in the British zone.

Nazi organisations, laws and courts were abolished and no Nazis were to be retained in or appointed to any position of authority. The destruction of the Nazi Party was a Police responsibility, and they seized party officials and records.

While responsibility for this lay with Counter-Intelligence, the Military Government was responsible for purging the Police themselves. Legal sanctions fell under Military Government Law No. 5, 'Dissolution of the Nazi Party'. This declared illegal, and prohibited the activities of the Nazi Party and subsidiary organisations. It prohibited recruitment to para-military organisations, and provided that these should be disbanded and dissolved. It provided for the seizure of all funds, property and records of the Nazi Party and subsidiary organisations. Any offence against this law was punishable by death, or any lesser penalty. Party officials were arrested in accordance with a list drawn up by Military Government staff. The list included senior Party officials, all members of the Gestapo, the S.S., the S.A., the Hitler Youth, all officers of the *Waffen* S.S. and the *Allgemeine* S.S., and senior ranks of other para-military organisations. This led to the arrest of over 60,000 people in the British zone, each of whom had to complete a questionnaire to determine their Nazi Party activities, and those of their relatives. A Special Branch at each Military Government centre evaluated the questionnaires.

The task was Herculean. If the Military Government followed Roosevelt's wishes, German administration of food and water, and public health would come to a halt, followed by disease and anarchy, with far-reaching repercussions for the occupying forces, within and beyond Germany's borders. The Military Government exercised common sense, accepting that everyone had had to belong to the Nazi Party to gain employment and feed their families. Knowledge of Germany and the language was essential to make a realistic assessment of the degree of enthusiasm with which interviewees had, or had not, embraced Nazi ideology and participated in its activities.

Usher understood the Germans in 1945, and could compare them with how they had been in the Kaiser's time. It was a challenge to differentiate between those who had risked their lives to oppose Nazism, those who might claim to be anti-Nazis, and those who were just nominal Nazis.

Schools and youth organisations created by the Nazis were closed, Nazi text books and those glorifying militarism confiscated, after which schools were reopened. The ideas of freedom to think for oneself, free speech, a free press and freedom of religion, alien concepts to many, were promoted.

The first task of the Military Government was to establish the rule of law, so all German Courts were suspended until the Military Government reopened them. All Nazi Courts and Tribunals were abolished. Military Government Courts were set up in the interim.

As 1945 wore on, Usher supervised all activities and encouraged German local government officials to carry out their tasks honestly and efficiently. It was not easy to get defeated and demoralised communities to believe in themselves and overcome difficulties, but Usher was always there, urging them on and encouraging them to help themselves and rebuild their lives. The obstacles and difficulties were very real, but Usher's desire and drive to overcome them were just as real.

Because of the priority to get industry in the Ruhr up and running again there was no coal for domestic heating and cooking, so timber had to be located and felled to provide wood for burning. At first people were reluctant to damage municipal trees, and they were scared to fell State ones. It took much persuasion by Usher to get them to take saws and axes to trees, but necessity overcame their scruples. The next matter was 'The Battle of the Winter'. Should the winter of 1945/6 prove harsh the Administration would face a major problem, and it became a matter of urgency to call all the *Oberbürgemeister* and *Landräten* of *Regierungsbezirk* Minden to a meeting in the *Regierungsgebäude* where Usher addressed them.

I do not want to make a long speech but I wish to tell you that I am fully alive to all your difficulties. You must always remember the reason for those difficulties and also the aims of the Military Government

First you must put your own house in order. You must feed yourselves, and also you must pay for the war which was of your own making. At the moment you are not in a position to feed yourselves much less to pay what you owe.

The Military Government will help you to get on your feet and there you must work, not only to liquidate your debts, but to find your own salvation. This winter will be hard. You will get a sufficient ration—nothing extra. You will sometimes be cold, but I have already made the necessary arrangements for a supply of wood, which you must collect yourselves.

It is your duty to co-operate closely with the Military Government, especially in the care and education of the young. In this way you will be able to ensure that the children of the present generation will not suffer as their fathers and grandfathers have done.

The way ahead will be hard, but you must remember that all the other nations will suffer as you will, and that the suffering has been caused solely because Germany has forced two wars on the world. We have no exultation in victory. The conditions are too serious. But the occupation troops will conduct themselves as wise conquerors. As we were strong in battle so will we be wise in peace.

Today the world does not trust Germany. You must make it your life's work to strive, day and night, in order to regain this trust for your Fatherland.

Fortunately, unlike the following winter, that one was relatively mild, but even so it was touch and go. The problems were two-fold. The first military responsibility was transport, with rail and road systems in chaos after the bombing and fighting, and the second was the question of who should get what rations. Throughout the war Germany had been supplied by the countries she had conquered, but now that she could not live off the fat of other lands she was faced with the very real prospect of starvation. The Allies could not give them more than they could scrape together for themselves or the liberated territories.

Requisitioning for British Headquarters at Bad Oeynhausen was one of Usher's tasks. Repeated demands made it hard for the Germans to plan. This did not concern many at Headquarters, who showed a lack of concern for Germans who would not have spared civilians in occupied territories. Usher stated bluntly that he did not think the fact that the Germans had behaved badly was any reason why he should behave badly in turn, and he always did his best to play fair with them. As a consequence he never had any problems with German officials or the people.

Usher visited the Nuremberg trials, with Lieutenant-Colonel Barnes. They travelled in the big Detachment Maybach, with two German drivers in smart chauffeur uniforms, to see the War Trial in progress, and to visit the vast 250,000 seat stadium where Hitler had harangued the party rallies.

Usher recorded his impressions of the visit, which started on 26th February, 1946. They set off in thick mist, over roads slippery with snow and ice, going by Warburg, in the south of the Detachment area, where they spent the night, then through Kassel, Fulda, Bad Kissingen and Schweinfurt along narrow roads with precipices and snowdrifts on either side, across the Rohn Mountains. A Polish car driven at great speed came out of the mist heading straight for them and forced them off the road.

> However I got a horse and sleigh and it pulled us out. Finally, at 8pm, we arrived at the Grand Hotel Nuremberg, a swagger hotel. However, to reach our bedrooms we had to go through the bombed part of the hotel—open to the air—to my room, which was very comfortable with private bathroom, shower, sitting room, telephone and valet! Meals were excellent—two eggs for breakfast! Dancing every night with cabaret-orchestra. Nuremberg is in the U.S. Zone and everything is done in the American way so I tasted the delights of U.S. rations[2] again.

---

[2] To anyone living in wartime Britain the U.S. seemed an almost unimaginable land of milk and honey, hence, among other things, the G.I. brides.

Those attending the International Military Tribunal Court were given a plan of the courtroom, a seating plan of the accused and biographical details of the twenty-one war criminals on trial.

The business of the court consisted of the indictment of the S.S., S.A. and Gestapo as criminal organisations. It was led off by Mr Justice Jackson (they say he will be next President of the U.S.A.) who is the leading U.S. Prosecutor. He was followed by Maxwell-Fyffe for us and then the Russian and the French. There are 2,000 people employed in connection with the Trial.

G.D. Roberts K.C. (England and Harlequins) was No. 3 of the Prosecution to Lord Lawrence and Maxwell-Fyffe—I used to play [rugby] against him. We had a great chat and he stood me lunch. He was No. 2 but with the Socialist Government, he had had to go down one. Last year he had to pay £12,000 in tax! The Court is not very big. Every word is taken down in shorthand, and also sound recorded. You can hear every word spoken on the gramophone in a special room down stairs. Through the earphones one can hear any of the four languages, English, Russian, German and French. You simply switch the needle round the dial of your apparatus. I tried to listen through one earphone and so got two languages. This was interesting as the translation is in commentary form. The Speaker does not stop talking for them to translate, but if he goes too quick a white light shows on the Judge's desk—a red light if the loudspeaker for the earphones goes wrong. Then everything stops till it is put right.

Guards, typists and interpreters are only on duty for an hour at a time. They slip out when their relief comes and there is no general change over, but it means there is continual movement in Court. One policeman fainted next to Goering and without looking Goering caught him by the belt and held him up till he was carted out.

The prisoners live in small cells with most austere furnishings. They have to do everything in their cells and are observed every 30 seconds day and night by the guards through the peephole in the door. Their clothes are taken away every night, brushed, pressed and given back in the morning so that they will not look dishevelled. They get Prisoner-of-War rations, so are better off than the civilians outside in that respect.

Goering has tremendous personality and they say he has made a great mistake not defending himself instead of having a second-rate Counsel. All the best German Lawyers were Nazis and so are inside themselves, and so only not so good ones are available. Although Goering is probably for it anyway he could have had a lot of fun jumping up and objecting, and his personality might have had some effect on the court.

Hess looks nothing—very pale and depressed. The two sailors, Raeder and Doenitz look inconspicuous in their ill-fitting blue suits. Keitel does not look bad in grey uniform without any medals and decorations—Jodl looks unimpressive—von Ribbentrop looks very scruffy and aged a lot—Rosenberg looks very nervous. Sauckel and Frank took a lot of interest and were quite bright looking. Von Papen and von Neurath looked more distinguished than the others with their grey hair—Seyss-Inquart looked like a bank clerk—Streicher looked awful—not an impressive lot.

They took my *skean dhu* away in the afternoon. They did not spot it in the morning.

In mid-1946 Usher's time as a Civil Affairs Officer came to an end and he was ordered back to Britain. On June 14th, 1946 he bade farewell to Minden. Addressing the members of the *Regierungsbezirk* in German he said:

I will not make a long speech especially as it is my Farewell Speech. I would like to say that I am very pleased with the co-operation of the *Regierungspräsident* and his staff in the *Regierungsgebäude* and of all the *Landräte*, *Oberbürgermeisteren* and *Oberkreisdirekteren*.

I am convinced that *Regierungsbezirk* Minden has made good progress and has nothing to fear from comparison with other *Regierungsbezirken*. The road that lies before you is long and hard, but at the end of the road stands success.

This road leads through democracy. I know well that in the hearts of many of you democracy does not appear to be the solution of your problems. But I state definitely that democracy is the only way to freedom and peace. So, gentlemen, you must study democracy and believe in it, and educate the German people in this belief. It is the only way!

Every day I got to know the German people better, and I am convinced that the German people can have a good future.

In every one of us there is a streak of cruelty. Undoubtedly, among your former leaders this streak was very pronounced. Hitler and his helpers made good use of mass psychology. We have seen the result in the concentration camps of Auschwitz, Belsen etc. I will not go into details, they are too cruel and disgusting. But, gentlemen, you must leave no stone unturned to prevent a repetition. I have spoken of mass psychology but how often have I heard, "Herr Oberst give us an order"? Every member of the population must think and speak for himself and use his initiative, and not always wait for an order. You love family life. From now on you must live in peace in the family of the world. Banish every streak of cruelty, banish mass psychology.

In conclusion I would like to thank you, *Herr Regierungspräsident,* for your willing co-operation at all times. You have always done everything possible to work with me. Nevertheless, you have remained a good German. Your task has been hard, but you have filled your duty well.

For you, gentlemen, your work has been just as hard, and I would like to tell you that I have always had the most satisfactory reports over your co-operation from my *Kreis* Commanders, and I thank each individual one of you.

From Scotland I will watch your progress with great interest—*Lieben Sie wohl!*

Dr. Zenz's reply, in English, was a testament to Usher's character, integrity and ability.

Commander, Colonel, Ladies and Gentlemen!

When you, highly honourable Commander, with your Military Government on April 10th of last year, in the name of the occupation forces, took the administration of the *Regierungsbezirk* Minden in your hands, the sound of guns of the Second World War had not yet died away. Fourteen difficult months of work and of anxiety have since then elapsed. During this time, we all gathered together here have worked with you and your Military Government as German advisers. In doing so we were guided by our conscience and hoped to help our German people. We are grateful to hear from you the confirmation that we have done our duty, that we have made a contribution to a remarkable progress visible in the *Regierunsbezirk*, and yet preserved fully our honour as

Germans. It is this last word of your address that fills our hearts with pride.

A nation that abandons its national honour has no right of existence and no esteem in the world, especially not with your proud nation. I believe, therefore, to be fully understood, particularly by you as a soldier, when I state that the population of the Minden–Ravensberger *Land* consider the occupation as a misfortune that distresses us. What mitigated considerably the occupation in its form and effect, is the fact that you, highly honourable Colonel, have always exhibited good will and a kind heart as head of the Military Government. You had, though, as a soldier, the duty to give hard orders to us, and to pass on to us orders received from your superiors which you felt to be heavy. But we all know from daily experience, that the war had come to an end for you on that day when you took upon yourself the position as a Commander of *Bezirks*-Military-Government, that you always were anxious—more than generally known—to help the population of this district, to soften their sufferings and to give them a new vital energy after the collapse.

From the many things you did for the population I can only mention some ones.

The town of Lugde will never forget that after the horrible storm-water, which befell the town, you were present as first man and helped with advice and assistance as much as possible. The village of Fürstenau knows that you must be thanked that after the attack of the Poles they were able to rebuild the destroyed houses in spite of the building restrictions and the scarcity of materials.

We all know how carefully you dealt with the problem of refugees and how much you regretted to be forced to impose Refugee burdens upon the district in increasing numbers. The fact, that according to your words the *Regierungsbezirk* Minden need not fear a comparison with other *Bezirken*, proved that you selected and approved democratic persons as representatives of the population and good experts as heads of the administration.

Therefore we thank you with all our heart. We will do our utmost in this beautiful land of Minden–Ravensberg to fasten the democratic thoughts within the population and to take care that never again any tyrants will put the world into war and distress against the will of the people.

One sentence of your speech specially met our hearts, the sentence that you became more acquainted with the German people and that you believe in a good future for the German people. That is a special joy for us in this desperate time. This word encourages us in our work and facilitates the co-operation with Military Government. This also will make sure that you and the Gentlemen of your Military Government have gained the confidence by virtue of personal knowledge of the population of the *Land* Minden Ravensberg.

All of us ask you also to sponsor this confidence in our nation, even when you have entered on your high and responsible office in Scotland[3]. It will be your merit, if the torn connections between your country and ours will be taken up again, and thereby the way into the peaceful family of the world will be opened again in future.

In this sense we take leave from you together with the population of my district, dear Colonel, First Commander of Military Government of *Regierungsbezirk* Minden. We are glad that you will follow up the further progress of *Regierungsbezirk* with the greatest interest. May this modest collection of photos of the *Kreise* and towns of *Regierungsbezirk* Minden remind you of the place of your work in the beautiful Westphalia.

I greet you, Sir Colonel MacGregor, in the name of the representatives of the Minden-Ravensberger population and its authority as the new Commander of the *Regierungsbezirk*. We also ask you to accept the confidence that we were honoured to have received in the past months by your predecessor. We shall thank you by entire fulfilment of our duty in the knowing to do this to the best for our people.

The following year Dr Zenz wrote in English:

Dear Colonel C.M. Usher,

When writing to you today, I do it in grateful memory of the 22nd of April 1945, the date on which by your confidence, I was appointed to take over the office of

---

[3] This remark of Zenz's shows that not only British and Americans who served under Usher, but also Germans who had seen him exercise high authority with humanity and humility, expected that the British Army would reward his efforts with higher rank and even greater responsibility.

Regierungspräsident of the *Regierungsbezirk* Minden. I often think back with pleasure and gratitude to the fourteen months for which, with your benevolent assistance, we were allowed to work. Also the *Regierungsbezirk* Minden and its population have not forgotten your kindness and help, which you have demonstrated on so many occasions. Often thereafter your name has been mentioned when, in the *Regierungsbezirk*, I went to see those gentlemen who were allowed to work under you. May I assure you that your being the first Commander of Military Government in *Regierungsbezirk* Minden will always be remembered.

You were quite right in saying to me on the occasion of your departure that many and great difficulties for the German people and the *Regierungsbezirk* Minden were still to come and would be charged to us in the future. Our general hope that our conditions would improve and that, by the economic rise, we would again become more hopeful has not been fulfilled up to the present; on the contrary the difficulties became greater and greater. There has been an incessant influx of refugees from the East into the *Regierungsbezirk*. Including the evacuees from the West it has now approximately 300,000 refugees and is very limited with regard to accommodation, and the state of industry has become worse and worse because the raw materials are running short. As far as they were still available in 1945, they have been almost entirely consumed in the meantime. A bad winter which, apart from the difficulties of food-supply brought us a serious shortage of fuel, is behind us. And yet, when I look back now, we administrative authorities are proud that, during all this time, we have, together with Military Government, been able to maintain the hope for the improvement of the conditions among our population so that they remained appeased. On the occasion of our meetings we always assured ourselves that we would have complied fully with our duties if we would succeed in keeping the hope of the population alive until the slow recovery of the people would be evident.

You have certainly been informed by the gentlemen of Military Government that, in the meantime and since your departure, the *Regierungsbezirk* Minden has undergone a steady change.

I had the pleasure of knowing, in your successor, Colonel MacGregor, a gentleman who, like you, cared with great love for the *Regierungsbezirk* Minden and gave his assistance whenever he could.

At the larger conference of the *Regierungspräsidents* I could therefore, with pride, always point to the fact that, in many matters, *Regierungsbezirk* Minden could already show results where other *Regierungsbezirken* were only starting work. Also my ladies and gentlemen of the *Regierung* have always emphasized in my presence the good relations with Military Government. Therefore it was not surprising when numerous gentlemen of other *Regierungen* attempted to come to Minden.

The reconstruction is slow. In consequence of the coal-shortage the building industry cannot work to the extent required. In spite of that, many desirable projects, even though unofficially, have been completed.

I could write about much more, Sir, but I do not know in how far it is admissible. I have to restrain myself to giving general information. If your way should once more lead you to Germany, my wife and I would be very pleased to welcome both you and Mrs. Usher. We would then have an opportunity to recall the common interest during the time of your activity here and to enjoy the progress which, thanks to the efforts of you and your successor, the *Regierungsbezirk* has been able to achieve. I hope that this will come true some day. I will be pleased to write to you about my future activities.

May I heartily thank you for your letter which was a very great pleasure to me.

I am, Sir,
    Very sincerely,
        Yours, P. Zenz.

This was the experience at all levels where British and German opposite numbers developed a respect and affection for each other.

Members of Usher's Military Government staff wrote in a similar vein, thanking him for what he had taught them. They kept in touch over Caen and Minden for many years, until shortly before Usher died. Usher particularly treasured one letter from Lieutenant-Colonel Douglas MacOlive, his Civil Affairs

Officer in Bielefeld, who had been in the fish trade in Hull before the war and went on to found an engineering company in Krugersdorp, South Africa. This letter read:

Dear Colonel Usher,

I have served under many commanders but wish to record that during the execution of the most interesting and important job of my life I have had the privilege of serving under the best commander. Trust, sympathy, help and friendship on your part have helped me over many a stile. What success I have attained has been largely due to the wise counsel and treatment I have received your hands. Thank you.

Good luck and happiness to you in the future.

Yours ever,

D. MacOlive

Usher made many friends in France and Germany, people who appreciated his warmth, empathy and encouragement. His success, both in Caen and in Minden, in winning people over and gaining their willing support in rebuilding shattered communities and lost self-confidence was a tribute to his own self-belief, his moral integrity, instinctive sympathy for those who had suffered and most of all, his personal charm and character, which had warmed the most reserved, mistrusting and suspicious to him. He had shown that diplomacy, understanding and common humanity could achieve wonders where a more formalised and rigid approach might fail. Both French and German administrations pressed farewell gifts of books and other special mementos of their regions on him when the time came for him to leave them. Colonel Charles Usher had repaid the trust put in him when he was called back to the Army from the Home Guard, and had greatly enhanced Britain's standing in the eyes of the respective local communities.

CHAPTER 9

BACK IN EDINBURGH

IN June 1946 Usher returned to Britain to find that, after 35 years service as a Gordon Highlander, there was no place for him in an Army that was visibly shrinking as all the 'hostilities only' men were demobilised. For a man who had done so much to rebuild French and German self-respect, civic responsibility and self-confidence, there was to be no official recognition, either military or civil. He had been made an O.B.E. for his work with prisoners in prison camps during the First World War, while his activities in smuggling intelligence on German troop movements, which could have led to charges of spying if caught, were ignored. The D.S.O. he received for the defence of Bergues in 1940, so vital to the successful evacuation of the B.E.F., seemed a poor substitute for the higher rank and award that so many believed should have been his, and which went to others. These, however would have to suffice if his outstanding work from June 1944 to June 1946 was to be so callously ignored. He was 55 years old and had to retire, having reached the normal retirement age for his rank.

In all those years he had never had a house of his own, and he retired with just a Colonel's pension. No higher office had come his way, despite the well-meant hopes and prediction of Dr. Zenz and many others, and he now had to find some form of paid employment. Higher rank, or a title might have secured a commercial directorship in return for a name on a firm's letterhead, or a position on a Public body, but with no such prospect, Usher had to find a job where his experience would be valued. His achievements in re-establishing public services, local administration and law and order in Germany might have been suitable for a Chief Constable's position, but such posts were filled by candidates with more relevant police qualifications. Lieutenant-General Sir Andrew Thorne[1] urged the War Office that should there be a mission to Russia, Usher would be ideal for inclusion. However, as good fortune would have it, a

---

[1] Who had commanded 48 Division, in which Usherforce had defended Bergues in 1940.

successor was required for Colonel Ronald Campbell, who was retiring as the first Director of the Department of Physical Education at Edinburgh University, a position he had held since 1929. His former protégé and fellow Gordon Highlander, Charles Usher, had ideal credentials for the job. This was the perfect vocation for Usher, and he and the University were fortunate in such a good match. It was heaven-sent, and the culmination of a lifetime's achievement.

The first task was to find somewhere to live in Edinburgh, and a flat was purchased at 14 Royal Circus, a strikingly handsome row of elegant classical Georgian buildings in Stockbridge. The flat was at the top of a common stair surrounding an echoing well, and was next to the Royal Circus Hotel, with which it shared a ghost that travelled happily back and forth through the dividing wall! This was the third place where Madge had come across ghosts, and she just had to put up with it, but fortunately it was a benign spirit. The flat was home throughout Usher's time at Edinburgh University.

In Germany there had been no shortage of food or drink, or luxuries such as nylon stockings for wives or girlfriends, purchased in the American PX (Post Exchange). In Britain, however, a severe Labour Government ran an impoverished country, and oversaw unavoidably severe rationing of coal, food and clothing. There were electricity blackouts, and miners' disputes in the newly nationalised mining industry. Chatting to one respected English trade unionist, Usher received the confidential reply, 'Boogers won't work and nowt'll make 'em'. Industrial disputes were rife. Foreign currency was severely limited, and imported goods were a rare luxury.

1947 saw the inauguration of the imaginative and innovative Edinburgh International Festival of Music and Drama, a declaration to the world that Britain, and particularly Scotland, despite the privations of the past eight years, was still a beacon of culture, a home for the Arts, and an inspiration to the peoples of war-weary Europe. Responding to a call to accommodate an opera singer, Usher offered a room for an Italian tenor. The country was in the grip of austerity, a problem for a singer who required a raw egg in a glass of sherry before every performance. Neither sherry nor egg was easy to come by, but Usher's military connections saved the day, sherry and eggs being somehow obtained. (For most, the only alcohol readily obtainable was rum, and the usual offering at cocktail parties was rum and orange.)

In a landmark speech in March 1946 Churchill warned, 'An iron curtain has descended on Europe'. The Cold War had begun, and the Red Army seemed poised to sweep across Europe unopposed, Western manpower being insufficient to contain it. It was believed that it could reach the English Channel within a week. No sooner had an exhausted Britain seen off one threat than it was confronted by another, the spectre bolstered by fears of 'Reds under the bed'.

The War Office saw a possibility, remote though it might be, of invasion, and in 1952 Usher received an active commission in the Home Guard, resuscitated after disbanding at the end of the Second War. The Warsaw Pact formed a counter to NATO, the Hungarian rising was crushed by the Red Army, and the development of nuclear weapons led to an uneasy truce between America and Russia, sustained by the nightmare scenario of Mutual Assured Destruction. In 1956 Usher's appointment came to an end when the Home Guard finally stood down and was disbanded. He derived great satisfaction from having served under five Sovereigns[2] and held a commission under four.

Usher's work at the University gave him great pleasure and satisfaction. The Department of Physical Education and the University Gymnasium, incorporating the University Fencing Club, was in the Pollock Institute at 46, The Pleasance[3]. The object was to give all students the opportunity to keep the body fit and the mind alert, thus helping them with their studies.

There were two distinct tasks. First, to help the men's and women's Athletic Clubs' student office bearers with administrative work that might otherwise interfere with their studies, (e.g. finance, grounds and ground staff), and help with any sporting advice (but not coaching, which was too big a task to be feasible for such a small staff).

His successor, L.E. Liddell, in *The Story of Edinburgh Athletic Club*, summarised the origins and purpose of the Department:

> At this point it is useful to review the complementary and supplementary functions of the Department of Physical

---

[2]   Edward VII, George V, Edward VIII, George VI and Elizabeth.

[3]   Today the home, during the Edinburgh International Festival, of many Fringe acts, some of them in the theatre constructed in what used to be the Gymnasium, frequented so regularly by Usher.

Education as they have developed with the Men's and Women's Athletic Clubs under the aegis of the Athletics Committee of Court. In appointing Colonel R.B. Campbell (1929-1946) and Colonel C.M. Usher (1946-1959) as its first and second Directors of Physical Education, the University foresaw two discrete needs—to help the Athletic Clubs and to encourage the main mass of students less naturally disposed to exercise to take a sensible amount of healthful recreation. Accordingly these distinguished soldier-athletes brought the forces of their personality, experience and enthusiasm to bear upon the problems. Colonel Campbell, the pioneer, did much to provide interesting alternatives to conventional games and physical training programmes that most students had experienced at school. He realised that, with the possible exception of the naturally gifted athletes, to seek to compel intelligent young people to take part in physical activities for which they had neither ability nor enthusiasm, resulted in their pronounced and often lasting opposition to most forms of exercise. During the period of economic depression and shoestring budgets into and through the years of World War II, Colonel Campbell strove unremittingly to widen the scope and attractiveness of the subject and, later, their contribution to the nation at war. He succeeded by means of harvest camps, rambling clubs and a novel and objective system of indoor training, manifestly different from run-of-the-mill 'P.T.', and calculated to appeal to all except the physically idle. He inaugurated in 1938 a Certificate of Physical Proficiency, an acknowledgement to those students who were prepared to attend regularly enough at the Gymnasium to achieve an above average standard of general 'fitness'. At the same time he continued, with a small and enthusiastic staff of former Army P.T. instructors and a leading Scottish gymnast, to identify his Department with the Athletic Club activities.

During Colonel Usher's directorship Colonel Campbell's indoor training scheme was adapted to provide continuous recreational classes, so that students, at any convenient gap in their lecture and laboratory programme, could join in and have some exercise. This 'Floor Show', was without audience but with a sizeable if frequently changing male cast, and throughout Colonel Usher's period of office, it served many athletes as training whilst at the same time providing sufficiently intensive exercise for the less physically skilled.

Usher knew that if every joint was moved, every muscle would be conditioned, and the exercises were so arranged that, in twenty minutes, an individual could have a complete work-out without having to wait for an opportune moment, as he joined in immediately on arrival and therefore could never be late! The variety of exercises avoided repetition, and he could stay as long as he chose, without risk of boredom or over-fatigue.

The Department of Physical Education greatly aided the Athletic Club. The approach was considerate, with no interference, but willingness to help when required. It could never be said that the athlete was more welcome than anyone else, yet all found exactly what they wanted under the best possible conditions. The Athletic Club could train in the gymnasium without detriment to other users. The happy and carefree atmosphere concealed a discipline that passed unnoticed, and never needed to be enforced.

The high-achieving members of the Athletic Club were fully catered for, and it was heartening to see a physical illiterate striving happily with a rugby internationalist, both enjoying themselves to the full.

All this was second nature to Usher, who had developed and run similar, if less ambitious and polished, programmes in the prisoner-of-war camps of 1914-18.

Two excellent instructors were inherited, Major Charlie Mather and Tom Houston. One would stay on the floor for three-quarters of an hour. He was then relieved and rested for three-quarters of an hour. He was dressed like the students and was the playing captain of his team, which was his class. Work was by imitation, and words of command, thanks to floor markings to guide the students, were minimal and always given in a conversational manner.

There was no subscription. All that was required was to bring a small padlock and key for the locker provided. Showers and refreshments were available. The number of women students at the University had so increased by 1947 that Miss Sheila Cater, qualified at Bedford College, was appointed the first Director of Physical Education for women students.

There was an excellent secretary, Miss Muir, and an able Janitor, Sandy Bruce, an ex-Gordon Highlander, described as 'a most efficient Cerberus', who served for many years.

The Certificate of Physical Proficiency could be obtained by matriculated students who had attended the gym not less than 30 times in the two terms from October to March for men, and 25 times for women. They had to get 60% in the basic tests and swim one length of the swimming pool. The Examination for the Certificate was conducted by two external examiners. Training was given during the summer term. The Certificate came in an impressive red tube at the Graduation Ceremony, as did the Academic Degree, and this earned Usher a place on the platform with the robed and gowned academics.

Keeping the attendance up at the gymnasium was hard work. Student membership remained fairly constant for the next thirteen years despite many attempts to expand it. At the beginning of each Academic Year Usher would visit all the lecture halls and, thrusting the microphone aside, exhort the audience to visit the gym. He would tell them that:

> '. . . there is no such condition known to science as a state of chronic fatigue due to mental overwork. If you feel tired, you think your fatigue will vanish if you rest. You will be wrong. What you need is the right kind of exercise scientifically applied. This is available for you under most pleasant conditions in the University Gymnasium. Some exercise followed by a shower will make you feel both refreshed and exhilarated.'

He told them about the Certificate of Physical Proficiency, which was not difficult to obtain if they attended the gymnasium regularly, and that, as an additional qualification to a degree, was of considerable value when seeking employment on graduation.[4]

The distinguished Professor of Political Economy, Sir Alexander Gray, C.B.E., M.A., L.L.D. whose hobby was translating Goethe into Lallans, always followed Usher. With tousled grey hair, and endeavouring to look as though he had had a particularly heavy night, he took the microphone after Usher had gone and croaked,

> 'When I was young I just *wurrked* and look at me now!'

A contributor to the student magazine under an article headed *Elders and Betters* wrote:

---

[4]   Usher's younger son, Kenneth, gained the Certificate of Physical Proficiency, the scroll signed by his own father. He recalled 'I collected *two* red tubes on Graduation Day watched by parent, white moustache bristling proudly!'

. . . with an element of surprise that is purely military he breaks in upon our daydreams. Who has not heard, either at the entrance to the Old or the New Quad, his queries as to whether we are constipated, and if we are, his further exhortation to come to the gym. What person who has been properly brought up to have an enquiring mind could resist a trip to the Gym, in view of these commands, even though it be only to see what manner of man it is who so ruins our reveries? If he did yield to his curiosity and visited the Gym he would meet a complete enthusiast, as Colonel Usher is interested in all branches of University Sport. He would meet a man who is prepared to face a gale at Gullane to watch golf, or who appears in the guise of a Police Constable at Easter Road in order to make sure that he saw the Hibs v East Fife game. In all he would meet a man who has brought a distinguished sporting name to Athletic Club activities and who at all times does his best for students and their sports.[5]

This was a time of austerity in Britain, and there was seldom a fat man to be seen. It was noticeable that when 'the Yanks' came, they all looked over-fed compared with the British. Perhaps three-quarters of the male students had served in the armed forces, and started fit. Some were married, and the Further Education and Training Scheme grants they enjoyed, while quite generous, were not designed to permit an indulgent life style.

Exercises were intended to tone the muscles, not to reduce weight. There were the usual pieces of apparatus standard in any gym, and innovative activities. There was a wall up to a balcony at one end, and the task was to run at it and pull oneself over. Some students volunteered to help in the gym at Saughton Prison, where this exercise proved most popular! Businessmen were invited to attend during their lunch hour, and were guaranteed to increase their height by an inch if they did so!

The student magazine mentioned Usher attending professional football matches 'disguised' as a Police Constable. He was, in fact, a Special Constable, and one of the perks of the job, as well as a free uniform, was free entry to football matches, which he much preferred to parading his medals with the Royal Company of Archers! As a 'Special' operating out of Gayfield

---

5   This description bears an uncanny resemblance to the 'Jerxpert' of internment in Holland in 1918.

Square[6] there were domestic disputes to be settled at flats leading off the common stairs in the tenement blocks familiar to readers of Edinburgh alumnus Ian Rankin fifty years on.

In 1950 Usher, whose ability as a sportsman, trainer, administrator and diplomat was widely acknowledged in Scottish sporting circles, was appointed as Manager of the Scottish Team at the Empire Games at Eden Park, Auckland, New Zealand.[7]

In 1956 Usher's fluency in Russian was called upon when, during the visit of Russian Prime Minister Nikolai Bulganin and Secretary of the Communist Party, Nikita Kruschev, the Soviet Navy visited the Firth of Forth. Sailors were taken on a tour of Edinburgh and to a football match. 'They were not at all like the Russians I knew' was Usher's wistful comment.

In 1958 Usher was invited to return to Caen, where the award of the *Grand Prix du Dirigeant Sportif* was presented by a group of distinguished French sporting writers. In addition to his contacts in Caen were friendships forged at Dunkirk. General Barthélémy, who had commanded the French garrison at Bergues in 1940, was a visitor to Edinburgh, and Brigadier Sir Colin Jardine, D.S.O., M.C., Military Secretary of the B.E.F. in 1940, was a guest gun at the erstwhile family shoot at Johnstounburn[8].

Edinburgh University's athletes became a second family. What better challenge could there be than ensuring pride of place for Edinburgh among Scotland's Universities? Help, encouragement and experience was given on pitches, courts, pools and ringsides, and also in personal matters and everyday life problems. Professors threatening to exclude students struggling with academic studies were charmed into keeping them on when their retention was vital to the success of a team!

Together with Colonel P.L. Lelan, Professor of Public Health, who took a great interest in the Athletic Club and, working behind the scenes, generally helped those in trouble, it was

---

[6] The Police Station so familiar to Ian Rankin's Inspector Rebus.

[7] Details of this appointment and the trip to New Zealand can be found in Appendix 2.

[8] Johnstounburn, near the village of Humbie in East Lothian, was acquired by Andrew Usher, the donor of the Usher Hall, in 1894. It was originally an inn, built about 1625, known as the Highwayman's Haunt, as the robbers were believed to meet there prior to moving to Soutra Hill where they held up the coaches.

sometimes necessary to bail out students who, in desperation, pawned trophies won at Powderhall sprint track and were unable to redeem their pledges, or who pawned desirable books from the library. Considerable time was spent with the groundsmen, and in the search for better playing fields and facilities.

During this time, on winter holidays in Majorca, curiosity about his family, past and present, led to him editing a collection of memoirs and reminiscences. These were printed and published privately in 1956 under the title of *The Usher Family in Scotland.*

In 1959, when he was 68, the Senatus Academicus decided Usher had to retire. That he could still stand on his head on a raised beam, arms outstretched, made no difference to their decision. It was small compensation for a still-active man to be awarded an Honorary Degree of Master of Arts. The Athletic Club made him an honorary Blue and Life Member, but another forced retirement was hard to bear, and rather than spend his retirement idling away the time, he spent the next seven years contributing to and editing *The Story of Edinburgh Athletic Club (from its origin in 1866).*

In the foreword Sir Edward Appleton, Late Principal and Vice Chancellor wrote:-

> I respond most readily to a request that I should commend this Volume to its readers. For here is a chapter of our own University history, a record of the prowess of our students, generation after generation, in sports and games. We are told that, in ancient Greece, the victors of such contests were decked with garlands of wild olive; their names were inscribed in public records; heralds proclaimed their deeds, while poets sang their praises. Our student athletes, a notably modest section of our University society, would surely be embarrassed by such fulsome acclamation. It has been enough for them to have 'played for the University'.
>
> But we don't want the tide of oblivion to wash over their athletic triumphs. That is why this story about them has been written, proudly and affectionately, by Colonel Charles Usher, whose priceless service to the University as Director of Physical Training will never be forgotten. Besides serving as an inspiration to the athletes of today, I trust that these pages will also appeal to those who are now, perforce, armchair sportsmen and sports-women. And I shall count

them understandably human if they experience a thrill at seeing their own past exploits recorded with such approval.

Many triumphs and anecdotes were unearthed and many great athletes immortalised. Some, whose names are omitted in Appendix 2 only because of the need to keep the narrative flowing, are to be found there.

Piping was an abiding interest, with membership of the Royal Scottish Pipers Society and the *Piobaireachd* Society, and in 1973 Usher was made Honorary President of the latter.

Having been Vice President since 1938, he was awarded the Honorary Presidency and Life Membership of the Scottish Amateur Fencing Union.

All his life, in the Army and throughout his retirement, Usher did what he could for ex-servicemen in distress, and in 1953 he became Chairman of the Executive Committee of the Edinburgh and Midlothian Branch of the Forces Help Society, and a member of the Board of Directors of the Lord Roberts Workshops, in Edinburgh. it was gratefully acknowledged that he had a 'happy knack' of inspiring enthusiasm amongst the voluntary workers, and that he had had a marked effect on the Branch's financial strength, by guiding and encouraging the Appeals Committee to raise considerable funds. The Lord Roberts Workshop provided well-paid employment for twenty disabled soldiers, sailors and airmen, some with 60% disability. The Edinburgh factory produced all types of brushes, but donations and legacies were essential because the disabled workers' output could not compete with mass production, and income from sales depended on the efforts of disabled but mobile ex-servicemen. When Usher finally retired, at the age of 80, in 1972, he was unanimously elected Honorary President.

During this time he had also taken on the unenviable task of keeping an eye on the bar management of the Gordon Highlanders Club in Edinburgh, where too frequent replacement of staff was required.

Home became part of The White House, at 24 Dirleton Avenue in North Berwick (where he and Madge had honeymooned in 1919), on the edge of the golf course, and only a short distance from Muirfield, where, between matches, he could reminisce with friends. When the Honourable Company of Edinburgh Golfers hosted the Open Championship in 1966 and 1972, Usher was a marshal.

As Usher grew even older, and the inevitable end loomed, he looked on great social changes that affected daily life. The gentlemanly pace of life was fast disappearing. The days when a manager would get to the office at 10.00 am and knock off for a game of golf at 4.00 pm were a dim memory of a slower-paced past. American-led business practices demanded long hours in the workplace to demonstrate commitment, even if productivity might suffer. This led to the demise of amateurism, which was the basis of Usher's sporting and physical education prowess through the years. It was increasingly difficult for young athletes to get time off to compete, particularly internationally, and the finance required could no longer be funded by jumble sales or a whip round. The tide of commercialism gradually crept in under the unsatisfactory form of 'shamateurism', where sportsmen were unofficially paid for their efforts, until the inevitable result was that payment was accepted. It was a sad day for Usher.

Usher welcomed some of the technical results of progress. He certainly approved of the rugby ball made of synthetic waterproof material. Since the 1850's the ball had been made of four pieces of leather stitched together with waxed hemp thread. The best balls were made from cow-hide, free of warble marks, taken near the backbone at the butt end where the hide is much tighter in grain. But, however good the hide or the workmanship, the balls got wet, and when wet lost shape and became rounder. They also became heavy, and were soon almost indistinguishable from a medicine ball! When they were new they could be kicked prodigious distances. The new type of ball maintained its shape, could be better handled in wet conditions, and offered a consistency that had never previously been possible.

There were great changes in the construction of golf balls. The Dunlop 65, or its junior partner the Warwick, both beautifully wrapped in cellophane, were the pinnacle of the amateur golfer's ambition. It could be a major financial decision to unwrap the Dunlop 65, and winning one was a coveted prize. The covers were inevitably cut over time but this never prevented Usher deriving great satisfaction playing his disgracefully battered ball to defeat his opponent's pristine one!

Colonel Charles 'Dougie' Usher never lost his affection for the Regiment into which he had been commissioned in 1911, and he attended and helped to organise the annual Gordon Highlanders Officers Dinners held in Edinburgh, usually at the North British Hotel. On one such occasion there was confusion over the number attending, due to a misunderstanding between Regimental Headquarters and the Hotel. The formally dressed Head Waiter was adamant that the extra numbers could not be squeezed into the dining room, for 'Health and Safety' reasons, and for a time it appeared that some disappointed subalterns would have to leave and find somewhere else to dine. On becoming aware of the situation Usher took the Head Waiter aside and, with a fatherly arm around his shoulders, chatted softly and amicably to him. In no time at all the Head Waiter had been charmed into opening a nearby room, fitting it out with a properly set dining table, and sitting the delighted young officers in a room of their own where they could enjoy themselves away from the eyes of the 'old and bold'. They came through to the main dining room for the speeches and were vociferous in their praise of the old soldier who had given them such a splendid evening. It was yet another example of the charm, diplomacy and powers of persuasion of a remarkable man.

Time and tide wait for no man, and on 21st January, 1981, at the age of 89, Charles Usher died, followed a few months later by his beloved wife, Madge. He had lived life to the full, and in the words of his favourite poem, he had met 'with Triumph and Disaster' and had treated 'those two impostors just the same.' In adversity and triumph he had maintained the high standards he had set himself from the very beginning. He had served his country, his fellow men, and above all, his beloved Gordon Highlanders, faithfully, loyally and with total commitment. His many friends in all walks of life mourned his passing, but gloried in having shared a life lived so well. He was, indeed, an inspiration to all who knew him and those who came after, in every way 'A Remarkable Man'.

APPENDIX 1

WHO WERE THE USHERS?

IN the 1950s, during his time as Director of Physical Education at Edinburgh University, Charles Usher and his wife Madge spent winter holidays in Majorca, where Usher started to edit a collection of memoirs and reminiscences by earlier members of the Usher family. He was assisted in this venture by his distinguished cousin, Graham Usher. These were printed and published privately in 1956 under the title *The Usher Family in Scotland*. The book is an interesting account of the various branches of the family, full of events and personalities, but these are of little direct relevance to the career of Charles Milne Usher. The genealogy of the line, however, is covered below.

Charles Usher's great-grandfather, Andrew Usher (1782-1855), wrote 'Certain it is that the Usher family came from Ireland'. Those Irish Ushers came originally from England in the 13th century. Tancred of Weems, in *The People of Rulewater* (1907), said 'Two men of the name of Usher, who were masons, came over to Scotland from Ireland c.1400 and settled in Eildon. By their industry they prospered and became possessors of land in Darnick.' Over some 250 years those Ushers became substantial proprietors. There is, however, evidence that Ushers were already present in Scotland in the 14th century. An Usher who was in high favour with, and a personal friend of King David II of Scotland (d. 1370), married a daughter of Aymer de Macuswell, progenitor of the present family of Maxwell. Later Scottish Ushers intermarried with the Ramsay and Wardrop families.[1] The name 'Usher' stood out as different from all the great Border families of the day. There are Ushers in Northern Ireland but they went over there from Scotland during the 'Plantation' era of the 17th century.

Recorded in the Exchequer Rolls of Scotland for 1330 is Robert Usher, Provost of Peebles, and in the Close Roll of the fourth year of the reign of England's King Richard II, Finlay

---

[1] Andrew Usher, brother of Charles Usher's grandfather, who gifted the Usher Hall to Edinburgh, had a coat of arms that included the motto of both the Ramsays and the Wardrops.

Usher, a Scottish Merchant is named. The earliest Usher to whom Charles Usher's family could date their ancestry was the Border Laird, Usher of Faftenfield (c. 1547), a presumed descendant of one of the two masons. This Laird Usher was a brother-in-law of Gibbie Hateley of Gattonside, who, in his Will of 1547 stated that Usher was to receive 'a hunder merks Scotis and my nobbler and two auld pricklers which I took frae the lads o' the Border when they came ae nicht to harrie me'.[2] An unnamed family member was hanged in the Grassmarket in Edinburgh for cattle reiving, and another appeared to get off by bribing the hangman with a shilling.

Being Presbyterians could have been hazardous for Laird Usher's grandson, John, born 1651, and his son James, born 1672, because of religious persecution. Scotland had supported the monarchy, and after the beheading of Charles I, had crowned Charles II King in 1651. Scotland welcomed the Restoration, but was less happy in accepting the religion imposed by the Crown. Presbyterianism held that man owes his allegiance directly to God with no need for intercession from King, bishops and prelacy. The King, of Roman Catholic sympathies, but wise enough to keep these to himself, wished to impose the Episcopal form of religion on Scotland. He said Presbyterianism was not a religion 'for gentlemen' and left the English Church to impose bishops and priests on Scottish parishes, but congregations melted away along with their Presbyterian ministers.

Ministers who did not conform were removed from their charges. Many left their parishes, their manses and stipends and took to the hills, where they preached to their congregations in outdoor 'conventicles'. Inspired by the National Covenant of 1638, that Charles II had repudiated in 1661, they were known as Covenanters, and when they preached, the gatherings were considered treason. Covenanters emigrated or were pursued, cut down, shot, captured and imprisoned in the Tolbooth or the Bass Rock, where they were tortured. Many were hanged at the Mercat Cross in Edinburgh's Grassmarket. They died, many cheerfully, as martyrs entering into glory. Giving shelter to Covenanters was treason, punishable by death.

---

[2] This came from a document entitled 'A Literary Curiosity'. The family copy was lost in a fire, but it is just possible another copy exists somewhere.

For the Ushers, things began to look up when James' son, John, acquired lands in Darnick, including Toftfield. John's only son, James, married a hardy lady, Margaret Grieve, who produced 11 children. One of these, Andrew, was an intrepid businessman who saw many successes and reversals. The family was closely associated with neighbour Sir Walter Scott.

The West Indies provided drama and ill-fortune to Ushers who ventured there over the centuries. Hugh Usher was drowned returning from Jamaica in 1832. Thomas and George, who grew coffee in Ceder Valley in Jamaica, died there, George of yellow fever. James drowned in 1807 when his ship, the brig *Margaritta*, foundered between South America and the West Indies. William[3] also drowned, as a one-year-old baby.

Andrew, son of James Usher and Margaret Grieve, finally found himself in the spirit trade, and took his two youngest sons, Andrew and John, into partnership, while he helped his eldest son, James, to set up as a brewer in Merchant Street, Edinburgh. James was later joined by his younger brother, Thomas, to form the brewing company known as James and Thomas Usher. James gained fame as the inventor of the first steam-powered plough[4] (a model of which is in the Science Museum), for which he was honoured by the Highland Agricultural Society. James had ten children, including Andrew James b. 1839 and Robert Henry. One of the daughters, Charles Usher's Aunt Carrie, was a friend of Robert Louis Stevenson.

Robert Henry (Harry) Usher, Master Brewer, the company's London representative, married Alexandrina Law Milne (Ina), the daughter of John Milne and his wife Elizabeth Sara. Harry was 39 years old, and lived at 2 Castle Terrace, Richmond. He was third Captain of the Royal Wimbledon Golf Club, a member

---

[3] Hugh, Thomas, George, James and William were all brothers of Andrew Usher.

[4] The steam plough contributed to James' early demise. The plough was on show at an exhibition on the Meadows in Edinburgh but James, on account of illness, had not been able to go and see it. The Show authorities decided to run the machine down to James's house for the inventor to see. By coincidence, James, feeling better, determined to visit the Exhibition in his dog-cart. The plough and the dogcart met in Lothian Road. The horse, 'spooked' by the noise and the appearance of the plough, threw James out of the trap on to the road. He was very badly shaken and died shortly afterwards.

of C Company, the London Scottish Rifle Volunteers, a keen shot and fisherman. Alexandrina was 25. Her parents lived at Trinity Grove, Leith. The family firm, John Milne and Son, of Edinburgh, were brass founders, gas meter and gas apparatus manufacturers, and they had a London branch.

Alexandrina's mother, a staunch member of the Church of Scotland, was worried that her daughter's suitor might prefer golf to church on Sunday. Harry hoped she would understand that, after a week in London, he had to get out into the fresh air, rather than sit in a stuffy church, but he did reassure her that on the matter of belief he was in agreement with the Church's doctrine—with the exception of predestination, which he could not fathom. In any case his view of God transcended any mere form, Presbyterian, Episcopalian, Greek or Roman. It was touch and go, but he stuck to his guns and, fortunately, everybody who met Harry thought highly of him. She was won over. Harry and Ina were married on 18th June 1879 at North Leith.

The union produced two daughters, Ina and Elsa, and three sons, James, John and Charles (born 1891), who were later known in Edinburgh as the 'rugger brothers'. Harry returned to Scotland in 1895, when he and his brother Andrew James left the Brewery, and settled at Glenord, 8 Spylaw Road, Edinburgh. The firm had lost money in the London market, but Andrew James and Harry opposed a policy of granting loans in the Scottish trade, while their uncle, Thomas, favoured making advances, with due caution, to expand trade. James and Harry were bought out in 1895, and the firm became Thomas Usher and Son with limited liability. Thomas was Chairman and Managing Director.

Three years later Harry caught a bad cold while fishing on the Tweed. The cold turned to pneumonia, and he died, leaving Alexandrina to bring up the family on her own.

As if the early death of their father were not enough, the family suffered further, tragic, setbacks. Early one morning the elder daughter Ina, aged 7, found she was unable to stand. The diagnosis was polio. The medical procedure, undergone on the kitchen table, was horrific. Without anaesthetic a nail was driven through her left heel to 'deaden the pain' and bone and flesh were removed and replaced with cork! Despite having to wear long lace-up boots and walk on two sticks, she went to school in Brussels, and worked gruelling hours in Military Hospitals during World War I, making beds and lifting patients. In World War II she was Assistant County Director for Midlothian, with rank equivalent to Lieutenant-Colonel. She adored her youngest brother and kept newspaper reports of every rugby match he played in a bulging scrap book over four inches thick. Very personable, she turned down numerous offers of marriage, as she felt that she would be a burden on her spouse. Elsa, the second daughter, was, sadly, 'slow', but a valued child minder.

Charles 'Dougie' Usher and his wife, Madge, had two sons, Iain Douglas (born 1920) and Kenneth Milne Douglas (born 1927). Iain was commissioned into the Royal Engineers in 1939. He served with the 4th Indian Division in North Africa and cleared mines at El Alamein. He commanded a Field Company in Burma and was present at the surrender of the Japanese in Singapore. After the war he served in Germany and Cyprus and was a graduate of the Staff College. Iain shared Charles Usher's talent for languages. When in India he learned Urdu, passing at the Higher level when all his contemporaries were still struggling with the first grade. He could write Urdu and Hindi. He left the Army in 1957, and died in 2004.

Usher's younger son, Kenneth, volunteered in March 1945, aged 17, despite being deaf in one ear. His father had 'schooled' him in how to get past his medical! He enlisted at Cameron Barracks, Inverness, and was posted to India, where he was commissioned into The Gordon Highlanders from the Officer Training School, Bangalore. He served with the 1st Battalion in Germany until 1948, when he was demobbed. While at Edinburgh University he joined the 4th/7th Gordons. He served as ADC to HRH The Duke of Gloucester in 1949 when the Duke was Lord High Commissioner to the General Assembly of the Church of Scotland. While in Edinburgh he trained with the 9th Battalion, The Royal Scots, but went to annual camp with 4th/7th Gordons. He left the Territorial Army when posted by his employer to Southern Rhodesia in 1951.

Charles Usher therefore had the profound satisfaction of seeing both his sons have successful careers in the British Army, with one of them serving in his beloved Gordon Highlanders. Another great source of pride was that both his sons possessed university degrees, Iain with a BSc from the Military College of Science[5], Shrivenham, (as well as his psc from the Staff College) and Kenneth with an MA (Hons) from Edinburgh.

---

[5] The Military College of Science moved to Shrivenham in 1946. It became the Royal Military College of Science in 1953.

APPENDIX 2

SPORTING PROWESS

The Merchiston Years

A T Merchiston Castle School, Charles Usher starred in inter-school rugby matches, against The Royal High School and George Watson's College, from the age of 14 onwards, scoring many tries. He was 'a good and enthusiastic forward, who plays football of the best Scotch type, never sparing himself and always going hard, winning or losing'. 'Would we had more of them' the commentator added. He was Captain of the XV in 1909/10, his last season, and in the following year the success of the team was to a great extent due to the discipline he had left behind. It was tough going; shorts remained unwashed from the beginning of term to the end, and got so muddy that they could stand up on their own! One unfortunate result of this cavalier approach to laundry was a number of cases of impetigo! So accomplished was Usher at rugby, that in his last year at Merchiston the Scottish Rugby Union wanted him to play for Scotland. His mentors, however, felt that he should wait until he was physically more mature, and the offer was, regretfully, declined.

He was very fast on his feet, which was in part the secret of his success on the rugby pitch (he won the half-mile open in his penultimate year). His strength, power and fleetness of foot on the rugby field and athletics track were matched by his suppleness, sense of balance and agility in gymnastics, where he stood out from his peers. It was no surprise when he was selected for the Gym VIII and Display Team. He was noted as a good goalkeeper at hockey, and was an International trialist, but he did not follow it up because rugby took precedence, and the two sports were effectively mutually exclusive.

He gained his cricket colours in his last year. Reviews did not spare players, but spurred them on to greater endeavour. Of Usher they said, 'not a smart wicket keeper, but sound in most respects except stumping, being able to take catches and put down the wicket quite well, is no batsman, but has considerable scoring powers and always made runs when wanted'. Match reports said of him:

Usher going in first hit with such power that he made 65 not out in a very short time, and he had the bowling honours to his credit, for he took 6 wickets. (1907, 4th XI v Watsons)

Usher played magnificently for 103 not out, which was obtained in a very short time as a result of very hard hitting. He also had 3 wickets. (1907, 4th XI v Watsons)

He was last man in, top scorer for 35 not out and scored the winning hit. (2nd XI v. Edinburgh University 'B')

While still at school he was selected to play cricket for the Grange Cricket Club.

Rugby

The fiercely competitive sport of rugby was character-building. Rugby demanded a combination of all the virtues, courage, discipline and stamina, and fighting on when all seems lost. In the rough and tumble of such a physical sport there were inevitable clashes between players on opposing sides, but there was seldom any sending off. There were no replacements, and if a player was injured, his team had to play on without him. There were no substitutes. The ethos differentiated the game developed in the public schools from commercial Association Football. One of the first questions the senior partners of august legal firms in Edinburgh, great trading houses of Empire, Shell Oil, the Indian and Sudan Civil Services, and Service Chiefs would ask their aspiring cadets was 'Play rugby?'

The Pre-First War Years

Usher played for London Scottish in 1911/12, and for the Army against the Navy in 1912. On 16th March 1912 came his first cap for Scotland as back row lock forward against England at Inverleith. A pre-match *Scotsman* said:

It is difficult to see how Scotland can escape defeat. If it does it will be a surprise indeed; if Scotland wins it will be little short of a sensation.

Scotland v England, 1912

The cynics were wrong. In a hard game the English pack lost J.A. King with two broken ribs, and their full-back W.R. Johnston, suffered concussion after two hard tackles. With England playing one man short, the Scottish forwards dominated, and there was good passing by their backs, but the

English tackling was sound. The half-time score was 0-0. Early in the second half, with the Scotland pack dominating, J.L. Boyd passed the ball down the line to W.R. Sutherland, who scored in the corner. A dash from H. Broughham from the English 25, hotly pursued by J.G. Will, led to a sensational equaliser. Will caught up with and tackled Brougham, but the ball went loose and J.G.G. Birkett dribbled it over the line for D. Holland to touch down. The depleted English pack redoubled their efforts and got more possession, and it looked as though they might win. However, a bad pass in front of the posts was picked up by Usher, who scored the winning try, converted by the Captain, J.C. MacCallum. Scotland, against the odds, had secured a famous victory, winning 8-3 (1 goal, 1 try to 1 try) to claim the Calcutta Cup.

Scotland:

W.M. Dickson (Blackheath), W.R. Sutherland (Hawick), W. Burnet (Hawick), A.W. Angus (Watsonians), J.G. Will (Cambridge University), J.L. Boyd (United Services), E. Milroy (Watsonians), J.M.B. Scott (Edinburgh Academicals), F.H. Turner (Liverpool), C.M. Usher (London Scottish), D.M. Bain (Edinburgh Academicals), J.C. MacCallum (Watsonians), L. Robertson (United Services), J. Dobson (Glasgow Academicals), D.D. Howie (Kirkcaldy).

England:

W.R. Johnston (Bristol), A.D. Roberts (Northern), R.W. Poulton (Harlequins), J.J.G. Birkett (Harlequins), H. Brougham (Harlequins), A.D. Stoop (Harlequins), J.A. Pym (Blackheath), A.H. MacIlwaine (United Services), J.H. Eddison (Headingley), R.C. Stafford (Bedford), J.A. King (Headingley), D. Holland (Devonport Albion), R. Dibble (Newport), N.A. Wodehouse (United Services), A.L. Kewney (Rockcliffe).

Referee: Mr F. Gardiner (Ireland).

Amongst the formidable players in those teams were Wattie Sutherland, who won 13 caps between 1910 and 1913. A superb wing three-quarter, worshipped in the Borders, and rated together with W.E. Kyle as the greatest of Border players, Wattie was killed in the war. Another to die was Milroy, Scotland's brilliant scrum half, who won 12 caps between 1912 and 1914.

F.H. Turner, with 15 caps, and one of the very best forwards, from Sedbergh was also killed. J.G. Will was a great wing, handy and fast. J.M.B. Scott won 21 caps between 1907 and 1913. He typified the best sort of hard working Scottish forward.

On the English side was the Irishman W.R. Johnston at full back who caught and kicked outstandingly well. He won 16 caps. R.W. Poulton was a first class centre three-quarter, light on his feet, with an uncanny ability to spot the gap. He was killed in the Great War, to England's great loss. J.G.G. Birkett was the biggest centre in international rugby at the time, thrusting in attack and excellent in defence. A.D. (Adrian) Stoop was one of the greatest stand-offs ever. J.A. (Jack) King, killed in August 1916, was possibly the best of the small-size forwards. R. Dibble was a hefty, indefatigable forward, while N.A. Wodehouse was a superb scrum leader who survived the First War only to be lost as an Admiral commanding a convoy in the Second. A.L. Kewney, a great red-headed forward from Northumberland, won 16 caps between 1906 and 1912.

France v Scotland, 1913

On 1st January, 1913, Usher ran on to the *Parc des Princes* for the fourth International between France and Scotland. On a lovely sunny day with hardly any wind, and 25,000 supporters, the largest and most enthusiastic crowd to watch a rugby match in France so far, the Scottish team was piped on to the field to a great welcome, and kicked off. They attacked and for the first ten minutes occupied the French 25, but the French tackled well and their scrums held. The French went on the offensive, and a fine run by Dufau nearly led to a score, with Burgun missing a dropped goal. Soon they were back in Scotland's half, and three minutes later the stadium erupted as Mauriat scored the first try. Seven minutes later, Stewart scored two tries in rapid succession, the first between the posts. Turner converted the first.

At half time the score was France 3-Scotland 8, (1 try to 1 goal, 1 try).

Scotland dominated the second half, most of which was spent in the French 25. Gordon scored after a magnificent run, and Turner converted. Sutherland missed a try by inches, and Abercrombie attempted a penalty that struck the post. With five minutes left, Abercrombie, after a long run, passed to Gordon who sent Stewart in for the touchdown. Before the final whistle Gordon scored a try, converted by Turner.

The final score was France 3-Scotland 21, (1 try to 3 goals, 2 tries)

There was an unpleasant incident when the match ended. In the first half the French were awarded a number of penalty kicks, but in the second half most of the penalties were against them. The French crowd protested vociferously at every decision against them. When the game ended the referee was manhandled by irate French fans, and a French N.C.O. in uniform, who felt that the referee, '*un Anglais*', had favoured the Scottish team, approached him so menacingly that the police arrested him. The soldier, who was liberated almost immediately, was cheered by the crowd, and carried shoulder high around the field. When tempers cooled, however, good nature prevailed and nothing more came of the protest.

France:

F. Dutour (Stade Toulousain), Dufau (Stade Bordelaise Université Club), G. Lane (Racing Club de France,), J. Sentilles (Stadoceste Tarbais), P. Jaurreguy (Stade Toulousain), Hebenbaight (Aviron Bayonnais), M. Burgun (Racing Club de France), P. Mauriat (Football Club de Lyon), M. Pascare (Toulouse Olympique), J. Sebedio (Stadoceste Tarbais), M. Thil (Stade Bordelais Université Club), G. Lieuveille (Stade Bordelais Université Club), M. Legrain (Racing Club de France), M. Mounie (Stade Toulousain), Fernano Forgues (Aviron Bayonnais).

Scotland:

W.M. Dickson (Oxford University), W.A. Stewart (London Hospital), A.W. Angus (Watsonians), R.E. Gordon (Woolwich), W.R. Sutherland (Hawick), E. Milroy (Watsonians), A.W. Gunn (Royal High School), F.H. Turner (Liverpool), C.M. Usher (London Scottish), P.C.B. Blair (Cambridge University), C.H. Abercrombie (United Services), G.A. Ledingham (Aberdeen Grammar School F.P.), D.D. Howie (Kirkcaldy), D.M. Bain (Oxford University), J.B. McDougal (Greenock Wanderers).

Referee: T. Baxter (England).

Burgun was a clever stand-off, who also played centre and on the wing. He was killed in the War, as was the great Scottish forward, Abercrombie.

Scotland v Wales, 1913

On 1st February 1913, Wales came to Inverleith. Snow fell from Friday evening to Saturday mid-day. The ground was muddy, but it was a bright day with a cold wind blowing towards Ferry Road. The crowd of about 18,000 included many Welsh supporters, bedecked with leeks and daffodils and in full voice, superbly confident of victory.

Scotland won the toss and played with the wind, but Dickson's kick was charged down, and in the eighth minute Clem Lewis scored. Profiting by a smart tackle by Angus on Trew, the Scots attacked, but lacked cohesion. Usher made a commendable effort to improve the Scottish position, and Stewart dashed down the touch-line, but was overwhelmed by the Welsh defence. The ball came out to Howie, who called a mark in a good position, but Turner failed at goal. It was at this stage that Scotland did best. They hovered on the visitors' line, but Trew was a potent threat, while Williams saved an awkward situation with a good mark. A free kick midfield gave Abercrombie a chance to test his powers at goal, but the effort, though splendidly directed, fell short of the mark. From then till the interval the Scots defended desperately. Dickson showed great pluck in stopping a Welsh invasion, but with Angus handling badly, the Scottish line was in danger, until Scott and Robertson stemmed the flood, and Sutherland, stepping into the picture for the first time, improved matters with a good kick to touch. At the interval Wales led by a try to nil.

For most of the second half Scotland were pinned in their own half, with the Welsh in control. Angus failed to take a pass from Lockhart; the Welsh seized the ball and Hirst had an inspiring run on the touch line. He was well supported, but the attack was smothered by effective tackling, while a few minutes later a brilliant tackle by Stewart kept H. Lewis out. Scrum followed scrum, free kicks were plentiful but the play was unimpressive. Welsh supporters were jubilant as the Scottish line endured one trial after another. H. Lewis looked certain to score, but a forward pass robbed Wales of their reward. Then Dickson found touch with a magnificent kick, but the Scottish advantage was lost, and they were immediately on the defensive again. There were a couple of drop goal attempts by J.C.M. Lewis, the second going wide and dropping behind the Scottish line. Both Stewart and Bruce-Lockhart failed to judge the bounce and H.

Lewis won the race to the ball to score a try, converted by J.C.M. Lewis.

Final score: Scotland 0-Wales 8 (1 goal, 1 try).

Scotland:

W.M. Dickson (Oxford University), W.A. Stewart (London Hospital), R.E. Gordon (London Scottish), A.W. Angus (Watsonians), W.R. Sutherland (Hawick), J.H. Bruce-Lockhart (London Scottish), E. Milroy (Watsonians), F.H. Turner (Liverpool), L. Robertson (London Scottish), C.M. Usher (London Scottish), P.C.B. Blair (Cambridge University), C.H. Abercrombie (United Services), D.M. Bain (Oxford University), J.M.B. Scott (Edinburgh Academicals), D.D. Howie (Kirkcaldy).

Wales:

R.F. Williams (Cardiff), H. Lewis (Swansea), W.J. Trew (Swansea), T. Jones (Pontypool), G.L. Hirst (Newport), J.C.M. Lewis (Cardiff), R. Lloyd (Pontypool), H. Uzzell (Newport), G. Stephens (Neath), F. Perrett (Neath), Rev. A. Davies (Swansea), P. Jones (Newport), F. Andrews (Pontypool), R. Richards (Aberavon), W. Jenkins (Cardiff).

Referee: Mr S.H. Crawford (Ireland).

Edinburgh Academical J.M.B. Scott was an outstanding forward who had won 21 caps by 1913. It was this bruising encounter against Wales that led Usher to pack his stockings with newspaper when playing against Wales! On the Welsh side was Dicky Lloyd, one of the best ever to punt, drop or place kick a rugby ball.

Scotland v Ireland, 1913

On 22nd February, 1913, Usher was back at Inverleith to do battle with the Irish. This time Scotland won easily in a free scoring match by 29 points to 14.

Weather conditions were perfect, bright sunshine prevailing throughout the day, with a light breeze blowing towards the Ferry Road end. Attendance was around 18,000, with a fairly small number from Ireland, and some Irish students from Edinburgh University, congregated below the Press box, singing and waving green banners. Dr Guthrie's School bandsmen played the Irish side on to the field, and their pipers played on the Scottish XV.

Ireland kicked off and their backs immediately got to work, but Bennett was crowded out. Effective dribbling by Blair led the Scots to the other end, where Bowie's cross-kick was followed up by Sutherland, who crossed the Irish line, but was held up by sheer force of numbers. However, after five minutes the ball passed swiftly through Milroy, Bowie, and Gordon, to Stewart, for the London Hospital player to score a fine try, converted by Turner. McIvor led the Irish to Scottish territory, and although their backs were not impressive, Lloyd consistently gained ground. After the Scottish defence had been almost breached by Boyd Campbell, Minch made a clever dash for the line. He was frustrated, but from the ensuing scrum on the Scottish line, Shute stole over for a try converted by Lloyd. It was an exciting game and the Scots regained the lead when Stewart, getting the ball in midfield, outran the opposition for a roundly applauded try, converted by Turner.

Disaster followed when Dickson dislocated his shoulder, leaving the team a man short, there being no substitutes in those days. Pearson took over at full-back and Scott moved from the scrum to the three-quarter line. The side coped well. Bain got the ball out to Gordon who was overtaken by McIvor, but managed to pass to Stewart, who scored his third try between the posts for Turner to convert. Scotland were in control, and Usher scored after a forward rush. At half-time Scotland led 18-5 (3 goals, 1 try to 1 goal).

In the second half Scott moved to full back and Pearson to three-quarter. Quick ball from Milroy set Pearson darting down the wing to outwit the defence and pass to Bowie who scored. Turner converted. (Pearson, Milroy and Bowie were Watsonians.) Scott kicked a long ball to touch. From the resulting line-out the ball went along the three-quarter line to Stewart, who went in for a try at the corner flag. This time, Turner could not get the distance with his kick.

The Irish forwards broke away and Stokes scored, for Lloyd to convert. Holmes broke through and Lloyd dropped a goal. The Scots rallied after this Irish onslaught, the forwards pushed on and Purves touched down for a try, to jubilation from the ecstatic crowd.

The final score was, Scotland 29-Ireland 14, (4 goals, 3 tries to 3 goals, 1 of them dropped).[1]

Scotland:

W.M. Dickson (Oxford University), W.A. Stewart (London Hospital), R.E. Gordon (London Scottish), J. Pearson (Watsonians), W.R. Sutherland (Hawick), T.C. Bowie (Watsonians), E. Milroy (Watsonians), F.H. Turner (Liverpool), J.M.B. Scott (Edinburgh Academicals), G.H.H.P Maxwell (Edinburgh Academicals), L. Robertson (London Scottish), C.M. Usher, (London Scottish), W.D.C.L. Purves (London Scottish), D.M. Bain (Oxford University), P.C.B. Blair (Cambridge University).

Ireland:

W.G. McConnell (Landsdown), C.V. McIvor (Dublin University), G. Holmes (Dublin University), J.B. Minch (Bective Rangers), F. Bennett (Belfast Collegians), R.A. Lloyd (Liverpool), H.M. Read (Dublin University), G.Shute (Dublin University), G.V. Killeen (Garryowen), S.B.B. Campbell (Derry and Edinburgh University), J.E. Finlay (Queen's College, Belfast), E.W. Jeffares (Dublin Wanderers), P. Stokes (Blackrock College).

Referee: Mr J.Baxter (England).

Pearson of Watsonians was another to die in the coming conflict. A very good centre despite slight build, he won 12 caps up to 1913.

England v Scotland, 1913

Next was Twickenham on 15th March, 1913, where England won the Calcutta Cup and their first Grand Slam, in front of the Prince of Wales and 25-30,000 spectators. They won 3-0 (1 try to nil) in one of the hardest games ever played between these two sides, with Usher, Turner and Purves 'conspicuous in good work'. It was a fast match, but resolute defence by both sides

---

[1] A 'goal' was scored when the ball was kicked through the goalposts, over the cross-bar. An unconverted try was shown as a 'try', worth 3 points, but a successful conversion earned 2 points, which turned the try to a 'goal', worth 5 points. A drop goal was also marked down as a 'goal', but its value was 4 points.

restricted scoring, and the English backs were kept at bay by Scotland save for the thickset L.G. Brown fighting his way through to the corner flag for his try in the first half.

England:

W.R. Johnston (Bristol), C.N. Lowe (Cambridge University), F.N. Tarr (Leicester), R.W. Poulton (Harlequins), V.H.M. Coates (Bath), W.J.A. Davies (R.N./United Services), F.E. Oakley (R.N./United Services), J.A.S. Ritson (Northern), J.A. King (Headingley), J.E. Greenwood (Cambridge University), L.G. Brown (Oxford University), N.A. Wodehouse, (R.N./United Services), S. Smart (Gloucester), G. Ward (Leicester), C.H. Pilman (Blackheath).

Scotland:

W.M. Wallace (Cambridge University), W.R. Sutherland (Hawick), E.G. Loudon-Shand (Oxford University), J. Pearson (Watsonians), J.B. Sweet (Glasgow High School F.P.), T.C. Bowie (Watsonians), E. Milroy (Watsonians), J.M.B. Scott (Edinburgh Academicals), F.H. Turner (Liverpool), C.M. Usher (London Scottish), P.C.B. Blair (Cambridge University), D.M. Bain (Oxford University), G.H.H.P. Maxwell (Edinburgh Academicals), W.D.C.L. Purves (London Scottish), L. Robertson (London Scottish).

Referee: Mr T.D. Schofield (Wales).

For England, C.N. Lowe was very fast and a fearless tackler. He was one of the small band who played both before and after the first war, winning 25 caps. F.N. Tarr, a great centre, could take a pass at speed, had a long stride and was good in defence. W.J.A. Davies handled the ball well and kicked well. F.E. Oakley was a grand naval forward, first class with the ball at his feet. His submarine was sunk in the first months of the 1914 war. S. Smart was capped 12 times between 1913 and 1920, being another of the few to play before and after the First War. C.H. Pillman was the best in the England team, a true wing forward, first class in attack and defence.

In 1913 Usher played for London Scottish v London Hospital at Richmond. Scottish Scorers were Turner and Usher, but Hospital won 9-6 (2 goals, 1 dropped to 2 tries).

Scotland v England, 1914

Usher appeared for the Army against the Navy, but played in only one International in 1914, at Inverleith on Saturday, 21st March, when England won by the narrowest of margins, 16-15 (2 goals, 2 tries to 1 goal, 1 dropped goal, 2 tries), and in doing so won the Championship and Triple Crown for the second successive season. Friday's rain had left the ground heavy, but the weather was good except for a strong north wind. With 25,000 spectators, probably the biggest crowd ever seen at Inverleith, there was not a seat in the stand or enclosure left unoccupied. Special trains brought enthusiasts from England. The proceedings were enlivened by the brass and pipe bands from Dr Guthrie's Industrial School, who played the teams on to the field, the English team coming on first to the strains of *John Peel* and the Scots following to *Scotland the Brave*, both 'heartily received', although the latter probably not by Usher who had a particular aversion to it! The crowd was rewarded with a thrilling, fast 'classic' game with a brilliant display of rugby by both sides, who were to have eleven players, over a third of their number, killed in the coming war.

After twenty minutes, Turner passed to Will who scored at the left corner but Lowe soon equalised for England. In the second half Scotland's forwards went furiously into action and Turner sent Huggan over to score on the right corner flag. The worried English supporters were rewarded by their team getting three good tries. Lowe touched down between the posts and Harrison converted, Lowe scored his third try and Poulton the next, to put England ahead. Scotland were not finished, and a strong run by Huggan led to a dropped goal by Bowie. Will made a couple of outstanding sprints for the line and on the second touched down for Turner to convert. The result was on a knife-edge but full time ended Scotland's chance to reverse the score.

Scotland:

W.M. Wallace (Cambridge University), J.L. Huggan (London Scottish), A.W. Angus (Watsonians), R.M. Scobie (R.M.C./London Scottish), J.G. Will (Cambridge University), T.C. Bowie (Watsonians), E. Milroy (Watsonians), C.M. Usher (London Scottish), A.W. Symington (Cambridge University), A.D. Laing (Royal High School F.P.), G.H.H.P.

Maxwell (Edinburgh Academicals), E.T. Young (Glasgow Academicals), F.H. Turner (Liverpool), A.R. Ross (Edinburgh University), I.M. Pender (London Scottish).

England:

W.R. Johnston (Bristol), C.N. Lowe (Cambridge University), J.H.D. Watson (Blackheath), R.W. Poulton (Liverpool), A.J. Dingle (Hartlepool Rovers), H.C. Harrison (R.N./United Services), A.F. Maynard (Cambridge University), J.E. Greenwood (Cambridge University), L.G. Brown (London H./Blackheath), J. Brunton (North Durham), S. Smart (Gloucester), G. Ward (Leicester), C.H. Pillman (Blackheath).

Referee: Mr T.D. Schofield (Wales).

Usher met J.E. Greenwood and L.G. Brown in the pack. Greenwood, a grand forward, had 13 caps and Brown was one of the best in the scrum and in the loose. He was another to play before and after the war as was S. Smart, with 12 caps between 1913 and 1920.

Irrespective of whom they played for, those amateurs were the greatest friends and enjoyed each others' company. When Edgar Mobbs (wing and centre three-quarter who ran in such a way that his knees got the chins of those tackling him), Jack King, (the best small forward of his time), L.A.N. Slocock (one of the best big forwards) and others, including Usher, hijacked a hansom-cab and bundled the driver into the back, Mobbs got into the driver's seat, King leapt on to the horse, and they drove the length of Piccadilly and back without incident. In 1917 Mobbs, a Lieutenant-Colonel, was killed at Zillebeke while personally attacking a machine-gun post. Jack King fell at Guillemont in 1916, and Slocock was also killed in the War. Usher and his fellow-internationalists mourned the loss of these fine men with whom they had played alongside or battled against fiercely but fairly on the pitch.

The War Years

Usher was a prisoner-of-war from 27th August, 1914 until the end of the war. Throughout those years he encouraged prisoners to keep fit through a programme of physical training and sports. The sports extended to international matches in the prison camps, reported in the news sheets produced by the prisoners.

While they might not compare with pre-war internationals, they were hotly contested, and the teams often contained players of much sporting ability.

The first sports reports appeared in *The Torgau Lyre*. These include an account of an International football match between England and France on 13th October, 1914. The term 'England' used here actually denotes Great Britain, as the team sheet shows. Usher, the consummate rugby player, was more than happy to play in this game, in goal.

England v France

The weather conditions were favourable for a fast, sporting game. The teams were

France:

Dugli (goal), Vandeburch, Floquet, Cloy, Chamboredon, Khan, Ragou, Catou, Beaumont, Dellague, Romain.

England:

Usher (G.H.) goal, Carthew (Suffolk), Burrows (5D.G.), Beaman (R.A.M.C.), Roach (Connaught R.), Nicholls (Suffolk), Robertson (G.H.), Bowering (E. Surrey), Constable (Warwick), Pereira (Suffolk), Mackie (R.D.F.).

Referee. *M.* Wiullaume (Boulognis F.C.).

Constable started the game for the Islanders. There was fine play on both sides in the first period, Chamboredon, Beaumont and Dellague conspicuous on the French side while Burrows, Roach, Constable and Bowering put in sterling work for the Englishmen. Half time score, England 0-France 0.

After the restart the English bombarded the French goal and Dugli made some magnificent saves. Finally Bowering netted from a beautiful pass from Beaman. The stalwart 'medico' was on top form in the latter stages and proved a stumbling block to many of the French attacks. Time came soon after with the score unaltered. Result: England 1-France 0.

Usher took part in any sport played in the prison camps. He even played, with two other Gordon Highlanders, Lieutenants

D.W. Hunter-Blair and A.W.M. Robertson, in the Eton Field Game, in total ignorance of the rules.

The Post-First War Years

Usher was soon back on the rugby field. On 5th April, 1919 the Mother Country (a team from the home countries, forerunner of the British and Irish Lions) met New Zealand at Inverleith in the Inter-Services and Dominion Tournament.

A crowd of 15,000 saw a great fight from start to finish. New Zealand led at half-time by two tries to nil. Their strong forwards followed up under high balls and handled like backs, while their speedy backs, Storey and Ford outplayed Day and Sloan. Fine handling by Lewis, Pickles and Cullen let Day touch down in the corner, but the New Zealanders were in Mother Country territory throughout the second half, and won the day. The final score was New Zealand 6-Mother Country 3 (2 tries to 1 try).

Mother Country:

Major B.S. Cumberlege, Lieut. H.L.V. Day, Capt. W.J. Cullen, Lieut. M.C. Pickles, Major A.T. Sloan, Lieut. J.C.M. Lewis, Capt. J.A. Pym, Lieut.-Colonel L.G. Brown, Capt. C.M. Usher, Lieut.-Colonel J. Brunton, Capt. C.H. Pillman, Capt, A.D. Laing, CSMI. Jones, Major Lawless and Capt. R.A. Gallie.

New Zealand:

J. O'Brien, J. Ford, J. Stohr, L.P. Storey, J. Ryan, J. McNaught, C. Brown, A. Wilson, R. Sellers, E. Hazell, E. Bellis, J. Kissick, J. Cookcroft, W. Fogarty, A. Singe.

Referee: Mr J.G. Cunningham (Watsonians).

On 12th April, 1919 at Twickenham the Mother Country drew level with New Zealand by beating South Africa, 21-12 (3 goals, 2 tries to 1 goal, 1 dropped goal, 1 try). Sloan, Cullen, Usher, Pickles and Dickson all scored tries, three of them converted by Brown. Harris and Townshend scored tries for South Africa, the latter's converted by Villiers.

Scotland v France, 1920

Scotland played France in drizzling rain on 31st January, 1920 at *Parc des Princes* before 30,000 spectators. Usher led the Scots on to the field to a rousing welcome, wearing the kilt over his shorts and playing the pipes. There was a great roar when he removed his kilt.

In a dour game on a heavy ground, the French kicked off. Angus and Fahmy carried the ball into the French 25. The Scots dominated but were held off by the halves Billac and Struxiano. The Scots pack was heavier, but the French kept control and only Thom and Usher played up to international standards. The half time score was 0-0.

In the second half French pressure was countered by good Scottish play that pushed them back into their own half. Kennedy missed a penalty kick at goal, but a second penalty took the ball into the French corner, where Fahmy collected and passed to Crole, who kicked ahead, followed up and touched down for a try, converted by Laing.

The French struggled to prevent the Scots from adding to their score. Their three-quarter play was excellent, but their forwards could not match the Scots. The match was marked by good sportsmanship on both sides, and the French carried the referee shoulder high off the field. The final score was Scotland 5-France 0 (1 goal to nil).

Scotland:

G.C. Patullo (Panmure), A.T. Sloan (Edinburgh Academicals), Dr. E.C. Fahmy (late Edinburgh University), A.W. Angus (Watsonians), G.B. Crole (Oxford University), J.H. Hume (Royal High School F.P.), A.S. Hamilton (Headingly), D.D. Duncan (Oxford University), H.A. Gallie (Glasgow Academicals), F. Kennedy (Stewart's College F.P.), A.D. Laing (Royal High School F.P.), W.A.K. Murray (London Scottish), G. Thom (Kirkcaldy), C.M. Usher (London Scottish), A. Wemyss (Edinburgh Wanderers).

France:

Chilo (Racing Club), Jaurreguy (Racing Club), Lasserre (Bayonne), Crabos (Racing Club), Serre (Perpignan), Billac (Bayonne), Struxiano (Toulouse), Pons (Stade Toulousain), Sebedio (A.S. Biterroise), Lubin (Stade Toulousain), Cussayet (Stade Tarbais), Puech (Stade Toulousain), Thierry (Racing Club), Marchand (Stade Portevin), Lausent (Bayonne).

Referee: Mr. Potter Irwin (England).

Scotland v Wales, 1920

The match on 7th February, 1920 was at Inverleith, where demand for tickets was high, and had not the Hearts-Falkirk cup tie been on at Tynecastle, the crowds would have been too great for the ground. Usher captained Scotland, the first serving officer to lead an International side, in an exciting, bruising game, the result in doubt to the final five minutes.

The Welsh kicked off with the wind behind them, and were soon on the Scottish 25, with heavy mauling until Maxwell kicked a penalty into touch. The Scots took play into the Welsh half, but Rees cleared, Wetter got the ball out to their three-quarters and Jenkins scored a try, which he converted. Despite a concerted effort by the Scots, Wales held the lead 5-0 at half time.

Welsh scrum half, Wetter, was offside, and Kennedy's penalty kick from the touch-line near the half-way line narrowed the Welsh lead to 5-3. Fahmy injured an ankle and went out to the wing. A wild pass by Wetter was taken on by the Scots pack, the ball went to Sloan, who, ignoring an injury, scored in the corner. Scotland led by a point.

The Scottish three-quarters lacked the pace to penetrate the Welsh defences, and this was compounded when Mackay, in attempting to score, damaged tendons in his leg and was carried off. His place was taken by Macpherson, depleting the pack up against the powerful Welsh, and leaving the Scots at considerable disadvantage. Once again, however, the Welsh had a penalty given against them, successfully taken from a wide angle by Kennedy.

With ten minutes to go, the Welsh, numerically superior in the scrum, and with Scotland's defence weakened by injury, threw everything into the attack. A converted try would be enough to win the match. Twice they nearly scored, but they were up against a determined Scottish defence, and Uzzell and Jones were injured. When the final whistle went the crowd was ecstatic, the pitch was invaded and the Scottish players carried off shoulder high.

Result: Scotland 9-Wales 5 (2 penalty goals, 1 try to 1 goal).

Scotland:

G.L. Patullo (Panmure), E.B. Mackay (Glasgow Academicals), A.W. Angus (Watsonians), E.C. Fahmy

(Abertillery), G.B. Crole (Oxford University), A.T. Sloan (Edinburgh Academicals), J.R. Selby (Watsonians), C.M. Usher (London Scottish), D.D. Duncan (Oxford University), G.H.H.P. Maxwell (R.A.F.), G. Thom (Kirkcaldy), R.A. Gallie (Glasgow Academicals), N.C. Macpherson (Newport), F. Kennedy (Stewart's College F.P.), A.D. Laing (Royal High School F.P.).

Wales:

J. Rees (Swansea), W.J. Powell (Cardiff), J. Shea (Newport), A. Jenkins (Llanelli), B. Williams (Llanelli), B. Benyon (Swansea), J. Wetter (Newport), H. Uzzell (Newport), T. Parker (Swansea), J. Jones (Aberavon)), C. Jones (Bridgend), J. Williams (Blaina), H. Whitfield (Newport), S. Morris (Cross Keys), G. Oliver (Pontypool).

Referee: Mr Crawford (Ireland).

Scotland v Ireland, 1920

A 25,000 crowd at Inverleith saw Scotland start well against Ireland on 28th February, 1920. In the first minutes Crole punted over Crawford's head, collected the ball and touched down near the posts for Kennedy to convert.

Fahmy made some good touch kicks and Crole, Angus and Browning took the play up to the Irish posts, but a scrum infringement gave the Irish a free kick that got to their 25. An Irish infringement led to a penalty, taken by Kennedy, who kicked a magnificent goal. The score was now 8-0. Crole again punted over Crawford to touch down between the posts for Kennedy to convert, leaving the Scots 13 points ahead at half time.

The Irish took advantage of a following wind in the second half. Wallace kicked ahead and play went to the Scottish 25. The Scottish pack responded with strong rushes to take the game back to the Irish 25. Fahmy sold a dummy, broke through and was tackled. He repeated the move and kicked across to Angus, who scored. This was followed by good handling, resulting in another try for Browning. Neither of these tries was converted.

G.B. Crole was outstanding, his punts ahead and follow-up brilliant, and Fahmy at stand-off handled accurately, drew the defence and in the closing stages sold another dummy to break through the Irish defence. Angus was superb in defence and

Browning, a newcomer to the side, was notable for his speed both in defence and attack.

Scotland was now the only undefeated national side of the season. Next stop was Twickenham.

Result: Scotland 19-Ireland 0 (2 goals, 1 penalty goal, 2 two tries to nil).

Scotland:

G L. Pattullo (Panmure), A. Browning (Glasgow High School F.P.), A.W. Angus (Watsonians), A.T. Sloan (Edinburgh Academicals), G.B. Crole (Oxford University), E.C. Fahmy (Abertillery), J.A.R. Selby (Watsonians), C.M. Usher (London Scottish), F. Kennedy (Stewarts College F.P.), D.D. Duncan (Oxford University), A.D. Laing (Royal High School F.P.), G. Thom (Kirkcaldy), N.C. Macpherson (Newport), R.A. Gallie (Glasgow Academicals), W.A.K. Murray (London Scottish).

Ireland:

W.E. Crawford (Lansdowne), B.A.T. McFarland (Derry), P. Roddy (Bective Rangers), T. Wallace (Cardiff), C.H. Bryant (Cardiff), W. Duggan (University College, Cork), J.B. O'Neill (Queen's University, Belfast), H. Coulter (Queen's University, Belfast), A.H. Courtney (University College, Dublin), R.Y. Crichton (Dublin University), W.D. Docherty (Guy's Hospital), J.E. Finlay (Cardiff), W.J. Roche (University College, Cork), A.H. Price (Dublin University), P.T. Stokes (Garry Owen).

Referee: Mr. J. Baxter (England).

W.E. Crawford was considered the best Irish back between 1919 and 1939.

England v Scotland, 1920

The England v Scotland Calcutta Cup match on 20th March, 1920 was played at Twickenham before a record crowd of 40,000, including King George V, the Prince of Wales, the Duke of Gloucester (whom Usher had taught to box at Sandhurst), and Prince and Princess Arthur of Connaught. The King, the Prince of Wales and the Duke of Gloucester shook hands with the players.

The excited anticipation in the glorious spring (the Scottish commentator described it as summer) weather was palpable. Scotland had beaten France, Wales and Ireland and was in line for the Triple Crown. England had beaten France and Ireland narrowly but had lost to Wales, so it was a determined Usher, captain for the third time, who led his team on to the pitch and kicked off. Play was fast and furious, and the Scottish pack attacked relentlessly. The English three-quarters tackled ferociously. They passed wide and kicked across repeatedly, while B.S. Cumberlege at full back kicked well and gained much ground.

At half time the score was 10-4 to England (Scotland's score a dropped goal by Bruce-Lockhart).

At the beginning of the second half play was halted briefly to allow Usher to recover from injury, but thereafter the Scots were always in the English half, with Usher and Maxwell furiously trying to bore their way through. But the reality was that Scotland were outplayed by a faster more enterprising English team. It was not for want of trying, but the English had done their homework.

Play was fast throughout (said a Scottish report). England won, and won well. The victory was not so much due to superiority in play as to a faculty for making openings. Each of England's tries were achieved in this manner, and the Scottish defenders had little chance of preventing them. The Scots put in the bulk of the aggressive work, but by a slavish regard for orthodox methods had every move anticipated, and threes could never shake off the English defenders, whose marking and tackling were very fine, and very effective.

The Scottish team changes did not make for improvement. The forwards, strengthened by the return of G.H.H.P. Maxwell and A. Wemyss had the pull in the fight, but in the loose they were not as effective as we have seen this season. C.M. Usher made an inspiring leader, and among others who caught the eye were Duncan, Thom, Wemyss, and Macpherson. Maxwell was good if not so prominent as in the Welsh match.

With matters going so well for the Scots in the scrums it was unfortunate that there should be a lack of understanding between the half-backs, who did not 'hit it off' until the game was well advanced, by which time the Englishmen were playing with confidence. Repeatedly, C.S. Nimmo failed to locate his partner, E.C. Fahmy, and it was from one of his wild passes that England were enabled to open the scoring. Later, the partnership improved, but another weak link was at centre-threequarter, where J.H. Bruce-Lockhart gave a far from satisfactory display. He neither took nor gave his passes well, with the result that G.B. Crole was handicapped, especially as he was faced by the speedy Blackheath man, C.N. Lowe. The Oxford university man did well under the circumstances, but he could not shake off Lowe, and when he resorted to the kick ahead, tactics that were so successful against Ireland, he was beaten for pace. A.W. Angus, the Watsonian captain, was serviceable but slow, and his partner A.T. Sloan, the speediest man on the Scottish side, was too well marked and seldom had room to develop his pace. G. Pattullo, at full back, was not at his best. His kicking fell short, and he often failed to find touch.

On the English side, B.S. Cumberlege at full back fielded the ball with sureness, kicked strongly, and rarely failed to gain ground. The threes were seen less often in combination than the Scottish line, but were more effective. They indulged in wide passing, and exploited the cross kick. Lowe, Myers, and Harris were the pick of the four, but Hammett, who played his best international game, was not far behind. In defence they were great, and their kicking was always sound. Davies was the better of the halves, and could not have been far short of being the best player on the field. The forwards did not match up to the Scottish pack, but were more than useful, with Greenwood, Voyce and Wakefield outstanding.

England's strength lay in the back division, where they were faster than the Scots. The greatest difference was at centre-three-quarter, where Myers and Hammett were superior. Their speed was particularly useful in defence, neutralising much good work by the Scottish forwards. The Scottish 'threes' were not good enough for the occasion.

The Triple Crown and Calcutta Cup had almost been 'in the bag'. Their loss must have been on Usher's mind for his final appearance at Twickenham two years later.

Result: England 13-Scotland 4 (2 goals, 1 try to 1 dropped goal).

Scotland:

G.L. Pattullo (Panmure), A.T. Sloan (Edinburgh Academicals), A.W. Angus (Watsonians), J.H. Bruce-Lockhart (London Scottish), G.B. Crole (Oxford University), E.C. Fahmy (Abertillery), C.S. Nimmo (Watsonians), G.H.H.P. Maxwell (R.A.F.), A. Wemyss (Edinburgh Wanderers), F. Kennedy (Stewart's College F.P.), G. Thom (Kirkcaldy), C.M. Usher (London Scottish), N.C. Macpherson (Newport), D.D. Duncan (Oxford University), R.A. Gallie (Glasgow Academicals).

England:

B.S. Cumberlege (Blackheath), C.N. Lowe (Blackheath), E. Myers (Bradford), E.D.G. Hammett (Newport), S.W. Harris (Blackheath), W.J.A. Davies (United Services/R.N.), C.A. Kershaw (United Services/R.N.), T. Woods, (R.N.), G.S. Conway (Cambridge University), S. Smart (Gloucester), A.F. Blakiston (Northampton), A.T. Voyce (Gloucester), F.W. Mellish (Blackheath), W.W. Wakefield (Harlequins), J.E. Greenwood (Cambridge University).

Referee: T. D. Schofield (Wales).

Scotland v Wales, 1921

On 5th February, 1921 Scotland met Wales at St. Helens ground, Swansea, before 40–50,000 spectators. It was their first win in Wales for 29 years, described as 'one of the most memorable struggles in the annals of International Rugby', but marred by the crowd swarming on to the pitch. The view from parts of the enclosure was obscured by the people along the touchline, and when the players formed up for the kick-off, many spectators climbed over the barriers and crowded the touch line. When Wales got a penalty kick near the Scottish line, several hundred, who could not see what was going on, pelted the press with ash and stones, climbed over their tables and invaded the pitch. The teams returned to the pavilion for five minutes while the police, foot and mounted, cleared the ground. The touchline crowd was twelve deep with those at the back, unable to see anything, pushing those in front on to the field of play.

In the second half the pitch was again invaded leading to play being halted for a further twelve minutes.

T.H. Vile, the veteran Welsh captain, won the toss, chose to play into the wind and faced hard and skilful play both in the scrum and the three-quarter line, with Scotland building a lead of eight points in the first twenty minutes. F. Evans had to leave the field to have his head bandaged while Carmichael was left stunned by the ball.

From a loose scrum in midfield, Sloan passed to Thomson who scored, then Buchanan got a try, converted by Maxwell, who also kicked a penalty before the interval, bringing the Scottish lead to 11-0.

In the second half, Jenkins dropped two goals and the Welsh forwards took charge, but Scotland displayed better pace and teamwork. There was a great battle between the opposing packs; 'now the Welshmen were on top, now it was C.M. Usher and his team who held the mastery'. Towards the end, Jenkins left the field with a knee injury.

The Scottish backs were superior, and among the forwards the powerful G.H.H.P. Maxwell was always to the fore, whilst 'C.M. Usher more than justified his return to the side. Against Wales he can be depended upon to give of his best . . . and there was no better forward on the field'.

J. Hume was an inspiring leader, combining with R.L.H. Donald to outplay Vile. In the closing minutes Sloan went through a crowd of players for a great try.

Result: Wales 8-Scotland 14 (2 dropped goals to 1 goal, 1 penalty goal, 2 tries).

Scotland:

H.H. Forsayth (Oxford University), A.T. Sloan (Edinburgh Academicals), A.E. Thomson (United Services), A.L. Gracie (Harlequins), J.H. Carmichael (Watsonians), R.L.H. Donald (Glasgow High School F.P.), J.H. Hume (Royal High School F.P.), C.M. Usher (London Scottish), G.H.H.P. Maxwell (London Scottish), J.M. Bannerman (Glasgow High School F.P.), R.S. Cumming (Aberdeen University), R.A. Gallie (Glasgow Academicals), J.C.R. Buchanan (Stewart's College F.P.), G. Douglas (Jedforest), J.N. Shaw (Edinburgh Academicals).

Wales:

J. Rees (Swansea), M. Thomas (Bartholomew's Hospital), A. Jenkins (Llanelli), P. Baker-Jones (Newport), F. Evans

(Llanelli), W. Bowen (Swansea), T.H. Vile (Newport), T. Parker (Swansea), E. Morgan (Llanelli), W. Hodder (Pontypool), J. Williams (Blaina), T. Roberts (Risca), L.A. Attwell (Newport), S. Winmill (Cross Keys), J. Jones (Aberavon).

Referee: Mr. J. Baxter (England).

The struggle for Home Rule in Ireland prevented selection for the match at Lansdowne Park, Dublin on 25th February. One of the branch post offices had been the subject of an armed raid. There was a strong police presence in and around the ground and a company of soldiers with armoured cars was stationed near the entrance gates. The Scottish backs played well but the Irish scrum triumphed. An account stated 'In the circumstances the last minute changes among the Scottish forwards were unfortunate. No pack could afford to lose such strenuous players as C.M. Usher and N.C. Macpherson without being materially weakened. Usher's leadership would have been invaluable and Macpherson's experience of fast, open play might have made matters less unequal in front'. Scotland lost 8-9.

Usher knew and admired Eric Liddell, the fastest international wing in the game, and they played together in the Scottish teams of 1922 which beat Ireland 6-3 and drew 9-9 against Wales at Inverleith. Liddell had a rare combination of pace, a fine rugby brain, and good hands. He could spot a gap and he could sell a dummy to perfection, he never funked a tackle and was brilliant in defence. It was in athletics, however, that his world-wide fame was based. In the 1924 Olympics he won gold for the 400 metres and bronze for the 200 metres. He did not compete in the 100 metres because the qualifying heats took place on a Sunday, and as a devout Christian he withdrew from the race, which was then won by Harold Abrahams. The rivalry between the two athletes was the subject of the 1981 film *Chariots of Fire*. A missionary caring for, and inspiring, his fellow prisoners to the end, he was to die in a Japanese internment camp in China in 1945.

England v Scotland, 1922

The sun shone brightly on Twickenham for the Calcutta Cup Match on 18th March, 1922. Both captains, C.M. Usher and W.J.A. Davies, presented their teams to the King and the Duke of York in front of the 40,000 crowd. Usher always said there seemed to be a hoodoo for the Scots playing at Twickenham and, true to form on this day, England scored their fifth successive Calcutta Cup victory against the seemingly invincible Scotland, who came into the game unbeaten and with a strong pack.

Scotland dominated for the first half hour and from a line-out on the English 25, the ball passed out along the three-quarter line to Mackay, who penetrated their opponent's defence and passed back to Dykes for the touch down, converted by Bertram.

Although Scotland were again in charge for around ten minutes after half time, Davies, the English captain and fly-half suddenly transformed the game with inspirational play, making a spectacular run for the corner flag with C.N. Lowe breaking out from the loose to score. Almost immediately afterwards Davies dodged a tackle by Bryce, passed the ball down the line for Myers to brush off the Scottish defence and pass out to Lowe who had come down the right at speed to score by the posts. Conway converted.

With ten minutes to go the situation for Scotland was desperate. They gave everything they had, and there was a tense hush as they were awarded a penalty from an English infringement in the scrum. It was taken by Maxwell, but agonisingly, it hit the cross bar.

To round off his spectacular play, Davies then kept Scotland at bay with a great kick up the touchline and, from the line-out, made a brilliant run, swerved past Forsayth and scored, an individual effort that was acknowledged by applause from supporters of both sides.

The final score was England 11-Scotland 5 (1 goal, 2 tries to 1 goal).

Scottish commentators felt the team was handicapped by the absence of E.H. Liddell and A. Browning. Perhaps the pack had tired themselves too early; Lawrie, Bannerman, Usher and Buchanan were not at their best, Bryce, was criticised for taking too much on himself. Fettesian G.P.S. Macpherson and Gracie came in for the most praise.

Scotland:

H.H. Forsayth (Oxford University), E.B. Mackay (Glasgow Academicals), G.P.S. Macpherson (Oxford University), A.L. Gracie (Harlequins), J.M. Tolmie (Glasgow High School F.P.), J.C. Dykes (Glasgow Academicals), W.E. Bryce (Selkirk), C.M. Usher (Edinburgh Wanderers), G.H.H.P

Maxwell (London Scottish), J.M. Bannerman (Glasgow High School F.P.), D.M. Bertram (Watsonians), W.G. Dobson (Heriot's), D.S. Davies (Hawick), J.R. Lawrie (Melrose), J.C.R. Buchanan (Stewart's College F.P.).

England:

J.A. Middleton (Army and Richmond), C.N. Lowe (Blackheath), A.M. Smallwood (Leicester), E.R. Myers (Bradford), I.J. Pitman (Oxford University), W.J.A. Davies (United Services), C. A. Kershaw (United Services), W.W. Wakefield (Cambridge University), G.S. Conway (Cambridge University), T. Voyce (Gloucester), J. Maxwell-Hyslop (Oxford University), R.F.H. Duncan (Guy's Hospital), H.L. Price (Oxford University), P.B. William-Powlett (United Services).

Referee: Mr. R. A. Lloyd (Ireland).

In this strong England team were G.S. Conway, Fettes and Cambridge, credited as the best player in the English pack between 1920-24. W.J.A. Davies at stand off had great hands and kicking ability. C.A. Kershaw was a very strong scrum half who had good hands and a fast, accurate pass. W.W. Wakefield won 31 caps between 1920 and 1927. The fastest forward ever to have played for England, he might have made an outstanding three-quarter.

Sadly this was Usher's last International match. He had captained his country in all four encounters and he felt it was now time to stand down when he had reached the peak of his form. He was exactly 6'0" tall and weighed 14 stone.

Usher was in much demand on the rugby field elsewhere. Reference to his play can be found in John McLaren's *The History of Army Rugby*. At Queen's Club, on 6th March, 1920, the Army beat the R.A.F. 21-9 in the presence of King George V, Prince Albert and Prince Henry. 'C.M. Usher made a colossal difference to the pack, leading it well and inspiring his fellows with the excellence of his play' and 'The best forwards on the field were Usher and Wakefield, who led a fine R.A.F. pack.' He captained the Army against the Navy on 4th March, 1922 when the Navy captain, Davies, dropped a goal to win the match 7-3.

On 11th April, 1922, the Army beat the R.A.F. 23-8. 'It was a fitting match for Usher to bow out as he played his usual forceful game in the forwards, well supported by Young, Ross (HLI) and

MacNamara (Royal Enniskillen Fusiliers)'. Usher played against the French Army in 1920, 1922, 1923 and captained the 1924 Army team.

He was described as a dashing and tireless forward, covering the ground like lightning. Special mention was made that he had been severely wounded but recovered so well that he captained the Mother Country XV in 1919. At the age of 42 while attending an Army match at Blackheath as one of the Selection Committee, an Army player failed to turn up and Usher stood in. The Army won 21-11 and according to the *Times* 'Usher had a splendid game'.

Amongst other matches in 1922 was Edinburgh Wanderers v Hillhead High School F.P. at Inverleith, where Usher scored the opening try after good work by G.P.S. Macpherson, and kicked two goals.

The best of the Edinburgh Wanderers at this time were Usher and Andrew Wemyss who, as a member of the Gala XV, made his reputation as a powerfully built, hard working player, game to the last, and invaluable in the scrimmage. 'Greatest of them all, however, was Charlie Usher of whom it has been written: "Some would find their ideal forward in C.M. Usher. He had the football brain and evolved a game which was a cross between that of the Englishman, C.H. Pillman and Mark Morrison, but short by a bit of that of J.D. Boswell, who reputedly reduced the art of pushing and not pushing to a science." Rarely equalled as a pack leader, Usher had the art of inspiring forwards to do their utmost, even to surpass themselves. By individual brilliance he won many matches'.

In *Rugger: The Man's Game*, E.H.D. Sewell lists his choices for a best ever Scotland XV, from the players who featured between 1890 and 1939. The team was:

W.T. Forrest, K.G. Macleod, R.E. Gordon, H.J. Stevenson, E.H. Liddell, A.R. Don-Wauchope, P. Munns, M.C. McEwan, M. Morrison, W.E. Kyle, W.P. Scott, D.R. Bedell-Sivright, C.M. Usher, H.G. Monteith.

While serving with the 2nd Battalion, the Gordon Highlanders in Fort George, Usher turned out for the Highland Rugby Football Club and in a match against Aberdeen University helped Highland to win 23-5 (1 goal, 6 tries) to (1 goal). Usher scored three tries and kicked a goal, while fellow Gordon Highlander Jack Robertson also scored three. Usher captained the 2nd Battalion, Gordon Highlanders against the 1st Battalion, KOSB in the first round of the Army Rugby Championship at Inverness this time losing 9-0, despite his best efforts, to the experienced side from the traditionally rugby-playing regiment.

Usher was a member of some distinguished rugby clubs— Barbarians, Army, United Services, London Scottish, Surrey, Edinburgh Wanderers, Selkirk and Merchistonians. Players were amateurs and, irrespective of nationality or team, upheld the sporting traditions of the game. Lasting friendships were born.

One good friend was Andrew Wemyss[2] who lost an eye while instructing on the hand grenade. Usher ascribed his good fortune in escaping serious injury throughout his rugby career to 'Andra' who on many occasions would hasten to protect him, apart from providing valuable information about his opponents. On one occasion he remarked to Usher, 'Charlie we've got one man with one eye on our side but the others have two one-eyed men!'

None who heard Wemyss commentate on radio would forget his trenchant comments. Failure to run for the corner flag fast enough brought forth damning criticism, and then a grudging admission afterwards that the player had a broken collarbone or leg, or something, which, however, barely counted as a valid excuse! Usher did not like the telephone much but when 'Andra' came on the conversation never seemed to end.

Fencing

Usher had always enjoyed fencing, and it was his firmly held view that all young men and women should be taught to fence. The Society of Scottish Swordsmen was founded by Sir William Hope of Balcomie at the end of the 17th Century, but fencing in Scotland virtually ceased to exist until artist and explorer William Gordon Burn Murdoch[3], John French W.S., John Gordon Jamieson and Patrick Johnston Ford, together with Maria Steuart founded the Scottish Fencing Club in 1909 in Edinburgh. The first *Maître d'Armes* was Léon Crosnier, who had had a brilliant career at the famous military fencing school

---

[2]   Andrew Wemyss, better known as 'Jock' Wemyss, was a well-known sports reporter in Scotland, writing in Edinburgh and national newspapers and commentating on matches on the radio.

[3]   William Gordon Burn Murdoch was married to Jane, daughter of Andrew Usher, brother of Charles Usher's grandfather, James.

of Joinville-le-Pont. The French were supreme with the foil and the épée so Professor Crosnier was the ideal man for the job.

In 1923 when a U.S.A. fencing team was due to meet a British team in London, Usher and a few other enthusiastic Scottish fencers decided that the Americans should be invited to Edinburgh for a match against Scotland. There were some 20 clubs but no representative organisation, so the Scottish Amateur Fencing Union came into being, with the Duke of Atholl as President and Usher as Honorary Secretary and Treasurer.

It was a great occasion, although U.S.A. won by 35-11. Usher was a member of the Scottish sabre team. A contemporary newspaper report recorded that he defeated Macpherson 4-1 with a characteristically dashing display of fencing, and Schoomaker 4-2, winning two out of Scotland's four sabre victories.

Usher was awarded a medal in Paris from the *Societé Militaire d'Escrime* at the *Championnat Militaire d'Europe*. He took part in the Scottish Command Bronze Medal Tournament at Redford Barracks in Edinburgh in March 1925, winning the sabre and taking second place in the épée and foil after a run-off for first place.

Boxing

Usher had boxed since he was a boy at Merchiston, and kept his hand in at Sandhurst, in the Gordon Highlanders and even in the prisoner-of-war camps. As an instructor at Sandhurst after the First War he taught Prince Henry, Duke of Gloucester, to box. It was not surprising that, when posted to the 2nd Battalion at Fort George in 1924, he should become involved with the Battalion boxing team.

Battalion boxing in 1924 began to emerge from a low with the assistance of Usher's friend Tom Berry (light-heavyweight champion of the British Empire, 1925-27) as trainer, and Ronald Campbell. They won the Novices Aldershot Boxing Shield in 1926, the Aldershot Command Inter-Unit Novices Boxing Championship in 1927/28 and the Aldershot Command Open Boys' Inter-Unit Team Championship in 1928. The star was Belfast-born Boy (Private) John (Jack) Garland, bantam-weight winner of the Army Boxing Championship in 1927, the 1928 Amateur Boxing Association (ABA) Bantam Weight Championship and Imperial Services Boxing Association Championship. In the same year, he reached the quarter-finals of the Amsterdam Olympics, defeated only due to the highly unorthodox methods of the gold medal winner Vittorio Tamagnini. Having one of his boxers, whom he had trained, encouraged and brought to believe that he could beat anyone, representing The Gordon Highlanders in the Olympic Games was a great personal satisfaction for Usher and testament to his leadership and inspirational character.

Amsterdam was Garland's first time abroad. He was accompanied by his trainer, Private Tim Kelly, and kitted out with Panama hat and smart blazer. It was exciting finding himself quartered with the rest of Great Britain's boxing team, and chief trainer Johnny Hill, at Harlow prior to sailing. His account was fascinating.

> The Channel crossing, one of the roughest for years, took a lot out of me. I never want to be a sailor. We were glad to see Amsterdam on Sunday, August 5th, at about 7.30 am, lost no time in getting ashore, and after being quizzed by Customs were identified with our passports, and allowed to proceed. Tim Kelly tried to speak Dutch when he referred to the Customs' official opening his bag, but everybody laughed as we got aboard our motor for our Olympic headquarters at Lloyds Hotel, where we were very well treated. I expected to have all sorts of foreign food served me, but was agreeably surprised to get ordinary fare—porridge, bacon and eggs, etc. We had an inspection of Amsterdam, and first impressions were good. We changed our money into gulden, worth 1s.8d. each, and soon mastered it. I was told the beer was fine. It wasn't cheap, but as I had none it didn't trouble me.

> We went to see the Stadium, but although there were other events on, we did not concern ourselves with anything except the job in hand. The Boxing Stadium holds 9,000, and the ring is an ordinary 24-feet raised dais, but with a soft floor, which sagged with the boxer's weight and prevented any good footwork. It resembled a spring mattress, and was rather disconcerting.

> The judges, of whom so much has been written, sat one on each of three sides of the ring, and wrote their slips out just as in Army boxing.

> The seconds dressed as their fancy dictated, whilst all were allowed to talk and shout advice during the boxing. The crowd added their advice continuously, and fought amongst themselves until the police, who resemble soldiers, quelled

the disorder with their swords. During one of Mallin's fights the uproar was so great that the ring fight had to be stopped until the 'crowd' fight outside the ropes was over.

This unruly element rattled the judges, who were of different nationality to the contestants, so much so that they even changed their decisions, not as our Army referees might do, instantly, perhaps on account of picking up the red instead of the green flag, but in the case of Isaacs and Daly (U.S.A.) half an hour later! Isaacs won fairly, and got the verdict. The U.S.A. section of the crowd booed so much that the judges reversed their decision and awarded the fight to Daly.

My first opponent was Mignard, a Frenchman, a neatly-built man of about twenty-four, who gave me the fight of my life; a real gruelling contest which kept me busy at all times. He was a skilful boxer, with good hands and heart, and in perfect condition, but I had his measure, although his rushes and spectacular hitting out seemed to captivate the crowd. Here, I might say, the British team went to the Olympiad as boxers, and fought as such, and the U.S.A. and Argentinians had the same idea, but the other countries had different ideas, and their methods embraced everything known of punch and slog, butt, boring, holding, thumbing, and palming, and sometimes kneeing; anything except kicking, and that would have been regarded as fair by their partisans.

The judges, too, appeared to agree with these tenets, whilst the finer points of boxing, unless accompanied by noise and gore, failed to impress them.

I give Mignard full marks though, for he was a fair fighter, and I was relieved when it was over and a win for Great Britain announced.

I spent the time until my next contest the following day watching the others, and saw some curious decisions. For example, those against Goyder, Great Britain heavy; Webster, light-weight; Taylor, fly-weight (he wept when the adverse decision was announced, as he was a winner all the way of the three three-minute rounds); and also against Mallin, the British middle-weight.

I was full of confidence when I found my next opponent was Tamagnini, the Italian, an extraordinary stocky youth of twenty-one, who looked much heavier than a bantam. The system of weighing in the day before the first contest, and not bothering about it again, does not make a boxer seriously attempt to keep his weight to his proper class limit. Some bantams there scaled 9 st. 9 lb. two days after weigh in!

We started off in the afternoon session, and I soon found that my opponent did not intend to box, but preferred to bore in, head down, with arms swinging, and if he failed to connect to clinch and butt. If it is allowed, then I am not complaining, but he did not do much damage, though a head against one's chin continually is annoying. At the end of the first round he had me in a corner, slogging wildly, sometimes hitting me, sometimes the ropes or post, when I slipped past him, and, half turning, caught one on the side of the jaw which caused my knees to rock and sag. I slipped down, but immediately attempted to rise, when Joe Bowker, ex-welter-weight champion, who was in my corner with Private Kelly, said 'Take a breather; you have plenty of time'. As they do not count aloud there, I thought I would not risk it too long, so got up when I thought about five seconds had gone and continued. In the next two rounds I had the Italian well in hand, and evaded his rushes but could not do much with a straight left; it merely hit the top of his head. As only two bandages of 10 inches were allowed, and I had both of them on my left, they were insufficient, and each left to his crown hurt me more than it did Tamagnini. His 'hay-makers,' and he was tireless in throwing them, were ineffectual, but looked as if he was worrying me. I boxed him, and decidedly had the better of it. A boxer knows when he is beaten or outboxed. I was confident, increasingly so, as the first round ended, and was happy about it, but when 'Italy won' was announced I did feel sore! The crowd apparently were also, for there followed a terrific uproar in all languages, only one of which I understood, but there was no mistaking the meaning.

So ended my Olympic career. I had done my best, but, of course, I was sorry I hadn't won for Great Britain and the Regiment.

Hockey

Usher played hockey at school, where he showed much promise, but gave it up as it was a straightforward choice between rugby and hockey. He played at Sandhurst and when with the 1st Battalion before the First War, but never to the detriment of rugby. He often turned out for the Depot hockey team when he commanded the Depot at Castlehill from 1928 to 1933.

On February 23rd, 1929 the Depot played the Richmond Hockey Club on the Links, and won 5-0. The *Tiger and Sphinx* recorded:

> Our forward line was considerably strengthened by the return of Major Usher as centre-forward, who hit three of the five goals. Cpl. Jardine, as outside-left, proved a strong member of the side, and when he learns to vary the strength of his centres will be a valuable addition to the team.
>
> The halves were strong, having the additional service of L./Cpl. Restarick, 1st Battalion, as left half. The defence was also greatly strengthened by the services of R.S.M. Russell, 5th/7th Battalion, in goal.
>
> The Richmond Team were fast, and if their centre-forward had received a few more accurate passes might have lessened the Depot lead.

The Post-Second War Years

Usher's years at Edinburgh University after he had left the Army saw him involved in a wide range of sports and physical training activities. As Director of Physical Education he was in his element, helping young men and women to develop their sporting abilities, and in many cases demonstrating that they had abilities they had never suspected, and encouraging those who were prepared to make the effort to keep their fitness levels as high as possible.

British Empire and Commonwealth Games

Usher's talents were recognised nationally, and in 1950 he was appointed manager of the Scottish team at the British Empire Games at Eden Park, Auckland, New Zealand.

The Scottish Team included:

> Duncan McDougall Clark (Scottish Team Captain), Detective Sergeant, Royal Ulster Constabulary, hammer and shot putt. Champion of Scotland, all-Ireland, Ulster and the British Police, and British National, Scottish Native and British Police record holder.
>
> John G.M. Hart (Edinburgh University), high and low hurdles, Scottish Champion, Scottish Native and Universities Champion.

Jack Paterson, 6 miles and marathon, champion and record holder in the Scottish A.A.A. Marathon, Liverpool City Marathon and Edinburgh Highland Games.

Emma Hoppit Anderson, P.E. teacher and Women's Captain, broad jump, 1st place in the S.A.A. Sports, Hampden in June 1949 and 2nd place in the British A.A. Sports, White City July 1949. She had a good name for someone who specialised in the long jump!

Dr Alan S. Lindsay, medical practitioner, triple jump, S.A.A. Champion and record holder.

Hugh Riley, apprentice plumber, flyweight boxer, Champion and record holder Scottish and British A.B.A.

T.G. Muller, bantam-weight boxer, British A.B.A., Scottish and Western District Champion and British N.C.B. Champion.

Henry Gilliland, baker, feather-weight boxer, Scottish and British A.B.A. Champion.

James Hamilton, colliery electrical engineer, cyclist all events except sprint, champion Ayrshire and other club championships.

Peter Heatly (Edinburgh University), electrical engineer, diving, 110 yards free style, 110 yards backstroke, British and Scottish Champion.

Albert D. Kinnear, P.E. lecturer, 110 yards backstroke, 110 yards free style, English A.S.A., British Inter-Services Champion, Scottish Record Holder.

Margaret T. Girvan, 17 years old, shorthand typist, 110 yards back stroke, 110 yards free style, 440 yards free style and medley relay. Scottish and Western District Champion.

Helen O. Gordon[4], 16 years old, schoolgirl, 200 yards breast stroke and medley relay. British Junior, Scottish Junior and Senior, Western Counties Junior and Senior Champion.

Elizabeth M. Turner, 17 years old, shorthand typist, 110 yards freestyle and medley relay. British, Scottish,

---

[4] Helen Orr Gordon was commonly known as 'Elenor', running together her first and middle names. She died in 2014, just weeks before she was due to present swimming medals at the 20th Commonwealth Games in Glasgow.

Eastern District and Border Counties Ladies Champion.

G.S. Henry, circulation assistant, Scottish Champion welter-weight and middle-weight Western Champion.

Hugh Morrison, bricklayer, who held many Scottish, British and other records for weightlifting.

Alan G. Patterson, high jump, British and Scottish Champion and British and Scottish Native record holder.

Andrew Forbes, 3 miles, Scottish record holder.

Apart from Alan Patterson and Andrew Forbes, who flew, and Hugh Morrison who lived in New Zealand, the 21-strong Scottish party (the largest Scotland had ever sent overseas), together with English, Welsh and Nigerian athletes and officials, 71 in all, set sail in the SS *Tamaroa* owned by the Shaw Savill Line, known by the athletes as the 'Slow Starvation and Agony Line'.

Accompanying the Scottish Party were the trainer, Ken Shaw, Scottish professional heavyweight boxing champion, chaperones Madge Usher, and Mrs Todd, volunteer chaperone to the British Girl Swimmers, accompanied by her husband, who was Past President of the Scottish Swimming Association.

On the way they called at Curaçao in the Netherlands Antilles, where Usher enjoyed a reunion with wartime friends, and after passing through the Panama Canal finally berthed in Auckland on January 28th, 1950 in brilliant sunshine. They were welcomed by a Scottish Pipe Band, and in turn Usher piped the welcoming party on board. The reception for the team, all in tartan, was overwhelming, due to the large numbers of Scottish émigrés. Private George Harper of D Company, 1st Gordons in 1914, came from Hawke's Bay to see Usher. They had both been captured at Le Cateau and Usher remembered him well. It was a touching moment. The team was given a tremendous welcome on South Island at Dunedin, where the mayor, Sir Donald Cameron, was a generous host.

The Scottish team performed respectably and won 5 gold medals, 3 silver and 2 bronze. The winners were:

Gold:

Elenor Gordon, 220 yards breast stroke.

Duncan McDougall Clark, record breaking hammer throw of 163' 10¼".

> Hugh Riley, fly-weight boxing.
> Henry Gilliland, feather-weight boxing.
> Peter Heatly, 10 metres platform dive.
>
> Silver:
> Peter Heatly, 3 metres springboard.
> Andrew Forbes, 6 miles.
> Alan Patterson, high jump.
>
> Bronze:
> Albert Kinnear, 110 yards backstroke.
> Elizabeth Turner, Elenor Gordon and Margaret Girvan, medley relay.

At short notice Usher stood in and represented Scotland in the individual épée. With 3 wins he came 5th in the elimination pools, fighting for the first time with an electric épée. He eventually lost to Charles de Beaumont, eleven years his junior, captain of the British Olympic Fencing team in 1936 and 1948 and Épée Champion of Great Britain in 1936. Too short a flex did not help but his chances had always been slim.

He managed the Scottish team (which won 6 gold, 2 silver and 5 bronze medals) in 1954 for the 5th British Empire and Commonwealth Games in Vancouver.

> Gold
> Joe McGhee, marathon[5].
> Dick Currie, boxing, flyweight.
> John Smilie, boxing, bantam-weight.
> Peter Heatly, diving, 3 metres springboard.[6]
> Elenor Gordon, swimming, 220 yard backstroke.
> Elenor Gordon, Margaret McDowell, and Margaret Girvan, swimming, 3 x 110 yards medley.
>
> Silver
> Frank McQuillan, boxing, lightweight.
> John Wardrop, swimming, 440 yard freestyle.
>
> Bronze

---

[5] This was the race, in which the favourite, Jim Peters of England, ran himself to exhaustion and could not complete the final lap, the race then being won by the strongly finishing Joe McGhee.

[6] In 2014, at the age of 90, Sir Peter Heatly watched his grandson, 17 year old George Watsons pupil James Heatly, compete for Scotland in the diving competion at the 20th Commonwealth Games (the Glasgow Games) in the Commonwealth Pool in Edinburgh.

Ewan Douglas, hammer.

George Bridge and John Caswell, bowls.

John Wardrop, John Service and Robert Wardrop, swimming, 3 x 110 Medley.

Margaret Girvan, swimming, 110 yards free style.

Peter Heatly, diving, 10 metres board (platform).

While in Vancouver Usher read a paper on Physical Education in the University of Edinburgh.

On the return flight from Vancouver boredom was relieved by the discovery that the landing wheels were stuck, so the team lifted the floorboards to disengage them manually, enabling the aircraft to land safely.

A hangover from the war, in both Vancouver and Auckland, was that because the womenfolk were concerned that returning soldiers would get into drunken brawls, restrictive local bylaws had been introduced. These caused some problems. In Vancouver, an inspection of the celebration dinner venue revealed the place settings with no wine glasses, 'What beverage will you be requiring Sir? Tea or Coffee?' This was disconcerting, but a reconnaissance by Usher revealed a group of men in earnest discussion, each with a glass of amber liquid beside them. This was a privilege extended only to the Vancouver Parks Committee, so Life Membership was immediately extended and a dram readily accepted.

In New Zealand, the pubs closed half an hour after the offices, which perhaps explained why the All Blacks were such good forwards—if you did not move fast enough or forcibly enough you would not get to the bar in time to be served! In one town, after closing his office door, the Mayor opened the safe so that he could offer some much needed hospitality!

The Edinburgh University Years

University Athletics

In 1946 the Edinburgh University athletics team was stronger in field events than track. In a contest against Glasgow, Edinburgh lost 55-59 but there were some outstanding performances, with K. Maksimczyk winning the discus (124' 10½") and the shot putt (37' 4½"). He also won the pole vault, hammer and triple jump! J.G.S. Millhench won the javelin with a throw of 136' 10½".

Edinburgh won the Scottish Inter-Universities championships by 3 points. A. Lindsay won the triple jump with 42' 5" to beat the 1875 record of 41' 11". J.G.M. Hart won the 120 yards hurdles in the Scottish Hurdles Championship, and went on to win the event seven times, then a unique feat in Scottish athletics. His time of 15.3 seconds at the 1949 Scottish Championships beat his own Scottish Native record and qualified him for the Scottish team for the Empire Games in New Zealand in 1950.

In 1948 Edinburgh beat Trinity College Dublin 69-44 and Queens University Belfast by 58½-43½ .

There were many great contests with Victoria Park, a leading Scottish harrier Club with Hart, K. Maksimczyk, C.J.M. Hall, Quamina Cofie, John L. Hunter, David Mackenzie, Alistair Caskey and T. Braid producing outstanding performances.

J.G.M. Hart set a new Scottish Native record for the 120 yards hurdles with a time of 15.5 seconds (which he broke the following year in 15.3 seconds).

Ewan Douglas (heavy events) and David Mackenzie made the British Olympic team in 1948 and 1952.

In 1951 Harry Duguid established a British record with a discus throw of 155' 3". In 1955 he set a new British National record with a hammer throw of 192' 6". In 1955 D.W.R. Mackenzie threw the javelin 204' 11" for a new Scottish Native record.

Between 1946 and 1959 Edinburgh won the Scottish Universities Championships fourteen times, tied with Glasgow once and lost to Glasgow once.

University Football

The University beat Queens Park in 1945/46, with Otto Johnson the outstanding player, and applied to join the East of Scotland League. This meant much travelling, so when the 1st XI were so engaged their place was taken by the 2nd XI. The Queens Park Shield was won in 1947/48. The Captain A.T. (Sandy) Bruce scored 78 goals in the season but then signed for Hibernian. Between 1945/46 and 1958/59 the Queen's Park Football Society Trophy was won by Aberdeen (7), Edinburgh (4) and Glasgow (3).

The Spartans Football Club was formed in 1951 by former University players, and the University Athletic Club allowed them to play at Craiglockhart and the Canal Field.

University Rowing

Rowing at Edinburgh University is faced with problems of weed, silt, varying water levels and the narrowness of the Union Canal. However, there was some good rowing in 1950, and, under J.C. Paterson, the Edinburgh University first crew won the Maclay Cup at the Western Regatta, the U.A.U. Championship at Chester, the Scott-Skirving Cup at its own regatta and the Edinburgh v Durham race. In 1954 the first crew won the Clyde Head, Scottish Championships, U.A.U. Championships and the City of Chester Challenge Cup. In 1957/58 with G.C. Cowley as Captain, a crew competed in the Scottish Championships.

This event had more than usual significance, as it was agreed by the Scottish Amateur Rowing Association that the winner would represent Scotland in the British Empire and Commonwealth Games in Wales in 1958. The first crew (R.N.T. Thin, R.F. Rintoul, W.K. Millar, G.C. Cowley and J. Tait) settled down to prolonged and intensive training, under Mr. R. Tinning, F.R.C.S., an Australian Olympic oarsman living in Edinburgh. They trained throughout the winter, and in the Easter vacation camped at Dullatur on the Forth and Clyde canal, covering in training 220 miles in 10 days. Their efforts were rewarded when, on a foul June day, the championships were rowed on Loch Lomond and the crew, as clear winners despite stiff competition, was selected to represent Scotland in the coxed IVs event at Llyn Padarn.

In 1958/59 the first crew won both the Scottish Universities and the Corporation Plate at Worcester. In 1959/60 it won the Aberdeen University, Glasgow Printers, Loch Lomond and (for the fourth successive year) the Scottish Universities Regatta, as well as the Scottish Four-Oared Championship.

The Boating Section of the Women's Athletic Club restarted in 1946/47, and ventured south for competitive rowing. In May their 'A' crew won a race against Durham. The first crew in 1948, made up of Joyce Lisle, Sìne MacLachlainn, Arnie Bury, Lois Phillips and Valmai Lewis (cox), after losing to Cambridge, beat Reading and won the Rowantrees Challenge Bowl for ladies 4-oared race at York City Regatta.

In 1947 Miss Hillcoat presented a cup for competition in Edinburgh between Edinburgh University crews and those from English Universities. The first Hillcoat Regatta was held in May 1949, a vintage year for the Section, and the Edinburgh crew

(Kathleen Robb, Sine MacLachlainn, Kathleen Harkness, Winnie Dickson and Joyce Lisle (cox)) were winners, defeating King's College, Newcastle, Durham Colleges, Durham University and Leeds. Later they completed this triumphant year by beating London University on the Thames, Cambridge University on the Cam and Reading University on the Thames.

The following year the first crew (Athole McNeil, Winnie Dickson, Sine MacLachlainn, Dorothy Grieve, and Joyce Lisle (cox)) again won the Hillcoat Cup, won the Durham Regatta, and defeated Reading in the final of the University Women's Rowing Association Regatta at Blaydon, Newcastle.

During these successful years the crews were coached by expert oarsmen, David Stephens, A.M. MacLachlainn, A.F. Berkeley, John Watt and C.A. Forsyth. On one occasion the coach's concentration was so great that he cycled into the canal, to the consternation of the crew but the delight of a pigeon breeder who 'hated' the women's crew for disturbing his birds during early morning practices, which began at 7 a.m.

University Boxing

The winners of the Scottish Universities Boxing Championship are awarded the McIntosh Cup, presented by Emeritus Professor McIntosh F.R.S. in 1926. From 1946 to 1959 Glasgow were the winners nine times and twice tied with St. Andrews who themselves won three times. Edinburgh won once, in 1949, when the Championship was held in Aberdeen, with George Ferguson as Captain and Joe McLaughlin as Vice Captain. The team was George Ferguson (fly-weight), I.C. Hunter (welter-weight), Joe McLaughlin (light-heavy), John Hughes (heavy-weight).

George Ferguson was, despite his lack of inches, an inspiring leader in and out of the ring. In a team contest, nothing boosts morale more than winning the first fight, and George as fly-weight invariably obliged, usually within the distance. As far as is known, he is the only Edinburgh University boxer to wear contact lenses in the ring. On one occasion, when he had been examined just before entering the ring, the M.O. slowly shook his head and said, 'My God man, I don't know how you even find your way to the ring'. George decided to slip the contacts in and they were so difficult to see when worn that the referee never even knew they were there, in spite of looking closely into his eyes before the first bell. George was Scottish Universities Champion three times and runner-up in both the East of Scotland

and British Universities Championships. The team was not specially endowed with boxing ability, but every member trained assiduously, and few Edinburgh University boxers have ever been fitter. All were in peak condition in the ring. In addition, there was a strong team spirit engendered by the discipline of training and the leadership of the Captain. An unusual feature of the training schedule was that most of the team were blood donors and thought nothing of giving a pint of blood before going to the gym for training and sparring, with no ill effect.

University Cricket

In 1937 the McKerron Cup for Cricket, for the winners of the Scottish Universities Championship, was presented by the final year medical students of Aberdeen University in memory of their Professor, R.G.M. McKerron. Edinburgh won it six times between 1946 and 1959 and shared it once with St. Andrews; St. Andrews won it outright five times and shared it with Glasgow once.

P.J. Walker, a very useful medium-pace bowler (also Captain of Soccer), was the first post-war captain. In the team were C.M. Wheatley, I.C.W. Bigland, R.D. Merson, C.J.R. Mair, A.M. Atta, M.E.S. Dickenson and New Zealander A.A. Rayner. They won the Championship. Merson played for Scotland and Bigland was a reserve.

Merson, a Merchistonian, followed Walker as Captain for two years. He was a much better bat than he ever got credit for, despite his Scottish cap. An unselfish partner at the wicket, he did not try to bat at both ends while surviving at the wicket. J.I. Cunningham was a tower of strength, as was H.O. Crosskill from the West Indies, one of the University's best cricketers. Other valuable recruits who gave long service were Arthur Laird, Harry Seed, J.R. (Jim) Taylor and J.W. (John) Everett, who played Squash for Scotland and won the British Universities Championship. Laird and Seed also played for the University at soccer and hockey respectively. Perhaps best of all was prolific run-getter Jim Taylor, a delight to watch and among the University's greatest batsmen. One century against Durham University was a classic. He was picked for Scotland in 1949.

Roy Watts was captain for two years. He was enthusiastic and successful. An above average fast bowler, he could also get runs when required. Both years the Championship was won and there was also victory over an exceptionally strong Grange side by 3 wickets. There were some interesting personalities in Watts' time. In came T. Sivagnanam (Siva for short) from Ceylon, A. Barron, a good fast bowler, A.G. Collington, an entertaining bat, and J.N.G. (Norman) Davidson. Davidson was a fine batsman and as quick in the field as at fly-half for the University, the Royal Navy, Barbarians and Scotland.

The next year, the other Norman, N.G.R. Mair joined the team. Both Normans were equally good at rugby and share the distinction with A.W. Duncan and M.R. Dickson of representing their country at both games. Mair was a stubborn left-hand opening batsman, particularly strong on the off-side. He had infinite patience, and opposing teams were glad to see his back. The outstanding performance was when Taylor and Siva put on 100 runs in 40 minutes.

In 1951 the XI under A.W. Henderson, later to play for Scotland, contained four future University captains—I.A.B. Mackenzie-Ross, Norman Mair, J.F. (Jim) Cowan and J.W. (Jimmie) Meikle—and R. Singh from India and D.L. (David) Norrie from Dollar Academy, a first-class wicket-keeper, who played for the Royal Navy. An exciting match with Stirling County was won by one wicket. The University entered the newly founded East of Scotland league.

In 1952 Hugh Trotter, a brilliant batsman from South Africa, helped the University regain the Universities Championship. At the end of the season, with no grant forthcoming, a tour of Lancashire was undertaken. The three matches against strong League teams could well have been drawn, but the University always went out for a win. R.S. Phillips kept wicket extremely well and Margetson spun the ball as well as any of the professionals fielded by the opposition, if not better.

On the next tour Norman Mair scored a century against Southport and Ainsdale. Norman's year started auspiciously with an easy win against Leith Franklin. J.W. Meikle scored 110 not out, Don Morton, rugby three-quarter, took 6 wickets for 19 runs and A.D. Audain from the West Indies was a top all rounder.

In 1954 with Jim Cowan as Captain, two fast bowlers, P.D.F. James and K.D. Robinson, and a good slow bowler, P.E.H. Brown, Edinburgh won the Championship.

For the third year running, the XI toured in Lancashire. The match against Manchester University was lost, but Liverpool University, who the previous day had nearly beaten Lancashire 2nd XI, were held to a draw. There were moral victories over

Chorley and Southport, while Western Command were routed. Norman Mair had an average of 72.8 and Audain 68.8. On the hard wickets only a bowler who could keep a length like Audain or spin the ball like Jim Cowan had any chance of success.

Hugh Trotter led the side in 1955, and the season began with a splendid win over Aberdeenshire. The Universities Championship was retained. 1956 saw a good victory over Stirling County, but the Championship was surrendered to St. Andrews. There was a crumb of comfort in the fact that Edinburgh beat them. In 1957, Keith Robinson showed a captain's example by bowling very well, and a word is due for G.H. Pagan, surely one of the best Secretaries that the University ever had. There was a good win over Perthshire and a draw with Grange. The outstanding team member was undoubtedly D.J. (Dion) Walles from Ceylon. He was thought by many good judges to be of Test standard.

Even by Scottish standards, the weather was shocking in Robinson's second year as captain. It washed out two attempts to play Glasgow and curtailed the St. Andrews' match to two overs.

University Fencing

Edinburgh was extremely successful in fencing for many years, until 1956/57 and 1958/59 when the St. Andrews and Edinburgh Croughly Cup was won by the former. In 1947/48, when W.F. Coulson was Captain, Professor A.M. Drennan, President and Dr. W.R. Mathewson Vice President, Coulson won the Fort Cup for épée, Z.K. Czajkowski won the Seton Trophy for foil and the Leveson-Gower Cup for sabre. The team won the Scottish Universities Championship, winning all the individual titles.

Czajkowski succeeded Coulson as captain, and the international, Colonel T.P. Saunders, warden of Cameron House, greatly improved the standard of sabre fencing. W.P. Mazur became Scottish Universities Sabre Champion and R.F. Rosenberger represented Scotland at sabre.

David Mends was an excellent captain the following year, both by precept and example. He had a long reach, of which he made excellent use, and an ideal temperament. Major W. Segda, who had represented Poland with the sabre at the Olympic Games, also arrived. He had served with the Polish Forces in the West of Scotland, and took over as *Maître d'Armes* to the great satisfaction of the Club.

In 1950/51, Undergraduate Colonel Saunders was captain. This had a beneficial effect on the sartorial turn-out of the team. The captain was impeccably dressed, with David Mends following suit. D.E. (David) Warren, however, took the prize with his white knee-breeches and silk stockings. Major Segda obtained his teaching diploma and thus became a chairless professor. All this led to a happy and successful season, Mends winning the Scottish Open Foil and Junior Sabre Championships, with Warren as runner-up in foil. In the Scottish Universities Individual Championships all three titles were won by Edinburgh, David Mends having a double in foil and épée, while Rosenberger won the sabre.

All was now set for an extended run of success, during which Edinburgh University were undoubtedly the leading club in Scotland until 1956. Mends and J.D.A. Henshaw represented Scotland for the first time in 1952, and in the photograph of that year it was good to see Colonel Ronald Campbell in his place as Honorary President. Success breeds success, and the Club was reinforced by many promising fencers, most of whom had graduated from the Novices' Class. Among them were A.G. (Graham) Meikle and A.G. (Tony) Watson. Both brought great credit on the University, but N.St.C. (Neil) L'Amie as captain stood no nonsense from his turbulent band of champions. In 1952/53 the outstanding victory was over Durham University, who had beaten all the Universities in the North of England. Meikle won the Scottish Junior Foil and Coulson the Junior Sabre. A journey was made to Leamington Spa, that Mecca of fencing. To the astonishment of the large assembled company, the University épée team, consisting of Meikle, Mends and Warren, beat Salle Paul, who had two English Internationalists, but in the second round Birmingham proved too strong. It was some consolation later in the season when the Edinburgh team was chosen *en bloc* to represent Scottish Universities against the Rest of Scotland. The following season all matches were won, as were the three individual titles at the Inter-Universities Championships.

In 1954/55, the Fencing Section again carried all before them. R.A.N. Napier won the Scottish Sabre Championship and O. van Eichstorff was Scottish Champion. In the Individual Inter-Universities Championships, J.D.A. Henshaw won the foil and Napier the sabre. Meikle, Henshaw and Napier were invited to fence for Scotland.

In the following season the 'Old Guard' were still to the fore and proved themselves too strong for the other Universities. In the 1955/56 Individual Championships, Edinburgh provided all three winners; Henshaw (épée), Meikle (foil) and Napier (sabre). All three again fenced for Scotland. In the British Universities Championships, Meikle was 4th in épée, while Henshaw (foil) and Chan (sabre) reached the semi-final pool.

The installation of the electric épée was a great encouragement to the fencers. It does away with the need for judges and signals hits by means of a bell and an electric light. It is most useful and popular with fencers, with the exception of the French, who sum it up as follows: *'Ce n'est pas amusant de discuter avec une ampoule électrique!'*[7] Charlie Mather retired in 1955 and his mantle fell on Captain S. T. Garner.

In 1956/57 several of the older fencers were in their final year of medicine and unable to take part in all the matches. Professor Segda had to retire owning to ill-health and his presence was greatly missed. This, of course, affected results. The team now had practical experience of the old adage 'We are but half men until we taste defeat', a new experience. The season was successful, but with foreboding for the future. Meikle, Tony Watson and Coulson represented Scotland. Meikle won the Scottish Universities Épée and Coulson the Sabre Championship. In addition, the former was a finalist in the British Universities Foil and the latter was runner-up in the Scottish Sabre Championship. Watson reached the final of the British Universities Épée and D.G.S. Reid was runner-up in both Scottish Universities and Scottish Junior Foil. These individual successes compensated in some measure for losing the Scottish Inter-Universities Championship, which in the event was to spend only one year away from home! Only three members, all épéeists, travelled to the next Individual Championships at Aberdeen, where they took the first three places. T.G Phemister was the winner. Watson won the Ford Cup at the Scottish Fencing Club and was selected to represent Scotland at the British Empire and Commonwealth Games. The season 1958/59 was a quiet one, although the Captain, A.C.H. Watson (no relation to Tony) fenced for Scotland in the Quadrangular Tournament and was Scottish Universities Épée Champion.

---

[7] It's not fun to chat with a light bulb!

University Golf

Edinburgh University competed for many cups, between members and against other teams. Between 1946 and 1959 Glasgow University dominated the Scottish Universities Team Championships, winning ten times. Edinburgh won twice, while St. Andrews and Aberdeen each won once. Edinburgh's Hector Maclean won the Scottish Inter-Universities individual Championship in 1947.

Outwith the Scottish Inter-Universities contests Edinburgh played at home and away with golfers from south of the border.

The team ventured into England in 1953, a real challenge in the days before motorways, when, in winter, chains had to be strapped on to wheels with frozen hands when snow and ice were encountered. One of the car drivers once ran out of petrol and got stuck in a snowstorm in Yorkshire. They lost 5-7 against Oxford and against Cambridge at the Royal West Norfolk. Cambridge's team was described by *Golf Monthly* as one of the best of all time. Edinburgh won against London. Later in the year return matches were played at Gullane, with a draw against Oxford, but a 5-7 defeat against Cambridge. The following year they scored a cliff-hanger win, decided on the last hole between Pat Smythe, the Edinburgh Champion, and the London Secretary Rice. Oxford was held to a draw and Cambridge won on their home course at Mildenhall.

C. N. (Clifford) Hastings was perhaps the best natural striker of a golf ball at Edinburgh since the war. In 1955 and 1956 he played against David Marsh and Gordon Huddy, two of the best Cambridge players, who both subsequently became Walker Cup players. Playing over Gullane No. 1 Clifford had 31 on the first nine and defeated Marsh by 7 and 6. In 1956 he defeated Gordon Huddy, holder of the President's Putter, by 3 and 2.

A.D.M. Gorrie captained the team on 31st March 1955, when Edinburgh won the Scottish University Championship for the first time since 1939.

Clifford Hastings and D.I. Purdie deserve special mention from the circumstances of their victories. Not content with the victory at Sandmoor Golf Club, Leeds, on 9th September, the team won the British Universities Championship and brought the Trent Cup to Edinburgh. This trophy is awarded to the University with the lowest aggregate medal score of any four players out of a nominated team of five. The Edinburgh team had a total of 626 strokes for eight rounds and were 23 strokes better than Manchester, the runners-up. The team was A. M. (Miller) Forbes, A.H.H. (Alistair) Campbell, J.L. Finlay, R.G. Rangecroft and F. Stewart.

The British Universities Championship was retained in 1956 with a total of 599, six strokes ahead of runners-up Cambridge. A.C.N. (Sandy) Ferguson with 146 was Edinburgh's best scorer. The other team members were A.P. Ritchie, R.S. Leslie, P.L. (Peter) Binns and Miller Forbes. Forbes' score was highest of Edinburgh's five by 5 strokes, but he went on to win the Individual Championship. Forbes' win is the more remarkable as this was the first time the Championship came to Scotland. This necessitated 5 matches, and in the semi-final he beat his own team-mate, Peter Binns.

The 1955/56 English tour was a great success. In poor conditions of snow and frost, Edinburgh defeated Oxford at Woking by 6 games to 4, with two games halved. The best performances were by the captain, A.M. Forbes, who started his match against Shepperson, the 1953 Boys' Champion, with a 2 and a 3, reached the turn in 35 and won comfortably. Alastair Cochrane went out in 35 and was one under fours when he won at the 16th.

The match against London University should have been played at the Berkshire Club, but overnight snow prevented play and the venue was changed to West Hill. Edinburgh won, thanks to the splendid play of their tail-enders, W.B.M. (Barry) Laird, R.S. (Bobby) Leslie and A.H.H. Campbell. For once Alastair Cochrane fell from grace. He was 4 up with 7 to play, but owing to bad putting lost on the last green. Later in the season Cambridge were defeated at Gullane, by 7 games to 5, and once again the tail wagged. Peter Binns had a 3, 3, 3 finish to demolish his opponent, while Barry Laird sank a 12-yarder at the 17th and proceeded to play the 18th in immaculate style.

Undefeated on their English tour, the team covered themselves with glory by winning the Lothians Team Title. The team, A.J. Cochrane, A.C.N. Ferguson and A.P. Ritchie, won by 3 strokes from Dalmahoy. In the British Youth Championship at Barnton, Peter Binns was runner-up after tying twice with A.F. Bussell, the winner. Binns and D.M. (Duncan) Lawrie represented Scotland in the Youth International match versus England. Alas, the British Universities Champions failed to retain their Scottish title.

1956/57 was disappointing. It was impossible to defend the Trent Cup, as it had been decided to hold the British Universities Championship near London, and the expense was too great. The Scottish Universities team was revived, and five Edinburgh players were selected. The outstanding performance of the season was by R.P. White, who, by leading the qualifiers in the Eden Tournament, won both the Victory and the Duke of York cups. R.O. Aitken was runner-up in the Scottish Universities Individual Championship.

1957/58, with Alistair Campbell as captain, was a notable year, with victories in both the British and Scottish Universities Championships. Campbell won the British Universities Individual title. In the matches against Oxford and Cambridge at Gullane, the former were beaten by 9 matches to 3, but the latter once again emerged triumphant by 11 matches to 9. A noticeable feature of this successful season was the fine team spirit throughout.

The British Universities title was retained the following year at Moortown, near Leeds, by 9 shots, but the Scottish title was surrendered. The English tour had to be cancelled, owing to an unfortunate accident to the Dormobile on the way back from Aberdeen, and the cost of towing and repairs used up all the money earmarked for the tour. There was some compensation when wins at home were recorded against Dublin, Durham, London, Oxford and Cambridge Universities. The greatest surprise was in the match against Cambridge, which consisted of two rounds of foursomes. Edinburgh led 4-0 at lunch and the final result was 6-2. The crowning glory was when Alistair Campbell beat Alan MacGregor, the Merchants' golfer at the 38th hole at Bruntsfield, to become Lothian's Amateur Champion for 1959. When presenting the trophy to Alastair, Mr. Steve Wright who had donated the Trophy in 1947 said he had never seen any final played in so gentlemanly a way.

Usher, Director of Physical Education, who seized every opportunity to promote physical fitness, said at the end of the most successful season 'it is sometimes asked how athletes who devote much time to games fare in their final examinations. With regard to golf in recent years Alastair Cochrane got a 1st and a PhD in Physics while Alistair Campbell got a 1st and a PhD in mining'.

University Running

The season 1946/47 marked the beginning of an undreamed of run of success for the Hare and Hounds section led by the physicist T.H. (Tom) Braid, Eastern District Champion and R.R. (Ron) Rowles, who reinforced the nucleus trained by Ian Stokoe. In 1948/49, with Ron Rowles as captain, the Hare and Hounds won the Scottish Universities Championship and R.F. (Ron) Wilby was Scottish Universities Individual Champion. By Rowles' inspiration, leadership, example, innovation and organisation Edinburgh University reigned as Scottish Universities Champions for many seasons.

In 1950, during Ron Rowles' second year came the crowning glory. At Sheffield the Hare and Hounds won the U.A.U. (British Universities Championship). Tom Braid and young George Walker laid the foundation by brilliant running. Sixteen Universities, with 132 competitors, took part in the 6¾ mile race, won in 39 mins. 19 sec. Edinburgh's counting six were: 3rd Braid, 5th Walker, 17th R.J. (Bob) Sherwin, 21st A.C. (Andy) Ross, 25th Rowles and 26th J.P. (Winkie) Waterston. The winning score was 97 points to London's 140 and Cambridge's 190. The team also won the Eastern District League (Sandilands Shield), Eastern District Championship (Fraser Trophy), Scottish Universities Championship and Scottish Union Championship. George Walker was Scottish Universities Champion, and the team of Ross, Sherwin, McRoberts, Hunt, Walker and Brydie were Scottish Universities Champions, Scottish Junior Champions and East of Scotland Champions.

Jimmie Brydie took over in 1953/54, a most successful season. There were outstanding recruits in Adrian Jackson, Hunter Watson, Noel Allsop, Alan Ravenscroft, Adrian Horne and Alan Cumming. Hunter Watson won the Eastern District Youth Championship and came 2nd in the national event. Adrian Jackson won the Club Championship, which he retained in each of his six years at the University. The Frazer Trophy, the Sandilands Shield and the Scottish Junior Championship were regained, with Adrian winning all three League races in the Shield event. He was 2nd in the U.A.U. Championship, and first man home in the Scottish Inter-Universities Championship.

J. Crawford succeeded Jimmie Brydie and led another outstanding team. Andy Ross returned after service in the R.A.F. All the trophies were retained, with the addition of the

MacKenzie Trophy (Eastern District Relay Championship). Ross then became captain, and the trophies were retained except for the Scottish Junior Championship. Adrian Jackson was 1st in the U.A.U. at Wimbledon, the first from a Scottish University to do so. In 1958/59 the Hare and Hounds won the Scottish Universities Championship for the 11th successive year.

University Hockey

Hockey was of special interest for Usher, a former Scottish trialist, although he had been unable to play, as the hockey internationals took place on the same day as the rugby internationals, and rugby had taken precedence.

There was a steady build up of the team from 1946 to 1949, but in 1948 T.L. Allan was capped for Scotland, the first of five caps, and in the following year S.T. Theobald won the first of his eight caps. In 1949, with David Dix Perkin as captain, 29 matches were played of which 25 were won, 3 drawn and 1 lost. Edinburgh won the Inter-Universities Championship, but the highlight was beating Cambridge University Wanderers 2-0 at the Folkestone Festival. Dix Perkin was elected President of the Athletic Club, to be succeeded as captain by Henry MacIntosh, who, after hard work in the gymnasium, improved his footwork and was capped for Scotland in 1951, together with W.T.M. Luff. Despite some excellent new players there were few successes in the next four years, but good use of the facilities in the gym resulted in increased fitness in the field, and the Championship was regained in 1955/56, under John McArdle. In 1956/57 Bryan Stack from Ireland, where the standard was higher, took over (he later became President of the Athletic Club). Of 31 matches played 20 were won, 6 lost and 5 drawn. In March 1958 a Jumble Sale was held to raise funds for a tour of Holland, in which all seven matches were won. J.M. Asumang then took over, the record being 21 matches played, 14 won, 3 drawn and 4 lost. Eight of the Edinburgh team were picked for the Scottish Universities Championship.

University Rugby

Many fine rugby players were in place in the 1946/7 season when Usher took up his appointment. The captain was T.B.M. Norman, an English trialist, and despite not being capped he was invited to play for the Barbarians. He captained a combined Yorkshire and Cumberland XV against Australia, and played for the Royal Navy, Hampshire and Harlequins. Also in the team were Colin Mair, Gus Black, David Mackenzie, Ian Wilson, Joe Newall, Ian Fraser and J. Wiltshire. The aim was fast, open rugby, and kicking for touch, so prevalent in post-war rugby, was spurned. Other University players in the Barbarians included R. Macdonald, D.D. Mackenzie, and M.R. (Mickey) Steele-Bodger (who gained nine England caps).

Twelve University players represented their countries in the twelve years following World War II, and there was at least one International in every Edinburgh University XV. They were Scotland players J.G. (Gibbie) Abercrombie, J.L. (Les) Allan, A.W (Gus) Black, I.F. (Ian) Cordial, J.N.G. (Norman) Davidson, A.K. (Kelso) Fulton, J.G.M. (John) Hart, D.C. (Donald) Macdonald, Ranald Macdonald, David Mackenzie, N.G.R. (Norman) Mair, and, playing for England, M.R. (Mickey) Steele-Bodger. Ian Wilson, a majestic place kicker, was reserve against the Wallabies in November 1947.

Olympic athlete David Mackenzie, when captain, introduced numbering of players, and programmes for Club matches for the first time in Scotland. The programmes, printed in the Department of Physical Education, were a constant source of revenue. White shorts were introduced in place of blue, and a laundry service ensured the team always turned out with spotless kit. Great interest was taken in the junior teams, and they were known by names instead of numbers. The XXX Club was unchanged, the 3rd XV became the Vikings, and all the others had names beginning with the letter V—Vandals, Vagabonds, Vampires, etc. This was a popular innovation, and the standard of play improved. Blues helped to coach the junior teams, and it was a thrill for the Fresher in the most junior team to find a current Blue, possibly also an Internationalist, giving him tips.

There was a great match in David Mackenzie's year when the XV played beautiful rugby against Hawick, one of the giants of Scottish rugby, at Mansfield Park. The result was a win for the University by two goals and a try to a penalty goal and two tries. So pleased were the sporting Hawick spectators with the play of the University team, which they said was the best seen at Hawick for a very long time, that they carried Mackenzie off the field.

David Mackenzie was an inspiration on the field and off. It gave great satisfaction to the Club when he gained his first Scotland cap in 1947. He, with Gus Black, had played in the Service Internationals. An extraordinary feature was the number of first-class scrum-halves produced. They started with Gus Black, who, besides playing for Scotland, was selected with Ranald Macdonald to tour New Zealand with the British Lions in 1950. Black had an extremely long pass from the scrum. When Black left, A.K. (Kelso) Fulton (like Gus Black, a product of Dollar Academy) came into his own and duly played for Scotland.

On Wednesday 2nd April 1947, the Edinburgh University XV squad, made up of T.B.M. Norman (Captain), D.D. Mackenzie (Hon. Secretary), A.W. Black, R. Burnett, J.P. Crowdy, J.I.M. Forsyth, I.G.P. Fraser, I.B. Grant, J. Inglis, J.D.O. Loudon, C. Lutton, R. Macdonald, C.J.R. Mair, J.E. Murray, J. Newall, J. Nicholson, A.G.B. Poole, D.I.T. Wilson, J. Wiltshire and C.M. Usher (Honorary Manager) undertook their first foreign tour against Agen (Champions of France) and the combined Universities of Paris and Bordeaux at Bordeaux.

At Calais the team was met by *M.* Girard, who had been a liaison officer in World War I. He was a delightful and valuable friend who became the team's mascot. There were many *mal entendus*, blamed on the *vacances des Universités*, but *M.* Girard straightened things out and any contretemps were forgotten in the laughter that ensued.

Arriving in Paris, the team spent the night in three small hotels used as 'digs' for students, near the *Gare d'Austerlitz*. The next morning there was a mix-up over seats in the train, as the reserved seats for the party were in *Wagon 16*, which in the event did not exist! The train was packed owing to the Easter holidays, but fluent French speaker Usher solved one difficulty most efficiently, as he gallantly offered his place to a charming girl, who was loath to accept; a compromise was reached and she sat happily on his knee from Paris to Bordeaux! All were tired on arrival after travelling for the best part of three days. The warm reception, an excellent hotel and a good meal revived the team's spirits, although it was disappointing that no runabout was possible before the next day's match, as the XV had not had a game for two and a half months.

The match against the combined Universities of Paris and Bordeaux was lost 34-18, but the team took some credit from it. Colin Mair at full back played on after his nose was broken, and dropped a goal from near half-way with his left foot. Black at scrum-half was greatly admired by all, and David Mackenzie showed great speed on the wing. Wiltshire was outstanding among the forwards and scored two tries, but the fatigue of the journey, combined with the heat and the hard ground, told in the end.

There was an early start next morning, when, by a near miracle, everyone caught the train for Agen, where the *Hôtel du Midi* was most comfortable. Next morning there was an official reception at the *Mairie*.

There was a hard game against Agen. Tommy Norman scored a brilliant try and Ian Wilson kicked impressively so it was no disgrace to be beaten by the champions 26-14. This was followed by another banquet and a dance.

The next morning there was a reception at the *Préfecture de Lot et Garonne*, where the *Préfet* himself and his charming Australian wife received the team. Back at the hotel for a *vin d'honneur* from the Patron and then, loaded with gifts, everyone staggered to the station for the long journey to Paris. Again there was a mix-up about seats, and on arrival in Paris it was a shock to learn that no arrangements had been made for accommodation for the night. However, a bus was waiting, and after a wash and brush-up spirits rose again. A reception at the *Hôtel de Ville* was most enjoyable and gave Usher time to fix some accommodation. That evening a wonderful dinner at the 'Grenouille', near the *Place St. Marcel*, provided a fitting ending to the trip. Good-bye was said to *M.* Girard on the platform. Nobody could have worked harder, and he was remembered with affection by every member of the team.

In a return match played at Myreside, Edinburgh in 1948 Edinburgh were the winners.

A unique situation arose in 1948 during the Scotland v. England match at Murrayfield, which Scotland won by two tries to a penalty goal; at one period, the University provided both scrum-halves when Steele-Bodger moved to scrum-half for England in the place of the injured Madge, and Black was the Scots scrum-half.

There was a lack of really good experienced centre three-quarters, although there were several good ones. Ranald Macdonald alternated between fly-half and centre with success, but did not combine too well. (He finished up playing on the wing for the British Lions in a Test Match in New Zealand.) Tommy Norman came near to what was required, but was often taken to play for his county in England and so broke the continuity. There was a question as to whether Les Allan was a better full-back or centre three-quarter. J.G.M. Hart, the champion hurdler, was later capped for Scotland on the wing, but from London Scottish.

The most outstanding centre during the period was J.L. (Len) Gaunt, the Yorkshire cap. He was full of football and could be brilliant. In form, he could win almost any match on his own. T.L. (Tom) Johnston from Hawick was a very good centre, but was unfortunate with regard to injury. Another was the very good but sometimes erratic Ian Cordial. The fly half position was usually well filled; Ranald Macdonald and Bruce Mackenzie alternated between that position and centre three-quarter, but the most finished player was J.N.G. (Norman) Davidson for Hawick. Few better passers of the ball ever played for the University. An International cricketer, he had naturally a beautiful pair of hands. He was probably the youngest player ever to be chosen as the captain of Scotland, against France in Paris in 1954.

Two full-backs stood out, C.J.R. (Colin) Mair and J.W. Fisk. Colin, later Headmaster of Kelvinside Academy, was a convert from centre three-quarter and developed into a first-class full-back. Fisk used to play for Leicester. There were four outstanding forwards, Mickey Steele-Bodger, who came to Edinburgh after having been Captain of Cambridge, J.G. (Gibby) Abercrombie, N.G.R. (Norman) Mair, brother of Colin, and D.C. (Donald) Macdonald. Mickey Steele-Bodger was a colourful wing-forward and played many fine games for England. He had great difficulty in avoiding being put on the scales by the English selectors. Being very light for International rugby when the selectors were beginning to look for weight, had the English Union ever known his true weight his chances would have been jeopardised. Norman Mair was one of the best Captains the University ever had. Captain for three years between 1950 and 1955, he made way for Norman Davidson in season 1953/54. He ruled with a rod of iron. A great theorist, he deserved his nickname 'The Maestro', broadcasting on TV, and reviewing.

In 1950, in a match against Glasgow High School F.P., the Scottish Champions left their unbeaten record at Craiglockhart. The score was 16-9. This was Ian Cordial's match. In the closing minutes he ran right through the defence, which included the famous Angus Cameron. The next season, during Norman Mair's second year of captaincy, there was a thrilling game against Oxford shortly before the Oxford and Cambridge match.

The home team was at full strength, with Boobyer playing a great game. It was anybody's match, but Oxford got home 8-5. The high-light was a magnificent try by Kelso Fulton. Stealing away from a scrum on the half-way line, he made for the line. Those who saw the diminutive Kelso being chased by the entire Oxford team will never forget it! Later, Oxford visited Edinburgh on tour at Easter, when Edinburgh got their revenge 8-6. Before Christmas, at Craiglockhart, Edinburgh had drawn with Cambridge.

In 1953, during the tour of the south, Edinburgh defeated Bedford 18-11 and the United Hospitals 5-0.

The fixture with Bedford originated in 1949 from a suggestion by Mickey Steele-Bodger. It made a second match when every other year the University travelled south to play the old-established game against United Hospitals. Edinburgh won the first-ever match with Bedford, thanks to the unorthodox play of Ian Cordial. Bedford only once visited Edinburgh, at the end of season 1955/56, when they found Edinburgh in top form after beating Oxford in the previous match.

On 4th November 1953 H.R.H. Prince Philip, Duke of Edinburgh, Chancellor of the University, visited Craiglockhart and watched the match against the Co-optimists. He was received by George Buchanan-Smith, President of E.U.A.C. and vice-captain of Rugby. George presented Norman Davidson, captain of the XV, who then introduced all members of his team. He also presented Mr. George St. C. Murray, President of the Co-optimists, who was a good friend to University rugby. His Royal Highness took a keen interest in the game and formed the impression that a certain distinguished University player kicked too much!

George Buchanan-Smith was as dangerous on the rugby field as he was in his motor car. Larger than life, he was never deterred when cornered. On one occasion the XV could not afford the restaurant meals on the train to Aberdeen, so George cooked a meal for them, which resulted in British Rail complaining to the Department of Physical Education about the resulting conflagration. However, thanks to George's charm and Usher's persuasiveness, B.R. were happily mollified. Buchanan-Smith's sturdy bullnose Morris, with magneto, was also prone to catch fire, with no ill effect. It did so at the annual camp of the 4th/7th Battalion, The Gordon Highlanders. His sister, Mary, was in the same mould. One evening, returning home for dinner, she overturned her car in the drive but singlehandedly righted it and was only marginally late. George became Chaplain at Fettes and sadly died too young.

In 1957/58 Duncan Macdonald, a great wing forward, played against England and Ireland and his efforts largely contributed to Scotland forcing England to a draw.

Hugh Williams, a fine forward, captained the University in 1958/59, when Edinburgh regained the Scottish Universities Championship. He was followed by D.M. (Duncan) Lawrie, from Melrose, who in turn led the team to win in the following two years. The best match during Duncan's captaincy was a resounding victory over Cambridge at Craiglockhart in 1959 when Edinburgh could do no wrong. In a brilliant exhibition of scientific and fast-moving rugby, few sides could have stood up to them.

Throughout these years Usher's old friend, the radio commentator Andrew 'Jock' Wemyss, who came out of the First World War as a major with the M.C. despite losing an eye, was a great help, especially in scrummage technique[8]. The Club owed a lot to Dr. Neil Campbell as adviser and referee. The reports of Jack Dunn (*The Scotsman*), Reg Prophit (*Evening Despatch*) and John Robertson (*Evening News*) helped swell the gate takings at Craiglockhart.

University Shinty

In 1947 Archibald Lamond revived shinty on a new ground at East Fettes Avenue, and the next year the Committee entered the Senior League, deciding that the club should not be limited to hard-living, hard-drinking Gaelic speaking Highlanders. In 1949 the team won the Littlejohn Vase, a handsome trophy, for Inter-Universities Competition in sport, especially shinty. Although the trophy was lost to Aberdeen in 1950, it was regained in the next year by a strong team led by Iain MacPherson. In 1952 there was a match against Irish hurlers living in Glasgow, when

---

[8] Wemyss, like Usher, played rugby for Scotland before and after the First War. It was Wemyss who, in 1920, before his first international after the War, asked for a Scotland jersey, only to be met with a frosty inquiry as to the fate of the one he had been given in 1914! Wemyss was wounded in the war, and lost an eye. He reputedly carried a spare glass one, bloodshot, for use on Sunday mornings to match his real eye.

the first half was played under shinty 12-a-side rules and the second under hurling 15-a-side conventions. Edinburgh Corporation presented a cup for Inter-City competition with Glasgow. Glasgow only won once up to 1959 due to the preponderance of Edinburgh University players.

From 1950 the results were not so good, and from 1952 to 1959 Edinburgh only won the Littlejohn Vase once to Glasgow's three and Aberdeen's four victories. However, shinty was regarded as the most fun of all Athletic Club activities, with the losing captain having to present his team with a bottle of whisky. This replaced the old custom of giving the Littlejohn Vase winners a gold medal and a bottle of whisky, when they left for home after the match. The prices of whisky and *camans*, the curved Highland long-handled double-sided lofted-blade sticks, were too much for frugal Highlanders and Lowland converts to bear, especially when purchase tax was imposed on the latter!

University Swimming

It took time to rebuild the Swimming Club as top performers returned after the war ended, but there was a good nucleus in I.B. Grant, demobbed from the R.A.F., K. Madej from Poland, T. Birrell, D.C. Thomson, S. Drancz, T. Rabie, A. Gullies and P.G. Aungle. Ian Grant was captain in 1947/48, when Edinburgh won the Scottish Universities Championship and shared the Water Polo Championship. The following year under T. Brunel, the Universities Championship was retained, but Aberdeen then reigned until 1954/55. George Armitage became captain, George Hart and Iain Percy Robb joined and the Swimming and Water Polo Championships were won until 1958/59 when the latter was lost. J. R. Hutchinson, Captain of Water Polo became President of the Athletic Club.

At Aberdeen, E.B. (Brendan) Lynch, also a Rugby Blue, having played a strenuous game of rugby for Edinburgh University, went straight over to the baths to help the swimming team to victory by winning the 100 yards back-stroke, swimming in both relays and playing in the water polo match. Brendan scored a try in the rugby match and a goal at water polo. Iain Percy Robb was a fine breast-stroke swimmer, representing Great Britain as well as Scotland.

Seven members of the team represented Scottish Universities against England. Percy Robb won the British Universities Breast-Stroke Championship, G.D. Hart broke the 440 yards free-style record, while the 3 x 50 Medley Relay team also broke the record. Percy Robb went on to represent Scotland at the World Student Games at San Sebastian, where he won a gold medal as a member of the British team in the 4 x 200 Relay race.

On 28th October 1954, a notable event took place when, in the match between Scottish and English Universities, women's teams were introduced. Edinburgh organised the match at Coatbridge Baths and, to mark the occasion, arranged for the proceedings to be televised. This was a great success and a welcome boost to finances.

In the 1955 Scottish Universities Championship, Percy Robb broke the 200 yards breast-stroke record in 2 min. 34.8 sec., only 6 seconds outside the British record. In the British Universities Championships, Edinburgh were runners-up to London. Percy Robb won the 200 yards breast-stroke in the excellent time of 2 min. 33.4 sec., a new record for the meeting. He represented Great Britain against France, and also won the Scottish 200 yards Breast-Stroke Championship. He and Murdoch (breast-stroke), Hart (butterfly and 400 yards free-style), Lynch (100 yards back-stroke), Mekie (100 yards free-style), Hutchinson, Hart and Corbett (polo) represented Scottish Universities.

In 1956/57, Edinburgh was third in the British Universities Championship, after London and Manchester, but set up a new record in the Medley Relay. J.C.M. (Jim) Hill took Neil Tasker, the British Internationalist, to a touch in the 100 yards free-style. Percy Robb and Hill went to Moscow as Scottish representatives for the World Youth Festival. Roger King from London University, a British Polo Internationalist, arrived and seven members were selected for Scottish Universities.

The following year, both Scottish Universities Championships were retained, and two individual championships were won by Jim Hill (100 yards free-style) and Percy Robb (200 yards breast-stroke). Both represented Scotland at the British Empire and Commonwealth Games at Cardiff in 1958. In 1958/59 supremacy was maintained for the fifth successive year.

Peter Heatly was the outstanding University diver and swimmer of all time, and his fame spread throughout the swimming world. In the 1950 British Empire Games in New Zealand he won the Highboard event and he won the Springboard event in Vancouver in 1954. He captained the Scottish team at the British Empire and Commonwealth Games at Cardiff in 1958. He was Britain's best ever diver and

Scotland's leading swimmer between 1943 and 1948, holding every Scottish free-style championship from 50 to 880 yards. He created Scottish and Allcomers records from 440 to 1,000 yards.

University Tennis

At the end of the War, Edinburgh University Tennis Club, captained by D.A. Smith, were Scottish University Champions.

In 1947 E. Donald and New Zealander A.D.L. Hunter joined the team. In the four years when they played, they were unbeaten in any match against another University.

Two years later the Argentine D.C. (David) Kerr, who had seen war service with the Royal Navy, joined, and a productive partnership was formed with E.W. Mauchline. David represented the University at rugby, swimming and squash as well as tennis. Usher held him up as a 'shining example to those who gave up healthy exercise when "Finals" were in sight'. He was particularly delighted that David should describe his economic science course as a 'piece of cake'. Many years later as a Director of the Distillers Company, he famously stood up against Ernest Saunders in the notorious Guinness imbroglio.

During these years Edinburgh were Scottish Universities champions.

Succeeding years were not so fruitful, despite having some very good players, although G.J.M. Nairn's team won the 1952 Scottish Universities title and shared it in the following year. In 1958 M.C. Palmer-Jones and H.K. Lawrence were Scottish Universities Doubles Champions.

New University Sports

In 1948/9 three new sports were admitted to the Athletic Club. These were badminton, basketball and squash.

Badminton

With the influx of students from the Far East, the Scottish Universities Badminton Championship was won for the first time in 1951/52. The team was S.N. Chong (captain), T. Mahadervan, J.M. Louie, M. Macleod, J. Fleet and M. Tamin Yeop. Together, Mahadervan and Macleod won the Scottish Universities Doubles Championships. The team was in the First Division of the East of Scotland League. They won the Inter-Universities Championship again, and Y.W. Teh and E.C. Saw won the Doubles title. Clive Dennis, champion hurdler and President of the E.U.A.C., joined in. A tour was undertaken, with victories against Leeds and Birmingham, while the match against Manchester had to be left unfinished with the score 3-3. Their opponents were considerably surprised at the standard of play in Scotland, revealed to them for the first time. Teh and Saw were undefeated on the tour, and lost only one set which was to the Manchester first couple.

In 1957/58 the Inter-Universities title was regained, and in 1959/60 Hamilton won the Scottish Universities Singles title.

Basketball

The make-up of the Basketball team owed a lot to postgraduates from the U.S.A. It was very cosmopolitan, with Americans, Canadians, French, Germans, a Greek—and a few Scots!

In the first year they won the Scottish Universities Championship and the East of Scotland League. The team, F.E. (Francis) Adderley (captain), P.G. Banister, D. Spence, E. Morrison, A.C. Sutter, B.H. Bonnlander and H.H. Steele, won the Scottish Cup in 1950. The fearsomely red-bearded L.K. Davidson from Kentucky University was Captain and Coach in 1953/54. An all-British record was achieved against St. Andrew's University with a score of 141-37. They won the Scottish Universities Championship that year and the next. They lost to the Kirknewton Comets, the runners-up in the United States Air Force Championship, but the following year won one and lost one to the Comets, then virtually unbeatable, but Edinburgh won the Universities Championship.

The 1957/58 season was outstanding. The highlight was a play-off for the East of Scotland League. In this 'The Knights', an American Air Force Team, were defeated 59-39. The Universities Championship was retained and only two defeats suffered, at the hands of the Comets (United States Air Force Champions) and Oxford University. The best player was ace Phil Potts, who had been 'All American' in the United States two years previously. Other players were Mike Phillips, Stan Nealy, who also represented the University in the high jump, Dyck Couser and best all-round guard, Tony Batt. Keith Main, after his term as Captain, was a most efficient and energetic Secretary in season 1958/59 and much of the success of the team was due to his efforts. A notable victory was against Oxford at Oxford. The record in the Eastern District League was played 11, won 11; points for 755, against 249.

Unfortunately the final of the Scottish Cup was fixed for a date in the vacation, after 50 per cent of the team had returned to the United States. In the event the Cup was lost by the narrowest of margins. With a full team the University would probably have won without too much difficulty. The Scottish Universities Championship was retained, and the final record of the season was 28 matches won and only one lost. Arv Adell was a popular Captain as well as a fine player. The team was Carl Blomgre, Bill Zeckhausen, Norm Pott, Carl Proffer, Rick Starbuck, Keith Main (Honorary Secretary and coach), Don Mills, Leonard Grant, Arv Adell (Captain), Roger Carrington, Bill Kinkell and Curt Rehfuss. In 1959/60 the team did exceptionally well, winning the Scottish Cup and Eastern District League.

Squash

To begin with there were only two squash courts, but Mr T.J. Carlyle Gifford a former Edinburgh University Football Captain and Mr. R.G. Simpson, who jointly owned the first standard-size squash court in Scotland, presented it to the University for the use of both the women's and men's clubs. It was superbly equipped with changing rooms and bar. Thus, in 1951, the team won the Scottish Universities Championship, Peter Everett was the British Universities (U.A.U.) Champion and F.H. Borden won the Scottish Universities title.

In 1955/56 the team under Bill Matheson produced the best results ever up until then. George Chisholm, Olly Balfour and Bill Matheson represented Scotland, and Edinburgh provided the complete Scottish Universities team that beat the English Universities 3-2.

In the 10 years between 1950 and 1960 Edinburgh provided the individual champions in all except one year, Balfour, Brownlow, Chisholm, Everett, Matheson and D.W.D. Shaw, Captain of Scotland.

Judo

Judo was introduced in 1950, with R.F. Rosenberger, also an expert fencer, as the first captain. It had been a real struggle. The mat, composed of condemned army 'biscuit' mattresses covered with a tarpaulin and secured by ropes fastened to the walls, had to be laid out before and rolled up after each session, as the room was shared with the boxing and weight-lifting sections. Opponents were difficult to find but the club gave demonstrations to Territorial Army units and prison officers amongst others. The first contest recorded was a victory against Leeds University.

Weight-Lifting

Weight Lifting was admitted in 1951. Usher had a weight-lifting room constructed, but it was seven years before there was an Inter-Universities match, which was against Glasgow, who won. However, R.A. Findlay gave an outstanding performance with lifts totalling 535 lbs. In 1958/59 the first Blues were awarded. Glasgow were defeated twice and Findlay won the Mid-Heavy title with 620 lbs total in the Eastern District Championships.

Rifle Shooting

Last to join in 1956/57 was the Rifle Section, which won the long-range rifle match for the F.W. Jones Challenge Cup at Bisley. The team scored 818 against Cambridge's 807 and Oxford's 750. They were second to Cambridge in the following year, but K.C. Meldrum won the S.R. Wimbledon Challenge Cup against 967 competitors and the F.W. Jones Challenge Cup was regained next time round.

The overall picture

Re-establishing Edinburgh University as a major sporting institution in such a wide range of different disciplines was a remarkable testament to the determination, drive, and above all, knowledge of sport that defined Charles Milne Usher. From his earliest days at school through his long years in the Army to his successful tenure at Edinburgh University, Usher put physical fitness and a readiness to participate in sport at the forefront of his professional life. That this had enhanced his skills and ability as a soldier, as a leader of men, and as an inspirational Director of Physical Education was beyond doubt. Looking back over the years, so many men and women in military and academic spheres, from prison camps through parade grounds, sports fields and gymnasia, owed their success, and development into rounded and self-assured personalities to the example, encouragement and inspiration of this remarkable man.

APPENDIX 3

PRISON JOURNALISM

THE production of news-sheets, journals and magazines in prisoner-of-war camps during the First World War was not unique to any one camp. Much ingenuity and imagination went into producing these documents, and credit is due to the editorial teams, of all ranks, which put together entertaining, amusing and informative publications that did so much to raise the morale and stimulate the imagination of men facing seemingly endless years of incarceration. *The Torgau Lyre* and *The Iceberg* were two such publications, produced at Fort Brückenkopf near Torgau and Burg *bei* Magdeburg. They are examples of humour, irony, caricature and no little artistic ability.

There were no production runs to achieve high circulation, but single hand-written, hand-drawn copies passed round an avid readership. That some have survived in respectable condition is testimony to the care and respect in which they were held by prisoners-of-war. Reproductions of extracts from the first issue of *The Torgau Lyre* and from *The Iceberg* are shown in this Appendix, preceded by an account of their genesis, compiled from notes left by Charles Usher.

In October 1914 a group of officers decided to produce a magazine to entertain their fellow prisoners. The Editorial Staff comprised The Hon. Rupert Keppel, Coldstream Guards, who had been wounded at Landrecies, C.M. Usher, Gordon Highlanders, H.A. Cartwright, Middlesex Regiment, C.F. Ffrench, Royal Irish Regiment and L.F. Sloane-Stanley, Middlesex Regiment.

With no means of making copies, the task of scripting the text was given to Usher, who copied out each of the editions by hand. The title was *The Torgau Lyre*, and the first edition was produced on 17th October, with the information that it would appear every two weeks. The cover depicts a coat of arms below the title. Surmounted by a *wurst* there is a shield divided into quarters. The first shows a castellated tower representing Brückenkopf with a British officer facing left and a French officer facing right, both looking down at goose-stepping police carrying sloped rifles with fixed bayonets. The second, rain splashing into muddy puddles, the third, smoke drifting from crossed *meerschaum* pipes and lastly, an officer showering while another operates the wheel of a pump to produce the flow of water. To the left an elegant Guards officer leans his elbow nonchalantly on the shield. He has a stitched-up rent on his breeches and is contentedly puffing on his pipe. A smart French officer to the right uses the shield as a back support while reading and smoking a cigarette. The motto at the foot says '*Alles Verboten.*'

Many of the cartoons are signed 'Alice Kaput', a clear reference to the German '*alles kaput*' ('everything is broken'). The Editor tells his readers that producing the magazine has provided endless pleasure and amusement. Readers are asked to pay one penny for one hour's undisturbed possession of the magazine. He goes on to claim that it will live in history as the only British magazine ever published in Germany. 'The idea positively makes one come all over with excitement!'

Usher, who contributed many articles throughout the life of the journals, writes about *The Adventures of Lieutenant Filberte*. The unfortunate Trevor Filberte, perfectly attired as a swell, embarks on a disastrous mission to woo a pretty girl at a fashionable seaside resort. Rupert Keppel contributes a farce, *Lord Horace's Revenge*, sub-titled '*A Society Romance*'. The first sports reports appear, accounts of a football match between British Reserves and French Reserves, and an International England v. France match. An Eton Field Game was played, in which Usher, who had never before played this arcane and unique game, was one of five Gordon Highlanders who took part

The first of a series of scurrilous descriptions of prisoner personalities appears under the title *Bogus Biographies*. As well as his portrait, a coat of arms is devised for each personality representing the subject's best appreciated points, which are then elaborated upon. It is clear that whoever devised the armorials was well versed in heraldry. The second 'Biography' was of a fellow prisoner, 'Okey Belfour', an academic with an interesting past, which was elaborated upon and exaggerated to great effect.

Sloane-Stanley comes up with a long, gripping and utterly absurd tale, brilliantly illustrated by A. Kaput and George Brotchen (another alias, but we do not know his real name) entitled '*A Race for a Wife*—a Sporting Story throbbing with human interest'.

The hand-written pages and illustrations of the *Torgau Lyre* are a treasure trove of stories, verse, spoof advertisements and names of participants.

There were three editions of the *Torgau Lyre*, which speaks highly of the journalistic outflow and editorial drive of the team, which fulfilled its commitment of producing a fortnightly magazine. The three editions came out on 17th and 31st October, and 14th November. When the prisoners were moved to Burg *bei* Magdeburg the magazine was produced there, but it changed its name to *The Iceberg*.[1]

Undeterred by the bitter cold, ice and snow of the hard winter of 1914, Keppel and his companions from the *Torgau Lyre* carried on their journalistic efforts in Magdeburg, amending the title to *The Iceberg* and commencing with a Christmas number. Many of the illustrations were in colour. The cover, painted by Ian Hamilton[2] (known in the editorial team as 'the Office Boy') and 'Alice Kaput', showed Belgian *garde civique*, French, Highland and Russian officers all cavorting on an iceberg with the Editor, as would be expected from a Coldstream Guardsman, seated aloof, reading and smoking his pipe. All the while sentries stand guard. A Spring number followed in April 1915. The cover by Ian Hamilton depicts girls clad only as flowers, accompanied by captors and captives, sailing through the sea, with icebergs as a backdrop, in a scallop shell towed by a hippo, a fish, a seahorse and a goose. The hippo and the seahorse wear glengarries, and are clearly meant to represent Usher and Hamilton. Reproductions of the covers of these editions and some extracts and illustrations are shown in this Appendix.

The Christmas 1914 and Spring 1915 editions continued the mix of commentaries in prose and verse, portraying the trials and tribulations of daily life and the antics of the guards, as far as it was prudent to do so. In the Spring number, the Editor put out a note reading

---

[1]   Some editions of *The Torgau Lyre* and *The Iceberg* are held in The Gordon Highlanders Museum.

[2]   Ian Hamilton, a fellow Gordon Highlander, was a talented artist and the son of the distinguished artist Vereker Hamilton, General Sir Ian Hamilton's younger brother. Usher's fellow prisoner Ian Hamilton went on to design the Memorial to Sir Ian Hamilton in Glasgow Cathedral.

'In the event of any officer being arrested with *The Iceberg* in his possession, he will take immediate steps to ensure its safe and speedy return to the Editorial Office. The same Regulation will hold good in the not unlikely case of the Staff being arrested. We pride ourselves on our blue blood (which we often use instead of ink) and our aristocratic appearance.'

The Torgau Lyre — extracts

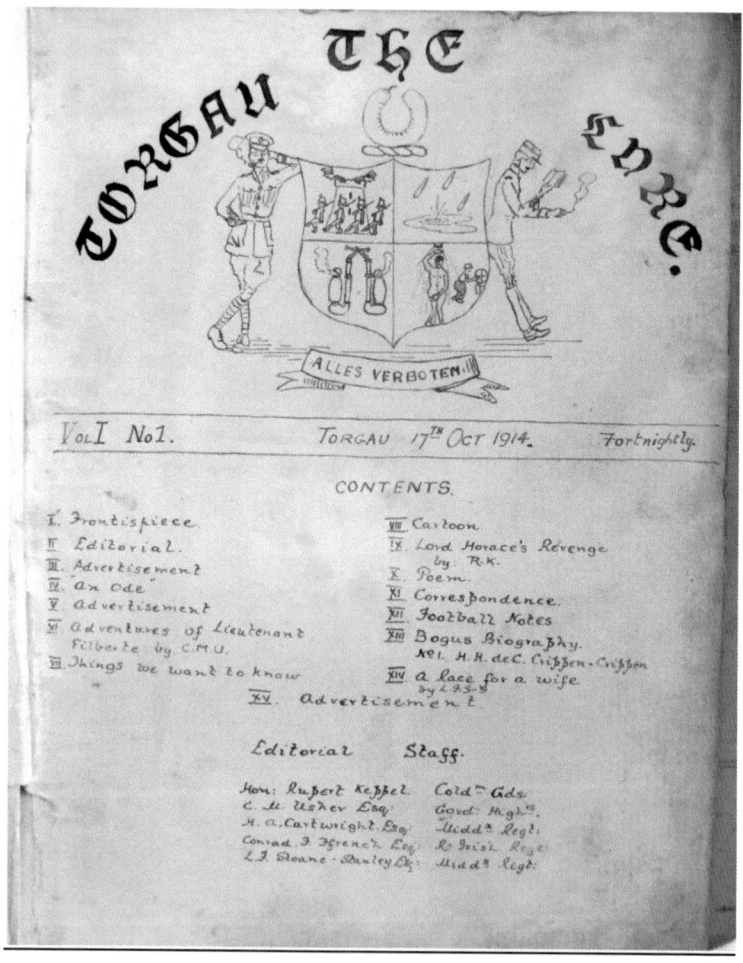

The Torgau Lyre - Issue 1

SCENE OUTSIDE OUR OFFICE AT 6 P.M. LAST SATURDAY

Editorial

It has been the custom from time immemorial for the Amateur Editor of a magazine to make the most abject apologies, or at any rate to try and throw the blame on someone else, on the appearance of his first number. In some cases a well-timed apology may perhaps have made the offence seem less of a crime, but nevertheless it is the action of a coward to apologize. We ourselves are no cowards: criminals of the worst type we may be, but we glory in it! Our Magazine may be futile and rotten, but it has given us endless pleasure and amusement getting it up, so what do we care. At any rate, WE are pleased, which is all that really matters. Our personal opinion of our Storyette writers, our Artists and our Poets mere words cannot adequately describe. Nat Gould, George Morrow, Harry Graham, appear cheap and ridiculous in comparison. Dickens, Romney and Tennyson cannot be compared with them.

And what do we ask for a glimpse of this wealth of talent? Do we ask gold? No! (because we know we couldn't get it) We ask you to pay one penny only* for the privilege of an hour's undisturbed possession of the first copy of the "Forgau Lyre" — the Magazine which will live in History as the only British magazine ever published in Germany! The idea of it positively makes one come all over queer with excitement!

The Editor.

✳ Money collected will be devoted to producing future editions on more sumptuous lines.

Editorial

Advertisement

THE ADVENTURES
OF
LIEUTENANT FILBERTE.

Nº I   HIS FIRST WEEK-END.

Lieutenant Filberte, newly joined, of the Blankshires arrived at Waveston-on-Sea, one sunny day in June, determined to give the local female population a treat. He drove to the Sea View Hotel, and having selected a suite of rooms, strolled out along the Esplanade. He was beautifully dressed in a cyclist's touring suit with knicker breeches, and brown button boots; the monotony of his indiarubber collar was relieved by a scarlet cravat, which hung loosely over his manly breast. His "Gents Boater" was cocked jauntily over one ear, while his gold albert glistened in the sun.

The Waveston season was at it's height, and everyone who was anyone was there and some of those who were not. Trevor Filberte soon espied a beautiful maiden coming towards him. She was clad in a sheath like gown of apricot gauze de soie, embroidered with flowers in natural colours, surmounted by a fox-skin boa. In her right hand she lightly balanced a purple parasol, while her châtelaine dangled languidly in her left. Just as she approached a puff of wind wafted the parasol from her tender grasp, carried it high above the heads of the gaudy throng, until it finally fetched up in a Corporation lamppost. With a cry she involuntarily turned to Trevor, but he, brave soul, was already in hot pursuit, and in less time than it takes to tell, had scaled the lamppost and restored the errant parasol, safe into

The Adventures of Lieutenant Filberte

①

the hands of its blushing owner. While the gushing words of thanks were still hot upon her lips, who should appear but Major Bounce, Trevor's platoon leader. His glance went right through Trevor and buttoned at his back.

The Major turned about smartly and offering his arm to the fair lady, they both retired in good order. Trevor stood stock still — his brain numb with pain and wrath. Suddenly the resounding clash of hotel gong brought him to his senses. He collected his wandering wits, turned on his heel and made straight for the Hotel Bar.

. . . .

Darkness was falling when Trevor woke up. He was lying prostrate on his bed (whither presumably he had been carried from the Bar by the Boots and Hotel Porter). Springing to his feet, he clasped his head between both hands, reeled towards the window, and flung it wide open. As the cool air beat upon his burning brow he automatically appreciated the situation. Involuntarily his eyes began to wander along the esplanade, where the darkness was so intense that it was impossible to perceive anything. The whole town lay wrapt in slumber. Not a sound was heard but the murmur of the billows as they broke upon the beach. Suddenly the silvery crescent of the moon slid slowly and silently from her hiding place, and cast a shimmer over the rippling waves.

Two figures were silhouetted against the sea strolling along arm in arm. Trevor immediately recognised the portly form of Major Bounce, and instinctively knew that his companion was the girl into whose eyes he had looked that very afternoon. He rushed to his suitcase — luckily his servant had packed his sword — his revolver. Seizing these he rushed down the stairs one at a time, hatred spouting out of every pore.

On he went across the tennis lawn. To spring lightly over the 12 foot wall, with burglar-proof entanglement, and reach the esplanade, unperceived, was the work of a moment. The unsuspecting lovers were sitting on a seat, his arm encircling her slender waist, her head reclining gently upon his shoulder. Little did they know what Fate had in store for them!

The Adventures of Lieutenant Filberte

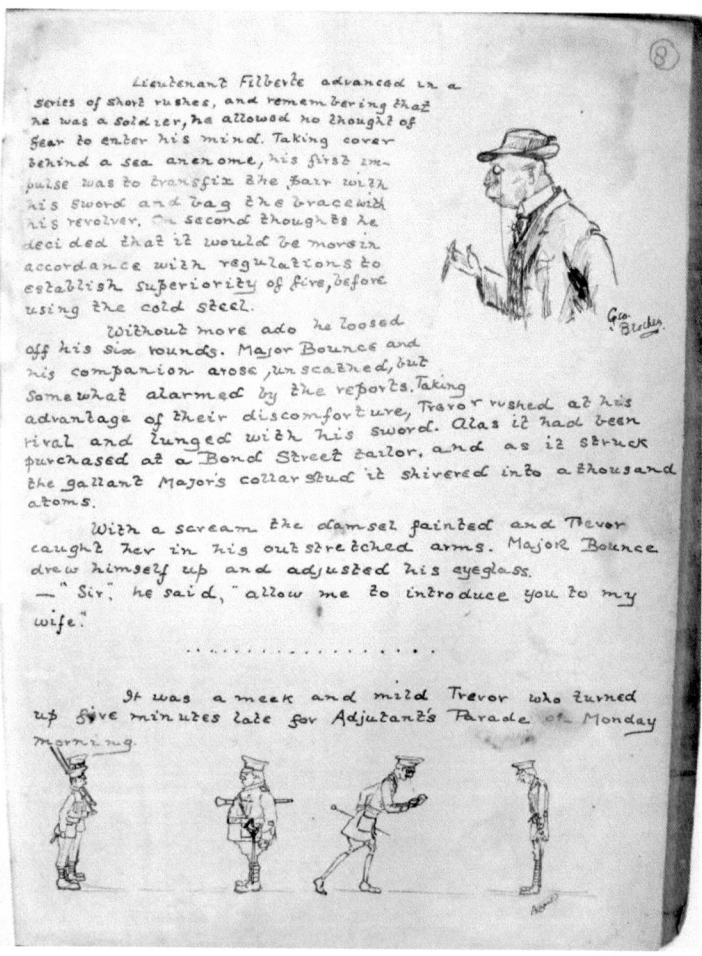

280

Lieutenant Filberte advanced in a series of short rushes, and remembering that he was a soldier, he allowed no thought of fear to enter his mind. Taking cover behind a sea anemone, his first impulse was to transfix the pair with his sword and bag the brace with his revolver. On second thoughts he decided that it would be more in accordance with regulations to establish superiority of fire, before using the cold steel.

Without more ado he loosed off his six rounds. Major Bounce and his companion arose, unscathed, but somewhat alarmed by the reports. Taking advantage of their discomforture, Trevor rushed at his rival and lunged with his sword. Alas it had been purchased at a Bond Street tailor, and as it struck the gallant Major's collar stud it shivered into a thousand atoms.

With a scream the damsel fainted and Trevor caught her in his outstretched arms. Major Bounce drew himself up and adjusted his eyeglass.

—"Sir," he said, "allow me to introduce you to my wife."

. . . .

It was a meek and mild Trevor who turned up five minutes late for Adjutant's Parade on Monday morning.

The Adventures of Lieutenant Filberte

He was beautifully dressed

The Adventures of Lieutenant Filberte

282

THINGS WE WANT TO KNOW.

The nature of the business which is being carried on at the FORUM and the names of the Senators. ?

and if it is not rather risky ?

The name of the gentleman who juggles with his false teeth outside Nº 5 Room every morning with various coloured liquids ?

Who is the gilded youth who is such a constant winner in the Baccarat Rooms ?

If it is not true that the Subalterns in Nº 2 Shed are overjoyed at the departure of a brother officer ?

Will they miss the smell of bacon in the morning ?

Who do our Allies call "épatant" and why ?

If the Choir appreciates the vocal assistance of the big gentleman with the bloodshot voice ?

Things we want to know

The name of the choirister whose voice was rather off colour last Sunday. And if the local bear had anything to do with it?

If the elderly Officer who is a pioneer inmate, was not rather open in his enquiries as to the whereabouts of the bath-room, yesterday?

If it is politic to discuss personalities in the Abort with the northern aspect?

Has a recent coolness between two gallant officers anything to do with this?

Where does the debonnaire cavalry doctor get his costs and why did he forget his brassard last week?

Why the "Gunner" Officer no longer goes to tea in No. 8 Room.?

If it is quite the thing to empty dirty water out of a top window?

Can any Field Officer enlighten us?

Things we want to know

LORD HORACE'S REVENGE.

a Society Romance.

Chapter I.

"James", said the Duchess, "remove the sausages." As she sat there, fingering her pearls, no woman could have looked more lovely than the Duchess of Pirbright, heiress to the vast Bulgeminster estates, with its acres of shooting and stalking,—where indeed every year the Duke would lead his house-party over the moors searching idly for pheasants or rabbits, before returning to the Hall for luncheon.

Tall and fair, with lovely eyes, Halma, Duchess of Pirbright, seemed to have been born under a lucky star. A large red wart on her neck went almost unnoticed, so dazzling was her beauty.

To-day her Grace was a bit out of sorts. "James," she whined, "hand the sausages." Lord Horace Frascati sidled up to her, and took her hand in his, looking into her eyes with that hungry stare, under which many a young girl had lost control of herself. The Duchess yawned, snapping her pearls, which rolled about the floor.

"Why do you look at me like that?" she said; I believe you want to borrow something." "No, Halma, darling, not now: it is because I

Lord Horace's Revenge

love you, — I adore you: Everything I have is yours if you will only fly with me!.

The Duchess lay back in her chair, pulling another necklace out of her bag, which she idly fastened round her neck.

"Horace", she whispered, with a little smile, "you know which is my bed-room, do you?" "Yes!" he answered eagerly, and a cunning smile lit up his handsome face; "Yes, darling ...?...

"Well, please will you fetch me a handkerchief?" Lord Horace's face darkened as he strode out of the room with a muttered curse. Halma should be his, even if he had to shoot the Duke of Pirbright like a dog!

As he crossed the hall he heard footsteps behind him. "Frascati", said a voice, what about that twenty thousand pounds you lost to me last night at billiards?"

Lord Horace turned, and a sickly smile stole across his face.

"Oh yes! Mount Carlton I had forgotten about it for the moment. What was it? ...thirty thousand pounds? I am just going upstairs to my room, I'll bring it down if you wait here!"

"Thanks old chap!" said the Marquis of Mount Carlton, opening a diamond - studded cigar-case, "I'll wait here."

Lord Horace's Revenge

Lord Horace Frascati passed the saloon, from which came a sound of dice and clinking of bottles, and made his way to the Duchess' bedroom. On the table lay her purse bulging with notes and gold, an old diamond tiara and a few necklaces in an untidy heap beside it.

An evil look came into Lord Horace Frascati's face. Glancing hastily round he clutched the purse, and with feverish fingers turned the contents out on the table, and began hurriedly counting the notes and gold. When he had finished he lay back in his chair, a cold sweat breaking out on his brow.

£50,000 - 7 - 2½! A fortune! Ruin stared him in the face if he failed to pay the Marquis by midday. He thought of all it would mean. Hounded out of the Automobile Club and the "Four Hundred" he would become a social outcast, — would perhaps have to leave the country. And there in front of him lay money enough to pay his debts, and nobody need know that he had stolen it! Nobody? Ah! but perhaps Halma would miss the money when she paid the local tradesmen at the end of the week. He must risk all that!

With another glance at the door he counted out £40,000 in notes and rushed from the room. As he descended the stairs, the notes in his hand a door suddenly burst open as he passed, and a lovely young

Lord Horace's Revenge

girl of eighteen rushed up to him and threw herself into his arms.

"Good morning, Dusty! (his old college nickname) she cried, "how are you darling!"

He bent down and kissed her, taking her hand in his; as he did so, a shower of notes fluttered to the ground, preceded by a couple of sapphire rings which he had picked off the table by mistake. Lady Ermyntrude Tudor looked at her fiancé with surprise. She had lent him tenpence only the night before, and knew that he had no money.

"Where did you get all those notes, darling?" she said at last. "Did you win it all at croquet from the Duke of Seven Dials?"

"I don't know what you mean," he cried hoarsely; "you dropped all this money yourself when you shook hands with me! It is your money, not mine! Where did you get it from, Ermyntrude?"

Lady Ermyntrude burst into tears and leant against the wall for support. "Ermyntrude!" hissed Lord Horace Frascati, "you stole that money from the Duchess of Rexbright. If you do not lend me £30,000 of it at once, I shall refuse to marry you, and shall expose you before the whole party at luncheon to-day!" He pulled out a revolver as he spoke, and leisurely adjusted the sights.

Lord Horace's Revenge

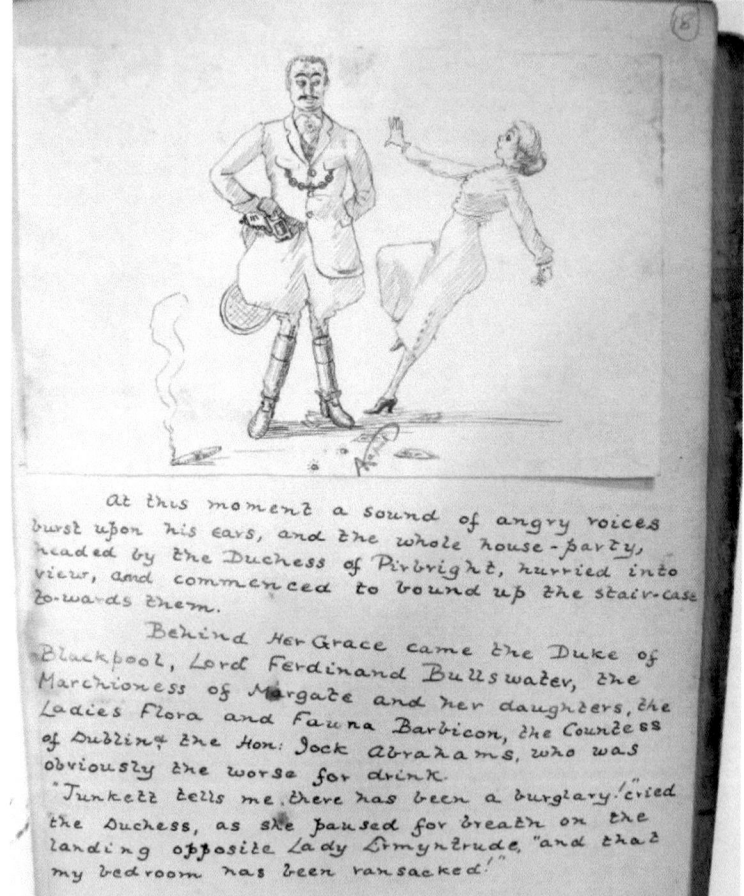

At this moment a sound of angry voices
burst upon his ears, and the whole house-party,
headed by the Duchess of Pirbright, hurried into
view, and commenced to bound up the stair-case
to-wards them.

Behind Her Grace came the Duke of
Blackpool, Lord Ferdinand Bullswater, the
Marchioness of Margate and her daughters, the
Ladies Flora and Fauna Barbicon, the Countess
of Dublin, the Hon: Jock Abrahams, who was
obviously the worse for drink.

"Junkett tells me there has been a burglary!" cried
the Duchess, as she paused for breath on the
landing opposite Lady Ermyntrude, "and that
my bedroom has been ransacked!"

Lord Horace's Revenge

Her eye fell on Lord Horace as he stood there fingering his revolver. "Ah! she cried, "my handkerchief! — I remember now! You are the thief, Dusty Frascati, you confounded blackguard! I know you did it, damn you!"

"You lie Halma!" he cried hoarsely "Lady Ermyntrude has confessed that she stole the money from your room, —— is that not so, Lady Ermyntrude?" and he turned to the young girl, who had sunk to the ground in a dead faint. "Look! cried he, "do you need further evidence of her guilt? And where did you get the notes from yourself, Halma?" He turned on her triumphantly. "Did I not give them to you myself in payment for the slight service you did me the night before last, when the Duke was away in London? Ah!" he pursued relentlessly, "you remember now, don't you? Shall I tell the whole sordid story to these people here?" And he pointed to the florid faces of the assembled house-party.

"No, not now!" shrieked the Duchess, "not now!" and she fell to the ground moaning pitifully.

"Stand back!" cried Frascati pointing his revolver at the Duke of Blackpool. He bent

Hon: Jack ABRAHAMS

Lord Horace's Revenge

rapidly down, and seizing the bank-notes thrust them in his pocket: then, lifting the Duchess in his arms, he pushed aside the Countess of Dublin, and strode down the stairs into the Front Hall. Outside the door stood three or four immense limousine motor-cars. Choosing the largest, Lord Horace Frascati placed the Duchess inside, and slammed the door. Already loud shouts could be heard coming towards them, with the trample of many feet! Up the park came the local policeman at the double. There was no time to be lost! Frascati turned hurriedly to wind up the engine, — THE HANDLE CAME OFF IN HIS HAND!

(To be continued.)

There was a young man who said "curst
Is the day when I bought that d—— wurst
    From the top of the tower
    Must I run every hour
To the opposite building —— or burst."

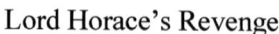

Lord Horace's Revenge

AN ODE.

An ancient clock above a muddy Square,
Now and for ages past beyond repair,
Owing to Time's incessant wear and tear.

It's works have been corroded through the years,
By th' Effluvium rising from the ——— ,
Hence it's excuse, when off the course it steers.

It's guardian, mossy-visage, bent and old,
With face empurpled 'gainst the Winter's cold,
Dispenser of the Naiad's gifts of old,

Toys with its guts with loving care,
Employing language quaint and rare,
Simile rich, Metaphor fair.

It's lingering hands persue their way,
It's bell strikes out wrong hours all day,
For ever in the old sweet way.

It counts with glee all those who go.
To pay their vows, through open door below.
Th' unbuttoning sprinter and the Costive slow.

Full soon may thou, old Timepiece, see
Thy courtyard from it's squatters free,
Ni Anglais ni Francais avec thee.

An ode

Football.

British Reserves ~ French Reserves.

A great game was witnessed by 2000 spectators including several gaily dressed ladies at Jorgau Park on Tuesday October 6th. Hepper winning the spin of the coin decided to play towards the Gas Works. The Opposing side therefore played in the opposite direction. The special trains from Halle which arrived rather late brought some 5000 more eager enthusiasts which brought the crowd up to nearly 10,000. (German enumeration). After a magnificent piece of combination on the right wing BOWERING the old "Spur" forward banged the spheroid into the fishing tackle. The Crowd rose like one man and cheered vociferously. Encouraged by this reverse the French played up bravely and bombarded the English defence. Carrying all before them, the English team charged down the field, Ansroux drove them back with a brilliant kick. The ball unfortunately completely defeated Giles his own custodian and went through the goal.

                  Half Time. England 2 goals
                           France Nil.

The second half was uneventful HEPPER and BOWERING each notching a goal for

Football

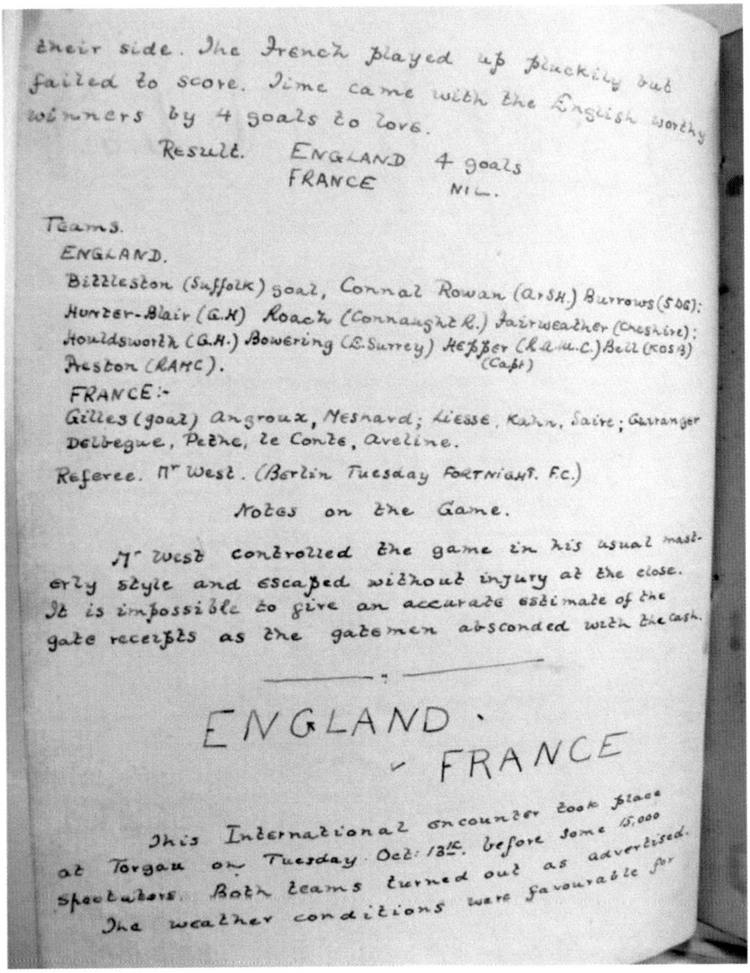

their side. The French played up pluckily but failed to score. Time came with the English worthy winners by 4 goals to love.

Result. ENGLAND 4 goals
FRANCE NIL.

Teams.

ENGLAND.

Bittleston (Suffolk) goal, Connal Rowan (arSH) Burrows (SDG): Hunter-Blair (G.H) Roach (Connaught R.) Fairweather (Cheshire): Houldsworth (G.H.) Bowering (E.Surrey) Hepper (Ch.d.u.C.) Bell (ROSB) Preston (RAMC).

FRANCE:-

Gilles (goal) Angroux, Mesnard; Liesse, Kahn, Saire; Gurranger Delbegue, Pethe, le Conte, Aveline.

Referee. Mr West. (Berlin Tuesday FORTNIGHT. F.C.)

Notes on the Game.

Mr West controlled the game in his usual masterly style and escaped without injury at the close. It is impossible to give an accurate estimate of the gate receipts as the gatemen absconded with the cash.

———:———

ENGLAND.

v FRANCE

This International encounter took place at Torgau on Tuesday. Oct. 13th. before some 15,000 spectators. Both teams turned out as advertised. The weather conditions were favourable for

Football

294

a fast, sporting game. The teams were.

FRANCE. Dugli (goal) Vandeburch Flogua: Cloy, Chamboredon, Kahn: Ragon, Cateau. Beaumont, Dellague, Romain.

ENGLAND. Usher (GK) Goal. Carthew (Suffolk) Burrows (SOG.) Beaman (R.A.M.C) Roach (Connaught) Nicholls (Suffolk). Robertson (GK.) Bowering (E Surrey) Constable (Warwick) Pereira (Suffolk) Mackie (R.D.F) Referee. M. Williaume (Boulognis F.C)

Constable started the game for the Islanders. There was some really fine play on both sides during the first period. Chamboredon, Beaumont and Dellague being very conspicuous on the French side while Burrows, Roach, Constable and Bowering put in some sterling work for the Englishmen. Honours were easy at Half-Time.

England nil.
France nil.

Soon after the re-start the Englishmen bombarded their opponents' goal and Dugli brought off some magnificent saves. Finally however BOWERING netted from a beautiful pass from Beaman. The stalwart "Medico" was on the top of his form in the latter stages and proved a stumbling block to many of the French attacks. Time came soon after with the score unaltered. Result:- ENGLAND 1 Goal
FRANCE NIL.

CHAMPIONSHIP TABLE.

	Played	Won	Lost	Drawn	Points
ENGLAND	4	2	0	2	6
FRANCE	4	0	2	2	2

2 points for a win, 1 point for a draw.

Touch FLAG.

Football

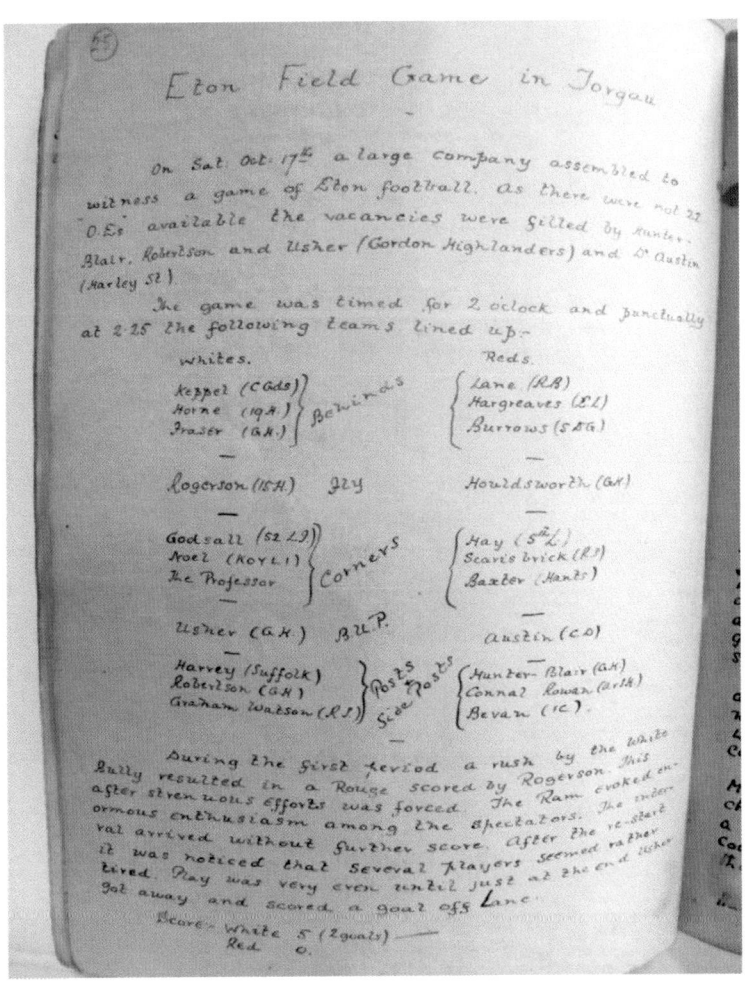

Eton Field Game

Bogus Biography - Okey Belfour

The real Okey Belfour, educated at Eton and Christchurch Oxford, was Head of English Language at Queens University, Belfast. On the outbreak of war he joined the Royal Engineers as a despatch rider and interpreter, although this appears to have been a cover. He was immediately given the rank of Corporal. With remarkable linguistic skills (in addition to English Language he lectured in Dutch, French, Norwegian, Swedish, Russian, Flemish, Greek, Latin, German and Hebrew) he was sent to Belgium to gather intelligence on German troop movements.

Bogus Biographies Nº 2

Professor A.O.J.S. Belfour M.A. N.B. K.C.B. P.T.O.

He beareth for coat armour:-

Dexter- On a field of oats a knight prickant at a man of learning couchant, a motor cycle stagnant interposed.

Sinister- Argent, Impedimenta of learning, proper.

Crest- Over two chevrons an obus bustant surmounted by a hat comic proper.

Motto- An oath puissant English unprintable.

Algernon Okey Jabez Spencer Balfour was born in Middlesex somewhere about 1882.

He survived his vaccination and in due course was educated at Eton and Oxford getting pluckily through this ordeal with the loss of no more than two or three teeth and his appendix. In choosing a profession poor Jabez made the first great mistake of his life,

Bogus Biography - Okey Belfour

His skill at languages was not replicated in his efforts to disguise himself as a Belgian peasant after the Battle of Mons. The Germans wasted no time on suspected spies and he was put against a wall to be shot. Before the order 'Fire' was given he said '*was du tust, das tue bald*' ('what you must do, do quickly') quoting the Luther translation of John 13.27. Amazed at such adept usage of German, the German officer held his fire. Realising that he was of more use alive as an interpreter, the Germans imprisoned him.

but bearing in mind that one of his ancest-
ors was a signatory to the somewhat infamous
death warrant of Charles I, every allowance must be
made for his conduct at his then early age, for he
entered the Stock Exchange. Here all went well
with him for many years till he unfortunately
became mixed up in an undertaking known as
the Liberator Building Society. Whoever this Society may have liberated it had the very reverse
effect upon Jabez, for although he escaped to the
Argentine he was seized, extradited and senten-
-ced to 15 years p.s. for his connection with it.

Released early in the present century
Jabez decided that a change of name and occupation was essential and accordingly he associated
himself for a time with Murray's New English
Dictionary, at the same time substituting an
"e" for the "a" in his surname and adding on
Algernon Okey in front. It is impossible to make
any excuse for the former though a touch of
pathos may be found in the latter choice when

Bogus Biography - Okey Belfour

The British War Office recognised his worth, even as a prisoner, and he was commissioned as a lieutenant in the Royal Engineers while at Magdeburg. He proved invaluable in dealings with the Germans throughout the War, after which his cover remained 'unblown'.

it is remembered that the name of Okey serves as a constant reminder of his only occupation during the first days of his imprisonment. But escape from the past seemed impossible, Algernon Okey was recognised, expelled from the office of the dictionary and driven to live upon his wits once more.

After a years wandering of which nothing definite is known, Algernon was lucky enough to get a billet as teacher of English to the natives of Belfast a town in the North of Ireland, but after five years he was again found out and sought oblivion (and very nearly found it) this time in a motor-cycling tour on the Continent.

Travelling through the Low Countries in the summer of 1914 Algernon was captured by brigands and the ransom demanded not being forthcoming, was on the point of being shot, when a somewhat risky story which he was relating to one of his executioners over

Bogus Biography - Okey Belfour

a glass of beer, so tickled the brigand chief that he forgot all about the execution and Algernon having found an opportunity of changing clothes with a friendly native escaped into the interior.

His present whereabouts are not generally known and it will be enough to end with the statement that he is now believed to be employed, in place of the more usual beautiful lady, in the receiving office of a Hydropathic Establishment at a certain well known Spa on the Elbe.

A Kaput

Bogus Biography - Okey Belfour

Note the silhouettes below - C.M. Usher in kilt.

Correspondence

To the Editor "Jorgan Lyre"

Sir,

It may be of interest to your readers to know that I have in my German garden now (October) a large grey fungus with blue spots. It is quite tame and submits to quiet stroking at meal times by myself and daughter — such a nice girl aged 18 and so good at Russian. She is putting her hair up next year and is passionately devoted to Wagnerian opera.

She is now home for the holidays from a convent school at Stückenheim (Board, fees & tuition, not including violincello) £30 per quarter. But the class rooms are steam heated which I think is so unhealthy & not quite the best thing for the complexion, although Lesbia's complexion is really very pretty, considering her love of sweet-meats.

If any of your readers would be charitable enough to lend £40 to a gentlewoman in distressed circumstances in order to start a ham & beef business in Saghalien, I should be eternally grateful

yours etc.

Constant Reader.

Sir,

While gazing at the sky on the morning of Oct. 9th 1914 I was surprised and not a little alarmed to notice that the firmament was filled with large floating specks. Perhaps some of your astronomically inclined readers can help me to elucidate the why and wherefore of this strange phenomenon.

Puzzled (Sozzled? Ed.)

Sir,

I wonder if you can help me in the following matter. How do I make a Batter pudding aux petits œufs noire de la chasse Polonaise. Is it necessary to baste it? How long should it be swizzled for & what won the St. Leger in 1909. Thanking you in anticipation.

yours very sincerely

Fungorius Mugwump

M.V.O.

Correspondence

A RACE FOR A WIFE

a sporting story throbbing with human interest.

"Egad", said Lieutenant Gatwick-Plumpton, lighting another fragrant Capstana-Capstana "I'm deuced heavily hit — simply devilishly."

The speaker, a handsome young giant, standing 6ft. 4 ins. in his socks, broad of shoulder with a face like a Greek god, sipped his crème de menthe, and glanced at his companion and brother officer, Gideon Growl by name.

The latter was a slim, well-built but intensely evil looking man. His dark villainous face was partially concealed by a black bushy beard, something like the third fence at Sandown Park. A lean hawk-like nose was flanked by two black, steely, glittering eyes, capable of spotting a dropped half-crown in the Silver Ring from the top of the Grand Stand. Add to this a hump back (acquired by riding "dud" finishes at flapper meetings) and a withered arm, caused by blood-poisoning, which set in after he was nearly stabbed to death by a three card trick-cum-jellied eel joint in a Hurst Park Race Special. Still, there was something debonnaire and dashing about Captain Growl. Few men could resist him, women fell before him like grass before the mower's scythe.

"Hard hit, are you Jack" said Gideon,

A Race for a Wife

The Derby is only three weeks off now!" He glanced warily round —

"Jack, why not run Harkaway and put yourself straight? Ride him yourself and we'll get any odds we like. He can give them all a stone and a beating. Why, the top weight this year is carrying 13 stone odd and Harkaway will certainly get in at about 11 st: 7lbs:"

"But" laughed Jacke "Harkaway is nearly twenty years old, and has never been raced in his life."

"So much the better, my lad," croaked Gideon "the handicapper will be completely at sea. So it, Jack! I'll train and you shall ride him!!"

Plumpton ran his fingers through his golden curls, stroked his dapper little imperial and thought hard. Not for nothing was he, Lieutenant Gatwick-Plumpton of the Pink Lancers, called "Daredevil Dick" by his messmates.

"Egad Gideon" quoth he, "it's a good idea. Damme I will!"

"Good on yer, boy. don't put it about though, it's a blooming pinch for us!" (Gideon be it noted was at times a little vulgar, but think of the company he usually kept! Bookies, card sellers, lobster merchants, and other swell mobsmen were his daily companions, and he invariably had a choice assortment of the foregoing race course pests to dine with him on guest-nights much to the disgust of the ladies)

A Race for a Wife

Have another bottle of the Boy and we'll toddle off to the "Gardenia". The ladies had, happily left the Mess and the remaining officers were engaged in playing ludo and other gambling games. The Lancers were one of the "swiftest" regiments in the Service.

"No, I thank you" said Jack, "I am off to see Euchrisma Odol — ah, that name !!!"

"Phffshah"! muttered Growl "sentimental fool! Hark-away WILL NOT WIN THE DERBY. I'll arrange to see Ikey, nobble him, and lay against him, and then — what Ho! as they say in Madrid!!"

Jack heaved his 14 stone of brawn and muscle out of the luxurious settee and adjusted his dolman and sabretache. "Good-night, Gideon dormez bien." he said, smiling.

"Good-night Daredevil Dick" rejoined Gideon heartily — then under his breath "curse you, curse you, curse you. Euchrisma and her fortune shall never be yours!

+   +   +   +   +   +

It was the night before the great race. Derby Town was full of life, the streets crowded with the flower of England's aristocracy. Prominent amongst them showed the Pink full dress kit of the Lancer officers who had come from Manœuvres to cheer their best loved subaltern on to victory or death, over the stiff fences which make the Derby the hardest race in the world to win.

A Race for a Wife

Meanwhile, masked and cloaked, in the Bar Parlour of the "Angry Rabbit" sat Gideon, talking in low whispers to Ikey, one of his creatures; wanted by the police of many countries on various charges.

On parting Gideon handed to Ikey an instrument like a garden syringe, a large bottle of Slowups famous dope for "Not wanted to-day" horses, two melinite bombs, a stiletto, a Browning pistol and a packet of "Beatalls Buckup Cocktail" powders for his (Ikey's) own benefit. In order to save the expense of stabling Harkaway it had been arranged that he should stay in his box all night; he required rest as he had been hunted with the famous Loamshire hounds on the previous Friday, when he and Plumpton, who sat a horse like a centaur, had negotiated the difficult leaps set by the M.F.H with ease and consummate skill.

A Race for a Wife

The plot was briefly this:— Ikey was to murder the entire station staff, blow in the doors of the horse box, dope Harkaway and also hamstring the horse, and then quietly escape. Nothing need be known of this nefarious deed, if quietly carried out, and the horse naturally would never get the course.

Gideon attired in a check suit, white bowler, polo breeches and patent leather boots was to stand in the 5/- Silver Ring and lay against Harkaway ad lib:. Now mark how this villainous plot was frustrated.

Ikey successfully reached the railway station and bought a ticket to Clapham. While the booking clerk was searching for the change Ikey beckoned to the collector and complained of being handed what he called a "snide half bar." The collector called the station-master, two or three idle porters chipped in and then — Ikey dropped a bomb.

There was a deafening report, a lurid flash. A column of acrid smoke rose to the hole in the roof through which the Derby Town Station staff had passed en route for the Golden Gates. Ikey walked quietly away to where the horse boxes lay. On the way he was obliged to stab two outside porters, and a signalman.

P.C. No 13C of the Derby County Constabulary, who was on duty at the station and discovered the outrage within an hour of its perpetration

Fragment of wood found near Derby station the day after the outrage

A Race for a Wife

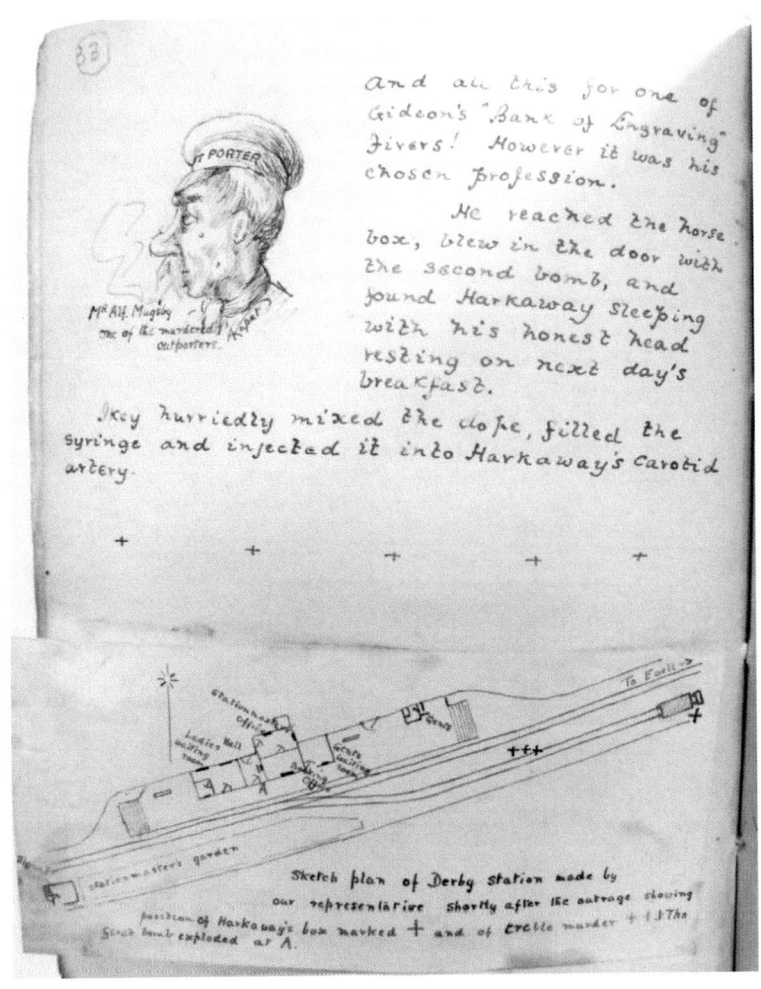

Mr. Alf Mugsby
one of the murdered
outporters.

IT PORTER

and all this for one of
Gideon's "Bank of Engraving"
fivers! However it was his
chosen profession.

He reached the horse
box, blew in the door with
the second bomb, and
found Harkaway sleeping
with his honest head
resting on next day's
breakfast.

Ikey hurriedly mixed the dope, filled the
syringe and injected it into Harkaway's carotid
artery.

✝   ✝   ✝   ✝   ✝

Sketch plan of Derby Station made by
our representative shortly after the outrage showing
position of Harkaway's box marked ✝ and of treble murder ✝✝✝ The
first bomb exploded at A.

A Race for a Wife

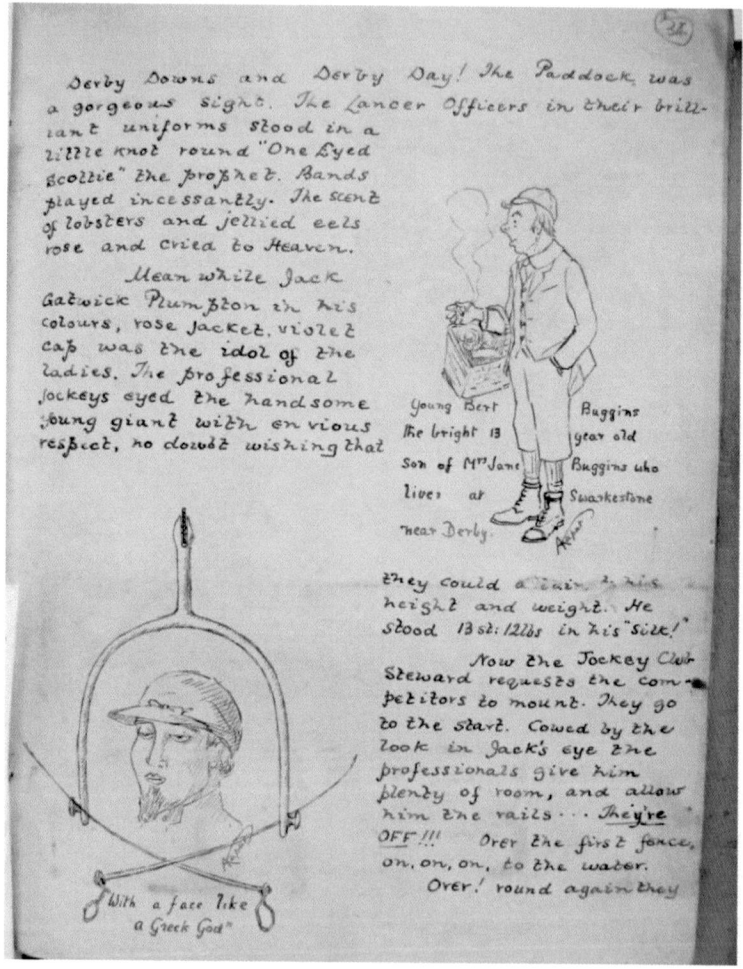

Derby Downs and Derby Day! The Paddock was a gorgeous sight. The Lancer Officers in their brilliant uniforms stood in a little knot round "One Eyed Scottie" the prophet. Bands played incessantly. The scent of lobsters and jellied eels rose and cried to Heaven.

Mean while Jack Gatwick Plumpton in his colours, rose jacket, violet cap was the idol of the ladies. The professional jockeys eyed the handsome young giant with envious respect, no doubt wishing that

Young Bert Buggins
The bright 13 year old
Son of Mrs Jane Buggins who
lives at Swarkestone
near Derby.

they could attain to his height and weight. He stood 13 st: 12 lbs in his "silk!"

Now the Jockey Club Steward requests the competitors to mount. They go to the start. Cowed by the look in Jack's eye the professionals give him plenty of room, and allow him the rails... They're OFF!!! Over the first fence, on, on, on, to the water.

Over! round again they

"With a face like a Greek God"

A Race for a Wife

35. On passing Tattenham Corner for the third and last time Jack gave Harkaway one touch with the whip — then throwing away all superfluous weight to ease him, he forged ahead and won the Derby by 40 lengths!

There was a sudden stir in the Silver Ring, a flash and a report! All that was mortal of Gideon Growl was carried off to the waiting room by a Metropolitan policeman to await the Coroners inquest.

For Ikey in his haste, had injected Harkaway with Beatalls Buckup Cocktail and had taken the dope himself !!! — and was now sleeping soundly in the local drunk and disorderly cell. No wonder Harkaway excelled himself

+   +   +   +   +

Daredevil Jack Plumpton led Euchrisma Odol to the altar three months later, pouched her banking account and lived happily ever after with Harkaway and Ikey, who gave up his bad ways and became Jacks confidential valet.

The End.

A Race for a Wife

Harkaway wins the Derby

A Race for a Wife

Ave Caesar

The Iceberg — extracts

The Iceberg - Christmas 1914

Random illustrations

'How you fell in with that horse-coping stiff.'

Over the jump

The Eastern Turret

A ghost story by C M Usher

The Eastern Turret
a Ghost Story

Nobody could have been more pleased than I was to receive Donald's invitation to spend Christmas at his old castle in Inverness-shire. I had often wished to see the ancestral home about which I had heard so much, and I had been wondering how I was going to spend the Yuletide Season all by myself in London. Thus both my wishes were gratified at the same time.

Donald met me at Kincraig Station in his trap and drove me through the snow, some six miles, to Tullockgribbean. It was just my idea of a highland castle, with its high-pitched roof and numerous turrets. It looked splendid as we first caught sight of it, wrapped in a mantle of snow and standing out in its solitude against the wild background of the Cairngorms.

I had met Donald's sister and his father and mother before, and so I felt quite at home

amongst the large party which had gathered to-
-gether for Christmas. After tea Donald showed me
over the castle which quite came up to my expect-
-ations. In some places the walls were ten feet
thick, and the winding staircases in the turrets
especially took my fancy. They seemed to wind
themselves upwards around the central column in
an eerie and uncanny manner. My room overlooked the loch, and from it I could see the eastern
turret, perched upon a crag of the rock on which
the castle was built.

    That evening most of the party
retired early, and Donald and I smoked a last
pipe to-gether before turning in. In a joking way
I asked him if he had not got a family ghost
to show me. He became very serious, and I at
once felt that I had talked too lightly of a
subject which my host desired to keep from me.
As he showed me up to my room he begged me
not to mention the subject again, as the castle
was indeed supposed to be haunted, and although
he himself had little faith in the story, his

The Eastern Turret

parents respected it. Moreover this was the time of year at which the ghost was supposed to appear. This naturally aroused my curiosity, and I determined to investigate the subject further on the morrow.

Next day was Christmas Eve, and Donald took me for a walk round the grounds. From the far side of the loch the main feature of the castle was the eastern turret, which I had noticed from my bedroom window. I asked Donald if there were any rooms in it. He looked rather troubled and replied that though there was a bedroom right at the top, nobody had slept there for a long time.

On further questioning him he acknowledged that this was the haunted room, and bit by bit I got its story out of him. Nobody had slept there since Donald was quite a small boy. On that occasion the unfortunate occupant had been found next morning dead on the floor, with a terrible gash in his throat, and his razor by his side. It appeared to be a clear case of suicide, but it was certainly a curious coincidence that the same thing had occured on four previous

The Eastern Turret

occasions and each time on Christmas Eve.

In the good old days an ancestor of Donald's was said to have murdered a man in this room, and later the ancestor himself fell a victim to the knife of an unknown assassin on the same spot at the same time — Christmas Eve. Donald was rather vague as to which of the two was still supposed to inhabit the room and to continue taking his revenge on peaceful strangers in the twentieth century. However I had no fear of committing suicide, nor was I afraid of a murdering ghost. On the other hand I should have been delighted to make the acquaintance, either of Donald's bloodthirsty ancestor, or of his victim, and therefore asked Donald if I might spend the next night in the room. At first he would not hear of it, but when he saw that I was perfectly serious he at length gave in and had my requisite belongings surreptitiously removed thither so that his parents should not know about it

The Eastern Turret

I certainly felt a little queer as I crept up the winding staircase on my way to bed in the eastern turret that night. The room was quite round and the stone walls bare, except for a faded piece of tapestry that hung at the head of the old fashioned bed. It was comfortable enough however, and contained nothing sufficiently suspicious to give a clue to its terrible story, except a general feeling of aloofness from the rest of the castle. I had had a long day and soon snuffed the candle and fell sound asleep.

I woke up about seven o'clock with a feeling of disappointment at having had a good night's rest. The sun was streaming in through the only window, and springing out of bed I saw the loch far below me gleaming in the winter sunshine. I began to shave in a leisurely manner, when suddenly I was overcome by an incredible fear. I felt conscious of someone standing behind me, and next moment I saw in the looking glass a

The Eastern Turret

face peering over my shoulder — not an evil de-
bauched face, but the face of a respectable middle
aged man, wearing side whiskers after the fashion
of the Mid-Victorian era. A badly tied stock
around his neck, ill disguised the horrible gash
that stretched almost from one ear to another.

An icy hand grasped my
wrist and slowly but surely my razor was
forced upwards and pressed against my throat.
In a moment I understood all. Donald's ancestor had been murdered by the ghost of his
own victim. and had haunted the room until
he himself had found another victim. And thus the
crime had been reenacted again and again, until
I myself was now being murdered by the ghost
of the man who had slept here when Donald
was a child, and would have to haunt this
room until another curious fool, like myself, chose
to sleep here.

Further and further the razor pressed into my flesh. I was powerless against the

The Eastern Turret

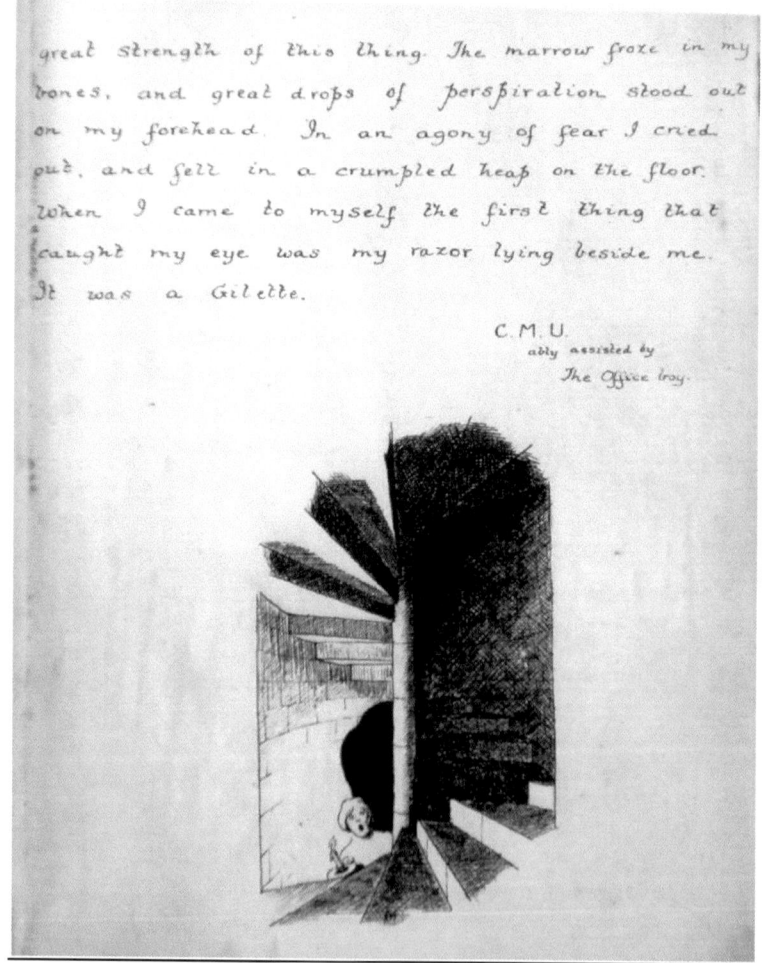

great strength of this thing. The marrow froze in my bones, and great drops of perspiration stood out on my forehead. In an agony of fear I cried out, and fell in a crumpled heap on the floor. When I came to myself the first thing that caught my eye was my razor lying beside me. It was a Gilette.

C. M. U.
ably assisted by
The Office boy.

The Eastern Turret

'The Office Boy' who 'ably assisted' Usher was Ian Hamilton.

Random illustrations

Winter - the pony trap

Night attack

Portrait of a monkey by Ian Hamilton

Mermaids

Prisoners exercising at Magdeburg by P Morel
(The kilted figure is almost certainly Usher)

Destroyers at sea

The Iceberg - Spring 1915

Sauve qui peut!

I wonder who's kissing her now?

Magdeburg

I thought I saw
A poem by C M Usher

I thought I saw!

a Poem

I thought I saw Adonis
Go striding down the path
I looked again and found it was
Breen, coming from his bath

I thought I was in Bond Street
So gaily did he strut
I looked again and found it was
That dapper Major — Nutt.

I thought I heard the thunder roll
I thought the world would smash
I looked again and found it was
An Ally goin' to 'crash'

I thought it was the sunshine
Was blinded by it's rays.
I looked again and found it was
That hat of Captain Grey's.

I thought I saw a phantom
Go racing through the snow
I looked again and found it was
"Herr Riding Master" Joe.

I thought I heard a fairy tale
Of ages dim and dark
I looked again and found it was
A yarn by dear old Clark.

I thought I saw

APPENDIX 4

HITLER'S ORDER OF THE DAY
10TH MAY 1940

Soldiers on the West Front!

THE hour has arrived for the most decisive battle for the future of the German Nation. For three hundred years the aims of both the English and French have been to retain power by preventing Europe consolidating, and by keeping Germany weak and impotent. To this end France has declared war on Germany 31 times in 200 years.

For years the British have sought world domination, preventing unification of the Reich and denying her the good things of life needed to sustain 80 million people. England and France have stuck to this policy without concerning themselves about the regime ruling Germany at any one time; it was always Germany they wanted to strike.

You too now know of those men responsible for these objectives—Germany should be crushed and broken up into little princely states. Then the Reich loses her political power and with it her ability to safeguard the right of the German people to live in this world.

This tells you the reasons for the rejection of all my wishes for peace, and explains the reasons for the war on September 3rd last year. The German nation has no hatred and no enmity towards the English or French nations.

Today the question is whether to live or go under.

In a few weeks the brave troops of our armies have suppressed the Polish enemy and the actions of England and France, and with these removed, the threat from the east. As a result England and France decided to seize Germany from the north.

Since 9th April the German armed forces have nipped that attempt in the bud.

What we have always seen for many months as an imminent danger to us has now happened. England and France are engaged in gigantic manoeuvres in Europe, aimed at striking the Rühr area through Holland and Belgium.

Soldiers of the West Front! With this your hour has come. Today the battle has begun for the fate of the German Nation for the next thousand years. Now is the call for you to do your duty.

The blessings and thoughts of the German people are with you.

Berlin, 10th May 1940.
Adolf Hitler

APPENDIX 5

THE CAPTURE OF BERGUES
GERMAN VERSION

WHEN Usher returned to Europe in 1944 he came across German publications celebrating the successes of their forces. One of these finds was a series of bound copies of *Die Wermacht* for 1940, 1941 and 1942. The 1940 publication describes the Germans' entry into Dunkirk as the last of the B.E.F. departed. It confirms the importance of Bergues, but ignores the stubborn defence that held them up for the best part of a week, from the first German attempts to cross the River Aa on 24th May to the withdrawal and evacuation of Usherforce on 31st May.

The Germans clearly recognised the importance of Bergues, and that taking the town would open the road to Dunkirk. That the only approach to Bergues by tanks was along the main road over open ground, exposed to anti-tank fire, undoubtedly influenced the German decision to capture the town by infantry assault. They did not know the paucity of anti-tank resources available to Usher.

The significance of Bergues to the Germans is shown by the article from the 1940 edition of '*Die Wehrmacht*'. It does not mention the attacks repulsed during the seven days when the defence was organised by Usher, but merely covers the attack that penetrated the gallant reduced French defences once Usherforce had been withdrawn to Dunkirk.

This publication ignores the German failure to destroy the B.E.F. and prevent its evacuation. While understandable in its triumphant lauding of the *blitzkrieg* campaign and the defeat of the B.E.F., it ignores the *Luftwaffe*'s failure in the Battle of Britain and Hitler's abandonment of Operation *Seelöwe* (Sealion), the seaborne invasion of Britain. Leaving Britain unconquered, an 'unsinkable aircraft carrier' from which Germany could be attacked, and which would ultimately prove the springboard for the Allied invasion of Europe that led to Germany's final defeat, was the end result of the German Army's thwarted attempt to take the B.E.F. out of the British

Army's order of battle, and its failure to open the route to Dunkirk through Bergues.

England's flight from the continent.

In the late evening of the 31st May a Silesian infantry division, coming in from the south pushed forward into the French defended port of Dunkirk. Entering from Poperinghe the fire from their batteries turned the withdrawal of the English forces to the sea into an incredible rout. The stationary British vehicles left in the streets and driven into the ditches along the route covered a distance of eight miles—entire batteries, lorries of all types, tanks, anti-tank guns and an incalculable amount of equipment which the English had abandoned before they could reach the rescue ships in the burning harbour of Dunkirk, either by swimming or in small boats.

The Division, an elite combatant formation of troops, had fought hard and successfully almost daily for 21 out of the 23 days of the campaign from the 10th May. Their main weapons, infantry, artillery and sappers had together with the other supporting troops of the division been used throughout with maximum effect and under assured, bold and determined leadership of their commander, contributed significantly to the success of the victorious campaign. Prisoner statements showed that the enemy of the Division which comprised Poles, Dutch, Belgians, English and French soldiers and who were constantly in retreat called the division 'The Blood Division'.[1] The shocking name the 'Blood Division' is understandable in that, despite the strong resistance by the French, the effective action by the Silesians at Bergues caused the defeat. The French were the aggressors here. As the French had the task of protecting the retreat of the British army to Dunkirk, the French could shed their blood for England as often as they themselves and soldiers of other central European states could expect to do, and when the prisoners were asked why that was they shrugged their shoulders and said they were not the leaders and they were

---

[1] An unlikely epithet to be used by British troops. Almost certainly the German interpreters would have come across many references to 'that bloody division' which means something completely different in British soldiers' colloquial language!

just to follow orders. The war-torn Flemish citizens looked up with fury in their eyes when they were asked about the flight of the English by the German soldiers. With contempt they spat out the words '*Ils sont parties*'—they've left!

As the weakening of resistance in the area around Bergues became more marked, the Division acted quickly with undiminished strength. The right regiment went east of Bergues on the canal, forcing a crossing despite the frenzied fire of the French, built a bridgehead on floating bridges and waded through the flooded meadows and fields, fighting onwards. At the same time, the left regiment attacked the area around Bergues, whilst the third stayed in reserve. However, the defence was so skilfully mounted, the individual infantry weapons and artillery were so difficult to bring close that the attack, not without painful losses, was held up in the 1st June. Artillery was mounted, they covered the ramparts with heavy fire, flame-throwers and assault detachments were deployed, however the resistance of the French was stubborn, because ramparts, many metres of thick stone walls, were ultimately a match for every infantry attack. The troops made a breach in the impregnable wall of the Bastion, as had been done at Dueppler Schanzen by the singing Pioneer Klinke, who died throwing a burning powder sack and so with his death enabled the infantry to storm through.

Now Stukas were used to create the breach in the same way, and with the same result. The Stukas were ordered in on 2nd June. At the same time the infantry regiment on the left got ready to follow the bombing attack. Raiding parties of the Pioneers under the leadership of Lieutenant V— were instructed to break through the breach, allowing the infantry free movement. Punctually at 15.00 hours the dive bombers appeared over the ramparts, made a few tight turns in the air and sent their bombs crashing on to the fortification.

The massing and descent of the Stukas had barely been noticed when the Pioneers advanced and hurtled down the last slope to the breach. An unknown Grenadier of the assault regiment showed them the place where a large bomb dropped by the Stukas had smashed the wall and in so doing had made the necessary opening for the storm troopers. One after another the Pioneers reached the breach and, panting, reached the summit, and as they reached the top the French came out from their cover and concealment, to counter-attack and retake the ramparts. The armed attack by the French was abandoned without a shot being fired, the leader of the Pioneers stood up at the head of his heavily armed troops and immediately went on the attack, using the surprise and shock, he called on the commander of the fortress, who was standing at the head of his men, and with his weapon in his hand indicated to them that further resistance would be useless and that the fortress was surrounded. The men put their hands up and the commander, a grey haired soldier who was wounded, realized that further resistance was impossible and agreed to the laying down of weapons. Within a short time nearly 10 officers and 500 men had surrendered and the fortress was in our hands.

Glowing silver around the peace and silence of the midnight hour, a thousand stars twinkled in the dark sky. Shots from enemy artillery flash brightly in the distance, here and there German machine-gun fire chatters on to the damp meadows towards suspected reconnaissance patrols, on the horizon the glowing light of the burning fortress of Dunkirk reddened the sky and illuminated the horrific defeat and destruction of the British soldier boys.

Throughout the Occupation there was a German war cemetery in the shadow of the ancient Abbaye St. Winoc, approached by a flight of stone steps with various colours of rhododendrons, and a swastika flag on a mast to the right hand side. Beyond these were flowerbeds with many species of flowering and evergreen shrubs and masses of French marigolds. There was a large Maltese cross created out of a little wall of red bricks 40cm high, covered in red rose bushes, outside of which were 1,000 graves each with an oak Maltese cross and a metal plaque inscribed with the rank, name, date of birth of the soldier and when he was killed. Overlooking the graveyard was a concrete tower riddled with shell holes surmounted by a sentry box also of concrete.

The Germans held Bergues until 1944, when the Allied advance after the Normandy landings and the taking of Paris forced them into retreat. But they left their mark on Bergues, and blew up the Belfry before they departed.

ACKNOWLEDGEMENTS

ABOVE all my heartfelt thanks to my wife Anne for her forbearance and help, at home and abroad, during the long gestation period, and to my daughter Cally for dissuading me from consigning all the fire-damaged source material to the skip and, together with my other daughter Juliet, generously sparing so much of their valuable time on the manuscript. Cally Shadbolt's expertise was also vital in relation to the photographs and maps.

I am deeply grateful to Lieutenant-General Sir Peter Graham, not only for convincing me that the memoir I had written for my grandchildren should be published, but also for marshalling the necessary people and resources required; chief of these is Lieutenant-Colonel Derek Napier, who gallantly volunteered as Editor. He is uniquely suited, as, having written the final volume of the history of The Gordon Highlanders, no one could have a better feel for the task. That is not all; he has an amazing array of associated technical skills in addition to boundless enthusiasm and generosity.

Early on the scene was Dundee author and journalist Graham Ogilvy who made a number of useful suggestions, as did Richard Bath of the *Scottish Field*.

Dr Duncan Anderson, Head of War Studies at R.M.A.[1] Sandhurst, provided essential background to everything that went on in Flanders in May 1940. The unstinting material help and friendship of André Heintz and his wife, Marie-Françoise, over very many years, have been indispensible for the behind-the-scenes account of affairs in Normandy at the time of the invasion. It is gratifying that André was awarded a long overdue *Chevalier de la Legion d'honneur* in 2012. Among his many kindnesses was his introduction to *Professeur* Claude-Jean Bertrand, who sent me his father's very private journal of his time as liaison officer during the Battle of Caen.

I am further grateful to:
The late Bill Leslie T.D., W.S. for access to his Regimental histories when mine were lost in the fire.

---

[1] R.M.A. Woolwich and R.M.C. Sandhurst amalgamated in 1947, becoming R.M.A. Sandhurst.

Jesper Ericsson, of the Gordon Highlanders Museum in Aberdeen, for drawing my attention to the wonderful stories, all painstakingly hand-written by my father, and the incredibly talented art work in *The Torgau Lyre* and *The Iceberg*.

Professor Charles Lock for supplying me with the true identity of Okey Belfour.

Svetlana at the Cathedral of the Dormition in Ennismore Gardens, London for deciphering the Cyrillic hand written names in a salvaged address book.

Jennifer Main at Merchiston Castle School for trawling through back copies of *The Merchistonian*, family copies having been lost in the fire.

Erica Darby for sundry extracts from the library of the Scottish Rugby Union, Murrayfield.

Mr Paul Brown of Reproset for great technical expertise in the recovery of damaged photographs.

Mrs Sue Sutherland for endless typing and retyping of the early manuscripts.

Hilary Fleming, John Sterk and Nicolas Oakley for sundry linguistic assistance.

Not least to our neighbour, Barry Horwood, and his niece Viv Goodchild, whose quick reactions saved our house from total destruction.

BIBLIOGRAPHY

Coulet, François. *Vertu des Temps Difficiles* © Librairie PLON, 1967.

Donnison, F.S.V., *Civil Affairs and Military Government North-West Europe 1944-1946*. London 1961 HMSO.

Ellis, Major L.F., *The War in France and Flanders 1939-1940*. London 1953. HMSO.

Fischer, Karl, *Die Wehrmacht 1940, Der Freiheitskampf des grossdeutschen Volkes heraus gegeben vom Oberkommando der Wehrmacht*. Copyright 1940 by Verlag., Berlin-Charlottenburg.

Guderian, General Heinz. *Panzer Leader*. First Futura Publications edition 1974.

Hay, Malcolm V., *Wounded and a Prisoner of War*. William Blackwood & Sons, Edinburgh.

Jessiman,William, *Diary of Sergeant William Jessiman*. Gordon Highlanders Museum.

McLaren, Lt. Col. John, *The History of Army Rugby* © The ARMY RFU, Aldershot 1986.

Miles,Wilfred. *The Life of a Regiment, Vol. V 1919-1945*. Aberdeen University Press.

Noote, Robert. *Mémoire en Images Bergues Saint-Winoc*. © Editions Alan Sutton 2007.

O'Rorke, Benjamin G., *In the Hands of the Enemy*. Longmans, Green and Co 1915.

Phillips, R.J., *The Story of Scottish Rugby*. T.N. Foulis Lt1925.

Poirier, Joseph. *La Bataille de Caen. Caen 8 décembre 1944*.

Seton, Colonel Sir Bruce, Bart., and Pipe-Major John Grant. *The Pipes of War*. Maclehose, Jackson & Co 1920.

Sewell, E.H.D., *Rugger the Man's Game*. Hollis and Carter Ltd. 1944.

Stewart, Alexander D.L., *Memoir of A.D.L. Stewart*. Gordon Highlanders Museum.

Usher, C.M., Editor, *History of the Usher Family in Scotland*. Edinburgh 1956.

Usher, C.M., Editor *The Story of Edinburgh University Athletic Club* © 1966 Edinburgh University Athletic Club.

Vannoorenberghe, René. *Flieger Alarm!*

Wilmot, Chester. *The Struggle for Europe*. Collins, London. 1952.

INDEX

Page numbers in *italics* refer to illustrations.
Illustration pages shown thus - (a)

Made in the USA
Charleston, SC
05 December 2014